1_{St}
1993

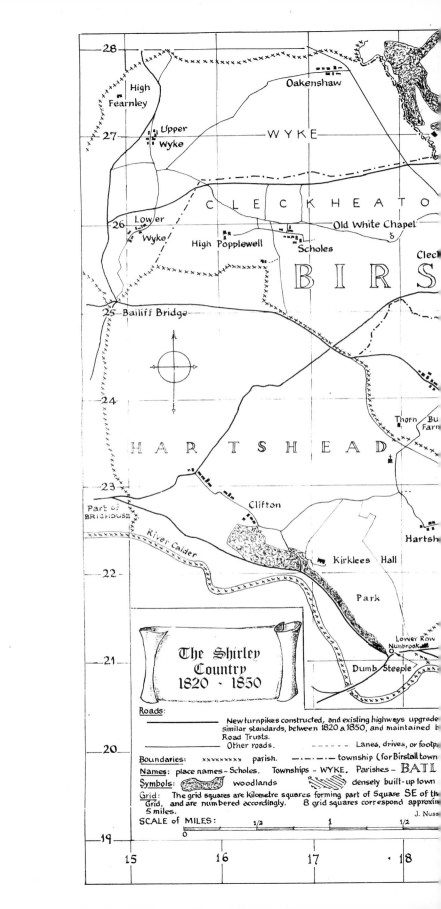

The Shirley
Country
1820 - 1850

Roads:

New turnpikes constructed, and existing highways upgrade[d]
similar standards, between 1820 & 1850, and maintained b[y]
Road Trusts.
Other roads.   ------ Lanes, drives, or footp[aths]

Boundaries: xxxxxxxx parish.   —.—.— township (for Birstall town[ship])

Names: place names – Scholes.   Townships – WYKE.   Parishes – BATL[EY]

Symbols: woodlands   densely built-up town

Grid: The grid squares are kilometre squares forming part of Square SE of th[e]
Grid, and are numbered accordingly.   8 grid squares correspond approxim[ately]
5 miles.

SCALE of MILES: 1/2   1   1/2

J. Nuss[ey]

0

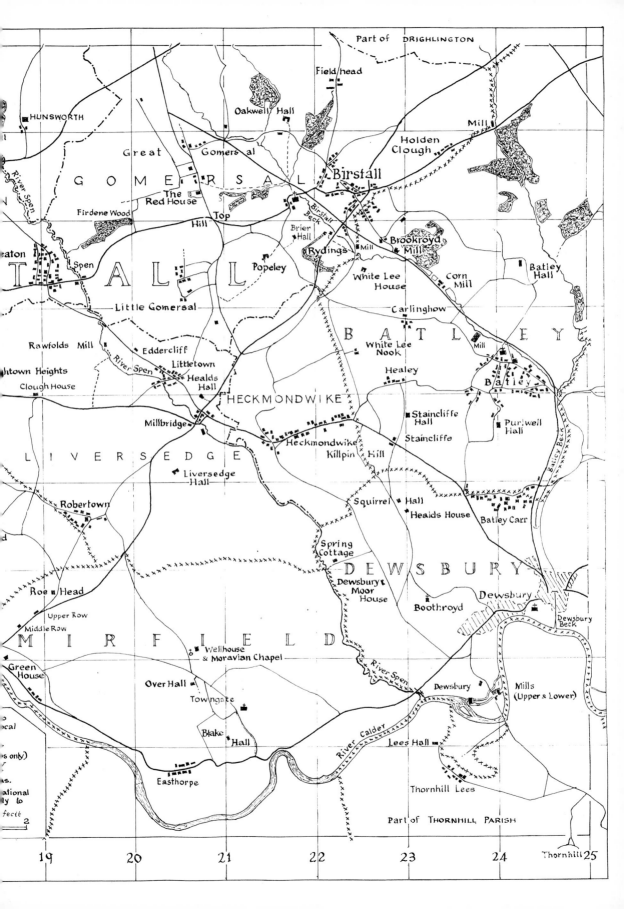

This book is dedicated to my friend and colleague
JOHN THEODORE MENET NUSSEY
1914 – 1992

He was a verray parfit gentil man

CHARLOTTE BRONTË AND HER 'DEAREST NELL'

Charlotte Brontë and her 'dearest Nell'

The story of a friendship

by
Barbara Whitehead

SMITH SETTLE
1993

First published in 1993 by

Smith Settle Ltd
Ilkley Road
Otley
West Yorkshire
LS21 3JP

ISBN Paperback 1 85825 010 2
Hardback 1 85825 011 0

British Library Cataloguing-in-Publication Data:
A catalogue record is available for this book
from the British Library.

Designed, printed and bound by
SMITH SETTLE
Ilkley Road, Otley, West Yorkshire LS21 3JP

CONTENTS

vi

ILLUSTRATIONS

ACKNOWLEDGMENTS

The research and writing of this book has spread over twelve years and during that time a host of people have been helpful and supportive. They all have my heartfelt thanks, even if not mentioned by name.

My friend the late John T M Nussey, referred to at his own request throughout this book as John Nussey, is the person to whom I owe most thanks. Without him this book would not have been written. It was the chance of our serving on the same committee in 1978 which led to a discussion of Ellen Nussey, John's great-great-aunt. I urged John to write about her life to vindicate her memory. He offered me the use of his family history research if I were willing to undertake the project. John also provided family photographs and drew the maps, read the manuscript and pointed out errors. He gave generous copyright permission for quotations from his own work and from family documents and took the non-driving author to see places where Ellen had lived and gave information about them. John was not always in agreement with me on the interpretation of the source material; where we differed, he consented to my interpretations appearing here.

Mr Goodes, the Walpole Librarian for King's School, Canterbury, and the school itself have been most generous in giving access to Ellen's *Reminiscences*, which they hold in manuscript, and copyright permission for long quotations therefrom. I cannot thank them enough for their kindness and co-operation.

Margaret Smith of Birmingham University very kindly read the manuscript and commented in detail, giving me the benefit of her immense scholarship in Brontë matters. Her fruitful suggestions brought about a great improvement in the work. Hugh Murray of York also spared time from a busy life to read through a wad of manuscript and indicate points which needed attention. My son Roger Howson displayed infinite patience in reading and commenting on the manuscript and suggesting better ways of presenting the mass of material.

Kim Brooker was an inspiring companion on much of the field research work and discovered that Henry Nussey's plans for extensions to the vicarage at Hathersage were in the archives at Chatsworth. Kim accompanied me on a visit to Hathersage when we were able to tour the empty vicarage during modernisation. We saw the bedroom grates Charlotte would have known, placed outside on the grass. We were able to envisage the building as it was when Charlotte and Ellen stayed there. He was also present when we found Ingwell House and went round it, as it was empty and up for sale.

Members of the Brontë Society have been very helpful, particularly Dr Juliet Barker and Sally Stonehouse when I was researching at the Brontë Society Museum. Jill Greenwood obtained a copy for me of *Haworth Parsonage, the home of the Brontës* by Jocelyn Kellett, published by the Brontë Society (1977), which is an excellent study of the architecture and history of the parsonage building, and she brightened my visits to Haworth. The Brontë Society kindly gave me permission to quote from documents in their care.

Chris Sumner welcomed me to her home, took me on a fascinating tour of the *Shirley* Country, and was always most kind and helpful. Thanks go to the then owner of one of the 'Sisters' Houses', who allowed me to look over it. Arnold Berry took me over Rydings, told me of its postwar history, and became a most helpful friend. The pleasant people then living in two of the flats into which Rydings had been divided allowed me to walk round their homes. Dr Richard Taylor of Leicester, a descendant of the Taylor family who were such close friends of the Brontës and Nusseys, welcomed me on a visit to his home and showed me one of the banknotes issued by their bank.

My thanks to Huddersfield reference library staff where I used the microfilm of Gomersal Moravian records, and to the archivist and staff of Moravian Church House, 5/7 Muswell Hill, London. Also thanks to Margaret L Connor for permission to use information on her family and for searching Fulneck records for me. Thanks also to Mrs Ives, and to other Moravian contacts, not least to Miss Connor's cousin Rosemary Outram, whose original enquiry to John Nussey about a tradition of former friendship between Connors, Brontës and Nusseys introduced a line of research which led, among other results, to the discovery of Mercy Nussey's connection with the Fairfield Moravian Settlement. Thanks also to the staff of the Museum of Education at the Brotherton Library building, Leeds University, for searching for records of the Moravian Ladies' Academy at Gomersal and finding an advertising handbill.

The Rev O A Beckerlegge was most helpful with advice on religious movements of the nineteenth century and with the loan of *A History of the Evangelical Party* by G R Balleine (Longmans 1909). Professors J A V Chapple and A Pollard generously gàve me their permission to quote from their invaluable and fascinating *The Letters of Mrs Gaskell* (Manchester University Press 1966). J G Sharps gave me permission to quote from his book *Mrs Gaskell's Observation and Invention* (Linden Press 1970) and also from documents in his possession, and was most helpful in reading and commenting on the manuscript. Ian Dewhirst, then of Keighley reference library, showed me resources there which I would never have located, helped me to avoid errors and told me the present name of the Devonshire Arms. The staff of York Library, both lending and reference, have willingly obtained books and information for me. Bernard Barr of the York Minster Library was, as always, a fount of information and help. The staff of the Fitzwilliam Museum at

Cambridge were most kind. Christopher Shepherd, of the Brotherton Collection at the Brotherton Library of Leeds University, explained their relevant holdings to me and was very helpful when I worked there. John Goodchild of the Wakefield reference library owns carbon copies of Ellen's letters to Mrs Atkinson, which I thank him for allowing me to see, and also at Huddersfield library is deposited the manuscript journal of William Carr, of which John Nussey transcribed relevant parts giving information which could not have been obtained from any other source.

Molly Bower, who is descended from Rose Bower, a sister of Tabitha Ackroyd, the Brontës' housekeeper, has allowed me to use information she found in the course of researching her family history. Sarah Fermi has delighted me with her conjectures and shared with me her knowledge of the 'High Water' cartoon in Emily Brontë's writing desk, and her research on it, as well as other information. Laurie Marriott allowed me to use information she found while researching her ancestors the Marriott family, who owned Roe Head.

And most of all – my husband Barry has been very patient as I worked at a subject which did not interest him, but which often caused him inconvenience.

ILLUSTRATIVE ACKNOWLEDGMENTS

The publishers would like to thank the following for permission to reproduce the illustrations listed below:

Brian Arundel, p84; the Brontë Parsonage Museum, pp2, 16, 18, 41, 55, 77, 82, 89, 103, 105, 107, 121, 139, 167, 173, 177, 183, 194, 207, 227, 239; Edward Garner, pp117, 120; Mrs A W Hall, p247; Brian Jackson, pp20, 71, 74, 160, 209, 212, 224, 241, 251; Trevor Mitchell, p134; National Library of Scotland, p83; National Portrait Gallery, pp133, 162, 163, 165; North Yorkshire County Library, pp148; the late John Nussey, pp22, 24, 25, 32, 33, 37, 44, 70, 128, 129, 132, 140, 215, 216, 218, 222, 223, 254; Scarborough Borough Council, p151; Barbara Whitehead, pp123, 147, 149, 208.

The endpaper map was drawn by the late John Nussey.

INTRODUCTION

I see the Brontës and their friends primarily as women of the nineteenth century, with both faults and virtues, living through the changes of their times as we live through ours, struggling with their lives as we struggle with ours. If I often adopt Ellen Nussey's viewpoint it is because this throws new light on the relationships, and because, while the facts or myths of the Brontës' lives are becoming hackneyed by frequent repetition, the facts of her life were still waiting to be discovered.

In concentrating on the relationship between Charlotte and Ellen Nussey, I have given a factual and chronological account of their story, feeling that this helps everyone to understand the lives of these two women who had such a close, deep and lasting emotional relationship. After Charlotte's death I have told the story of the survivor, Ellen, whose life continued to be dominated by her love for her friend.

Ellen Nussey was the closest outside friend of the Brontë family as a whole, and if it were not for her we would know little of their personal lives. Charlotte Brontë was the most influential person in Ellen's life, and it is Charlotte who is most illuminated by studying Ellen; but Ellen was beloved also by Emily and by Anne, liked by Mr Brontë, Aunt Branwell, Branwell Brontë, Tabby and the other members of the household.

Everyone interested in the Brontës owes Ellen Nussey a great debt; yet the view of her promulgated in her old age by the criminal, fraudster and conman T J Wise, to cover up his own conduct, has been the one adopted without thought by modern commentators. Most things written of her are either untrue or at best half-true. She was a woman of strong principles, great personal charm and intellectual interests; and above all, faithful unto death. Her family were in their own way as individualistic as the Brontës or their friends the Taylors; they had risen and altered in the changing world of the Industrial Revolution. Ellen suffered personal tragedies and bereavements parallel with Charlotte Brontë's and the frustrations common to capable women of her time. In their own right Ellen and her family are interesting. As an aid to understanding the Brontë family better, they are invaluable.

Because she was the guardian of Charlotte's letters to herself, dating from their schooldays to Charlotte's deathbed, many comments have been made on Ellen's later life and relationships, without much factual basis. In endeavouring to understand those years and set out their story, I am hoping that this part of the book will be valuable to many and will put her actions in a truer light.

I have become acquainted with Ellen, her family background, and her life; she and Charlotte seem now like dear friends of my own. As a family historian I can write about Ellen, as a novelist I can attempt to understand Charlotte. C S Forester wrote:

'It is not presumptious on the part of the most minor author to claim that he goes through the same physiological process as Goethe or Plato; the presumption is if he claims that his physiological processes produce as good results.'

Barbara Whitehead, York, 1993

MISS WOOLER'S YOUNG LIONS, 1831-2

On a fine winter's day, the 25th January 1831 in the West Riding of Yorkshire, a brother and sister drove the three miles from their home, Rydings at Birstall, to Roe Head House at Mirfield, the boarding school where the sister was to finish her education. The brother was eighteen year old Henry Nussey; the sister, Ellen Nussey, was thirteen. The school term was already into its second week – the young Nusseys perhaps had to wait until the family transport was available, or until there was a day with good weather. Ellen was not afraid of this new experience. This was her third school, a select one, and she already knew some of the people there. She was not to know that a momentous new chapter was opening up, for a friendship to be formed at Roe Head was to have a profound and lasting influence on her whole life.

In her early childhood she had gone to a school near her home, and on one memorable day the Rev Hammond Roberson had brought his horse into the schoolroom.[1] Later Ellen had attended the Moravian Ladies' Academy at Gomersal, a mile from Rydings, where Mary and Martha Taylor from the Red House, Gomersal – neighbours she had always known – were very likely to have been amongst her school fellows.[2] Her education might have been completed at this Ladies' Academy if it had not been for the departure of the much-loved Rev Richard Grimes, who seems to have been in overall charge of the school. After his departure Ellen's widowed mother, and possibly also the parents of the Taylor girls, were less happy with the Ladies' Academy and looked round for an alternative within their means. Miss Wooler's school at Roe Head was decided upon, and the three girls began there after the Christmas holidays.

As they approached Roe Head on that winter's day, Henry and Ellen saw a large, pleasant, detached house with two bays of windows extending up three floors to the roof, surrounded by its own gardens and stables. The house, which was only a short distance from the centre of Mirfield, had been built in 1740 by coal-owner George Marriott for his own use. Miss Wooler was leasing the property.[3] Roe Head was less than half the size of Ellen's previous school. It had an average of twelve pupils and a teaching staff of at least three, so there would be plenty of individual attention.

After the formalities of delivering his younger sister were over, Henry left to drive the short distance home and Ellen was taken into the classroom and asked to wait. At that time of day the other girls were playing outside and the room was, apparently, empty. Looking about, she found that, for a

A pencil drawing by Charlotte Brontë of Roe Head School, Mirfield, where she, Ellen Nussey and Mary Taylor met in January 1831.

schoolroom, it was pleasant. There was a bookcase against one wall so as she loved reading Ellen, thinking she was alone, intended to look at the books, but the opening and closing of the door and the few words that had been spoken had disturbed and shocked the other person in the room. Lying full length on the floor of the bay window was a girl who was crying her heart out, after a miserably unhappy first week. Realising that she was no longer by herself, this girl rose to her feet, turned her back on the newcomer, and tried to master her tears. Ellen then saw the silhouette of the small hunched figure against the winter light flooding in through the bay window, and saw only one thing about her – that she was unhappy. At once she went to try to bring comfort.

Charlotte Brontë had not wanted anyone to witness her breakdown. At the approach of this stranger she was mute and antagonistic, but that would not do for Ellen. Gently she asked what was the matter, and at last was given the grudging answer that Charlotte was homesick. 'Next week it will be your turn to comfort me,' said Ellen. 'I shall be homesick by then.'

The gentleness, the understanding, the charm, all of which were to be characteristic of Ellen throughout her life, had their effect. Unwillingly through her tears Charlotte gave a half-smile, and allowed Ellen to clasp her hand. The most important friendship of the two girls' lives had begun.[4]

Miss Wooler's school was not the most fashionable nor the most expensive school in the area. That palm had gone to Miss Richmal Mangnall's at Crofton;[5] among the pupils there had been Ellen Nussey's second cousins, the Walker girls from London; and also Charlotte Brontë's godmother, Elizabeth Firth.[6] The pupils were from wealthier and more far-flung families than those Miss Wooler attracted, although she was acknowledged as a fine teacher whose school gave her girls an exceptional training for the time.

Miss Wooler was the firstborn of the corn miller of Rouse Mill.[7] She was well educated, highly intelligent, and a notable leader within both her family and her school. It was something to be pre-eminent in a family that included two medical men and sisters who became teachers or the wives of clergymen. Throughout her life, Miss Wooler was always respectfully addressed by them as 'Sister'. She was a noted scholar of the Italian language. Although she was not tall, Miss Wooler was stately. She wore cream dresses decorated with embroidery, and coiled her hair high except for curls which fell on either side of her face in the style of the period. She was not above a little corporal punishment and was to box Martha Taylor's ears on occasion. It was Miss Wooler who originated the habit which both Ellen Nussey and the Brontë sisters were to maintain to the end of their lives – the habit of pacing round and round the room for exercise during the latter part of the evening. Miss Wooler walked in this manner at that time of day with her students, informally discussing various topics which she thought would be of benefit to them. The Brontë sisters were later to pace round and round discussing the plots, characters and events of their novels. Later still, when she was a very old woman, Ellen was to walk alone, the last survivor, looking at the framed photographs on her sitting-room walls and feeling that they kept her company as she passed on that lonely circular walking.

The school year was then divided up not into three terms but into two 'halves', which ran from January until midsummer and from the end of July or thereabouts until Christmas. Schools decided their own dates within this general framework, and Miss Wooler once left the decision of when to end the term to the last possible minute. There was often a short break at Easter.

At this school Charlotte Brontë had arrived on about the 18th January 1831 for her first 'half'. She had travelled humbly on the carrier's cart from Haworth, some twenty miles at a walking pace. Carrier's carts looked much like the covered wagons of the American west, and although the covers gave protection from the wind, there was no heating unless the traveller had a container filled with hot coals or charcoal to warm hands or feet. Frozen after hours of sitting virtually in the open air on that winter's day, Charlotte climbed down stiffly. Mary Taylor saw a girl looking drawn and old, dowdily dressed, too frozen to move other than slowly and awkwardly, peering about shortsightedly. Years later Mary, who carried the Yorkshire habit of plain speaking and love of truthfulness to extremes, described Charlotte's appearance and clothes on that first day at school with scorn. She herself was a very pretty girl – 'too pretty to live', Miss Wooler said – with the pink cheeks that all the Taylor children had, and she was too frank. She was later to apologise to Charlotte for having told her to her face that she was ugly. Charlotte replied gently that this outspokenness had done her good, but she cannot have enjoyed it. Even after Charlotte's death, Mary dismissed the Richmond portrait of her as flattering, sorry that the truth as she saw it should not be presented.[8]

In that January pretty Mary was smarting under the consequences of her father's bankruptcy, and this explains a great deal. It meant that Mary and Martha both had to go on wearing their clothes when they had grown out of them and the skirts and sleeves were too short. When they had new gloves, their mother made them stitch over the ends of the fingers for reinforcement so that they would last longer. Mary proudly ignored these petty humiliations.

When Charlotte made her appearance in the schoolroom, it was found that she had followed none of the regular courses of study, and knew less of some subjects than the youngest of the other girls. Charlotte was too short-sighted to play at ball games or to enjoy running about, for fear of bumping into things, and she was reluctant to wear her glasses, like so many schoolgirls before and since.

During the first week of term, Charlotte probably slept alone in a bed for the first time in her life. Now that it is normal to sleep alone, it is hard for us to realise the fear felt by someone who has never entered the hours of darkness without a fellow creature within touching distance. We forget how universal sharing a bed was. Nieces and aunts, sons and fathers, children of both sexes, sisters, brothers, friends, everyone shared beds as a matter of course. In wayside inns travellers often had to share with complete strangers, and much later, in her unfinished fragment 'Emma', Charlotte portrayed a favoured new pupil at a school sharing the bed of the headmistress. Most of the other pupils at Roe Head were pairs of sisters who would be accustomed to sleeping with one another.

The reactions of the girls on first meeting were typical. Mary saw the outside and criticised it, Ellen saw the unhappiness and comforted it, Charlotte, proud and hypersensitive, was hurt by the criticism and at first unwilling to accept the comfort. In time she grew to value Mary and accept her outspokenness, and to say of Ellen, 'no new friend . . . could be to me what Ellen is'.

Charlotte and Ellen were fairly unusual at Roe Head in going as singletons, and it seems certain that after Ellen arrived she shared a bed with Charlotte, as they did in later years when visiting each other. Charlotte looked forward to the 'calm sleep' she always enjoyed when sharing with Ellen. On the 17th May 1832, almost certainly in a school letter-writing exercise, Martha Taylor wrote a letter asking if, when Charlotte and Mary had both left, she, Martha, could sleep with Ellen.[9]

Ellen's arrival made all the difference to Charlotte. At first she could not unbend enough to feel a liking for this person who had surprised her in such a private moment – 'at first I did not like her; we were schoolfellows, that was all' – but knowing that in this newcomer she had if she wished a friend and ally as well as a bedfellow, she allowed the friendship to grow. When the class had their lesson in letter-writing in May 1831, Charlotte wrote affectionately to her schoolmate. With the friendship grew her confidence. She quickly caught up in the elementary studies which were part of Miss Wooler's curriculum and joined Ellen and Mary at the top of the class, sitting at the head of the table. Throughout the rest of their eighteen months schooling, the three girls were always together at the top of the class, varying the order of precedence only among themselves. At one point Ellen and Charlotte were joint firsts for an award and tossed a coin to see who was to take it. Ellen was delighted that it fell to Charlotte to carry the prize home.

One of the prizes at Roe Head was for neatness. Charlotte had been able to stitch neatly at the age of eight when she went to Cowan Bridge School, and during the intervening time she had come to set a high value on order and neatness, which were all part of duty. It irked her, in future years, to have relatively untidy visitors like Mrs Gaskell. Ellen was neat enough to be the winner of the Roe Head Neatness Prize, and this side of her character always pleased Charlotte.

Miss Wooler was soon to discover that in her intake of 1831 she had three girls of outstanding character and talent, three very different, individualistic girls – three young lions. Three girls at a boarding school in the West Riding of Yorkshire in 1831 would appear to be of very little importance in the England of William IV, yet nowadays the scanty evidence is combed over again and again for clues to their characters, because Charlotte Brontë became a writer of the first rank and of undoubted genius.

Mary Taylor was to become a teacher, a businesswoman in New Zealand, a pioneer in women's rights and in women's mountain climbing in the Alps, and also a writer with one novel (*Miss Miles*) and many articles to her credit. There was a long period during their schooldays when Charlotte and Mary were not on friendly terms, though both remained friendly with Ellen. Perhaps there was a little jealousy between them over the gentler girl. It took Charlotte some time to appreciate the vigorous astringency of Mary's character. Then she loved Mary deeply, for her independent truthfulness and integrity among other things. Mary was to love and prize her in return.

Ellen Nussey had less obvious achievements. She taught throughout her life but never took a paid post; she could write well and vividly but she wrote little for publication; she was an excellent craftswoman with an acute fashion sense, but those skills have always been under-rated; she had keen and true powers of observation, a love of literature and music, riding and walking, children and animals, and the ability to delight in life itself. But it was her spiritual life which marked her out. She developed a deep well-spring of religious devotion which was nurtured by the necessity of self-sacrifice to her family and constant sick-nursing within it. She was a rare and unusual person of great charm whose acquaintance we might never have made had she not recognised the highest when she saw it, and loved and supported Charlotte Brontë.

Charlotte was a year older than her two schoolfriends. In February 1831 Mary Taylor had her fourteenth birthday, on the 20th April Ellen Nussey was fourteen, and on the 21st April Charlotte Brontë was fifteen. This closeness of their birthdays was another little bond between Ellen and Charlotte, and meant that they usually remembered the anniversaries with a small gift and a letter, although Charlotte was quite likely to forget about both the birthdays or not be sure on which date they fell.[10]

We know that Miss Wooler's was a happy school, but of its curriculum we can only reconstruct an outline. French was important, and here Charlotte had a head start as she had been fascinated by the language early and was a reasonable French scholar before going to Roe Head. Mary Taylor, whose family traded on the Continent, also seems to have taken well to languages. Ellen had, of the three, the least gift for foreign languages, but she could read French to a high standard by the time she left Roe Head and was only held back by diffidence from writing it as fluently as she read it.

Music was part of the curriculum. Although we have no direct mention of Ellen playing the pianoforte, she had a good education in music at her previous school and in later life owned an excellent piano. Music was one of her greatest lifelong delights and she was a knowledgeable critic. She tells us how her friends played: Charlotte with such small tapering fingers that she could hardly span the keys, Mary with perfect execution but without feeling. Later, Ellen considered Emily Brontë's playing to be superb, outclassing everyone else.

Again we have no specific mention of Ellen drawing, but the pupils were taught drawing by Miss Wooler's sister, later Mrs Carter, and they may have had visits from an art master, because drawing and painting were fashionable accomplishments for young ladies. Charlotte is said to have done a great deal of drawing at Roe Head.

Reproductions of works of art were available to them. The magazines of the time reproduced engravings of famous paintings and Charlotte had already studied these and learned a great deal about painters, particularly of the Italian school. In addition she knew and loved Bewick's charming and shrewdly observed wood engravings. Mary Taylor was amazed that Charlotte could see so much to comment on as she pored over the reproduction of some picture held close to her eyes, and we have in Charlotte's childhood writings an example of the kind of criticism she had learned to make of such things.[11] 'She would study an engraving for a long time', said Mary, 'and could tell us much about it that we had not noticed.'

Charlotte in her earlier childhood had spent immense numbers of hours and taken great pains over copying engravings, every tiny line and stipple, but by the time she went to Roe Head she had become much freer in her work and very rapid. The rapidity is often remarked on. She would make drawing after drawing in an evening, throwing away the ones which did not satisfy her. She was the only one of the three girls to have academic artistic talent, but in applied art in the form of needlework and crafts it was Ellen who was outstanding.

The rigidity of Miss Wooler's curriculum is shown in many ways. Later, when she taught at Roe Head, Charlotte reminded Ellen that, being at the end of May, the school was in the thick of 'the Repetitions', of which Charlotte mentions 'the terrible fifth section'.

They did not have organised games, but had regular periods of outdoor exercise, which often consisted of racing round playing a game called 'French and English'. Short-sighted Charlotte would not join in these hectic activities and like many another bookish artistic child, preferred to stand dreaming under a tree, observing and thinking. The formal part of their days ended with prayers.

Mary said that when she went to Roe Head, Charlotte had an Irish accent. Mary's accounts are aimed at making the public impression of Charlotte more like the real woman, so presumably there was truth in this, although the influences on Charlotte's speech were fourfold. Apart from her father's Irish accent – which it is certain he would have tried to alleviate (his accent was not remarked on by later commentators) – there was her aunt's Cornish speech, the broad Yorkshire vernacular of the housekeeper Tabby, and the 'educated Yorkshire' which would be spoken by Mary and Ellen and acquaintances of Mr Brontë. We can hear Patrick Brontë's own accent as it was when he first arrived in England with that nasal northern Irish tone in his voice, reflected in the rendering of his name by a clerk at Cambridge as 'Branty'.

It is usual for people living in areas with strong local dialects to be bilingual and we know that Mary Taylor's father enjoyed speaking with a broad Yorkshire accent on occasion. In her letters to Emily, Charlotte affectionately used broad Yorkshire terms. She used to tease Ellen, who tried not to drop into the idiom of the area, by suggesting that Ellen could not understand slang or dialect expressions in common use. Charlotte had an intense awareness of speech patterns. She loved vernacular speech and reproduced it brilliantly; in her juvenilia[12] is a delicious example of the way uneducated southern speech sounds to a northerner. It was partly this love of the vigour of the speech of actual people which was later to earn her the castigation of coarseness.

It quickly became obvious to Charlotte's schoolfellows that she had an exceptional imagination. She told them about the writing the Brontë children did at home. Mary reported:

'She had a habit of writing in italics (printing characters) and said she had learnt it by writing in their magazine. They brought out a 'magazine' once a month, and wished it to look as like print as possible. She told us a tale out of it. No one wrote in it, and no one read it, but herself, her brother, and two sisters. She promised to show me some of these magazines, but retracted it soon afterwards, and would never be persuaded to do so.'

At school Charlotte showed Ellen her poetry, and Ellen said of the poem *Memory* that it was not regarded as of sufficient merit for publication in the volume of poems, yet it had an interest as depicting Charlotte's then desolate heart. Charlotte was still sorrowing for her dead sisters, Maria and Elizabeth.

She was always willing to make up stories for the amusement of the others. 'Make it out!' Mary would say. 'You know you can!'[13] Thus urged, Charlotte would give free range to her imagination. One night, weaving a story in the darkened dormitory, she was so carried away by her belief in the frightening tale she was telling that she collapsed through strain, and the other girls had to shout for help to bring her round.

It was the private, late-night hour which was to get Ellen and Charlotte into trouble – for the only time in their schooldays at Roe Head. Storytelling had been forbidden following the fainting episode, but they had not realised that all talking was forbidden, and when could Charlotte and Ellen resist talking together? When the girls were asked who had been talking, Charlotte and Ellen admitted this along with the rest of the pupils, and the verbal reprimand they received was one which Charlotte felt keenly.

As part of the life of the school the pupils acted out little dramas and plays on their half-holidays, and Charlotte wrote the words for one such celebration at the time of King William IV's coronation, when Miss Wooler's younger sister was crowned by the pupils.

The constant discussions which went on in Haworth Parsonage between her aunt and her father had stimulated Charlotte's powers of reasoning, and the fact that her father always spoke to his children as adults and expected them to be interested in politics and social questions as well as the latest movements in the arts, had given her the wide-ranging viewpoint of a citizen of the world. Mary, although her family hummed with intellectual activity and debate, had been repressed by a stern mother and the family emphasis was on practical matters. Ellen, in her position as the youngest of a large family, was much dominated over. She and Mary had not had Charlotte's mental 'forcing', and when they knew Charlotte better they began to regard her as an authority on life in general and on religion, art and literature in particular. Mary formed the habit of storing things up to tell Charlotte, so that she could have the benefit of her comment and opinion.

Arguments were rife between Charlotte and Mary on politics. In those days of the Reform Bill, of the Chartists and of far-reaching changes in society, few could avoid being political, and Charlotte and Mary found that their views were often at odds, Charlotte being Tory and Mary Whig. In religious matters they were more at one. Even Ellen, who already had a deep education in the Christian religion, was surprised by the greater knowledge of the Bible displayed by Charlotte and the way Biblical phrases and ideas permeated her thinking. At Roe Head the religious education of the three girls continued and the boarders regularly attended Church of England services in Mirfield. During her schooldays Charlotte was confirmed, and it is said that the Rev Edward N Carter, then a curate at Mirfield, prepared her for this. Mr Carter later married one of Miss Wooler's younger sisters, who was one of the staff at Roe Head, and the Carter family became lifelong acquaintances of all three of the girls.

On Sundays during the better weather, those boarders who were not too far from home were allowed to visit their families. Ellen and Mary both took Charlotte home with them, and they were able to attend the service at Birstall Church instead of Mirfield. Then they could have tea at Rydings or the Red House before walking back to Roe Head.

As well as being allowed to visit home, the boarders received visits from family and friends. Ellen mentioned the kindness of Mrs Ingham of Blake Hall in Mirfield who visited her and kept an eye on her welfare during her period at the school. (The Inghams were connections through Ellen's sister-in-law.) Charlotte's godmothers, Mrs Franks and Mrs Atkinson, also visited when they had the opportunity and sent welcome gifts including a gown and a shawl. Charlotte was twenty miles from home and a visit from her family meant a special effort on their part. Nevertheless it seems likely that she had visits that are not recorded. We hear how Branwell, aged only thirteen or fourteen at the time, walked the twenty miles to see her and then the twenty back again. Can we believe that Mr Brontë, who had had such a dreadful experience when sending his children to Cowan Bridge School for the Daughters of Clergymen which had resulted in the deaths of Maria and Elizabeth, would have left Charlotte for six months at a time without a visit, particularly when he had many friends in the neighbourhood? It is pleasant to imagine that he might have hired the Haworth gig and been driven over, complete with Emily and Anne, to spend an hour or two discussing Charlotte's progress with Miss Wooler and strolling round the garden.

It can only be conjecture, but to support the theory we have the fact that in Charlotte's first letters to Ellen after leaving school, Charlotte sends her sisters' love as though they and Ellen had already met. Emily and Anne asked to be remembered to Ellen in Charlotte's letter of the 1st January 1833, before Ellen had visited Haworth. Also, in his letter to Mrs Franks of the 6th July 1835, Mr Brontë says he had not been in Thornton for 'many years' but goes on to give details of a visit there which, if the 'many years' had been four, might well have taken place as a break in the journey to Roe Head, or returning from there.

The food at Roe Head was good. Like so many teenage girls today, Charlotte had given up the eating of meat, presumably for the same reason – a dislike of the idea of eating animals. At home she had been allowed to eat as she wished and, as nutrition was hardly understood at the time, it is likely that for some years she ate far too little protein. Probably this accounted for the shrunken look of her skin, which Ellen described as 'dried in', and the dryness of her hair. The staff at Roe Head and the other girls were concerned about the way Charlotte ate, and after some months they persuaded her to have gravy on her vegetables, and eventually to take a small amount of meat each day. When she was eating more normally, the appearance of her skin improved and she looked plumper.

Ellen was to write later:

'She never seemed to me the unattractive little person others designated her, but certainly she was at this time anything but PRETTY; even her good points were lost. Her naturally beautiful hair of soft silky brown being then dry and frizzy-looking, screwed up in tight little curls, showing features that were all the plainer from her exceeding thinness and want of complexion...A dark, rusty green stuff dress of old-fashioned make detracted still more from her appearance; but let her wear what she might, or do what she would, she had ever the demeanor of a born gentlewoman; vulgarity was an element that never won the slightest affinity with her nature.'

The absence of vital elements in her diet at this growing time may have been responsible for her small adult size, which was such a trial to her. She herself blamed it on the inadequate diet at her earlier school, Cowan Bridge, but she was there only a short time, and it is likely that bitter memory rather than fact influenced her in this opinion. Protein deprivation during the early teenage years was more likely to be responsible, but her mother and aunt were both small women and Charlotte, with an adult height said to be four feet ten inches, was no smaller than many women of her time and even of today – she was probably taller than her contemporary, Elizabeth Barrett Browning.

Charlotte, as she appeared at Roe Head, was unflatteringly described by Mary and more gently by Ellen. The daguerreotypes later taken of Charlotte, and apparently also of Emily and Anne, were nearly all broken and presumably are now lost,[14] so as positive and undoubted likenessess we have only those of her brother Branwell's well-known paintings which include her, and the Richmond chalk drawing.

Ellen is the only one of the three friends whose schoolgirl appearance is preserved for us, in the form of a professional chalk drawing. A visiting artist may have drawn this portrait which at the end of her life hung on the wall of her spare bedroom, and which has been much reproduced. She was also a small woman. Mrs Gaskell was to call her so, and in the early photograph where her hand rests on the back of a chair her lack of height is clear. We have later photographs of Ellen and a painting and drawing of her in old age. Although Charlotte did draw her, probably more than once, such a portrait has not yet been identified with any certainty. One drawing of Ellen by Charlotte was in later years given by Ellen to Wemyss Reid.

Mary's appearance survives for us in Charlotte's description in *Shirley*, rosy-cheeked, grey-eyed – 'Grey, remarkable eyes . . . so bright are the sparks of intelligence, which, at moments, flash from her glance and gleam in her language' – and in Ellen's description which she wrote for Clement Shorter: 'She was pretty, and very childish-looking, dressed in a red-coloured frock with short sleeves and low neck, as then worn by young girls'. Mary, said Ellen, 'never had the impromptu vivacity of her sister, but was lively in games that engaged her mind . . .' We have her serious-faced photograph in old age, and that is all.

Of Mary's younger sister Martha, Ellen said, 'Among her school

A portrait of Ellen Nussey as a young girl.

companions, Martha was called 'Miss Boisterous,' but was always a favourite, so piquant and fascinating were her ways. She was not in the least pretty, but something much better, full of change and variety, rudely outspoken, lively, and original, producing laughter with her own good-humour and affection.' Martha was particularly dear to the older girls, who petted her. All we know of Martha's attainments is that she could have won the Roe Head neatness prize if Ellen had not been there. Ellen added, 'Anything underhand was detestable to both Mary and Martha; they had no mean pride towards others, but accepted the incidents of life with imperturbably good-sense and insight.'

Altogether the three girls spent about eighteen months at Roe Head. It was an intensive, formative period in their lives. The other pupils of their time were always to be of interest to them.

The day came when, at the end of the first 'half' of 1832, the three were to leave. In the last weeks Charlotte and Mary had raced ahead and finished the syllabus ahead of time; Miss Wooler struggled to find things to occupy them, and Charlotte had obediently spent time on 'dead-end' studies, but the independent one, Mary, had refused to do this and was punished accordingly. She bore the punishment with the same haughty appearance of indifference she had borne when wearing her short, out-grown clothes.

At the very last, Charlotte regretted the sedate, hard-working way she had tackled her schooldays. Her father would not be able to afford more education for her. She longed for once to be an 'out-and-out' schoolgirl, to run, to get into mischief, perhaps to steal fruit from the kitchen garden or orchard, and asked Ellen to come with her on such an expedition – but she had left it too late. Going out into the garden with the intention of being a naughty schoolgirl, she realised that the time, the mood, had gone.

It was decided that Ellen should have more tuition in one or two subjects, and it was arranged that she return to Roe Head one day a week to continue a few classes, but once away from school, life claimed her. (Mary Taylor had also intended to return for more drawing lessons.) Her visits were few and soon given up altogether. Later she was to tell her friend Mrs Cortazzo that she had had no education after the age of fifteen and three months, but like her two school friends Ellen was a self-educator. Throughout life she never ceased from studying, meditating, and forming her own opinions on the issues of the day.

At the ages of sixteen and fifteen the three were to embark on their adult lives. To an outsider the similarities between them were more striking than the differences. They were all born into the same stratum of Yorkshire society, within a short distance of each other. They had the same education. Even before their births, threads had linked them, and the more the question is studied the more of these tenuous links are discovered.

The young doctor, William Carr, who rode over from Gomersal to Clough Lane, Hightown to attend Mrs Brontë in her first two childbirths, of Maria and Elizabeth, was the family doctor of the Taylor family of the Red House (years later they heard his ghost) and he married a first cousin of Ellen's,

Sarah Nussey. As adults, Ellen and Charlotte often walked over to visit him. Those dead sisters of Charlotte's were often the subjects of her conversation with Ellen when they were alone; they had been born only a mile from Ellen's home. Their goodness and intelligence and the hard fate they had suffered made them seem like saints in Charlotte's accounts.

The families we are concerned with were of the same social class, that of professional people and of self-employed business people. Numerically at the time it was a small class. Mr Brontë had been a teacher and was a clergyman, his wife's father was a merchant and some of her relatives were teachers and clergymen, and their children became teachers; Miss Wooler, daughter of a corn miller, had brothers who became doctors and sisters who were teachers and who married clergymen; Ellen Nussey's mother was the daughter of a corn miller, her father a partner in a woollen mill, two of her brothers became doctors and two clergymen, while three went into the woollen trade as partners in small mills; Mary Taylor's father had a woollen mill and a small bank, her brothers became partners in small woollen mills and a nephew became a doctor. In the case of both the Taylors and the Nusseys they employed about forty people per mill.

As the three had lived their short years, the social and economic fabric had changed. There had formerly been hardly a dwelling in that part of the West Riding without its spinning wheel to produce yarn and its loom for the hand weaving of woollen cloth. In the stretch of land ringed by Halifax, Huddersfield, Wakefield, Leeds and Bradford, the produce of the small sloping fields and the busy handlooms had supported a sparse but thriving population. It had been a region of craftsmen who spent part of their time dealing with cloth and the rest looking after their stock or their crops. It was a poor agricultural area, high and northerly, but oats could be relied upon to ripen and the basic food was either 'riddle' bread or 'haver' bread, both made from oats. Furniture, clothing, almost everything needed could be made locally. There was plenty of coal near the surface and peat to be dug on the moors, and the houses were built from the abundant stone and roofed by thin stone slabs.

The people of the area were noted for their independent character. This may have come from their ancestry, for this was part of the country settled by the Danes and the local dialect had many words in common with the Scandinavian languages. The people tended to nonconformity in religion. There were few aristocratic families, but there were many who occupied the roomy medieval and Jacobean halls scattered over the countryside and cheerfully mixed grandeur with wool. They were hardworking, thrifty, hospitable folk.

There was a network of broad stone pathways which linked hamlet to hamlet, market to market, the West Riding to the rest of England. Along these causeways came bales of wool and out went the lengths of woven cloth. All that was changing. Turnpike roads had been driven through and the horse-drawn coaches now ran swiftly from town to town. The mules, donkeys and packhorses with the bright woollen ornaments on their harness were being superseded. The small fulling and scribbling mills were being complemented by large weaving mills.[15] Industrialisation was not a rapid process, for even as late as the 1850s the Taylor family were acting as middlemen for many small weavers in the area, and the Nussey/Clapham partners in one mill are mentioned as still taking their cloth on donkeys to be fulled at Mirfield.

Smallpox could now be defeated by vaccination and this had already taken a brake off the growth of the population. Those who had the disease and survived used to be less fertile. Now, in inexorable progression the population was growing.

The three girls stood at the end of their schooldays poised to take their places in the grown-up world. They must have known how privileged they were. All around them, young people of their own age had been at work alongside their parents for ten years already. They themselves had never known what it was to be hungry or scantily-clad or to do strenuous physical work. They had been educated to a high standard where all around young people were growing up illiterate. They themselves had to face the dilemma of belonging to the caste called ladies, a caste whose members, however poor in money, must take care never to demean themselves by doing 'unsuitable' work for their own maintenance.

They must have felt regrets for the happy schooldays which were suddenly behind them, in which Charlotte had never romped and now wished she had. They turned to one another and, to soften the pain of parting, Ellen and Mary assured Charlotte that they would write to her, of course they would write; they had exchanged letters already during the previous Christmas holidays. She after all was the farthest away – seventeen miles from their own homes. They would write! they cried as they fluttered their handkerchiefs, but Charlotte was sure that they never would.

[1] This school has not been identified. There are several possibilities.
[2] The Taylor girls obviously had earlier education and the likeliest school is the Gomersal Moravian Ladies Academy, very near to their home. Hardly any records of the academy survive for the period. My opinion, based on probability and the closeness of the families, is that both Mary and Martha Taylor attended the academy with Ellen Nussey. On 26th July 1830 the academy admitted twenty-five boarders and four day pupils for the second half of the academic year. Mary and Martha Taylor were probably two of the four day pupils. Ellen Nussey could have been a third as her home was only some fifteen minutes walk away by field paths.
[3] Roe Head was owned by the Marriott family until the 1920s. The house, less the stables but with extensive additions, is still in educational use. In 1902 the College of the Resurrection, a Roman Catholic theological college run by the Verona Fathers, settled at Roe Head and have only recently left the premises, which now belong to the Holly Bank Trust as a refuge for physically and mentally handicapped people. The town of Mirfield is also the home, since 1898, of the Community of the Resurrection, a monastic establishment within the Church of England and a training centre for their novices. Its building stands high above the River Calder at the west end of the town and its great church dominates the Calder Valley. Among the community's many outstanding members is Father Trevor Huddleston, who spent a number of years at Mirfield. Confusion frequently arises between the Catholic College of the Resurrection and the Anglican Community of the Resurrection. Roe Head itself was occupied by the Catholic and not the Anglican institution.

[4] Ellen gave more than one account of her schooldays. I have tried to show here the truest representation of Ellen and Charlotte's first meeting and their later experiences. In her *Reminiscences* published by Scribner, Ellen glorified Charlotte for the American market and said that she was the first in the class during her time at Roe Head. In other reminiscences she gives a slightly different picture showing that the three friends shared the top place in the class, now one and now another taking precedence.

[5] Crofton continued as a school after Miss Richmal Mangnall's death in 1820. Her famous textbook, *Mangnall's Questions*, was widely used and possibly the source of the 'Repetitions' mentioned by Charlotte. This book is also mentioned by James Joyce in *A Portrait of the Artist as a Young Man*. Miss Mangnall's Christian name, said to have been first used in 1705 by Richard and Mary (Mal) Kay for their daughter, was later given to descendants of the Kay and related Openshaw families including teacher Richmal Crompton, author of the William books. See *Just Richmal* a biography of Richmal Crompton by Kay Williams (Genesis Publications Ltd, Guildford, 1986).

[6] Mr Brontë proposed marriage to Miss Firth after his wife's death, but she refused him. The two families had been very friendly when the Brontës were living in Thornton. It is said that Elizabeth Firth, by this time Mrs Franks, helped to pay for Charlotte's education at Roe Head.

[7] Rouse Mill was the cornmill for Soothill manor. The former manor house stood about a quarter of a mile east of where Batley station now is. Rouse Mill was in Rouse Mill Lane. The manor included Hanging Heaton.

[8] Mary stated in a letter to Mrs Gaskell, 28th January 1858, that she did not like misleading the public by publishing the portrait of Charlotte by Richmond. She thought the mouth and eyes should have been nearer together, the face squarer and the 'large disproportionate nose' more obvious.

[9] Ellen also left at the end of that half, so Martha was not able to sleep with her as requested in the letter.

[10] In the days before the civil registration of births, the parish register record was of baptism and the actual date of birth was often not noted, so that a surprising number of people were not sure of their date of birth. Ellen's is sometimes given as being on the 22nd.

[11] See Christine Alexander's *Charlotte Brontë; The Early Writings 1826-1832* page 282 *et subs* for some of Charlotte's art criticisms.

[12] Ibid

[13] Stevens, Joan: *Mary Taylor, Friend of Charlotte Brontë; Letters from New Zealand and Elsewhere.*

[14] Daguerreotypes of Charlotte, Emily and Anne belonging to Martha Brown's younger sister Mrs Ratcliffe are mentioned as existing although broken, in *A Springtime Saunter Round and About Brontëland* by Whiteley Turner. One of Charlotte is mentioned as belonging to Nancy Garrs, later Malone, in the *Leeds Mercury Supplement* of the 25th March 1893. In the newspaper reference the 'portrait' is described as 'taken on glass' with 'a pleasanter expression on the features than in the engraving attached to Mrs Gaskell's book'. Nancy's sister who also worked for the Brontës is said to have had a photograph. Daguerreotypes (1839-57) consist of a photographic image on a silvered metal plate, normally protected by a piece of glass which is sealed to it. The most common size is 2¾ by 3¼ inches. Their fragility is usually protected by placing them in a special frame, often very ornate, padded with velvet and with a cover, like a small book. If the glass covering of the silvered plate is broken, deterioration of the photographic image takes place and it can vanish altogether. Each daguerreotype was an individual photograph so multiple copies did not exist.

[15] Originally all the treatment of the wool shorn in late spring from the sheep's back would be carried out by the craftsmen themselves, using hand implements. Later the first small water or donkey driven mills carried out some of the processes and saved much labour. The wool needed to be washed (scoured), then the entanglements were taken out of it by passing it through rollers covered with brushes which worked one against the other (scribbling). Next it was carded - passed through rollers covered by short wires like the bristles of a brush. It was then soft and clean with all the fibres running the same way, and ready for spinning into yarn for the manufacture of woollen cloths. If the wool was to become worsted cloth it was combed and not carded. Combing was a skilled hand process using metal combs heated on a stove. The spinning of wool was being mechanised although this was more difficult than mechanising the spinning of cotton. Hand spinning of the warps (lengthways threads) went on for a long time as hand spun yarn was stronger. After the wool was spun it was woven on a loom. Again, it was more difficult to mechanise the production of wool fabrics than cotton, so hand-weaving ran parallel with machine innovations for decades, as the hand product was superior. Cloth was finished by being pounded in water with a wooden hammer (a fulling stock) which consolidated it. Fullers had previously trodden the cloth with their feet, hence the surname Walker; they trod the woolly vintage, or, as in the Scottish islands, pounded it to and fro with their hands.

CHARLOTTE'S, MARY'S AND ELLEN'S BACKGROUNDS

Before following the three girls on their paths through life, let us look back at the influences which shaped them. Their friendship was not a static but a dynamic one; it changed, it grew, it altered; but the material it had to work on was already formed by their family backgrounds.

First, Charlotte. The life of the Brontë family is well known. Patrick Brontë, from a poor Irish family, was a linen weaver in his youth, then progressed to being a teacher in a little village school and later he had travelled to Cambridge as a protégé of Anglican Rev Thomas Tighe, a friend of Wesley. At Cambridge Brontë studied under James Wood, was much influenced by Charles Simeon, and took orders as an Anglican clergyman. Brontë was of the evangelical wing of the church, which in the eighteenth century gave birth to the Methodist movement. Valentine Cunningham points out that 'The Evangelical Anglican, or Church-Methodist, old-boy network . . . was already visibly at work for Brontë'.[1]

After other posts, in 1811 Patrick Brontë became the curate of Hartshead-

The Reverend Patrick and Mrs Maria Brontë.

cum-Clifton in the West Riding of Yorkshire and took lodgings in the adjoining parish of Birstall. In 1812 he was appointed examiner at Woodhouse Grove Wesleyan Academy and met Maria Branwell, a Cornish woman and a Methodist, a niece of the headmaster's wife. They fell in love, married and lived first at Hightown (about a mile from Ellen Nussey's home), where their first two children were born. In May 1815 Patrick Brontë became the curate at Thornton near Bradford. He and his small family moved there, where Charlotte, Emily, Branwell and Anne were born in 1816, 1817, 1818 and 1820. They were still close to his old friends of the Birstall and Hartshead areas, and the years at Thornton were very happy ones for the Brontë family.

In February 1820, Patrick Brontë was appointed Perpetual Curate of Haworth in the West Riding of Yorkshire with a salary of £180 a year and a free house. Haworth had been the parish of the legendary Rev William Grimshaw, and from the point of view of the religious movement of which Brontë was part, it was a plum position. It also had the advantage of being a post in which he had secure lifetime tenure.[2] Patrick Brontë then moved his family some distance from the interwoven community into which the children had been born, but his friendships within it persisted through the years; his daughters reinforced the bonds in their lives, and in their novels appear people and places from this bustling area into which they had the *entrée*, but from which they were sufficiently removed to observe it objectively.

On Patrick Brontë's promotion to Haworth, the family must have moved with every hope of continuing prosperity and progress. The house was better than any they had had before, Brontë was in sole charge and could continue the work of the renowned Grimshaw, who had been both a Methodist and an Anglican in the days before the break between the two. Haworth might have been the stepping-stone to more remunerative parishes and further promotion. It cannot have been envisaged as a final resting place, although Patrick stressed his appreciation of its security. But Maria developed cancer and died. Although her husband made attempts to remarry, as nineteenth century widowers with small children normally did, he could not find a second wife and his sister-in-law Elizabeth Branwell came from Cornwall to run the household and bring up the children, as, again, nineteenth century sisters-in-law so often did. And Patrick Brontë's career came to a halt, although he was still a young man. Lively, talkative 'saucy Pat' was to become by slow degrees the eccentric who liked to spend time alone, and whose oddities were gossiped about. He was always liked and respected by the people around him, and when there was occasion to talk, he was talkative to the end of his days.

He was anxious to do his best for his children and knowing that his salary would die with him, he wanted to leave them capable of earning a living for themselves. This could be done by giving them a good education. Education had enabled him to rise from a dead-end job to his present respected eminence, and towards the goal of a good education he sent four of his little girls to Cowan Bridge School for the Daughters of Clergymen in 1824. It was unfortunate that the school was under the direction of the Rev Carus Wilson,

Cowan Bridge School for Clergy Daughters, where four of the Brontë daughters were sent in 1824; it later became the Lowood School of Jane Eyre.

a rigid and misguided man. The humanitarians among the teachers were appalled by the results of the regime there, and the two eldest Brontë children, Maria and Elizabeth, died of tuberculosis contracted at the school. Charlotte and Emily were taken away, Anne had been too young to go, and Branwell, the only son, was, as far as we know, always educated at home by his father.

After Cowan Bridge, the girls were at home for some years. Their aunt taught them, particularly needlework, they learned some French, and to an extent they shared in Branwell's lessons, even the classics, for they kept pace with him in most things. It has been said that Charlotte, if not the other two girls, went to a private school in North Street, Haworth, kept by a Miss Mary Wright.[3]

Patrick Brontë's role in educating his daughters is under-estimated. That he gave them tuition we know from his letter to Mrs Franks of 6th July 1835, in which he mentions his tuition of Anne while the others were absent. He bought as many of the latest books as he could, hoping they would be of benefit, and allowed the children to read everything in the house. He took a newspaper and shared other newspapers which were bought by his neighbours, so they saw the leading periodicals of the time. He bought prints and reproductions. Socially and intellectually the Brontë family were at the top of society in their area, but there do not seem to have been many children of the same social status with whom they could be friends.

Although the Brontë children did not play with the village children – who would be helping their parents in the woollen industry or in farm work for most of the day – they were very much part of village life. Perhaps the most surprising sections of Charlotte's juvenile writings are the vivid tavern scenes complete with genuine sounding dialogue and a robust attitude to death. She has conversations in taprooms to the life and murdered people are calmly interred under the flagstones of the pub floor, presumably on the analogy of burials inside churches. She was writing these scenes before the age of thirteen.[4] When the nine year old Charlotte was with her father on a visit to his printer in Keighley (Mr Brontë published several of his works himself), she is said to have checked through proofs for him while he conversed. If refreshment or rest was needed, he would have stopped at a wayside inn or gone to a hostelry in Keighley, and in those days there were no regulations banning children.

At last it was decided that the girls must have more formal education, and in January 1831 Charlotte was sent to Roe Head with the idea firmly in her mind that she must work hard there in order to teach whatever she learned to her younger sisters after her return home. Teaching was one of the very few respectable ways in which a woman of the gentle class could earn a living. Patrick had been a teacher, and essentially he always was. Learning and teaching were in the very air the Brontë children breathed. Their father also set them the example of being a published creative writer and so writing was also a natural part of life.

Haworth, the village which meant home to them, was an industrious place, as were most of the Pennine moorland villages. It was famous for the excellence of its handloom weavers, who were given high prices for their superior work until the 1860s, long after steam power and mechanisation had been introduced. Many of the houses lining the village street had a workshop at the front, either upstairs or down, with a loom busy through the day. Haworth was on one of the ancient packhorse routes over the Pennines from the West Riding of Yorkshire to the towns of Lancashire. It had been a healthy place in the past, whatever it was to become with the new pressure of population. The primitive sanitation which had been adequate became more and more dangerous as the population rose. The census figures for the chapelry of Haworth show a doubling of the area's population between 1801 and 1841. For Haworth village itself (the chapelry was a larger area) the population in 1841 was 2,434.

Next, Mary Taylor's background. The Taylor family, whose members were so important both to Charlotte Brontë and to Ellen Nussey, had been rooted in Gomersal township in the spreading parish of Birstall for a very long time. Lying on the eastern side of the Pennines between Halifax and Leeds, the area was crossed by rivers draining down from the high ground so that it was an uphill, downdale sort of place, a parish of hills and valleys. A John Taylour of Gomersal and his wife were assessed at fourpence for the poll tax in 1379. Because the Red House Taylors owned a field called Bawson Cliff,

The seventeenth century Red House, Gomersal, was the Taylor family home for generations. It is now a museum.

their individual family can be traced back to before 1560 through property deeds.[5] The Red House in Gomersal, built in 1660, had already been the family home for generations when Mary and Martha were born there. Mary Taylor's grandfather, who was a merchant in the woollen trade, built the small woollen mill at nearby Hunsworth with its house adjoining in 1788.

In religion the Taylor family tradition was to be independent. The desire for independence was such that they built their own chapel, and created their own private graveyard where they could be buried. They welcomed new trends – the Red House offered hospitality to John Wesley and Benjamin Ingham among others, and the family supported the new sect of Moravians.

Mary's father, Joshua, was a remarkable man. He was proud of the Yorkshire traditions which he inherited. Intelligent and enterprising, he travelled widely on business. Joshua Taylor was a banker as well as a woollen manufacturer, as many businessmen then were. He ran the small Gomersal Bank and printed his own banknotes. In this he was linked with his brother-in-law Abraham Dixon who had a bank in Birmingham, and it was the failure of Abraham Dixon's bank which brought about the downfall of Joshua Taylor's much smaller bank, and left him with debts which would take a lifetime to repay. He took out a mortgage and carried on with his business in the wool trade, as this was the only way in which he could support his children and tackle his debts. The family could always afford to travel and to pay for education, even though the financial stringency caused Mary and Martha's outgrown clothes and darned glove-fingers at Roe Head. The children were Joshua, born 1812; John, 1813; Joseph, 1815; Mary, 1817; Martha, 1819; and William Waring, 1820.

After the failure of their bank the Dixons went to live in Brussels and their home there formed a useful base for Joshua Taylor in his trading abroad. He loved travelling on the Continent, needed the knowledge of foreign languages, took a French newspaper, and bought vast quantities of French novels. Charlotte Brontë was fascinated by this household of cosmopolitan culture at the Red House. She admired their uncompromising honesty and apparent indifference to worldly advantage as a principal motivator in life. Even if she did not agree with their views, she found being at the Red House intellectually stimulating and arousing. She was not shy there; the boys in the family found that they could easily provoke her into fiery disputation. It has been said that Charlotte would sometimes dramatise when her spirits rose to the necessary pitch of excitement. She both charmed and fascinated her schoolfriends and their immediate connections when she did this – but unfortunately it was repeated to her when a meeting of young friends was in anticipation, that 'Martin York' (Joseph Taylor) had said, 'He was going to stir Miss Brontë up to the exhibiting point, and he should have a rare evening of enjoyment'. But Martin utterly failed then and thenceforward; Charlotte merely replied to her laughing informant, 'Is he!' But her resolve was taken, and it was immutable; her self-respect had received a blow, and no tactics on 'Martin's' part ever again prevailed to win the entertainment he coveted. She was so interested by the personality of Mary's father that she was to portray him both in *The Professor* and *Shirley*; in the latter she included the whole family, house and all.

Charlotte was a high Tory in politics; her views sometimes seem less liberal than her father's. Throughout his life at Haworth Mr Brontë campaigned for the betterment of social abuses. Some idea of the cause of Charlotte's political disputes and debates with the Taylor family can be gleaned from Mary Taylor's letter to Mrs Gaskell on the 30th July 1856:

'You give much too favourable an account of the blackcoated Tory savages that kept the people down, and provoked excesses in those days. Old Roberson said he "would wade to the knees in blood rather than the then state of things be altered." A state including Corn Law, Test Law, and a host of other oppressions.'

Thirdly, we can consider Ellen Nussey who, of the three girls, had the background which is the least known and the most misrepresented.

In beliefs, in standing, in long settlement in the area, the Nusseys and Taylors were similar. Their large detached houses were just over a mile apart. Both families depended on the woollen industry, with their menfolk travelling, acting as agents, and making contracts. They had been neck and neck in the establishment of their small mills of identical sizes. They were both involved

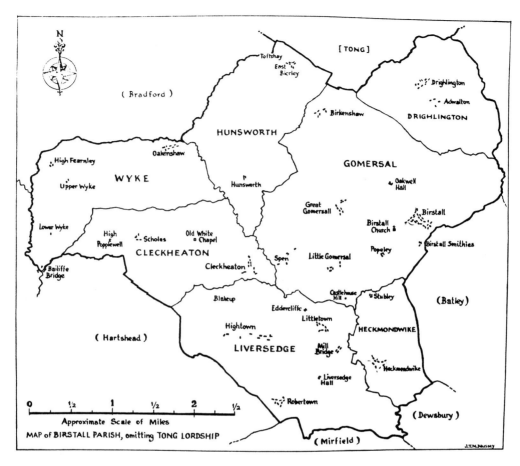

The ancient parishes of Birstall (omitting Tong).

with the Moravian community and with Birstall church. But there were differences.

The surname Nussey originated from the place-name of the bercary, or sheep station, set up by the monks of Bolton Priory on Appletreewick Moor in 1299. In the poll tax returns for Appletreewick in 1379 a Robertus de Nusse and a John de Nussay were assessed at fourpence each. The family increased and spread.

Ellen's great-grandfather George Nussey, a dyer, who married a Heck-mondwike girl, came to live in Birstall Smithies, then in 1711 took a part lease of Rydings hall and land and moved there. He later took over the complete lease and the couple spent the rest of their lives at Rydings. Their youngest son, Joshua, at the age of forty married his god-daughter, twenty-three-year-old Mercy Walker of Birstall Smithies. The Walkers, a yeoman and clothier family, had been established in the parish since before records began. Joshua and Mercy were Ellen's grandparents.[6] Joshua went into partnership with

Mercy's father and her brother John Walker in their business as clothiers. Clothiers acted as middle men in addition to manufacturing.

After living near the church for a few years, Mercy and Joshua Nussey and their children shared the house in Birstall Smithies with Mercy's parents. John Walker and his wife Elizabeth settled near Birstall market place, and most of their children were born there.

In two respects the Nussey/Walker family was different from the other clothier families of the area. One was their connection with the Hartleys. The other was the medical career of Richard Walker, younger brother of Mercy and John.

David Hartley, the philosopher who wrote *Observations on Man*,[7] a book which greatly influenced eighteenth century thought and the Romantic poets, was the maternal uncle of Elizabeth, John Walker's wife.[8] His two sons were both MPs. The elder, David Hartley Jnr, was an inventor and a friend of Benjamin Franklin, and later in 1783 with Franklin was to sign the peace treaty with America after the War of Independence.

The younger son, Winchcombe Hartley, was wealthy. Mary Hartley their sister was artistic and literary. These cousins kept in touch with John and Elizabeth Walker throughout their lives and were a very important influence. Mercy and John's younger brother, Richard Walker, broke from the family woollen tradition when, in 1763 aged fourteen, he was apprenticed for seven years to William Hey, a young apothecary-surgeon in Leeds. After this he spent the usual two years walking the hospitals in London. He had connections there, not only with his sister-in-law's cousins the Hartley family, but also with their friend Dr Joseph Priestley, who came from Birstall.[9]

It was almost certainly through these connections with Whig intellectual and political circles that Richard Walker gained the opportunity to go into a fashionable apothecary's business at 17 St James Street, London,[10] on a year's trial as manager of the shop. He was very successful in this post and as the years went on became first a partner, then at last the senior partner and head of the firm. As the business served the court, Richard held appointments as apothecary to various members of the royal family, becoming a personal friend of the Prince of Wales, better known as the Prince Regent, later George IV. Richard did not marry, and his home over the shop in St James Street became a little outpost of Yorkshire in London. The three branches of the Walker family – Mercy Nussey and her brothers John and Richard Walker – remained like this until the crisis year of 1776.

By 1776, due to the war with America, the Yorkshire woollen industry was in a period of intense depression. Unsold cloth was piling up by the thousand pieces in the cloth halls of Leeds and workers in the woollen trade were emigrating rather than face starvation. At this time Joshua and Mercy Nussey and John and Elizabeth Walker, in their joint business as clothiers, were faced with immense problems.

Fortunately family connections came to their aid. With the encouragement of his wife's cousins, the rich and influential Hartley family, John Walker left his ancestral trade and qualified himself for the church. He was then appointed curate in a parish near Bath. Later in life he was presented, additionally, to a living in the gift of the Hartley family.[11] This move on John Walker's part began the third strand in the interwoven Walker/Nussey families, the clerical, now added to the old tradition of the woollen trade and the newer one of medicine.

Left behind in Birstall Smithies, the Nusseys carried on the clothier business, which now had less mouths to feed. In this difficult time, 1776, Joshua Nussey's elder brother Joseph Nussey, who was living in the old hall of Rydings, died childless. Joshua then opportunely inherited the lease of the Rydings estate and at once sold it, breaking the Nussey connection with Rydings at this point. The proceeds of the sale of the lease helped the Nusseys to weather the economic storm.

More family support during the slump in the woollen industry came from Mercy Nussey's brother, Richard Walker, now well established in the

Richard Walker senior, royal apothecary and Ellen Nussey's great-uncle.

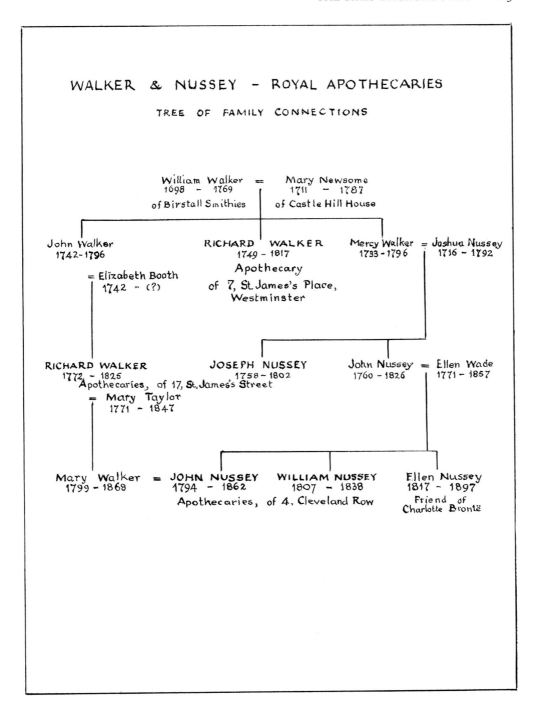

WALKER & NUSSEY - ROYAL APOTHECARIES

TREE OF FAMILY CONNECTIONS

apothecary business in London, who was becoming a glamorous and influential figure in his turn. Richard wished to help his nephews and nieces, who were very dear to him. He began to take his young nephews as apprentices, which would provide them with a good living for life. Choosing from amongst both his sister Mercy's children and his brother John's, he founded a medical dynasty which lasted nearly a hundred years.

Richard Walker's interests were wide, his conversation was enjoyable, and his patients sought his company even when they were well. His political allegiance had long been formed. 17 St James Street was the popular apothecary's shop among the Whig aristocrats who clustered round the Prince of Wales. Well-known names appear in the account book, Charles Fox, the Duke of Marlboro, Lord Palmerston, Lord John Russell and many others. The Whigs' favourite portrait painter was John Hoppner in Charles Street, St James Square, and Richard had a half-length portrait and a copy painted by him. The two portraits were passed down in the family, Ellen knew them, Charlotte Brontë saw one and probably both. In contrast to depression-hit Yorkshire, there could have been no more exciting, delicious time in the fashionable world of London than this last part of the eighteenth century and the early nineteenth. Beautiful, well-designed buildings were rising in streets and crescents, peopled by a society to whom elegance was everything. London was by later standards a small town. Illness there was, and medicine could do little to stay it; but the air was clean, the fields were close, the cries of London were heard on the streets and dairymaids milked their cows directly into customers' jugs in St James Park.

By 1790 one of Richard Walker's nephews, Joseph Nussey, was qualified and could be left in charge of the business when Richard journeyed on visits to Yorkshire with the other trainee nephew, his namesake (John's son, the second Richard Walker). At this time Richard had lived in London for twenty years and glittering though life there was, his thoughts were turning towards his Yorkshire roots. Although he was only forty he had made money. He had travelled on the continent, and had become accustomed to the best interiors. Preparing for his retirement now attracted him. He decided to look for a property in which, a few years hence, he might live and take his ease. The Rydings estate in Birstall, formerly leased by the Nusseys, was for sale, and in 1791, the year of the French Revolution, Richard bought it, and later bought additional property nearby.

Between the sale of the lease of the Rydings estate by Joshua Nussey in 1776 and the estate's purchase by Richard Walker, one John Beatson had sold the old hall's fittings for £2,000. Presumably these were panelling, fireplaces and carvings, which must have been of great richness. When Richard bought it the estate was described as 'a capital messuage commonly called Rydings. . . with one courtyard, three barns, three stables, three houses, three gardens, three orchards, sixty acres of land, ten acres of wood, commons or pasture for all manner of cattle'.

Nowhere had Richard seen anything he preferred to these woods and fields, murmuring brooks and rook-haunted trees, orchards, gardens, and homely farmyard, but the house itself was forlorn after the sale of its fittings. With deeds dating to the time of Henry IV, it was a solid medieval shell of a building firmly planted on outcropping rock.

For the next ten years, while still carrying on his London business, Richard renovated and restored Rydings. Leaving a good deal of it intact, he decided on a new front facade and an altered roof, partly doing away with the medieval three gables. He modernised the kitchen and re-fitted the rest of the house in the latest mode. He added battlements round the roof, partially concealing it. Then he filled the house with his choice of furniture and paintings. During his time in London, Richard had developed his naturally good eye and he collected notable works of art.

Both Richard Walker's sister, Mercy Nussey, and his brother, Rev John Walker, died in 1796. It seems that Richard Walker then offered a home at Rydings to John's widow, Elizabeth Walker, and her two daughters (her son, the second Richard Walker, was already working with him).

Next Richard used some of his recently bought land for the erection of a scribbling and fulling mill beside Smithies Beck near the entrance to the Rydings estate. The mechanisation of the means of production was coming fast, and it was a race in the valleys to see who could build a steam-powered mill first. Richard Walker ordered for Smithies Mill one of the first Boulton and Watt steam-driven engines, of which drawings and details still exist. One of Mercy's sons, Joseph Nussey, Richard had already trained as an apothecary, but the others were to form a partnership to run Smithies Mill.[12]

Richard Walker finally retired to Rydings in about 1802, the year in which his nephew and partner, Joseph Nussey, died at the age of 43. Joseph, Mercy's second son, who had been living over the shop at 17 St James Street, was a man with a very sweet nature. The Prince of Wales grew fond of him and when Joseph was in his last illness the Prince visited him and was seen to be in tears as he left the house.[13]

The second Richard Walker, John's son, therefore became the new head of the firm at 17 St James Street on his uncle's retirement, and took over the living quarters over the shop. While on visits to Yorkshire he met and married Mary Taylor from the affluent family at Purlwell Hall, Batley. It is said that Mary brought £20,000 to the marriage.

With the London firm in his nephew's capable hands, the first Richard Walker now began his life of leisure. He became an antiquarian, he wrote and published essays and poetry and translated Latin verse. He also wished to be of lasting benefit to his profession, and, remembering how difficult he had found it as a student to learn about the medical innovators of the past, he had researched and published *Memoirs of Medicine*. A copy of this book formed part of his great-niece Ellen's library. Richard gave free medical treatment to poor people who came to him on Sunday mornings before church service, and was once called to York to attend the Prince Regent who had fallen ill whilst at the races. He was also a justice of the peace.

His nephew John Nussey acted as his magistrate's clerk and an upper room in Rydings acquired the name 'The Justice Room'.

John Nussey was Mercy's third son and 'our' Ellen's father. While buying land for his uncle from John Wade, the miller at the manor corn mill at Carlinghow, Batley, John met and fell in love with the miller's pretty daughter Ellen. When they were married they lived sometimes at Birstall Smithies, but often in Rydings with Richard Walker. As far as is known, Ellen Wade did not bring any money or property to the marriage.

There can be no doubt that Richard enjoyed these retirement years. He made friends and had people to stay, ranging from his London great-nieces (Richard and Mary Walker's children) to Earl Fitzwilliam, then Viscount Milton, who stayed at Rydings for three weeks during the election campaign of 1807 when he was canvassing the county for the Whig faction. Richard Walker felt much honoured by the visit and Earl Fitzwilliam thanked him with the gift of a handsome and enormous silver wine-cooler. The wine-cooler later resided for many years in Coutts Bank, as none of the family could decide to whom it ought to belong.

As time went on, Richard Walker began to feel the indispositions of age. He was living a quiet invalid life at Rydings in April 1812 when the Luddite riots took place in the Birstall area. Rawfolds Mill, chosen by the rioters for their attack, was only a mile or so away over the hill in front of Rydings, down in the next valley. The attack was beaten off; four or five of the attackers were left in the yard of the mill, dead or dying. (These were the events used by Charlotte Brontë in *Shirley*.) The Rev Patrick Brontë at that time was minister at Hartshead barely two miles away. He condemned the violence, but is said to have had compassion on the victims and to have turned a blind eye when he saw that they were being buried secretly in the corner of his churchyard. Richard Walker, old and ill, took no part in these troubles and replied to Earl Fitzwilliam's enquiries by making light of the disturbances.[14] The active magistrate in the case was Joseph Radcliffe of Huddersfield. The ringleaders were arrested, condemned and hung at York.

At last Richard Walker's health deteriorated to the point where he decided to return to London, with easy access to medical treatment from nephew Richard. His legs troubled him a great deal. In London he lived with his niece Anne, and let off the Rydings estate. The nephew who was living at Rydings with him, John Nussey, had to move himself, wife Ellen, and their large family of children back to Birstall Smithies. Richard died in October 1817 and named as one of his executors Joshua Taylor of the Red House at Gomersal, father of our own Mary Taylor.

Our Ellen Nussey's life overlapped her great-uncle Richard Walker's by six months. She lived her life in the context of the Birstall area and of her family. To understand the framework of that life it has been necessary to look back in time, for people and events cast long shadows.

Her father John Nussey's career was a chequered one. Apart from his work for his uncle, he acted as an agent for cloth and for army contracts, and worked with his brothers in their mills and woollen businesses. His twelve children may have acted as a brake on his career – none of his brothers had so many. He was the only one of Mercy's children to be a beneficiary in Richard Walker's will, inheriting £300. He was later described by William Carr, his eldest brother's grandson, as 'improvident and unfortunate'.

When Charlotte met Ellen in January 1831, Ellen's influential great-uncle Richard Walker, 'Justice Walker', had been dead only a little over thirteen years. His life affected Charlotte a good deal, indirectly. She was to stay in the house he remodelled for himself and use it in her fiction; see his portrait, his papers and books. Some of his books took their place in Ellen's own library, to which Charlotte had access. When visiting Ellen, Charlotte probably used the furniture Richard Walker had chosen in rooms decorated as he had them, for in those days a house which remained in family hands changed little. Stories about him would have abounded. Ellen was very influenced by his life, for her family gained their livelihoods in ways which owed much to his support.

[1] *Everywhere Spoken Against*, 113ff.

[2] Patrick Brontë referred to himself as Minister of Haworth in the parish registers of Thornton at Anne's baptism.

[3] *Keighley News*, 28th June 1924

[4] We should remember how different the role of the public house was in that society. The coaching inns were the halts and distribution points for the Royal Mail and staging posts for travellers; newspapers were collected from pubs and inns, and parcels too by the carriers' carts; people called for dinner or afternoon tea; private rooms could be hired for an hour for business to be transacted, a letter written, or for weary travellers to recuperate.

[5] These deeds are amongst Hartley Thwaite's papers.

[6] Mercy's parents, William Walker and his wife Mary Newsome, had eleven children. Six sons died in infancy, one daughter did not marry, another married but was childless. Only three of the children, Mercy, John, and Richard, are of significance in this story.

[7] The Romantic poets were impressed by David Hartley's revolutionary theories and Coleridge named his son Hartley in his honour, although later the limitations of Hartley's pioneering work were realised. It was Hartley Coleridge who was sympathetic to Branwell Brontë.

[8] Elizabeth's mother was Elizabeth Hartley, wife of Francis Booth, a tanner of Littletown. The Booths were a locally important family, who held the lease of Popeley Hall at one time, and their connections were traced by John Nussey, to whom I am indebted for all my information about them. Elizabeth Firth (Mrs Franks), important to the Brontës, was also distantly descended from this Booth family.

[9] David Hartley II had trained as a doctor before becoming a politician. The Priestley family in the Birstall area had dealings with the Walkers, and for some years as a boy Joseph Priestley lived in the household of his teacher Rev Kirkby, who was married to Joshua Nussey's sister. Priestley was a close friend of William Hey (who became a famous surgeon and mayor of Leeds), and of Benjamin Franklin.

[10] The corner site is now covered by part of Lloyds Bank.

[11] John Walker matriculated at St Albans Hall, attached to Merton College where his wife's brother and cousin were fellows (Nathaniel Booth and David Hartley II). He became a curate at Mells. Winchcombe Henry Hartley (half-brother of David II) later gave Walker the living of Little Shefford. Duties there were light as there were hardly any houses in the parish, and the church was and is a tiny Saxon one in the middle of a field.

[12] *Smithies Mill, Birstall, the life and times of an 18th. century steam-driven scribbling and fulling mill in the Yorkshire heavy woollen district*, by John Nussey gives an excellent history of this mill. In the 1840 valuation of Gomersal township, Smithies Mill comprised mill, engine house, boiler house, counting house, out-warehouse, cart shed, food house, wool-warehouse, stable and lawn. Richard Nussey's report to the Parliamentary Commisioners on Smithies Mill gives: '44 persons employed in scribbling, carding, slubbing and fulling; 25 males, 12 under 21; 19 females, 16 under 21; 1 fuller and 1 slubber who each provided and paid his own assistant. The mill worked Monday start 7 am, Tuesday to Friday 6 am to 7.30 pm, Saturday finish 5 pm. Breakfast was 8-8.30 am, the mill stopped for the dinner break 12 noon to 1 pm, and there were 'drinks' at 4-4.30 pm. There were seven annual holidays, Christmas two and a half days, Birstall Feast in August one and a half, Easter and Whitsun one day each, Shrove Tuesday and New Year half a day. Sickness – there had been two cases of typhoid, both slubbers, and during the illnesses another member of the family took their place and received their wages.'

[13] Joseph Nussey became a partner in the firm at 17 St James Street in 1799 and in the same year was appointed apothecary to the Prince of Wales, holding this office until his death on the 30th January 1802.

[14] Richard Walker's letters to Earl Fitzwilliam about the Luddite disturbances are in Sheffield City Archives. The Radcliffe MSS in Leeds Archives at Sheepscar include the papers of the Huddersfield magistrate Sir Joseph Radcliffe.

ELLEN'S EARLY LIFE

The story can now be sketched in from the year of Ellen's birth in 1817 until her meeting with Charlotte Brontë in the schoolroom at Roe Head in 1831. Ellen, Mary Taylor and all the Brontës were born in the Regency period – that brief nine years which has given its name to the age. An open, elegant, breezy time when the population of the British Isles was low, its ideas free and its morals loose.

For Ellen's family, 1817 was to be a momentous year. She was the last child of John Nussey and his wife Ellen and was born in the hamlet of Birstall Smithies, in a house at the side of the drive leading into the estate of Rydings, to which estate the house belonged. This was her home for her first nine years and appears to have been a long, low stone-built house with a packhorse trail running between it and Smithies Mill and Beck at the front. The house may have been an old yeoman house, possibly lived in by earlier generations of the Walkers, but by 1817 it was divided into two dwellings.[1]

To Mrs Nussey, the advent of another baby was routine. She would be pleased to have a healthy normal child, and having paid her family dues by naming her other daughters after relatives, gave the baby her own name. She was a busy woman. She and her husband never seemed able to save money, and nine of her children were living at home as well as the new baby.

The eldest, John, had left home at fourteen to be apprenticed as an apothecary to his half-cousin, the second Richard Walker, in London. John was now qualified and still living as part of Richard's family, over the shop at 17 St James Street.

The next boy, Joseph, twenty, was working in the woollen industry with his father. Joshua, eighteen, was preparing to go to university where he hoped to take holy orders. Richard, fourteen, was to follow his father and brother Joseph into the woollen trade. All Mrs Nussey's boys seemed to be prospering; the younger ones, William, ten, and Henry, five, were schoolboys now, and little George, three, had got past babyhood.

It was her daughters that were the worry. Apart from the new baby there were three, Ann, twenty-two, Mary, sixteen, and Sarah, seven. We do not know what was wrong with Sarah, but something was amiss with her. There was the oddity of her being entered in the register of baptisms as Samuel – no doubt a slip on the vicar's part. Throughout her life Sarah needed unremitting care and attention. 'Death. . .would be a blessing to her', Charlotte Brontë was to write some years later. Whether she was a mongol, a spastic, or whether

THE CHILDREN OF
JOHN NUSSEY OF BIRSTALL SMITHIES   (1760–1826)
AND HIS WIFE
ELLEN, DAUGHTER OF JOHN WADE, CORNMILLER, OF CARLINGHOW

1 JOHN   1793 – 1862   Married Mary Walker, his second cousin, gd-dau. of his gd-mother Walker's brother John Walker.   Apothecary to George IV; Apothecary to the Household of William IV; Apothecary to Queen Victoria and to Household of Prince Albert.

2 ANN   1795 – 1878   Married, in 1849, Robert Clapham of Upper Batley, brother of John Clapham of Brookroyd Mill.

3 JOSEPH 1797 – 1846   Unmarried. Had an interest in the family firm Nussey and Walker, woollen manufacturers.

4 JOSHUA 1798 – 1871   Married Anne, sister of Henry Alexander, "an East Indies Director".   Ordained deacon 1823; some time chaplain to Lord Blaney; Rector of Poughill, Devon.

5 MERCY MARY 1801 – 1886   Unmarried.   Entered in March 1817 the Moravian Settlement at Fairfield, near Manchester, as "Great Girl". Possibly remained there until her father's death.

6 RICHARD 1803 – 1872   Married Elizabeth, dau. of John Charnock of Woodhouse Lane, Leeds. Inherited his uncle Richard Nussey's interest in the family's mills at Birstall; also leased New Mill, Holbeck. Later inherited father-in-law's two mills at Meadows Lane, Leeds.

✳

7 WILLIAM 1807 – 1838   Unmarried. Joined the family medical practice in London, 1823.   Joint Apothecary to the Royal Household with brother John from 1826. Drowned when in state of deep depression.

8 SARAH WALKER 1809 – 1843   Unmarried.   Appears to have been an invalid from infancy.

9 HENRY   1812 – 1867   Married Emily, daughter of Richard Prescott, of Eversley, Hampshire.   Curate successively at Birstall, Burton Agnes, Earnley.   Vicar of Hathersage 1844 – 1847

10 GEORGE 1814 – 1885   Unmarried.   Assisted his brothers in their woollen manufacturing activity.   In 1845 began to suffer from an illness ultimately diagnosed as mental. After an initial assessment at York by Dr Belcombe jnr., he spent the remainder of his days at a small private nursing home at Acomb (Dr Nelson).

11 ELLEN   1817 – 1897   Unmarried.   Friend of Charlotte Brontë.

✳   Between the births of Richard & William another son was born, named George. He died in Oct. 1812.

some childish ailment or accident had left her crippled or with other disabilities, we cannot know. But her condition was to be a burden to her young sister Ellen in the years to come.

It must have been of concern to their mother that at the age of twenty-two Ann was still unmarried, but she would be a great help. Ann was a practitioner of the little niceties of life and kept up social standards. In a family with so many energetic boys, that influence was valuable.

Ann and Mary had become involved in the Moravian community at nearby Gomersal, where the Rev Richard Grimes (Brother Grimes) was a man of great spiritual influence. In January 1817, Mary had applied to become a sister of the Moravian community at Fulneck, the largest Moravian settlement in the area. Brother Grimes vouched for the sincerity of her religious vocation. The Moravian practice was to draw lots so that the will of God could make the decision. The lot was against admitting Mary. She then applied to join the Single Sisters House at Fairfield near Manchester, although her family did not want her to go so far away. This time the lot fell in her favour and she became a sister there, taking the religious name of Mercy. She was known for the rest of her life as Mercy, and Charlotte Brontë was always to call her so, but sometimes she was called Mercy Mary, or Mary Mercy. Mercy did not remain a Moravian sister for life. By 1831 she was living at home again, but for how long she had remained in the Fairfield community and why she left, is not yet known.

It was in the autumn of the year 1817 that Richard Walker, royal apothecary, owner of the Rydings estate and Ellen's father's uncle, died, and

Ellen's parents: John and Ellen Nussey.

on the 6th November a traumatic event occurred to close the year. The Prince Regent's daughter Princess Charlotte, all England's hope, heiress presumptive to the throne, died in childbirth at the age of twenty-one together with her baby.

She had been a customer of the firm of apothecaries at 17 St James Street and Ellen's brother John, aged twenty-three, very junior as an apothecary at the time, had accompanied his half-cousin Richard Walker on medical visits to her. In later years John always spoke of the princess with regret. She inspired in all who knew her both respect and deep affection.

Ellen's memories went back to the time in 1819 when she was two years old and her family began to take her to services in the parish church. She thought it had been good discipline for her to learn to sit still and pay attention, and she soon grew to enjoy worship. At the time there were well-developed musical skills among the congregations of the area[2] and she began to love church music. Her baptism was delayed until she was four years old, as her brother Henry's had been. Late baptism is usually a sign of Low rather than High Church religious views. She remembered the valley in which she lived, 'with [only] two mills in it, when one could walk for miles by the beckside, and never see a soul but an occasional angler trying to tempt the wary trout'.

Worrying events were likely to pass above her head. Richard Walker had left the bulk of his property among the three children of his brother Rev John Walker: the second Richard, Mary and Anne. As Anne was married, her share, Smithies Mill, was left to her husband.[3] Richard had the Rydings estate, with the responsibility of providing his sister Mary with an annual income out of it.

The second Richard should have been rich. He had married a wealthy wife, was the head of a thriving business, a royal apothecary, and the only man who knew how to reach the fat Prince Regent's veins for bleeding. He was the doctor in whose arms the Duke of Devonshire died in 1811. When the Prince Regent was crowned in 1821 Richard's daughter Sarah was one of the charming group of 'Herb-maidens' who strewed herbs and flowers, in the coronation procession. Richard was in constant attendance on the king, and travelled with him to Ireland, Scotland and Hanover. Unfortunately, though he had the family good nature and charm, Richard was self-indulgent and careless. He had the right to embalm members of the Royal family, but on three occasions let others carry out this duty. Ellen's parents may have felt concern when they knew that Richard was raising a mortgage on his part of the Rydings estate.

In 1824 Richard's young half-cousin and partner, John Nussey, went on a journey to the Netherlands. This would be in Richard's stead, for he was no longer in good health, and in February 1825 he died. He thought highly of John, and a few short weeks before his death he saw the marriage between John and his own eldest daughter, Mary. The young couple went to live at 4 Cleveland Row, facing St James Palace, and this was to be the address of the medical practice, as opposed to the shop, until 1860. Joshua Nussey was by now a curate and he conducted the marriage ceremony for his brother.[4] George

IV was fond of John Nussey and kind to him, and so he prospered; he became the king's official apothecary in February 1825.[5] He and his wife were to give Mrs Nussey her only grandchildren.

Remote though these events seemed to the peaceful pastoral valley where Ellen was spending her early life, they had repercussions there. Within a year of the second Richard Walker's death, his widow had sold her part of the Rydings estate to Richard Nussey, Ellen's uncle. A strip of land was also sold for a new turnpike road, which cut straight through the Rydings parkland. Work started on two new turnpike roads[6] and Birstall Smithies became a crossroads in 1826.

In the same year, when she was nine years old, Ellen's father died. His bachelor brother Richard Nussey, who now owned Rydings, offered to share his home with Mrs Nussey and her family. They had lived at Rydings before, with old Richard Walker, and many of the family had been born there. Now they were to live there for the next ten years. It was probably at this point that Ellen, who had so far been educated at a little local school, was sent to the Moravian Ladies Academy a mile away at Gomersal.

Events went smoothly for the family until the year 1830, when in the same crucial summer weeks, the much-respected Brother Grimes left the Ladies' Academy at Gomersal – thus precipitating Ellen's move to Roe Head – and at the same time John Nussey in London was in attendance on the king, George IV, during his last illness.

John's wife Mary was on a visit to Yorkshire with their children, and when the king died on the 26th June, John wrote to her:

'I sat up with the poor King on Tuesday and Thursday nights. I thought he would have died during the latter night. I returned home on Friday [from Windsor] so completely exhausted and worn out that I could hardly support myself. . .and on Saturday morning was called up by Sir Astley Cooper, who communicated the sad tidings of what had happened in the night. . .'

John was then summoned to go back to Windsor with the ingredients for embalming the king. He was given royal mementos, as was the custom.[7]

Two days after the king's death, John Nussey was writing to his wife about his fears for their future. The Duke of Clarence, now William IV, had succeeded his brother. William was an old man and had his own medical attendants: John was afraid that there would be no place for him in the elevated circles he had frequented for so long. On the 30th June, Mary Nussey and her children visited Birstall Smithies, the first time Ellen's brother Henry remembered seeing her there. No doubt she told the household at Rydings about the events at Windsor. John Nussey was not to be completely out in the cold. He was appointed one of the two joint apothecaries to the royal household, which meant a drop in salary, but he was still a royal apothecary.

Ellen, now thirteen, must have listened wide-eyed to these details of the romantic far-off life led by her brother John. Years later when she visited London, Ellen was to see at first hand the royal relics treasured by the family, including the sword which barred Queen Caroline from entering the abbey at her husband's coronation, the collector's cabinet inlaid with the Prince of Wales' arms, and the gold watch with which the prince once paid his bill. She was to be given a pretty royal button, which had been George III's and was mounted as a brooch.

All this glamour gave the otherwise ordinary family at Rydings a sense of being special. It was noticeable in the case of Ellen's eldest sister Ann, who had a certain social snobbishness, even though she had been closely involved in the religious life of the Moravian community and should have had a mind above such emotions.

The Moravians influenced the Brontës, particularly Anne, and were to have a lifelong influence on Ellen and on Mary Taylor's family.[8] In the religious apathy of eighteenth century Britain the two Wesley brothers, John and Charles, and their friend Benjamin Ingham, were part of a movement of reform. They came into contact with the Moravians and were so impressed by them that for a while they worked together. It was after a Moravian meeting in London in 1738 that John Wesley felt 'his heart strangely warmed' and many of the Moravian customs, such as the Love-feast and the Decision by Lot, were adopted by early Methodists. In 1742 a Moravian Love-feast took place at Gomersal at which thousands of people were present, and two Moravian missionaries worked on afterwards in the West Riding. Fulneck, at Pudsey near Leeds, was the foundation community of the Moravians in the North of England and it is only a few miles from the parish of Birstall. A smaller congregation soon arose at Gomersal. This became a 'Settlement' in 1755. Both centres are still active today. Three interconnecting houses were built in Gomersal for a small group of Moravian Sisters, but the sisters did not continue there[9] although the church and the school (the Ladies' Academy) flourished.

As well as local girls like Ellen Nussey and the Taylors, pupils came to the school from all over the world. The curriculum was unusually wide, with special emphasis on needlework, embroidery and music. Religious instruction was stressed. Discipline was strict. It was said of the school that 'it sent out women who were patterns of courtesy and good manners and who remembered all their lives to behave like gentlewomen'.

There is an interesting link between the Brontë family and the Nusseys through the Moravians. The teacher at Cowan Bridge whom Charlotte was to immortalise as 'Miss Temple' in *Jane Eyre* was in real life Ann Evans, who married an Anglican minister, the Rev James Connor. His younger brother, Samuel Connor, was a Moravian minister who married Letitia Williams, a teacher at the Moravian Ladies Academy at Gomersal in the days when Ann and Mercy Nussey were closely associated with the community.[10] Charlotte's 'Miss Temple' and her husband are believed to have gone abroad, probably to Canada, for a number of years. On her return, 'Miss Temple' is said to have confirmed that the picture Charlotte gave of the school at Cowan Bridge was a true one.

The Moravians were a profound moral and religious influence on the

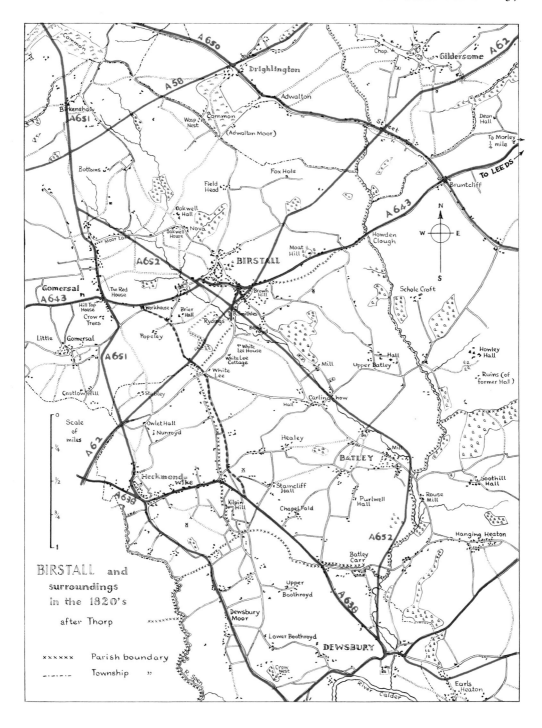

The present main road system is picked out in red, for help in identifying the locations of earlier features.

families of the Nusseys at Rydings and the Taylors at Red House, strengthening the bond between the two families. Mary Taylor and her brother Joe were closer in many ways to Ellen Nussey than her own brothers and sisters. At the end of her life, speaking of Charlotte's letters, Ellen said that she could not see that it mattered to whom a letter was addressed; it was the fact that it was by Charlotte Brontë which was important. Her actual words were, 'what does it matter if they are addressed to Mary or Joe?' Her choice of those two names betrays the intimacy which had existed between the young people so many years before. In thinking back to Charlotte, she automatically thought too of the Taylors.

There were a number of likenesses – sometimes reversed, mirrored – between Ellen's situation and Charlotte's. When she was five, Charlotte lost her mother; when Ellen was nine, she lost her father. As a result of these events, Charlotte's spinster aunt had come to live in the Brontë household, and Ellen's bachelor uncle had taken his widowed sister-in-law and her children into his household. Again pursuing the reverse image, Charlotte was, after her elder sisters' deaths in childhood, the oldest of her siblings; Ellen was the youngest of her much larger family. At Cowan Bridge School, Charlotte had witnessed outbreaks of 'typhus' and tuberculosis among the pupils; at Gomersal Ladies' Academy, there was an outbreak of 'black pox' brought there by a girl from abroad in 1829 when Ellen was almost certainly a pupil, and some of the villagers died.[11]

Charlotte knew that her home and livelihood depended on her father's life – there were no family resources. Ellen's home and livelihood depended on her uncle's life; but her elder brothers were making their way in the world, and would not have seen her starve or without a roof over her head. In spite of Joshua Taylor's bankruptcy, both Mary Taylor and Ellen Nussey faced the world with more financial security than did the Brontë children.

[1] The site of Ellen's birthplace is now covered by a small modern housing development.
[2] See *The History of Morley* by Scatcherd, p 138-139, for a discussion of the high musical standards of the area.
[3] Anne's part was left to Rev R H Chapman. This was usual in the case of married women because they and their property belonged to their husbands until the Married Women's Property Acts of the 1890s, unless special legal settlements gave them some control. In the event of Mr Chapman's death the property reverted to Anne. Her eldest son later owned Smithies Mill.
[4] In the church of St James, Piccadilly, all Richard Walker's children were baptised, his daughter Mary and John Nussey were married, and Richard was buried. Joshua Nussey was admitted sizar at St Catherines College, Cambridge, 1817, matriculated 1818, BA 1822, MA 1825, deacon May 1823, priest 1824. He was curate of St Margarets and St Johns, Westminster 1823-31.
[5] Succeeding his father-in-law, the second Richard Walker, in that post. It was probably to celebrate this event that a chimney, with a face and the date 1825 on it, was built at Smithies Mill; it can still be seen.
[6] The present Leeds/Huddersfield and Dewsbury/Bradford roads, the A62 and A652.

[7] Two tiny shirts prepared with exquisite handwork for Princess Charlotte's baby became heirlooms in the Nussey family. Together with the dress Sarah Walker wore as a Herb-maiden, the Nussey family's copy of the book of George IV's coronation, and most of John Nussey's mementoes of George IV given to him at the king's death (being the bedspread, nightshirt, and nightcap that the king used), they were placed on long-term loan to the Brighton Pavilion Museum by the Misses Nussey of the Ivy House, Chislehurst, Kent. The king's handkerchief of fine linen delicately embroidered with the royal monogram GR (George Rex) which the king held in his last hours, was given to the Society of Apothecaries, who prize it and preserve it carefully.

[8] The 'Unity of Brethren' (*Unitas Fratrum*) was the first Protestant church, originating in Bohemia in 1457. It prospered and the Bible was translated for the first time into the language of the people. Then in 1620 the *Unitas Fratrum* was overthrown and survived only among little groups in Moravia – hence the name Moravian. There they adopted a very simple and pure form of life and worship, and endured much persecution and many wanderings. At last refugees from these little communities reached Saxony, and established themselves there. Once with a secure and settled base, they had a spiritual reawakening and in 1732 began the missions which have been the main work of their church ever since.

[9] Known as the Sisters' Houses, these dwellings still exist. They were sold to Dr William Carr and continue to feature in this story. Among those who lived in the western house were Mary Taylor's brother Joshua and later her nephew Richard Alfred Taylor. The middle house was inhabited for a time by the two Misses Wooler and their niece Miss Marianne Allbutt.

[10] Information on the Connor family kindly given by Miss M Connor.

[11] *Two Hundred Years of Christian Witness at Gomersal, Mirfield and Wyke, 1755 to 1955* by T Heywood, a booklet which appears to have been privately printed by the congregation.

CHARLOTTE'S VISIT TO RYDINGS, 1832

If, after they parted at the end of their schooldays in the summer of 1832, Charlotte had feared that like many school and holiday friendships it would be out of sight out of mind for her with Ellen and Mary, she was mistaken. Ellen felt an affinity to Charlotte which she had never experienced before, which was beyond material things. She wrote and Charlotte was pleased and gratified. By July 1832 they had established their first custom, of writing every other month – six letters from each a year. Before parting they had promised to send one another locks of their hair as a keepsake, but, discovering the high cost of postage, neither of them did so. Charlotte hoped that Ellen would continue at Roe Head. Mr Brontë could not afford more education for herself so she craved it for Ellen, whose family could afford it. By now Charlotte's aunt was also sending love to Ellen, so it may be that Miss Branwell had been to Roe Head – though this must remain conjecture.

Letters between Charlotte and Mary are lost to us, because Mary destroyed them. Ellen and Mary, living within a quarter of an hour's walk and meeting often, only wrote when away from home. Ellen kept Mary and Martha's letters but they did not keep hers – the Taylors were not preservers of ephemera. Ellen's letters to Charlotte were destroyed, thanks to Arthur Bell Nicholls. It is on Charlotte's letters to Ellen that we rely for much of our knowledge both of Ellen and of the Brontë family, and although we are immensely lucky that so many letters survived, they can only provide a patchy and partial record.

At this time envelopes were not used. The address was written on the outside of the sheet of writing paper after it had been folded up and sealed with wax. Charlotte later used charming little seals with words on them giving messages or mottos.[1] Postage charges, which were levied on each sheet of paper, were paid on arrival. To avoid sending more than one sheet, people who had written all they could in the normal way often turned the paper through ninety degrees and then wrote across the paper again, at right angles to the first set of writing and over it. This is known as 'crossing' letters, and such a one would be called a 'crossed' letter. Ellen was particularly prone to use this method of sending the most words possible for the recipient's money. Crossed letters are difficult to read, and in the handwriting of Ellen's younger days, fiendishly puzzling. Charlotte and Mary complained constantly about the illegibility of Ellen's letters, but at least when deciphered they were worth reading.

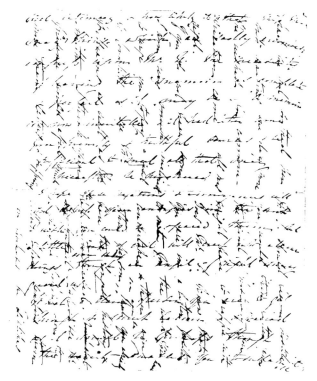

An example of a 'crossed' letter by Ellen Nussey (reduced in size).

Ellen's 'well-filled and interesting' letter of about the 4th September 1832 took the news to Haworth that Mr Brontë's old friend, Hammond Roberson, had suffered an attack of paralysis; that Ellen was taking lessons at Roe Head once a week (these lessons existed more in the promise than in the performance); and that a friend had turned out different from expectations. Charlotte informed Ellen that she was too sanguine about people's good qualities – but Ellen could not alter in that respect. She was to believe people good and true until they proved otherwise to the end of her life.

Although news from the outer world was welcome, there was plenty for the young Brontë girls to do in Haworth. Largely due to Mr Brontë, the school was newly erected. It was used as a Sunday school on Sundays and an ordinary National school on weekdays.[2] Charlotte mentions having 'all the Female teachers of the Sunday-school to tea'. Clergymen's families were expected to teach in Sunday school and some of their pupils recorded memories of Branwell's and Charlotte's teaching. We know that Anne taught there, and it is hard to believe that Emily escaped the duty completely. It was valuable teacher training and helped the family later to tackle posts as governesses and tutor.

Charlotte was also teaching her younger sisters, and soon we begin to sense the tone of the teacher in her general attitude. She was often didactic to Ellen. When Ellen expressed her detestation of one of Scott's villains, Charlotte, already that puppet-master, an experienced writer, laughed at her 'characteristic and naive manner'. Her own admiration was for Scott's skill in producing his effects. Had she known of the stream of discussion of the characters in the Brontës' books which has flowed ever since they were published, Charlotte would surely have indulged in sarcasm or laughter at the critics' expense. The creator and those who comment on the creation can hardly comprehend the point of view of the other, because as a craft the writing of fiction and the writing of literary criticism begin from opposite standpoints, as do the painting of a picture and the aesthetic criticism of the finished work.

The Brontës were leading an absorbing imaginary life and writing a great deal, discovering that a writer is two people in one; the craftsman who can use skill dispassionately,[3] and the emotional human being who feels life intensely and prizes that sensitivity and the ability to express experience. It does not make life easier to be sensitive, as the Brontës found, and creative writing can seem to come from outside oneself, as if the writer was only a channel.

Ellen tells us:

'It may be indicated here, for it belongs to this period, some of the Poems Charlotte had a preference for, and which, she used to repeat to herself when busy with her needle, in soft audible cadence. Heber's "Missionary Hymns", which was a very great favourite with her, and some of Moore's Poems such as —

> "O Thou who driest the mourner's tears"
> "The bird let loose in Eastern skies"

and

> "While here in shade and grief we roam."

She did not as yet know the gem of sacred poetry, Keble's "Christian Year," but afterwards, when she did know it, she felt the power and gentle influence of many of the Poems, and could not endure to hear anyone recite or read them who did not feel their beauty and meaning.'

In the late summer Mrs Nussey invited Charlotte to stay at Rydings. Charlotte accepted and the two friends were re-united when, in September 1832, Branwell Brontë escorted Charlotte the seventeen miles in the Haworth two-wheeled hired gig. Branwell, Ellen tells us, 'was THEN a very dear brother, as dear to Charlotte as her own soul; they were in perfect accord of taste and feeling, and it was mutual delight to be together.' They must have been close indeed; some sixteen months earlier, Branwell had made that forty mile round walk to see Charlotte. Ellen forgets that when she writes; 'Branwell probably had never been far from home before!' Certainly he had not visited a house with the same well-kept air, the atmosphere of affluence and comfort and the delightful position and lush gardens which Rydings, set among its trees and woods, had at that time. The fifteen year old Branwell:

'. . . was in wild ecstasy with everything. He walked about in unrestrained boyish enjoyment, taking views in every direction of the old turret-roofed house, the fine chestnut trees on the lawn (one tree especially interested him because it was "iron-garthed," having been split in storms, but still flourishing in great majesty), and a large rookery, which gave to the house a good background – all these he noted and commented upon with perfect enthusiasm. He told his sister he "was leaving her in Paradise, and if she were not intensely happy she never would be!" Happy indeed, she then was, IN HIMSELF, for she, with her own enthusiasms, looked forward to what her brother's great promise and talent might effect.'[4]

No outings were planned for the girls. They were left to make their own amusements and expected to take part in the normal life of the busy household of Ellen's uncle Richard Nussey. What they wanted most of all was to be together to talk.

'The visit passed without much to mark it, at this distance of time', wrote Ellen many years later, 'except that we crept away together from household life as much as we could. Charlotte liked to pace the plantations or seek seclusion in the fruit garden; she was safe from visitors in these retreats. She was so painfully shy she could not bear any special notice. One day, on being led in to dinner by a stranger, she trembled and nearly burst into tears; but notwithstanding her excessive shyness, which was often painful to others as well as herself, she won the respect and affection of all who had opportunity enough to become acquainted with her. Charlotte's shyness did not arise, I am sure, either from vanity or self-consciousness, as some suppose shyness to arise; its source was . . . in her "not being understood." She felt herself apart from others; they did not UNDERSTAND her, and she keenly felt the distance.'[5]

The experience of this and other visits to Rydings was to stand Charlotte in good stead in the years to come. Without her victory over this nervous alarm at being formally taken in to dinner by a stranger, she would have found such etiquette even harder later. The social round of the Nussey family, the comings and goings on business of the two Richards – Ellen's uncle and brother – and the company of Ellen's younger brothers Henry, twenty, home on vacation from Cambridge, and George, eighteen and involved like the two Richards in the woollen industry, cannot have been so repulsive to her, for she was to visit Ellen again and again, and feel almost as comfortable as she did in Haworth.

Ellen's other brothers were far from home on this occasion. John, William and Joshua were all in London, where Joshua had been married in March to a girl from a well-to-do family.[6] Ellen's mother, who became fond of Charlotte and Charlotte of her, was now in her early sixties. Ellen's sister Ann was in her late thirties, Mercy was thirty-one and the invalid Sarah was twenty-two. Charlotte respected Ann's abilities and developed an affection for Mercy.

Five years later, Rydings was sketched by Catherine Walker, Ellen's second cousin, as it was when Charlotte stayed there. Because Rydings was

Rydings, the Nussey family home, drawn by Catherine Walker, Ellen's second cousin.

the principal model for Thornfield in *Jane Eyre*, this contemporary evidence is of interest.[7]

No description exists of the internal furnishings of Rydings at this date. It is virtually certain that they were still mainly those of Richard Walker, Ellen's great-uncle. When at the end of his life he leased out the property, it would be furnished, so that if he recovered his health he could return to his home as he left it. When he died, small personal possessions might have been removed, but the fitments and the large furniture would have remained.

A later owner, Ellen's uncle Richard Nussey, would be glad to take over the existing furnishings at Rydings, because his sister Anne and brother William went on living at his former home, Brookroyd House, and its contents belonged to Anne. Whether Richard Walker's paintings were still on the walls of Rydings to interest Charlotte we cannot tell,[8] but his books and papers seem to have been so. (Richard Walker's notes on local history were used decades later by Michael Sheard.) We can be reasonably certain that the more bulky furniture had been installed in the house between 1790 and 1800. It was not practical to transport furniture long distances as the cost was so great.[9]

It was during this visit that Charlotte, impatient of restriction, was beginning to realise how much of a handicap it was to be a woman in their society. Ellen tells us: 'Charlotte probably had begun even now to contemplate the possibility of assuming a nom de plume at some future time, for she liked when in E[llen]'s home, to be playfully addressed as "Charles" and in cheerful moods would sign herself "Charles Thunder." ' Thunder was the meaning of the name Brontë.[10] She left for home with a present of apples for Emily and Anne, and the friends did not meet again until the following year. Charlotte was to write of her memory of Rydings:

'. . . a pleasant spot, one of the old family Halls of England, surrounded by Lawn and woodland speaking of past times and suggesting (to me at least) happy feelings.'

Charlotte wanted to practise her French and improve Ellen's, and tried to persuade her friend to correspond in that language, but Ellen was self-conscious and refused. She had taken her place now as one more daughter at home. In such a busy household, buzzing with social life, there was much to do and a handy fifteen year old was very useful. Now that Ellen was out of the schoolroom she could begin to learn household management. The family were doing well; there were few clouds on their horizon.

In the summer of 1833 Ellen paid her first visit to Haworth Parsonage, thus bringing about the next stage in her relationship with the Brontë family. Charlotte wrote on the 20th June with the formal invitation:

'Papa now desires me to present his respects to Mrs Nussey, and say that he would feel greatly obliged if she would allow us the pleasure of your company for a few weeks at Haworth.' It is an interesting letter. The health hazard of the season was influenza – health was a preoccupation then as now. An apparently slight illness could result in rapid death.

The letter begins: 'Dear Ellen, I know you will be very angry because I have not written sooner . . .' As their correspondence unrolled over the years, this was to be a constant note. Ellen's anger was not of the serious kind. Put together with other references, we can picture a kind of playful pettishness, a 'toss the head, stamp the foot' kind of anger. Charlotte was never – or hardly ever – to take Ellen's anger seriously, but she often teased her over it. It was characteristic that for what seemed good reasons Charlotte would leave Ellen without a letter for a long time, but if Ellen did not write to her as often as Charlotte wished, there was a frantic message from Haworth – 'Write SOON!'

A visit had often been suggested by Charlotte, but Aunt Branwell had insisted on waiting for good weather. 1833 had been a cold, bleak spring. This letter of Charlotte's on the 20th June was followed fairly quickly by Ellen's arrival, for she was invited for 'several weeks' and the surviving correspondence resumes with Charlotte's letter to her of the 21st July. Ellen may have been in Haworth for about a fortnight on this first occasion. It was a happy time.

[1] In Charlotte's juvenilia the Marquis of Douro gives his love a book 'wrapped in . . . paper sealed in green sealing wax, with the motto, "L'amour jamais."' On Charlotte's own letters to Ellen some of her mottoes were: 'Forget me not', 18.9.45; 'To You', 10.9.45; 'Absent not Forgotten', 28.12.46; 'Time Explains All', 10.8.46; 'Be Wise Today', 26.1.46; 'Remember Me', 30.12.45; 'Farewell', 29.11.45.

[2] The 'National' schools were not state schools as the later Board schools were, but schools organised by a society in London.

[3] It can be the cold truth that 'the technique which creates an effect is a wholly unemotional, almost purely mechanical process. It creates emotion, but that emotion is not part of the creative act'. From *Twelve Lectures on the Technique of Fiction Writing* by Kenneth McNichol.

[4] From Ellen Nussey's *Reminiscences* as published in *Scribner's Monthly* in May 1871, and reprinted in the Brontë Society's *Transactions* for 1898.

[5] Ibid

[6] The 3rd March 1832 'at Mary-la-bonne the Rev J[oshua] Nussey curate of St John's, Westminster, to Ann Elizabeth, eldest daughter of the late R Alexander, esq of Sussex-place, Regent's Park.' *Gentleman's Magazine*. Ann's brother Henry was a director of the East India Company between 1826 and 1853.

[7] See illustration.

[8] Richard Walker is known to have collected pictures and there were some very good quality paintings in the family.

[9] When Jane Austen's family moved to Bath from Hampshire they sold the furniture from their old home rather than attempt to transport it.

[10] Derived from the Greek for thunder, the name Brontë was well known at the time because it formed part of Lord Nelson's title. As it was close to Patrick's original name of Bronty or Pronty, he may have adopted it believing it to be a different form of the same name, or as a gesture of homage to Nelson.

ELLEN'S FIRST VISIT TO HAWORTH, 1833

Between the 20th June and the 21st July 1833, Ellen Nussey was in Haworth. Although in writing for publication Ellen's naturalness is a little lost, her account of the time is vivid[1]:

'My first visit to Haworth was full of novelty and freshness. The scenery for some miles before we reached Haworth was wild and uncultivated, with hardly any population; at last we came to what seemed a terrific hill, such a steep declivity no one thought of riding down it; the horse had to be carefully led. We no sooner reached the foot of this hill than we had to begin to mount again, over a narrow, rough, stone-paved road; the horses' feet seemed to catch at boulders, as if climbing. When we reached the top of the village there was apparently no outlet, but we were directed to drive into an entry which just admitted the gig; we wound round in this entry and then saw the church close at hand, and we entered on the short lane which led to the parsonage gateway.

Here Charlotte was waiting, having caught the sound of the approaching gig. When greetings and introductions were over, Miss Branwell. . .took possession of [me] and treated [me] with the care and solicitude due to a weary traveller.

Old Haworth from the south-east.

Mr Brontë, also, was stirred out of his usual retirement by his own kind consideration, for not only the guest but the manservant and the horse were to be made comfortable. He made enquiries about the man, of his length of service, etc, with the kind purpose of making a few moments of conversation agreeable to him. Even at this time, Mr Brontë struck me as looking very venerable, with his snow-white hair and powdered coat-collar. His manner and mode of speech always had the tone of high-bred courtesy. He was considered somewhat of an invalid, and always lived in the most abstemious and simple manner. His white cravat was not then so remarkable as it grew to be afterwards. He was in the habit of covering this cravat himself. We never saw the operation, but we always had to wind for him the white sewing-silk which he used. Charlotte said it was her father's one extravagance – he cut up yards and yards of white lutestring [a silk fabric] in covering his cravat; and like Dr Joseph Woolffe (the renowned and learned traveller) who, when on a visit and in a long fit of absence, "went into a clean shirt every day for a week, without taking one off," so Mr Brontë's cravat went into new silk and new size without taking any off, till at length nearly half his head was enveloped in cravat. His liability to bronchial attacks, no doubt, attached him to this increasing growth of cravat.

Miss Branwell was a very small, antiquated little lady. She wore caps large enough for half a dozen of the present fashion, and a front of light auburn curls over her forehead. She always dressed in silk. She had a horror of the climate so far north, and of the stone floors in the parsonage. She amused us by clicking about in pattens[2] whenever she had to go into the kitchen or look after household operations.

She talked a great deal of her younger days; the gaieties of her dear native town, Penzance, in Cornwall; the soft, warm climate, etc. The social life of her younger days she used to recall with regret; she gave one the idea that she had been a belle among her own home acquaintances. She took snuff out of a very pretty gold snuffbox, which she sometimes presented to you with a little laugh, as if she enjoyed the slight shock and astonishment visible in your countenance. In summer she spent part of the afternoon in reading aloud to Mr Brontë, and in winter, the evenings, she must have enjoyed this; for she and Mr Brontë had often to finish their discussions on what she had read when we all met for tea. She would be very lively and intelligent, and tilt arguments against Mr Brontë without fear.

"Tabby", the faithful, trustworthy old servant, was very quaint in appearance – very active, and, in these days, the general servant and factotum. We were all "childer" and "bairns" in her estimation. She still kept to her duty of walking out with the "childer", if they went any distance from home, unless Branwell were sent by his father as a protector. . .'

There are more details of Tabby from Whiteley Turner.

'Tabby had lived in Haworth in the days when the packhorses went through once a week with their tinkling bells and gay worsted adornment, carrying the produce of the county from Keighley over the hills to Colne and

Burnley. What is more, she had known the "bottoms" or valleys, in those primitive days when the fairies frequented the margin of the beck on moonlight nights, and had known folk who had seen them. But that was when there were no mills in the valley, and when all the wool spinning was done by hand in the farmhouses round. "It wur factories as had driven 'em away," she said. To a visitor to the parsonage it was a great thing to have Tabby's good word. She had the Yorkshire keenness of perception into character, and it was not everybody she liked.'[3]

Tabitha Aykroyd had come to be Mr Brontë's housekeeper when she was already fifty-four, and she was very much 'her own woman' as we would say today. She was a Methodist, a class leader, and had family connections in Haworth, including a sister and a nephew, William Wood, who was a joiner and cabinet maker and often carried out work for the Brontë family. One of Tabitha's sisters, Rose, had married John Bower of Harden, and lived there. Her son Jonas came over to visit Aunt Tabby from time to time and Branwell's outgrown shirts were passed on to his little boy John.

Ellen's narrative continues:

'Emily Brontë had by this time acquired a lithesome, graceful figure. She was the tallest person in the house, except her father. Her hair, which was naturally as beautiful as Charlotte's, was in the same unbecoming tight curl and frizz, and there was the same want of complexion. She had very beautiful eyes – kind, kindling, liquid eyes; but she did not often look at you; she was too reserved. Their colour might be said to be dark gray, at other times dark blue, they varied so. She talked very little. She and Anne were like twins – inseparable companions, and in the very closest sympathy, which never had any interruption.'

Both Charlotte and Emily had eyes whose colour interpretation varied. Several years later, in the course of the same few days, Charlotte was to meet Matthew Arnold and Mrs Gaskell. Arnold said her eyes were grey, Mrs Gaskell said they were brown, the colour of her hair, although it seems likely from the colouring of other members of the family that they were grey.

Ellen goes on:

'Anne – dear, gentle Anne – was quite different in appearance from the others. She was her aunt's favourite. Her hair was a very pretty, light brown, and fell on her neck in graceful curls. She had lovely violet-blue eyes, fine pencilled eyebrows, and clear, almost transparent complexion. She still pursued her studies, and especially her sewing, under the surveillance of her aunt. Emily had now begun to have the disposal of her own time.

Branwell studied regularly with his father, and used to paint in oils, which was regarded as study for what might be eventually his profession. All the household entertained the idea of his becoming an artist, and hoped he would be a distinguished one. In fine and suitable weather delightful rambles were made over the moors, and down into the glens and ravines that here and there broke the monotony of the moorland. The rugged bank and rippling brook were treasures of delight.

Emily, Anne, and Branwell used to ford the streams, and sometimes placed stepping-stones for the other two; there was always a lingering delight in these spots;- every moss, every flower, every tint and form, were noted and enjoyed. Emily especially had a gleesome delight in these nooks of beauty,- her reserve for the time vanished.

One long ramble made in these early days was far away over the moors to a spot familiar to Emily and Anne, which they called "The Meeting of the Waters". It was a small oasis of emerald green turf, broken here and there by small clear springs; a few large stones served as resting-places; seated here, we were hidden from all the world, nothing appearing in view but miles and miles of heather, a glorious blue sky, and brightening sun. A fresh breeze wafted on us its exhilarating influence; we laughed and made mirth of each other, and settled we would call ourselves the Quartette. Emily, half-reclining on a slab of stone, played like a young child with the tadpoles in the water, making them swim about, and then fell to moralizing on the strong and the weak, the brave and the cowardly, as she chased them with her hand. No serious care or sorrow had so far cast its gloom on nature's youth and buoyancy, and nature's simplest offerings were fountains of pleasure and enjoyment.'

Whiteley Turner noted down a comment of one of the local people on the Brontë girls' walks:

Main Street, Haworth, at the beginning of this century.

' "I've heard mi mother tell abaat when my father en her used to be sizin'
en stretchin their warps[4] et th' bottom o' the moor, near Wattery-loin top –
ya know yar folks wer handloom weeavers – theease Brontë lasses used to cum
past when art from a walk. They'd a bein eeather readin a bouk, er dooin sum
mak o' fancy work. They wod walk on just es if ther' worn't a soul i' th'
rooad, en never lift ther eyes nor speeak a word tiv yar fooaks, nor tiv onybody
they met; but 'e suppoose it wer' ther waa." '

Walking at Haworth, Ellen saw the Baptist chapel, which stood by the
route usually taken by the Brontës. Built in 1752, it had been enlarged in 1775.
Opposite to it was the old Wesleyan chapel, built by the Rev William
Grimshaw in 1758, but now too small for its burgeoning congregation and
soon to be replaced by a larger building elsewhere.

Describing the inside of the Brontë home, Ellen says:

'The interior of the now far-famed parsonage lacked drapery of all kinds.
Mr Brontë's horror of fire forbade curtains to the windows.[5]. . . There was
not much carpet anywhere except in the sitting-room, and on the study floor.
The hall floor and stairs were done with sand-stone, always beautifully clean,
as everything was about the house; the walls were not papered, but stained in
a pretty dove-coloured tint; hair-seated chairs and mahogany tables, bookshelves in the study, but not many of these elsewhere. Scant and bare indeed,
many will say, yet it was not a scantness that made itself felt. Mind and
thought, I had almost said elegance but certainly refinement, diffused
themselves over all, and made nothing really wanting . . .'

Ellen's bed was warmed, on this and on later occasions, by the glittering
warming-pan with a long polished handle.[6]

On her later visits, there was a piano at the parsonage. Ellen says: 'Emily,
after some application, played with precision and brilliancy. Anne played also,
but she preferred soft harmonies and vocal music. She sang a little; her voice
was weak, but very sweet in tone.'

Elsewhere, Ellen adds the fact that at twilight, she and Charlotte walked
with arms encircling one another round and round the table, and behind them
walked Emily and Anne in the old Roe Head custom.

From her *Reminiscences* again:

'Mr Brontë's health caused him to retire early. He assembled his
household for family worship at eight o'clock;[7] at nine he locked and barred
the front door, always giving as he passed the sitting-room door a kindly
admonition to the "children" not to be late; halfway up the stairs he stayed his
steps to wind up the clock. . . Every morning was heard the firing of a pistol
from Mr Brontë's room window,- it was the discharging of the loading which
was made every night. Mr Brontë's tastes led him to delight in the perusal of
battle-scenes, and in following the artifice of war; had he entered on military
service instead of ecclesiastical he would probably have had a very distinguished career. The self-denials and privations of camplife would have
agreed entirely with his nature, for he was remarkably independent of the
luxuries and comforts of life. The only dread he had was of FIRE, and this

dread was so intense it caused him to prohibit all but silk or woollen dresses for his daughters; indeed, for any one to wear any other kind of fabric was almost to forfeit his respect.'

Mr Brontë had very sound reasons for this prejudice. He had conducted the burial services of many children, and probably some women, who had been burned to death when their flimsy cotton garments caught fire.[8]

'Mr Brontë at times would relate strange stories, which had been told to him by some of the oldest inhabitants of the parish, of the extraordinary lives and doings of people who had resided in far-off, out-of-the-way places, but in contiguity with Haworth, – stories which made one shiver and shrink from hearing; but they were full of grim humour and interest to Mr Brontë and his children, as revealing the characteristics of a class in the human race. . .

Stories have been related of Mr Brontë and his method of working off powerful passions, which are considered incredible, but a good deal of the ugliness of these facts would vanish if people more fully knew the character of the man.

He could not be said to be a man of many sympathies; he never entered into details, they annoyed him, feeling [emotion] in most aspects was to him a weakness. If he analysed, it was in general principles, he ruled his opinions by maxims which made no allowance for idiosyncracies, unless it was that he had *one* exception – may we not be permitted to think that he *did understand* his *own* idiosyncracy, and so well too, that he thought it prudent to live the ascetic life which he adopted. He was quite capable of enforcing such rule upon himself when the time came for him to cease the unusual course of firing off pistols, etc. That he did *do* the things told of him, it is certain, for about the premises in early days were to be seen the bullet-holes in such objects as he had made targets of. Charlotte herself used to relate the story of the mutilated dress, as a strong proof of her father's iron will and determination to carry through his purpose – his wife was never again to wear the obnoxious dress which had been a present to her, and he made it impossible that she should wear it – he would quietly persuade himself that he was putting his gentle wife out of the reach of a very feminine temptation, and take no cognisance of his own hard and inflexible *will*, which ran itself into tyranny and cruelty. There is not the slightest doubt that he would have gained his object quite as surely by kinder and wiser methods of action, but it was not his nature to woo obedience, nor did he ever coerce it except as a general might, by stratagem. His outward demeanor was always perfectly under control and quiesent.

There was then but one dog, which was admitted to the parlour at stated times. Emily and Anne always gave him a portion of their breakfast, which was, by their own choice, the old north country diet of oatmeal porridge. . .'

Elsewhere Ellen describes the way in which at one end of the table sat Miss Branwell, on the other Charlotte, with Emily and Anne on either side, when Branwell was absent. Their food was simple: a single joint with vegetables, followed by some kind of milk pudding. They never had pastry.

Ellen knew the church as it then was, and would have wandered among

Haworth Church.

the gravestones noting the more interesting ones. She would see the flagstone under which lay interred a family of six, their ages being 86, 88, 95, 85, 70, and 85. 'Old milk and porridge undoubtedly had a part in the longevity', remarks Whiteley Turner. The tower of the church is now as it was then, but the body of the church has been rebuilt. There was a three-decker pulpit, hexagonal and black with age, which had been used by John Wesley and Rev W Grimshaw. Above the pulpit was a sounding board, carved with a sun-like shape, and round the rim the words: 'For I am determined not to know anything among you save Jesus Christ, and Him crucified. Grimshaw, B.A., 1742.' This was surmounted by a white dove. The village children used to keep their eyes on this dove, expecting it one day to take wing. There were two aisles, with graves the entire length of each. The black oak pews were high-backed, with the owners' names painted on the doors.[9] The communion table was close against the east wall of the nave, enclosed by a massive balustraded oak communion rail. The aisle was separated from the nave by a very lofty arcade and contained a gallery the full width of the aisle, the gallery being continuous across the west end of the nave.[10]

The Brontës had their own pew, where Emily sat with her back to the congregation, bolt upright in the corner and as still as a statue. Her 'solid, stoical' manner made a great impression on at least one small boy, who remembered her compressed mouth and drooping eyelids, and a slightly projecting tooth. Charlotte sat within a foot of the place where she was later to be buried.[11] Ellen tells us:

'The services in church in these days were such as can only be seen (if ever seen again) in localities like Haworth. The people assembled, but it was apparently to LISTEN. Any part beyond that was quite out of their reckoning. All through the prayers, a stolid look of apathy was fixed on the generality of their faces. There they sat, or leaned, in their pews; some few, perhaps, were resting, after a long walk over the moors. The children, many of them in clogs, pattering in from the school after service had commenced, and pattered out again before the sermon. The sexton, with a long staff, continually walked round in the aisles, "knobbing" sleepers when he dare, shaking his head at and threatening unruly children; but when the sermon began there was a change. Attitudes took the listening forms, eyes were turned on the preacher. It was curious, now, to note the expression. A rustic, untaught intelligence, gleamed in their faces; in some, a daring, doubting, questioning look, as if they would like to offer some defiant objection. Mr Brontë always addressed his hearers in extempore style. Very often he selected a parable from one of the Gospels, which he explained in the simplest manner – sometimes going over his own words and explaining them also, so as to be perfectly intelligible to the lowest comprehension. The parishioners respected Mr Brontë because, as one of them said, "he's a grand man; he lets other folks' business alone." '[12]

Mr Brontë was no gardener. The only thing in the garden in which he is recorded as taking an interest was the cherry tree. The climate has not changed to any appreciable extent since his day, and trees and gardens now flourish in the area, yet Ellen describes:

'The garden, which was nearly all grass, and possessed only a few stunted thorns and shrubs, and a few currant bushes which Emily and Anne treasured as their own bit of fruit garden . . . What the Brontës cared for and LIVED in most were the surroundings of nature, the free expanse of hill and mountain, the purple heather, the dells, and glens, and brooks, the broad sky view, the whistling winds, the snowy expanse, the starry heavens, and the charm of that solitude and seclusion which sees things from a distance without the disturbing atmosphere which lesser minds are apt to create . . . It was solitude and seclusion shared and enjoyed with intelligent companionship, and intense family affection.'

Ellen tells of one event during her visit:

'Charlotte and Anne Brontë were steady and faithful to their posts as Sunday-school teachers both now at this time, and whenever they were at home; some of the village girls as they grew up to womanhood evinced an affectionate appreciation of their labours – the female teachers also, in THEIR way, displayed a sense of the favours they enjoyed; they were all invited once a year to tea at the Parsonage. Their first visit was made when Charlotte's friend [Ellen] was staying with her. [Charlotte had mentioned to Ellen the Sunday school teachers' visit the previous year, the first year the school was in existence, so the visit Ellen witnessed must have been the second occasion.]

About four o'clock in the afternoon, half a dozen young women were ushered into the parlour; they were as fresh and buoyant as a moorland breeze, cheerful, healthy, bright complexioned young creatures, with an astonishing amount of brusquerie in their manner; they were nearly all earners of their daily bread at the factories, but manifested none of that deferential respect towards their employers which was the general tone of the well-employed in most other localities. They talked very freely of their masters but always by their Christian names, as "Jack" or "Joe"; when it was suggested that they should be taught better manners, the Brontës were greatly amused, Emily especially so, who said in her way, (which was always peculiarly quiet) "Vain attempt!"[13]

They showed however a rough respect to their entertainers, and great good nature also, for on discovering that the Miss Brontës were willing to play games with them but did not know HOW, they undertook to initiate them. The Brontë faces were worth anything as a study (if only an artist could have sketched them) during this attempt at learning to play; they had such a puzzled, amused, submissive expression, intently anxious though, to give pleasure and gratify others.'

When Ellen suggested that those pleasant, bracing Yorkshire lasses should speak of their employers with less freedom and independence, she can never have heard the workers near her home talking privately among themselves,

Charlotte's drawing believed to be of Bolton Abbey, which the Brontës and Ellen visited in mid-1833.

for there can be no doubt that they spoke in the same way. The Brontës had more direct contact with the working class than Ellen had at this time.

This first visit ended in the much publicised outing to Bolton Abbey. It is clear from Ellen's narrative what happened. She wrote:

'It was I believe at the close of this visit that, there was a clubbing together of pocket-money to secure an excursion to Bolton Abbey. Branwell Brontë undertook to procure a conveyance at a cheap rate which would carry ALL the party, and which, including the driver, would be six in number.[14] The daily anticipation of the coming treat, mixed with apprehensions about the weather, was perfect excitement to all. Branwell seemed to know every inch of the way, could tell the names of the hills that would be driven over, or walked over, their exact height above the sea, the views to be seen, and the places to be passed through; it was an event to each that, they were about to cross part of the range of hills which are designated the Backbone of England [the Pennines].'

The drive from Haworth to Bolton Abbey was about fifteen miles, over lovely undulating upland scenery and down into the valley of the River Wharfe. Wharfedale is one of the famous Yorkshire Dales and this is a very beautiful part of it. Turner painted a watercolour of the scene, and Ruskin described it in vivid and romantic prose. The ruins of the priory (it was never an abbey) stand in the calm green valley floor encircled by a curve of the river. The river passes through a narrow fast-flowing channel called the Strid, where fatal accidents have taken place when people and animals have tried to leap across, mainly because of the strong undercurrents.

Ellen explained:

'The party started from the Parsonage between five and six in the morning, in a small double gig or phaeton it was partly a loan as well as a hire to Branwell. They were to meet friends and relatives who were to take Charlotte's friend home. The Haworth party chanced to drive up to the Hotel [the Devonshire Arms Hotel, Bolton Bridge] just before them, but in plenty of time to note, and go through what to their young and enthusiastic hearts was a quite new experience, (i.e.) that, tho' the (rather) shabby conveyance . . . had been of no import whatever till now was regarded with disdain by the Hotel attendants, till they saw that they were cordially recognised by the handsome carriage-and-pair arrivals; all the party breakfasted, and then started on their stroll through the grounds . . . Emily and Anne hardly spoke during the whole excursion except to each other, but it was easy to see how they were drinking in pleasure and treasuring up the scenery in their minds. Charlotte who was acquainted with all the party, was less shy. Branwell who probably never knew the feeling of shyness, amused everyone; he was in a phrensy [sic] of pleasure, his eyes flashed with excitement, and he talked fast and brilliantly; a friend who was present and herself a great admirer of scenery[15] was so much amused by his ecstasies said, she had never passed such a day of enjoyment in her life;- She thought Branwell very eccentric, but recognised his rare talent and genius, she presaged though the DANGER of those flashing impulses, a danger which came so sorely and surely in after time. He had any amount of poetry ready for quotation, and this day he was well off in an appreciative audience whenever he chose to recite; it was one of the things he did well. (Branwell's appearance up to this time was grotesque rather than otherwise; he was neither fullgrown man nor yet a boy, and he had not acquired the art of attending to his appearance, none of the Brontës understood dress with its right and simple advantages, till Charlotte and Emily had been in Brussels; they then began to perceive the elegance of a well-fitting garment made with simplicity and neatness, when they adopted the better style for themselves it was a manifest improvement.)

The Haworth party were first started on their return journey – they left their friends (whose route lay in another direction) full of grateful pleasure and happiness for the days enjoyment which had proved to all, even a GREATER TREAT than had been anticipated.'

We know, from Charlotte's letter to Ellen on the 11th September, that the party who met them at Bolton Bridge included Ellen's brothers Richard and George, and Richard's fiancee Elizabeth Charnock. George was subsequently worried in case Branwell had not been sufficiently recompensed for Ellen's share of the hire of the gig. The Brontës for their part felt that as Richard had paid for their entertainment at the hotel, they themselves were the debtors if anything. The outing was a memorable end to a delightful visit.

NOTE: The sources for the quotations from Ellen in this chapter, unless otherwise attributed, are: a) Ellen's manuscript *Reminiscences* in the Walpole Collection of King's School, Canterbury; and b) Ellen's 'Reminiscences of the Brontës' as published by *Scribner's Monthly Magazine* in May 1871 and reprinted in the Brontë Society's *Transactions* for 1898.

[1] Ellen's manuscript *Reminiscences*, at King's School, Canterbury, which contains variations from the published version.
[2] Pattens consisted of a thick wooden sole, like a clog, with iron hoops on top. The wearer slipped their feet in normal shoes through the hoops and could then walk through wet or muddy places with clean shoes. Miss Branwell used pattens to protect her feet from the cold of the flagstone floors.
[3] Whiteley Turner, *A Spring-Time Saunter Round and About Brontëland*.
[4] The warp consists of the lengthways threads of the yarn which is being made into cloth. Before being put on the loom, the warp was 'sized' and stretched to help the threads bear the heavy work of having the weft threads woven into them. As warp threads are very long, the task of preparing them needs a lot of space.
[5] The parsonage windows were fitted with interior shutters. Anyone who has used wooden shutters inside old windows can testify to their good insulating properties, the warmth and the feeling of security and comfort which they bring. Later the parsonage windows are mentioned as being fitted with fabric blinds in addition, though when these were installed is not known.
[6] At the sale organised by Rev A B Nicholls after Mr Brontë's death, this warming-pan was bought by John Greenwood and carried home by one of his daughters.
[7] The eight o'clock evening worship of the household does not seem to have been widely remarked on.

[8] Regarding Mr Brontë's fear of fire and disapproval of cotton and linen clothing, see his letter to the *Leeds Mercury* on the 16th March 1844 about accidents to children when their clothing caught fire. He had, in twenty years at Haworth, read the burial service for between 90 and 100 children who had been burned to death in this way, and in every case enquiry had shown that their clothing had been of either linen or cotton. He recommended the wearing of silk or wool, which ignite less easily. The danger was so great that the *Times* also printed letters on the subject.

[9] Description from Whiteley Turner, *A Spring-Time Saunter Round and About Brontëland*.

[10] See *Haworth Past and Present* by J Horsfall Turner.

[11] *Bradford Observer*, 17th February 1894, published the memories of a man who, as a small boy, was obviously fascinated by the Brontë family.

[12] Ellen's narrative also gives: 'No doubt Mr Brontë's knowledge of human nature made him aware that this was the best course to pursue, till their independence had acquired a more civilised standard. There were exceptions, however, among them. Two or three individuals deserve particular note - they were men remarkable for self-culture and intelligence. One, it was said, vied with Mr Brontë himself in his knowledge of the dead languages. He and another had, in addition to their mental stamina, such stalwart frames and stature they looked capable of doing duty as guards to the whole village. The third individual was an ailing, suffering man; but he wrote such a critique on Charlotte's writings, when they became known, that it was valued more than any other coming from such a source.

The villagers would have liked Tabby to talk to them about the family in the parsonage; but Tabby was invincible and impenetrable. When they asked her "if they were not fearfully larn'd," she left them in a "huff;" but she did not deny her "childer" the laugh she knew they would have if she told them the village query . . .'

[13] It is only through others - through Ellen, Mary and Charlotte - that we can hear Emily Brontë speak; we have two speeches of Emily's verbatim - of which this 'Vain attempt!' is one.

[14] The six consisted of the driver, Charlotte, Branwell, Emily, Anne, and Ellen, and they were bound for the Devonshire Arms Hotel at Bolton Bridge.

[15] This lady was certainly Richard Nussey's future wife, Miss Elizabeth Charnock, daughter of John Charnock of Woodhouse Lane, Leeds.

ELLEN IN LONDON AND CHARLOTTE
IN HAWORTH, 1834-5

In December 1833, Ellen wrote telling Charlotte that she was not well and her doctor said she had a tendency to pulmonary infection. Charlotte did not reply for two months, and then wrote bracingly reminding her, in more veiled language, that she was a hypochondriac and always looked on the black side. Pulmonary infections usually meant tuberculosis and Charlotte was right to pooh-pooh this as a possibility, for although Ellen was to suffer for the rest of her life with a painful chest in winter weather, the problem seems to have been bronchitic and never took a tubercular form.

'Cheer up', wrote Charlotte, 'take constant and regular exercise . . .' and retailed the interesting fact that 'with us an unusual number of deaths have lately taken place'. Charlotte went on to say that she thought of 'my only UN-RELATED friend, my ci-devant school companion daily, nay almost hourly'. Charlotte's letter of the 11th February 1834 reached Birstall after Ellen had left for London on her first visit to the home of her eldest brother, John, at 4 Cleveland Row, facing St James Palace. Her fifth brother, William, had by now finished his medical training. He was working with John and living in the household. The medical practice was becoming increasingly separate from the shop.

Charlotte was apprehensive that Ellen, caught up in the sophisticated life of the capital, would lose interest in her old friends. No such thing happened, although the change of scene did Ellen good. Instead of her demanding invalid sister and bossy older sisters, she had little nieces and nephews to divert her. She must have been useful to her harassed sister-in-law, but a brilliant social life was not part of the programme. John was a very quiet man[1] and William a very religious one. Ellen visited St James Palace and saw the paintings of monarchs, but much of her time was spent peacefully reading. She recovered from her winter chest trouble and revelled in the freedom to read all the books in the house. At Birstall she was constantly in hot water for reading when she should have been doing something else.

Charlotte was in a fever of curiosity and astonishment:

'I was greatly amused by the tone of nonchalance which you assumed while treating of London, and its wonders, which seem to have excited anything rather than surprise in your mind; did you not feel awed while gazing at St Paul's and Westminster Abbey? had you no feeling of intense, and ardent interest, when in St James's you saw the Palace, where so many of England's

Kings, had held their courts, and beheld the representations of their persons on the walls?'

At that time London was still a fabled place to Charlotte, a greater version of Verropolis, her imaginary town. 'Almost as apocryphal', she wrote, 'as Babylon, or Nineveh, or ancient Rome.' She could hardly believe that Ellen was unchanged. In spite of Charlotte's much vaunted ability to read character, she went on to say that 'the minds of the rest of men and womenkind are to me as sealed volumes, hieroglyphical, which I cannot easily either unseal or decipher'. The imaginary town the Brontës had created, which began as homely Glasstown, a name reflecting nearby Hightown, Roberttown, and Glasshouse, places her father had known and which would enter his talk, this homely place had gradually become converted to Verropolis (later renamed Verdopolis), the place where Charlotte's hero, Wellington, ruled. In her imagination, London was as fabulous.

Ellen stayed away for the first half of the year. When she returned, Ellen was Ellen still. Now Charlotte felt that her friend's character was 'of a higher, a more steadfast order than I was once perfectly aware of. Few girls would have done as you have done – would have beheld the glare and glitter and dazzling display of London, with dispositions so unchanged, hearts so uncontaminated. I see no affectations in your letter, no trifling, no frivolous contempt of plain, and weak admiration of showy persons and things. . . . Put such a one as Amelia Walker [one of their school friends] in the same situation, and mark what a mighty difference there would be in the result!'

Ellen in reply asked Charlotte to stop flattering her and tell her her faults instead, and sent the present she had bought for her in London – a bonnet, 'pretty, neat and simple', which pleased Charlotte greatly, and brought her friend's 'fair, quiet face, brown eyes, and dark hair full to my remembrance'. The Rydings family news was that Ellen's mother was thinking of finding a new home, in anticipation of the day when Richard Nussey married the 'clever and amiable' lady whom Charlotte had met on the outing to Bolton Abbey. In fact the two were not to be married until 1848, but Richard did set up a household of his own by moving to Leeds around 1834. Mrs Nussey and family stayed at Rydings.

After her orgy of reading in London, Ellen was anxious to continue and, acknowledging Charlotte's superior knowledge of literature, asked her friend if she had any books to recommend. With this support she would be more able to defend her time spent reading. In reply she received Charlotte's famous didactic passage in the letter of the 4th July 1834 which biographers of Charlotte have used to suggest that Ellen had no opinions of her own. 'Now Ellen don't be startled at the names of Shakespeare and Byron . . . Scott's sweet, wild, romantic Poetry can do you no harm . . .'[2] Now aged seventeen, Ellen was living a busy and seemingly happy domestic existence, yet Charlotte always considered her friend's life to be unhappy. It is likely that as the youngest Nussey, daughter Ellen was the general 'dogsbody', and there was always Sarah to be looked after.

The Brontë Chair.

The working and social lives of the Nussey family mainly took place within the span of a few miles. Ellen, being naturally spritely and energetic, longed to dance; but her sister (presumably Ann) was against it, and brought in the weight of clerical opinion. The Rev Thomas Allbutt, who was engaged to marry Miss Marianne Wooler, was also against it. Ellen wrote to ask what Charlotte thought, and Charlotte was in favour. Later in their lives they were together at a number of dances and sometimes Ellen danced, but more often sat and watched with the sedentary Charlotte.

There were sadnesses in the Nussey family. Sarah, Ellen's invalid sister, was again ill, and on the 4th October 1834, unmarried Aunt Ann Nussey of Brookroyd House died at the age of seventy. Ann left all her household goods to her brother Richard, the owner of Rydings and lessee of Brookroyd. Presumably these remained *in situ* in Brookroyd. She divided her other property among her nieces and nephews, and Ellen's sisters Ann and Mercy both had legacies, though Ellen did not.[3]

In this, the year of the Tolpuddle Martyrs, the country was alive to the bad effects of the Industrial Revolution. Working conditions in the factories, and child labour for long hours, were now seen to be an evil. The mills were growing in size, and Parliamentary commissioners requested reports on each one. Brookroyd Mill, with which the Nussey family were concerned (in addition to Smithies Mill), employed 42 persons, only 15 of them over twenty-one. In these small early mills set in country valleys, conditions were very good compared to the large concerns in Manchester. Child labour was nothing new, for children had worked alongside their parents as long as there had been either children or parents, but working in the home or the fields was not obvious exploitation as was working in a mill.

In Dewsbury the firm of Halliley, Brooke and Halliley went bankrupt and the girls' old schoolfellows Leah and Maria Brooke were affected, as well as Mr Brontë's old acquaintances. On behalf of her father, Charlotte asked Ellen for particulars of how Mrs Brooke, Mrs Buckworth, Mrs Carter and Mrs Jackson were faring, sisters of John Halliley, the senior partner.

This seems to have been the year in which the parsonage at Haworth acquired its piano, as in Emily's diary letter of November 1834 she writes: 'Anne and I have not done our music exercise which consists of B major'. The Haworth domestic scene shown in this diary letter is a busy, happy one.

The year 1835 brought the girls together again when Charlotte accepted an invitation to Rydings, and travelled there in a hired gig during February, to be with 'ALMOST the only, and certainly the DEAREST friend I possess (out of our own family)'. She was invited for a month, but 'Papa and Aunt' thought a fortnight sufficient. Charlotte was sorry to leave. She was sent back to Haworth in a Rydings vehicle driven by one Kelly, an ex-seaman said to have been a manservant of the Nussey family, whose conversation entertained her on the journey. During this visit she thought she had managed to interest Ellen in politics, but although Ellen did express an opinion on occasion, in her girlhood she could never take the lively partisan interest shown by Charlotte Brontë and Mary Taylor.

The visitor had left behind her umbrella, and Ellen put a letter in its folds to save postage and sent it at Charlotte's request to Bradford, but as the Haworth carrier persistently forgot to ask for the umbrella, the letter was a very old one by the time it reached its destination. All manner of things had happened in the interval. The vicar of Dewsbury had died, and Thomas Allbutt, appointed to succeed him, could now afford to marry Marianne Wooler. Charlotte was on fire with election fever and wanted to know if Ellen's brothers were supporting the 'right' party.

The family at Haworth now came to the end of a very happy period – perhaps their happiest. But one memory later recorded by a village boy tells of a vivid, and less happy, episode in Branwell's life:

'When there was an election Rev Brontë and Branwell were on the Tory (blue) platform – the Liberal platform was opposite – When Mr Brontë began to question Lord Morpeth a regular "hullabaloo" was set up. Branwell in his impetuous way, rushed to the front, crying "if you won't let my father speak, you shan't speak." After that election, Branwell's effigy bearing a herring in

The Brontë Bridge.

one hand and a potato in the other, an allusion to his nationality, was carried through the main street of the village and afterwards burned. Branwell watched the procession from a shop in the village.'[4]

Ellen has left us a word picture of her friend's life at this time:

'Charlotte passed a great part of almost every day in drawing or painting; she would do one or the other, for nine hours with scarcely an interval, if she were greatly interested in her subject – her style was not bold or broad, it was minute and finished. At one period she set her heart on miniature painting but she did not succeed to her own approval, and sometimes, when a head or figure was nearly completed she would allow no remonstrances to prevent her committing it to the flames, if she failed in her own estimate her work was doomed, she did not however act in sullen wrath or disappointment, she cheerfully set to work again intent on achieving her ideal if possible. But few of her drawings or paintings survived her; she permitted acquaintances to carry them off as a loan, who forgot to return them; she regretted the loss of some, but she would not ASK to have them returned. Emily and Anne were fond of the pencil, but chiefly as a recreation, or for the sake of acquiring the art so as to be able to teach others when the need should arise.'

We know the rhythm of the Haworth days: the walk taken in the brightest part of the day if the weather was fine and suitable, under the escort of Tabby or Branwell; the good, simple food; the incomparable mental stimulus the siblings gave one another; the fantasy worlds in which they lived. They were full of life and hope and joy: 'A happy sunlit home', one observer called it.

Unique though the Brontës were in their character, their quality, their achievement, there have been a number of families who parallel them in the way the children have stimulated each other into creative endeavour, a subject which could be worthy of more study than it has received. The young John family in late nineteenth century Tenby, who had also lost their mother and who also numbered four, gave rise to Augustus and Gwen, two of the most original and outstanding artists of their time; and reading of their childhood situation and development brings the Brontës to mind. Augustus John, who used the English language prolifically and well, described his sister Gwen in words that could almost have described Charlotte Brontë: 'Few on meeting this retiring person in black, with her tiny hands and feet, a soft, almost inaudible voice, and delicate Pembrokeshire accent, would have guessed that here was the greatest woman artist of her age, or, as I think, of any other.'[5]

The Powys family in Dorset: 'seven of them wrote books, and of their books more than a hundred appeared in print between 1896 and 1960', provide another parallel. 'Three of the family won an enduring reputation; John Cowper Powys . . . Theodore Francis Powys . . . and Llewelyn Powys . . .'[6] Again one wonders what it was that stimulated such a flowering, and looks for likenesses.

But the most remarkable parallel is surely that of the Farjeon children, unfolded in Eleanor Farjeon's lovely book *A Nursery in the Nineties*. She tells us how she and one of her brothers played the game 'Tar' in which they took parts in a drama private to them; they could fall into it in a moment, as Emily and Anne once fell into their fantasy world of Gondal whilst on a train journey. Eleanor's emotional development was delayed because all her energies went into this marvellous game, which the two Farjeons carried on over years. There was no need for Eleanor to experience life, for in make-believe she had already experienced everything – every situation, every emotion.[7]

Returning to the Brontë family, the years they had just lived through had been a time in which their development took place unhindered in a congenial atmosphere, and they did their 'prentice work as creative beings. On the firm basis of these tranquil growing years, bound by family unity, they could found their future achievements and find the strength to weather their future storms. Now economic necessity took them out into the world, because they must learn to support themselves. It would only be Branwell, faced with stronger and different temptations to those of his sisters, who would find the basis insufficient.

[1] This characteristic was developed as much out of prudence as it was inborn by nature. In *Memoirs of Eighty Years*, Gordon Hake wrote: 'Nussey, whom I knew very intimately later in life, told me that the King [George IV] confided to him all his secrets, and that the knowledge, if written down, would set all England in a blaze.' Certainly no anecdotes of John's patients were passed down in the family.

[2] 'You ask me to recommend some books for your perusal; I will do so in as few words as I can. If you like poetry let it be first rate, Milton, Shakespeare, Thomson, Goldsmith, Pope (if you will though I don't admire him) Scott, Byron, Campbell, Wordsworth and Southey. Now Ellen don't be startled at the names of Shakespeare and Byron, both these were great men and their works are like themselves, You will know how to choose the good and avoid the evil, the finest passages are always the purest, the bad are invariably revolting you will never wish to read them over twice. Omit the *Comedies* of Shakespeare and the *Don Juan*, perhaps the *Cain* of Byron though the latter is a magnificent Poem and read the rest fearlessly. That must indeed be a depraved mind which can gather evil from *Henry the 8th* from *Richard 3rd* from *Macbeth* and *Hamlet* and *Julius Caesar*. Scott's sweet, wild, romantic Poetry can do you no harm nor can Wordsworth's nor Campbell's nor Southey's, the greater part at least of his, some is certainly exceptionable. For History read Hume, Rollin, and the *Universal History* if you can – *I* never did. For fiction – read Scott alone; all novels after his are worthless. For biography, read Johnson's *Lives of the Poets*, Boswell's *Life of Johnson*, Southey's *Life of Nelson*, Lockhart's *Life of Burns*, Moore's *Life of Sheridan*, Moore's *Life of Byron*, Wolfe's *Remains*. For Natural History, read Bewick, and Audubon, and Goldsmith and White – of Selborne. For divinity, but your brother Henry will advise you there. I only say adhere to standard authors and don't run after novelty.' Letter 32, Shakespeare Head edition of *The Brontës, Their Lives, Friendships And Correspondence*.

[3] 'Will of Ann Nussey of Brookroyd, 1834. [All] Household goods . . . to brother Richard. Interest on £1,000 to servant Mary Mills, if still in her service. Remainder of estate divided among nieces Ann and Mercy Nussey, late brother George's widow and daughter, and the family at White Lee. Executors, nephews John Nussey of White Lee and John Nussey of St James Street, London.'

[4] By his brilliant conversational powers Branwell became 'a favourite amongst the wealthier people in the district – he gave a bride a landscape painting and a sonnet, both his own work –' The informant was sent by Branwell on Sunday afternoons to the Shake Hands, a pub between Keighley and Oakworth, for a copy of *Bell's Life in London. Bradford Observer*, 17th February 1894, the boyhood memories of a Haworth man.

[5] Michael Holroyd's biography *Augustus John, the Years of Innocence*. Augustus John also appeared unsure of the date of his birthday, and Michael Holroyd suggests that this might have been due to the fact that Augustus' mother died when he was very young, as of course did Charlotte's.

[6] *The Brothers Powys* by Richard Perceval Graves.

[7] *A Nursery in the Nineties* by Eleanor Farjeon.

CHARLOTTE TEACHES AT ROE HEAD, 1835-8

Charlotte had meant to ask Ellen to come to Haworth during the late summer of 1835, but wrote on the 2nd July explaining that a new phase in the Brontës' lives had begun. She had accepted Miss Wooler's offer of a teaching post at Roe Head School, and this meant that her wages would support Emily there as a pupil, while Mr Brontë paid for Branwell's studies at the Royal Academy in London, and Anne stayed at home. These changes were to happen so quickly that there was no time for Ellen to go to Haworth. Instead, Charlotte asked her to visit Roe Head soon. 'If anything would cheer me, it is this idea of being so near you – surely you and Polly [Mary Taylor] will come to see me', she wrote. 'It would be wrong in me to doubt it – you were never unkind yet.'

At the time of this upheaval at Haworth, there was a parallel uncertainty and change at Rydings. Bachelor uncle Richard Nussey, with whom Mrs Nussey and her family lived, had not long survived his sister Ann of Brookroyd House. On his death his will made permanent provision for invalid Sarah, who was obviously much loved, by leaving her various investments. His share in the Smithies Mill business and the leasehold of property at Brookroyd passed to his nephew Richard, Ellen's fourth brother. Provision was made for his nephew John, the eldest brother, apothecary of Cleveland Row, to purchase Rydings if he wished.

John did wish to purchase Rydings, but not for himself, nor yet as a home for his mother, sisters and brothers, who had been living there for the last ten years. He had his mother-in-law, Mrs Mary Walker, and five of her daughters on his hands, and as she had originally come from Purlwell Hall, Batley, she wished to return to the area with her family and Rydings was a suitable home.

This meant that Mrs Nussey and those of her grown-up children still living with her must leave Rydings. Fortunately Brookroyd House was in family hands and furnished, and they could go to live there. Brookroyd did not have the same prestige, beauty or history as Rydings, but it was comfortable and substantial. The arrangements took some time – the will was not proved until 1837 - so they had months to get used to the idea and to rearrange their possessions. The distance between the two houses was small, and no doubt there was a great deal of to-ing and fro-ing in the interval, redecorating, overhauling of curtains and so on.

Three of Ellen's brothers were still at home – Joseph the second eldest, Henry who was five years older than Ellen, and George who was next to her in age. Joseph was involved in the family's manufacturing activities and for a time was a partner with his brother Richard in the latter's ventures in Leeds. George had dealings with the cloth market in Huddersfield and travelled there regularly, driving himself.

As for Henry, he had just finished university and was looking for a job. We are lucky in having his journal for the period before, during and immediately after his time at university.[1] In view of his role in Charlotte's life and the many suppositions about his character, a résumé of his career so far would be helpful.

Presumably he was not businesslike enough for the wool trade and did not have the makings of a doctor. Being a clergyman must have seemed the most suitable career open to him, and he certainly tried hard, and wrote many pious entries in his diary. He was a serious minded youth fond of describing people as 'worthy' and noting down facts and figures about events. At first, in his teens, he found it hard to be interested in religion or to think that he had a proper faith. 'I feel dark, dull, and unbelieving', he wrote at the age of eighteen, 'Instead of the service of God being a pleasure, I feel it a burden.' But he tried to sense more of the religious experience, and by the time he went to Cambridge he was sufficiently devout for the purpose. There he made friends with the groups of young men who sat at the feet of Simeon,[2] who had influenced Mr Brontë many years before.

It is often said that Henry wanted to be a missionary. It would not have been surprising if he had thought of this field, when we know how influenced the family were by the Moravian church which considered missions to be their principal work, and that Simeon regarded missionary activity as the ideal Christian function, but this was not Henry's interest. It was eight years later, during a crisis in his life, that he briefly considered the idea, and then Charlotte Brontë found the suggestion very amusing. She thought him totally unsuitable and pointed out his delicate health.

That she should model the diamond-hard determined St John Rivers in *Jane Eyre* on pleasant, indecisive, sociable Henry is a strange idea. Charlotte met literally dozens of clergymen and she did not need to know a person well to base a character on them – she had seen the Rev Hammond Roberson only once, when she was ten, yet made him into Helstone in *Shirley*. No doubt she met or heard someone, a clergyman or a lecturer, whose character had impressed her – and the memory was ready to hand when she needed such a person as St John Rivers.

Henry never found his real role in life. He had little religious vocation. He had some interest in paintings and sculpture, a delight in music, and a definite interest in poetry, which he wrote at length. At Cambridge his translations were the best of those submitted for the Halifax scholarship, which he won, and he came second in the first class of freshmen when classics and mathematics were combined.

Henry graduated in the summer of 1835 and became a curate, and by August he had found a post at Dewsbury with the Rev Thomas Allbutt, husband of Miss Wooler's sister Marianne. He worked there, signing the register regularly, until near the end of 1837. It was possible for him to commute from his home. Even if he took lodgings in Dewsbury parish, he could spend a good deal of time at home. He would inevitably come into contact with Charlotte, Emily and Anne Brontë whilst they were at Roe Head, for they were familiar visitors at Dewsbury Vicarage.

At more or less the same time that Henry Nussey was taking up this first post as a curate, Charlotte's brother Branwell made his abortive visit to London and failed to become a student at the Royal Academy. He returned home.

In mid-October Emily, unbearably homesick for Haworth, left Roe Head, and Anne took her place there.

The three years during which Charlotte taught for Miss Wooler were the time when she began to express her feelings for Ellen with passion. Vita Sackville-West[3] considered the surviving correspondence of this period to be love letters and believed the relationship to be lesbian whether Charlotte and Ellen realised it or not. She felt that Charlotte's true tendencies were towards her own sex. Virginia Woolf thought that in order to be great 'the artist must be in some sense androgynous'. Ann Thwaite says in her book on Edmund Gosse: 'It seems to me that the confession of strong feelings at one period for one person of the same sex does not qualify Edmund Gosse as "a secret homosexual" ',[4] and the fact that Charlotte and Ellen had strong feelings towards each other does not necessarily mean that they were lesbian.

The love between the two girls was certainly a deep, emotional experience for both of them. Charlotte played the suitor, Ellen the sought, but it is doubtful whether the relationship was what we would today define as lesbian. Ellen was eighteen in 1835, Charlotte nineteen; it may well have been a type of schoolgirl crush, an immature emotion, a try-out for adulthood, except that in a less extreme form it was to last for the rest of their lives. 'I am . . . trembling all over with excitement after reading your note; it is what I never received before – it is the unrestrained pouring out of a warm, gentle, generous heart', wrote Charlotte. And again: 'Your notes are meat and drink to me . . .' Ellen usually went to visit Charlotte on Saturdays; there would be the tap on the door, and then the servant would tell the young teacher, 'Miss Ellen Nussey is come'.

The strange thing is that throughout almost the whole of this three year period Charlotte was under the same roof as first one and then the other of her sisters. Their presence does not seem to have satisfied her in the least. They were pupils and she one of the staff and part of her wage was their tuition, so the relationship could not be a natural one. Neither could Charlotte's presence make absence from home tolerable to Emily, who left after three months; and Charlotte did not seem to be aware of Anne's later religious crisis or her ill-health until the situation grew extreme.[5]

Most of Charlotte's time was taken up by her duties, which she found more onerous than she expected. She resented having to serve the pupils in menial ways, such as mending for them, although she should have realised from her own experience at Roe Head what the duties of a teacher there involved. None of the other staff, kind though they were, stood in a relationship of equality with her – they were older and had been her own teachers. Though she had said that she loved Miss Wooler, working for her changed the relationship.

There was little free time, but Charlotte (perhaps accompanied by first Emily and later Anne), was able to walk to Birstall parish church for services on Sundays, where she could meet Ellen and Mary and visit Rydings or the Red House. Ellen and Mary went to see her at Roe Head – 'Can you come on Friday?' wrote Charlotte – and Ellen's brother George, who passed Roe Head when his business took him to Huddersfield, threw Ellen's messages into the garden for the lonely teacher. 'I wish you could know the thrill of delight which I experienced when, as I stood at the diningroom window, I saw your brother George as he whirled past toss your little packet over the wall.'

Ellen often invited Charlotte to stay at Rydings. 'You are far too kind and frequent in your invitations', wrote Charlotte. 'You puzzle me; I hardly know how to refuse, and it is still more embarrassing to accept. At any rate, I cannot come this week . . . on Sunday morning I will join you in church, if it be convenient, and stay at Rydings till Monday morning. There's a free and easy proposal!' When lonely and unhappy, Charlotte turned to her thoughts of Ellen, who had become increasingly devout. Hers was a faith Charlotte admired, and it helped Ellen to maintain her serenity through her own problems during this period. She was uncertain how long the family would be continuing to live at her beloved Rydings; her mother was unwell and her brother William was at home for a time, severely ill.

Charlotte could almost raise up a vision of Ellen by the power of her thought: 'There you sit upright and still in your black dress and white scarf [Ellen was wearing mourning for her uncle Richard], your pale marble-like face, looking so serene and kind and just like reality. It is from religion you derive your chief charm.'

For some time Charlotte had held an almost agnostic position, but this appeared to be changing. Ellen's character was less spritely and saucy at this time, more subdued. After referring to her friend's 'calm eye', Charlotte comments:

'You have been very kind to me of late, and gentle, and you have spared me those little sallies of ridicule which . . . used to make me wince . . . Ellen, I wish I could live with you always . . . If we had but a cottage and a competency of our own, I do think we might live and love on till Death..'

During these years Charlotte improved her acquaintanceship with the Healds. Old Rev William Margetson Heald retired in 1836 and his son, the Rev William Margetson Heald junior, became vicar of Birstall in his place. The Healds were close friends of the Nussey family, and Charlotte was to make use of them as models when she was writing *Shirley*. Usually Charlotte went with the schoolgirls to the church nearest to the school. Once Ellen's brother

The Reverend William Margetson Heald, vicar of Birstall.

attended also, and she wrote '..your brother George was at Mirfield church last Sunday. Of course I did not *see* him though I guessed his presence because I heard his cough (my shortsightedness makes my ear very acute) . . . [the girls] were quite smitten, he was the sole subject of their conversation during the whole of the subsequent evening.' George was notably handsome.

Charlotte and Anne had become acquainted with the prevalent Calvinistic doctrine that only those predestined to be saved would be spared hellfire, and no matter how great the efforts of the others to live good lives, it would not be possible for them to reach heaven. Although Mr Brontë was a very tolerant man, his tutor at Cambridge, Simeon, was Calvinistic, and the theories were widespread. From the horror they induced came the religious depression and crises both of the Brontë girls suffered, Anne in a more extreme form than Charlotte.[6] It was during her pupilhood at Miss Wooler's school that Anne underwent the crisis of religious doubt in which she requested a visit from the Rev James LaTrobe, the nearby Moravian minister from the chapel at Wellhouse in Mirfield. It is probable that Anne had heard of LaTrobe through Mercy Nussey, for a La Trobe was an elder at the Moravian settlement at Fairfield in 1817 when Mercy was admitted there. The uniquely humanitarian attitude of the Moravians was in sympathy with Anne's own ideas and she was much helped by the discussion she had with LaTrobe.

Anne was a pupil at Roe Head School longer than either of her elder sisters, and longer than Ellen Nussey or Mary Taylor. When in 1836 school broke up for the summer holidays, Charlotte and Anne visited Mrs Elizabeth Franks (*née* Firth, and Charlotte's godmother) at Huddersfield Vicarage, and saw old school friends of Charlotte's – Amelia Walker and her sister Jane. Also there were Amelia's parents, Mr and Mrs Joseph Walker, and brother William. The Walkers lived at Lascelles Hall. The visit included a trip to the hall, on the 21st June.

In the July of that summer Ellen visited Haworth again. Before the visit Charlotte was apprehensive, wondering if she would come after all:

'I hope no whim has got into your head which makes you consider your presence indispensable at home. I do think they could do without you for a little while. . .I hope no little touch of anger is still lingering in your mind . . .'

What Ellen might have been annoyed about, we do not know, but any uncertainty about Rydings had resolved itself; the Nusseys were about to move

Brookroyd House, Birstall, to which the Nussey family moved in September 1836.

to Brookroyd House. Ellen was unhappy and hated to leave her old home, but by the end of September 1836 the move had been made, and Mrs Nussey, daughters Mercy, Ellen and Sarah and sons Joseph, Henry and George were established at Brookroyd, in the house built near the farm and mill of the same name by Ellen's late uncle Richard Nussey. Ann Nussey stayed on at Rydings and lived with Mrs Walker and her five daughters for about two years.

During the 1836 Christmas holidays, Charlotte turned her thoughts to writing for publication and sent a letter to the poet Southey, enclosing some of her writing, to ask his advice and his opinion of her capabilities. It is worth noticing in the light of later events that she signed the letter with her true name. Branwell wrote at much the same time and for the same purpose to Wordsworth. It seems likely that the brother and sister, so close then, had conferred together about careers in writing and had decided to seek expert advice.[7]

In February 1837, Ellen was to stay once more in the household of her brother John in London, and might well be away for the whole of the rest of the school's half-year. Charlotte wrote to her on the 20th:

'I read your letter with dismay, Ellen – what shall I do without you? Why are we so to be denied each other's society? It is an inscrutable fatality . . . Why are we to be divided? Surely, Ellen, it must be because we are in danger of loving each other too well - of losing sight of the *Creator* in idolatry of the *creature*. At first I could not say, "Thy will be done." . . . Last Sunday I took up my Bible in a gloomy frame of mind; I began to read; a feeling stole over me such as I have not known for many long years – a sweet placid sensation like those that I remember used to visit me when I was a little child . . . I thought of my own Ellen – I wished she had been near me that I might have told her how happy I was . . . I must see you before you go, Ellen; if you cannot come to Roe Head I will contrive to walk over to Brookroyd, provided you will let me know the time of your departure. Should you not be at home at Easter I dare not promise to accept your mother's and sisters' invitation. I should be miserable at Brookroyd without you, yet I would contrive to visit them for a few hours if I could not for a few days. I love them for your sake . . .'

Charlotte was always welcome in the hospitable and unforbidding household now well-established at Brookroyd, but without Ellen she refused to stay there overnight. It was to be months before the two friends met again.

Ellen herself was far from happy. The move from Rydings had been a traumatic one for her, and she was not feeling well. On the 24th February her London sister-in-law had a new baby, John Thomas Hartley Nussey, the third attempt to continue the name John, and – a heavy burden for baby shoulders! – the infant also intended to commemorate the Hartley family, who in the previous century had been so influential. It was probably to help with the older children during the arrival of the baby that Ellen's presence was so urgently requested. There can be no doubt that the family had begun to regard her as a tower of strength to be called on, particularly in nursing emergencies. While this says a great deal for Ellen's capabilities, it also shows a lack of regard for what she herself might wish to do or be.

Thrown on her own resources at Roe Head, Charlotte's longing to escape from teaching by writing came back in full force, and she continued her correspondence with Southey with a letter to him on the 16th March. Writing to Ellen in London, she wanted reactions to various books she had been reading herself: 'Get the book, Ellen, read it, and tell me what you think of it'. And to know how her friend's spirits were faring. 'Are you happier than you were? Try to reconcile your mind to circumstances and exert the quiet fortitude of which I know you are not destitute . . . I do not forget ten o'clock, I remember it every night.' (Perhaps they prayed for one another at that time.) Charlotte sends a kiss for Ellen's 'little favourite niece Georgiana' and in return Georgiana wrote a baby letter to her. A good deal of Ellen's life in the next two years was to be spent in the households of her married brothers John and Joshua.

In Yorkshire the industrial unrest which was to continue for over ten years had begun in the Batley and Spen valleys. Distress among the handloom weavers, and feelings aggravated by the threatened implementation of the cruel Poor Law Amendment Act of 1834, produced unrest which found a voice in the Chartist movement. Dewsbury, which in itself was a small market town but around which were particularly large numbers of handloom weavers, was badly hit. It became increasingly difficult for these weavers to find work, and many of them had good cause to concern themselves about the provisions to be made for the poor. During May a great Chartist meeting was held on Hartshead Moor within a mile of Roe Head, and it is very possible that Charlotte – perhaps with Anne – went to a spot from which they could observe the proceedings. When she came to write the novel *Shirley*, Charlotte put in passages which suggest that she had been close to rioters, or at least close to excited crowds:

'You never heard that sound, perhaps, reader?', she writes in *Shirley*. 'A rioter's yell – a North-of-England, a Yorkshire, a West Riding – a West-Riding-clothing-district-of-Yorkshire rioter's yell? So much the better for your ears – perhaps for your heart.'

The Poor Law Amendment Act, legislation which was to affect the lives of ordinary people more than any other, had been passed in 1834. It came into force gradually throughout the country, in the teeth of much opposition. Humanitarians were against it with reason, for it was to bring widespread suffering and inhuman treatment of the old and the helpless. Instead of local provision of help from the poor rate, it demanded large workhouses to serve the whole of the new 'unions' of parishes. These workhouses were at the time called 'Bastilles' and they were indeed like prisons in their government and regulations. The Rev Patrick Brontë made a great speech against the act early in 1837, a slashing indictment, and this speech had been selected by *The Times* for publication. The arguments in favour of the act were that large numbers had for generations received relief out of the poor rates, and thought it no shame to do so. There was a school of thought which considered it the people's own fault if they needed help and that if obtaining help was sufficiently unpleasant, if asking for assistance was shameful and humiliating, then people in need would stand on their own feet and cope without being a burden on the community. The implementation of the act was to mean forcible separation of old couples who had lived their lives together; the complete lack of privacy, decency and such small luxuries as a cup of tea or a pipe of tobacco; the exaction of hard physical work from the ill, old and infirm; poor and inadequate food; the lack of heating, adequate clothing or bedding; the separation of husbands, wives and children of all ages; and the loss of their homes, their dignity, their few household goods, their own clothing, their last few remnants of self-respect.

Events for Ellen in London were far removed from this industrial and social unrest. The interest of the household at Cleveland Row must have centred on the decline of King William IV's health; he died on the 20th June 1837. Intimately involved as John Nussey was with the royal family, this and the future professional outcome was of immense importance to him. Since the death of George IV, to whom he was apothecary to the person, he had had to be content with a lesser appointment to the royal household.

The Elizabethan Healds House on Dewsbury Moor was the new site of Miss Wooler's school after the summer of 1837. Charlotte was a teacher here until 1838, and Anne was believed to be a pupil.

The death of the king brought about the accession of Queen Victoria. To Charlotte and her sisters, to Ellen and to Mary, this was a thrilling event. They had always lived under the reign of aging *roués*; now a girl younger than themselves was the Queen of England. At the accession of Victoria, Charlotte was twenty-one, Ellen Nussey, Mary Taylor and Branwell Brontë were twenty, Emily Brontë nineteen and Anne Brontë seventeen. The Brontës had lived half their lives already. The first years of Victoria's reign were – in royal circles – lightness and joy; the young girl-queen loved dancing the night away and horse-riding during the day, flirting innocently with the men of the court, singing in her silver voice, dressing in light fabrics and pretty pale colours, decorating herself with flowers and leaves.

Much to the relief of John Nussey and his family, he was appointed apothecary to the person – one of the people in day-to-day charge of the young queen's health.[8] In the security of this prestigious new royal appointment, John completed the formalities of his purchase of Rydings, a matter which had been unresolved since the death of his uncle in 1835.

During the summer holidays of 1837, Miss Wooler moved her school to Dewsbury Moor and established it in the building called Healds House. This was an old Elizabethan dwelling which took its name from its recent occupiers. The last of them, John Heald, had left to live with his nephew, the recently-appointed Vicar of Birstall. Charlotte and Anne Brontë rejoined the school in early August (*see note 5*).

It is likely that Ellen, her brother John and his wife came north that summer, bringing with them John's son Edward, aged nine, for he now went to school not far from Dewsbury at Healds Hall, Liversedge. This was Hammond Roberson's well known school for boys, run by his nephew Henry Roberson, as Hammond had suffered a paralytic stroke some years earlier. Little Edward Nussey remained for one 'half' at Healds Hall School.[9]

Since leaving Roe Head, Emily Brontë had remained happily at home. Then, in September or October of 1837, she took a post as teacher at Law Hill, a school near Halifax. It was hard work, and she found it difficult (*see note 5*).

Things were not well at Dewsbury. Little Edward Nussey was not the only one who left the area in December. At Miss Wooler's school, Anne Brontë was ill and in December Charlotte, who feared that Anne's chest was affected, had a quarrel with her employer, then took Anne home and almost severed all connection with Miss Wooler. Ellen remembered that poor Charlotte was full of agony for her suffering sister, seeing and feeling much further than Miss Wooler, who never had a day's illness in her life . . . so Charlotte thought her hard and unfeeling – 'they "had it out", as people say, and were all the better friends afterwards.'[10] It was at the same time that Henry Nussey's health worsened into a severe illness and he too left Dewsbury and his post as curate there.

During the Christmas holidays of 1837, Ellen was to have visited Haworth, but the housekeeper, Tabitha, broke her leg and the visit was not possible; the Brontë family were looking after the house themselves in addition to nursing Tabitha. 'I am not the only one who is disappointed', wrote Charlotte. 'All in the house were looking forward to your visit with eagerness.' Charlotte made up her quarrel with Miss Wooler, and in the new year, 1838, she returned to teach again.

Anne Brontë's health improved quickly once at home, but Henry Nussey took longer to return to normal, because during his convalescence he had a road accident in which he sustained an injury to the head. Later he looked back and remembered the occasion; '. . . before recovery from the consequences of my illness . . . [I thank God for] again preserving me from death instantaneous by a fall from a spirited horse. My head was very much affected, by this misfortune, and my ministerial work much impeded . . . This probably operated to make me so excited at the time of the missionary meetings. The bad effects in my head only disappeared with my last illness.'

We understand head injuries much better today, when many young people are in Henry's position after motorcycle or car accidents. In the first half of 1838 while he was recovering from his illness and the accident, Henry was taken onto the team of curates working under his friend, Rev W M Heald jnr; but Henry was not fit enough to work well and did not expect to be paid for this six months casual employment.

When he went to preach a trial sermon in a Leeds parish in February 1838 he was criticised for his poor articulation of the words; he was advised to open his mouth and be more distinct, and he was not offered a post. When in the early summer he obtained a place as curate in Burton Agnes with Rev Charles Henry Lutwidge he still had great difficulty in public speaking, and at a missionary meeting could not bring out the words of the motion he was proposing, almost seeming to have a seizure. Lutwidge later dismissed him, saying that Henry's health was not good enough for him to carry out his duties. Yet while at Cambridge Henry had read out the lessons for a week, and during singing tuition was told that his was a good general voice, and he had no problem at Dewsbury – so it is certain that these troubles were the result of the head injury.

Emily Brontë had left her post at Law Hill School in April 1838, for what reason we do not know; Ellen tells us Emily taught there for six months. Charlotte, with more persistence, was still in Dewsbury in the early summer, towards the time of Queen Victoria's coronation, and feeling even more alone, for now both her sisters were at home in Haworth and Ellen, after enduring a family tragedy in London, was spending some months with her brother Joshua and his wife at Batheaston, a village near Bath, where for some four years Joshua was the curate.

It had been a very distressing time for the Nussey family. William, who had been sick and dejected the previous autumn, had died at the age of thirty-one. Henry records that William had been ill from February of 'some malady of the brain'; we would now call it clinical depression. 'He laboured under a deep conviction of sin and became very silent and absorbed in his own thoughts.' It seems that John, the eldest brother, hushed up the manner of

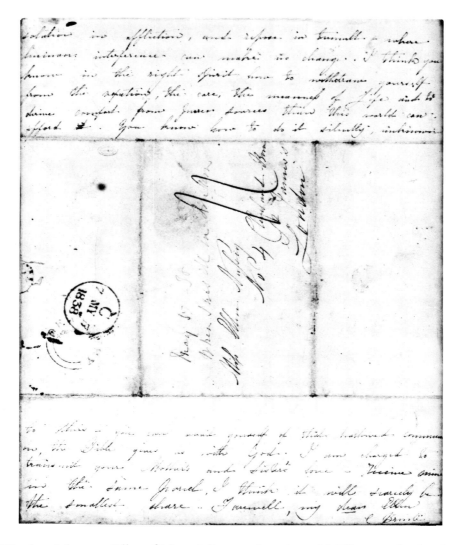

Charlotte's letter to Ellen of May 1838, commiserating with Ellen over her brother William's illness.

William's death by disguising the details on the death certificate. In fact William threw himself into the Thames on the 7th June. Henry in Burton Agnes was not aware of the true facts, and it is possible that even Ellen, in London, did not know exactly what had happened. In any case, she was very distressed and this is probably why she was sent to Batheaston.

The isolation of Dewsbury Moor with both Ellen Nussey and Anne Brontë away, combined with the cumulative effect of hard work, proved too much for Charlotte and she became very run down and exhausted. She had to abandon teaching and go home to Haworth, probably in the middle of May; by the 9th June 1838 she began to feel a little recovered. Her three years of teaching for Miss Wooler were over, the longest period she was ever to spend in an employment.

In London it was fortunate that the imminent coronation helped to turn the thoughts of John Nussey away from the traumatic loss of his brother and partner. He hunted out old recipes for richly perfumed oils to be used in the ceremony, but the young queen sent him a message to ask for something very lightly scented. On the coronation day, 28th June, the weather all over England was superb and everywhere celebrations were taking place. There was a procession at Batheaston, including the Rev Joshua Nussey, watched by Ellen;[11] in Burton Agnes near Bridlington curate Henry Nussey recorded the treat of tea, cakes and sweetmeats given to the local children and teachers by his vicar, Charles Henry Lutwidge. A party of Lutwidge relations, sisters, aunt and cousins, had arrived. Henry was much struck by the good looks and evident cleverness of the visiting ladies, and particularly by two of Lutwidge's sisters, Henrietta Mary and Margaret Ann.[12]

In contrast to the coronation jollifications, which distracted and amused the population during June, unrest over the implementation of the Poor Law Act flared up again in the West Riding during August with riots in Dewsbury.[13] The parliamentary commissioners were pressing for enforcement, and implementation rested with the guardians of the Dewsbury Poor Law Union. Those against the act included Robert Clapham, who represented Batley on the board of the Dewsbury union, and was the local agent for the Wilton estate. His farm was near Brookroyd and he and his wife were friends of the Nusseys and of Charlotte, who once enquired whether Mrs Clapham had had her baby yet. (Much later, Ellen's sister Ann was to become Clapham's second wife.)

The Dewsbury Poor Law union covered the parishes of which Charlotte was later to write in *Shirley*, and in this union it was Joshua Ingham, later Anne Brontë's employer, whose evidence as spokesman for the Dewsbury guardians enabled the Poor Law Commissioners to enforce the new act. John Beswicke Greenwood supported him.[14] There were only eight of the Dewsbury guardians in favour of the act and nineteen against, but Ingham and Greenwood forced it through. The act's opponents were furious with Ingham, made threats against his life, and later he was stoned by a mob. Ingham and Greenwood were both rich and had no sympathy with the poor; Patrick Brontë and Robert Clapham were in closer touch with the people and knew just what the implementation of the act would entail. Mr Brontë in particular worked constantly for the improvement of the lot of his parishioners and others. After the Dewsbury riots, local unrest manifested itself through support for the Chartist movement, and later, in October, another large Chartist meeting was held on Hartshead Moor.

At home in Haworth, Charlotte was visited by Mary and Martha Taylor who stayed for a few happy days.

Ellen's brother Joshua left Batheaston during October 1838 to take up an appointment as Rector of Poughill, Devon, a post he had been given some months before. It seems likely that his removal to Devon was the occasion of Ellen's returning home. Certainly she was back by the end of October 1838 and Charlotte was able to stay with her at Brookroyd. This visit was one of the times when Charlotte led a busy social life. She had already made the acquaintance of many people in the area, poorer families as well as the more comfortable. Among them were the Knowles family, who established the first post office and druggist's shop in Birstall. In 1977 Miss Knowles, then an old lady, told John Nussey that 'Ellen Nussey was an old friend of my grandmother and often visited her at the post office where we had been established since 1775 until my brother's retirement in 1965. She always brought Charlotte Brontë to Gran's for tea whenever she came over to Birstall'. Charlotte visited many of the houses of Ellen's relatives and friends, including Dr Carr at Gomersal, the clerical family of Heald, and Ellen's distant cousin Joshua Walker and his family at Oakwell House. Charlotte knew many people so well that before returning to Haworth she made a round of goodbyes. In the parishes of Birstall, Batley and Dewsbury, she was now as much at ease as she was at home.

In Burton Agnes, Henry Nussey was also saying goodbye. He had been there less than three months when his vicar decided that Henry's health was not good enough, and suggested an alternative curacy. Henry was then ill again, and during these weeks heard through Heald of a vacancy for a curate to take charge of Earnley parish, near Chichester in Sussex, where the vicar was non-resident. Although Earnley was expected to be a short-term post, Henry accepted it and left Burton Agnes on the 29th November for Hull and the ship to London. Once settled in Sussex the quiet life and peaceful surroundings brought about an improvement in Henry's physical condition. 'Through the goodness of my God I am now in better health and have better nights of rest than I have had for almost years back . . .', Henry wrote at the end of 1838.

These were stirring years to have lived through and more changes were ahead. 1838 was the year in which the regular Atlantic steam-ship service began. Railways were being organised all over the country, and with other inventions were to make great differences to life. The Brontë family were now all resident again in Haworth after their various experiences out in the world. Emily's knowledge of Law Hill is said to have contributed to the ambience of *Wuthering Heights*. Charlotte's experiences of the Chartist agitation determined her theme in *Shirley*. Their friend Ellen Nussey was once more in her home area and becoming reconciled to living at Brookroyd, and her brother Henry was happy at last, down in Sussex.

[1] Henry Nussey's *Journal*, 3268A, ff 1–65v, is in the Ashley Collection, Manuscript Room, British Museum. Henry was admitted 'pensioner' aged nineteen at Magdalene college, Cambridge, stating that he had been at school at Leeds. He matriculated 1831, became BA 1835, and after posts at Dewsbury, Birstall and Burton Agnes, became curate of Earnley with Almodington 1839–44, next rector of Hathersage, 1845–7. He then appears in the Clergy Lists with no address until 1866.

[2] Charles Simeon, 1759–1836, a fellow of Kings College, Cambridge, became an acknowledged leader among evangelical churchmen and was one of the founders of the Church Missionary Society.

[3] *Vita; the life of V Sackville-West* by Victoria Glendinning, pp 169, 207.

[4] *Edmund Gosse; a Literary Landscape* by Ann Thwaite, p 534.

[5] It has recently been suggested that the accepted dating of this period is mistaken, and that Anne had only one illness, at Roe Head, and that the move to Dewsbury Moor was after she had left the school. This seems to be proved by Ellen's endorsement to Charlotte's letter of January 1838. There is also doubt about the exact period Emily spent at Law Hill.

[6] In letter 53 in the Shakespeare Head edition of Charlotte's letters is a deleted word which has been read as 'Your' by Dr Winnifrith, making the phrase 'your ghastly Calvinistic Doctrines'. As the letter is to Ellen, who did not apparently hold Calvinistic doctrines, and whose religious outlook is frequently lauded by Charlotte, this 'your' (if that is the correct reading) must be rhetorical. Probably Ellen deleted it to avoid confusion.

[7] Later when the identity of the author of *Jane Eyre* was much speculated upon, the name Brontë was one of the 'possibles' mentioned in the Martineau/Gaskell circles.

[8] John Nussey (1794–1862) held the office jointly with Edward Duke Moore until October 1857, then alone until his retirement in 1860. The apothecary's role was similar to that of our GPs. John Nussey attended Queen Victoria at several of her confinements including the birth of the future Edward VII, and one of his sons recalled being present with his brothers outside the palace when his father held the infant prince up to a window for the crowd to see. Information from John Nussey.

[9] Edward's second cousin, William Carr, also aged nine, was at Healds Hall at the same time. An exercise book listing the boys' names, ages, and heights, belonging to a Mrs Trench (now deceased), was seen by John Nussey. Edward wrote a letter to 'Willy' the following Christmas.

[10] Letter from Ellen to Clement Shorter 22 April 1896.

[11] The *Bath Chronicle* gives details of Coronation Day at Batheaston.

[12] Rev Charles Henry Lutwidge's sister Frances Jane married their first cousin Charles Dodgson in 1827 and had eleven children including Charles Lutwidge Dodgson, who was later the writer 'Lewis Carroll'. Whether or not Lewis Carroll ever went to Burton Agnes is a matter often debated. The wording of Henry Nussey's *Journal*, 'sisters, aunt and cousins', seems to imply that the whole family came, in which case Carroll was there, at the age of six, and Henry met him.

[13] There were many newspaper reports of these riots, including one in the *York Herald*, 11th August 1838.

[14] Both were connected with Ellen through her brother John's mother-in-law, Mary Walker, who was now living at Rydings. Beswicke Greenwood was Mary Walker's nephew, Ingham her half-cousin.

LOVE AFFAIRS AND GOVERNESSHIPS, 1839-41

The next few years of muddled change and development saw all the girls except Emily Brontë becoming romantically involved, and all of them casting around for their true careers and roles in life.

The first proposal of marriage Charlotte Brontë received was from Henry Nussey, and it is worth looking at this episode.

When Henry was dismissed from his post at Burton Agnes, he was comforted by the memory of the Moravian custom of putting decisions to the lot so that God's will could be made known. He quoted in his journal, 'that though man devised his way, the whole disposing of the lot was of the Lord'. The dismissal did prove a blessing in disguise. When later he was living in the small, quiet village of Earnley, close to the sea and within walking distance of Chichester, Henry's health began to improve for the first time since his severe illness and head injury. By February 1839 he was feeling so well that he decided to marry and form a small boarding school to supplement his income.

He had been much attracted to the Rev Charles Henry Lutwidge's sister, Margaret Ann, when she stayed at Burton Agnes the previous summer, and now wrote to her on the 18th February 1839, proposing marriage. She was

Henry Nussey became curate of Earnley Church, Sussex, at the end of 1838.

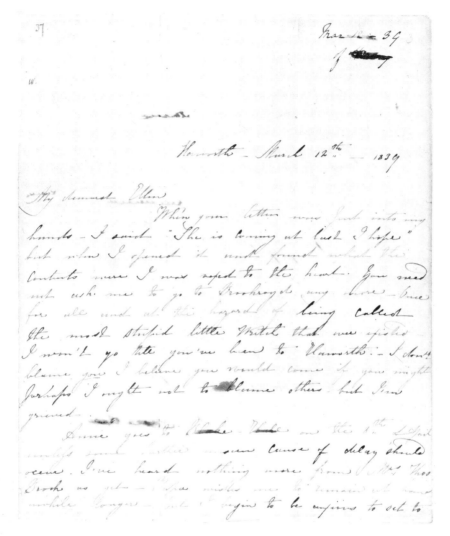

The letter from Charlotte to Ellen, dated the 12th March 1839, saying that Anne is going to Blake Hall.

almost three years his senior. Margaret Ann passed the letter to her father, Mr Charles Lutwidge, and he replied refusing the offer on her behalf. Henry was sure that she was attracted to him, so he wrote a second time, but again her father wrote with a refusal.[1] This hit Henry hard, and although he received the second refusal on the Tuesday the 26th February, it was not until the Friday that he could bear to record it in his diary.

In the Moravian community, couples wishing to marry put the decision to the lot and accepted the decision of God declared through it; if the decision went against them, they chose another partner. Henry was determined to abide by the will of God. Having been refused by Lewis Carroll's aunt, he proposed to Charlotte Brontë on the 1st March – possibly a uniquely literary double proposal. He was refused by Charlotte too. Her letter reached him on the 9th of March 1839.

Henry should not be condemned. His behavior was not very different from that of the Rev Patrick Brontë after the death of his wife, when he wrote to one after another of the women who he thought had a 'tendresse' for him. In looking round for a clergyman's wife, Henry behaved very responsibly, valuing the qualities of steadiness, intelligence and good sense, which he felt she would need.

Henry and Charlotte liked one another. The friendship was seven years old and there was some affection between them. Charlotte refused him kindly. She liked him physically well enough to be willing to go to bed with him ('I have no personal repugnance to the idea of a union with you'), but knew that she was too lively for his serious nature ('he is grave, quiet . . . amiable, well-disposed' but, alas, not 'clever'), and she wanted to fall in love with the man she married. The most amazing thing she said about the proposal was that she was tempted to accept so that she could have Ellen to live with them.

In spite of Charlotte's refusal, the two went on corresponding spasmodically. Charlotte was always friendly towards Henry, though he was both less

Anne Brontë was governess for the Inghams of Blake Hall, Mirfield, between April and December 1839. The hall, pictured here about 1900 with (on the right) the extensions made to the east façade by Joshua Ingham in 1845, appears in Agnes Grey *as* Wellwood House.

Anne Brontë's employer as governess at Blake Hall, Mrs Mary Ingham. She casually remarked in later life that she 'had once employed a very unsuitable governess called Miss Brontë'.

intelligent and less sprightly than her beloved Ellen. He had a great admiration for Charlotte's intellect, her abilities, and her literary taste.[2]

On the 8th April, Anne Brontë went to Blake Hall, Mirfield, as a governess to the children of Joshua Ingham. Anne's fellow pupil at Roe Head had been Mrs Ingham's younger sister, Harriet Cunliffe Lister, so Anne may well have heard of the post through her. The Inghams used the Blake Hall pew in Mirfield church, so Anne would certainly know them by sight.

Joshua Ingham, the target of popular hate in the previous year during the agitation over the Poor Law, had a personality of the worst possible kind for association with someone of Anne's temperament. The tone of his household seems to have been taken from him, also the character of his children, as his wife was a 'placid, mild woman' and the children were wild and uncontrollable. His mother, Martha Ingham, who had been so kind in visiting Ellen Nussey during her time at Roe Head, comes reasonably well out of Anne's subsequent novel *Agnes Grey* (written in 1846), part of which is based closely and recognisably on Anne's time with the Inghams. But even Mrs Martha

Ingham does not escape censure, being called capricious and portrayed strengthening Ingham's prejudice against the governess. Anne stayed in this uncongenial post until December.

Ellen's family seemed very reluctant to allow her to visit Haworth. The reason given was Ellen's poor health. It has been suggested that they feared she might become attached to Branwell, but as he had set up a studio in Bradford and was living there, trying to succeed as a portrait painter, this seems unlikely. Charlotte was always more than welcome at Brookroyd, but she would not accept constant hospitality without returning it. Inheriting her father's interest in medicine, she prescribed for Ellen. Fresh air and exercise were to be the remedies, and she was arranging to hire a donkey during a projected visit, so that Ellen could be led over the moorland paths without becoming overtired. It would not be Charlotte leading the donkey, for she had a fear of large strange animals. Ellen later recalled, about Emily Brontë, that she used to tease the shortsighted Charlotte (in the days before Charlotte became resigned to wearing spectacles), by taking her close to strange cows or horses and then telling her what she had done, in order to be amused at Charlotte's consequent alarm.

The Nussey family may have felt afraid of losing Ellen, because she entered so whole-heartedly into the life of Haworth Parsonage. The family had decided her role in life. Her sister Sarah needed care, Mrs Nussey and Mercy were frequently ill and Ellen herself had one illness after another. The family were happy for Ellen to work hard at home or visit her brothers, less happy for her to stray outside the family fold. Visits to relatives were to be a constant feature of her life, as they were of so many single Victorian women. They did not visit for a day, but for two or three months, often in response to need in the host family, illness or the care of children, but sometimes simply to live their lives in company with their near ones.

In May any opportunity for the two friends to be together was lost when Charlotte took up a temporary post as governess. Miss Hoby, governess to the Sidgwick family at Stonegappe in Lothersdale, was to be away for some weeks and might even be giving up the position. In the event Charlotte was with the Sidgwicks for about two months, in which she showed for the first time the unfortunate pattern which was to cause her so much unhappiness – she far preferred the master of the house to his wife. About Mrs Sidgwick she wrote: 'she cares nothing in the world about me except to contrive how the greatest possible quantity of labour may be squeezed out of me', whereas Mr Sidgwick 'is in my opinion a hundred times better . . . It is very seldom that he speaks to me, but when he does I always feel happier and more settled for some minutes after'. She describes a walk with him and the children as 'one of the pleasantest afternoons I have spent here'. Her loneliness was a little cheered by seeing something of the Carter family. The Rev Edward Nicholl Carter, who had been curate at Mirfield from 1827-38, was now perpetual curate at Lothersdale. 'At home I should not care for them, but here they are friends', she wrote, and she became fond of Anne Carter, probably a younger sister of the Rev Carter, who was a 'young, beautiful and happy girl', whose death at the end of the year was much to sadden Charlotte.

Once Charlotte was back at home, in July, she and Ellen had the intense excitement of a proposed holiday together to think about. The Nusseys had decided that three weeks by the sea might improve Ellen's health, and she asked Charlotte to go with her. There were endless obstacles in the way – whether they could go at all - how long Charlotte could stay (her family felt two weeks was the maximum) – where to go – how Charlotte was to travel to meet Ellen – at last it all seemed impossible.

A diversion was provided by a most surprising letter proposing marriage to Charlotte, which arrived from a clergyman, Mr Bryce, who visited the parsonage only once, in August. Charlotte obviously had that mysterious quality, sex appeal. She had allowed herself to be uninhibited with Mr Bryce and laugh at his jokes. Charlotte's shortsightedness may also have played a part. Shortsighted people not wearing glasses tend to look earnestly into the eyes of others and this can be misconstrued. Once again Charlotte sent a letter of refusal.

At last, at the beginning of September, Ellen, thoroughly exasperated with waiting, persuaded one of her brothers to loan her a carriage and set off to Haworth to collect Charlotte, without notice. The spritely young woman encountered no opposition – she took everyone by surprise and charmed them into parting with Charlotte in the time it took for the horse to rest. From Leeds the two young ladies travelled as far as they could by the new railway, their first experience of it. The railway came as a blessing to both of them; for the first time they were able to travel freely and at a price they could afford. There was no suggestion that it was 'not ladylike' to travel alone in a railway carriage – they were both to do so frequently. They had decided to go to Bridlington, but they were not to escape the superintendence of well-meaning relatives. The joy with which they looked forward to being independent was sharply dashed. Henry's curacy at Burton Agnes had been very close to Bridlington and the Nusseys had written ahead to tell friends he had there of the girls' arrival. They were captured by those generous and good-hearted people, the Hudsons, and taken to stay at their house at Easton for a month. At last they were allowed to go into lodgings at Bridlington, but the Hudsons still kept an eye on them and brought foodstuffs over. Ellen and Charlotte enjoyed their one week of real freedom every bit as much as they thought they would. The two friends had never before been quite alone and left to their own devices. It answered all their expectations and they were very happy.

Although, in coming to Haworth, Ellen had shown herself capable of enterprise and exertion worthy of a Victorian youth rather than a Victorian maiden, it was Charlotte, irked throughout her life by the second-class treatment women received, who longed to have the freedom of a man. The two girls were amused by the evening 'parade' the other visitors took on the little pier, which became so crowded that it was like a ballroom, and they only joined this throng once. But when they did what they really wanted to do, walking on the headlands by moonlight, they were overcome by fear and went back. Then, safe in their lodgings, they heard the:

'. . . sounds which came from a Ranters' meeting-house across the street, there was violent excitement within its walls, and Charlotte was wild to go in amongst the congregation and see as she said, "What they were up to"; but was restrained by the reflection that those people who were making such awful noises were acting as they believed on religious impulse, and ought neither to be criticised nor ridiculed in their midst.'[3]

This episode was used in her novel *Shirley*.

Charlotte found the sight and presence of the sea an overpowering emotional experience. The holiday did the girls good and was often remembered, even the visit to the Hudsons which had made them feel so constrained at the time. Charlotte wrote:

'Have you forgotten the sea by this time Ellen? is it grown dim in your mind? or can you still see it dark blue and green and foamwhite and hear it – roaring roughly when the wind [is] high or rushing softly when it is calm? . . . I think of Easton very often and of worthy Mr Hudson and his kind-hearted helpmate and of our pleasant walks to Harlequin-wood – to Boynton – our merry evenings – our romps with Fancheon – etc. etc. if we both live this period of our lives will long be a theme of pleasant recollection.'[4]

The two girls were surrounded during their holiday by friends Henry Nussey had made the previous year, and while on a day-trip to Burton Agnes had visited two of his parishioners. At the end of the holiday they went to Ellen's home. Charlotte stayed at Brookroyd House at least overnight and possibly for a day or two. It was the busy centre of a sociable family. 'Whenever I go there', Charlotte wrote, 'I am unavoidably forced into society – clerical society chiefly'. After breaking her journey, she left Ellen and made her way back to Haworth via Dewsbury and the Keighley coach.

Soon after their return, Charlotte had a letter from Henry. He had fallen in love with a penniless girl and wrote to Charlotte about it, but this did not end in marriage either. He did take scholars to live in the rectory house at Earnley, and over the next years his sisters kept house for him in turns.[5]

The year 1839 had been a year for love – Queen Victoria announced her engagement to Prince Albert in mid-October. She had been reluctant to marry – she was enjoying herself too much – but the isolation of her position, and Albert's charms, changed her mind. 1839 had also been the year in which William Weightman had come to Haworth as a curate. Although he had accepted the post in May, he did not come until August, and it is likely that Charlotte hardly noticed him until after her return from Bridlington in October. He became very important to the Brontë family, and the happy tone of Charlotte's letters at the end of the year shows the influence of the presence in her circle of this light-hearted and attractive man.

In the parish of Birstall, too, events had moved on. Ellen's three brothers in the wool trade, Richard, Joseph and George, had been having severe trading problems during the year. In the Taylor family, there was mention for the first time in 1839 of Mary's father being ill.

The New Year is a time for new beginnings and Branwell Brontë became a tutor at Broughton-in-Furness on the 1st January 1840. So far he had not succeeded in anything. His portrait painting in Bradford had been unremunerative and he had given it up. Now he was to live in another family and teach – which meant that for most of December 1839 his sisters had been busy sewing new clothes for him. It has been forgotten how important a part of every woman's life was the hand sewing of garments and of household furnishings. The 'work' constantly referred to in Victorian novels was sewing and knitting. Ellen and her friends never sat idle. If they were chatting, they were at the same time making or embellishing something, 'working'. So before every departure of one of the family from home, the Brontë sisters spent hours making and mending the lighter garments, shirts and underwear. Tailors were patronised for heavy male outer garments. Mr Brontë, although he made a point of using the local tradesmen, still had his new coats made by the tailor who had made them when he was at Cambridge. When, after twelve months wear, they began to look shabby, he would have them 'turned' by one of the Haworth tailors so that they looked as good as new. He used to stitch on two pockets himself, to house his pistols.[6]

At the beginning of 1840 Charlotte, Emily and Anne were all living at home, and Branwell had settled into his post as tutor. In addition to their sewing and writing, the Brontë sisters were also busy doing housework, because Tabby, who now had an ulcerated leg, had gone to live with her sister in a little house nearby, which Tabby had bought from her savings.

Charlotte was looking for another teaching post, but her attempts were not bearing fruit. Ellen thought of working as a governess. 'I know not whether to encourage you in your plan of going out or not', wrote Charlotte, pointing out that Ellen's health was the obstacle. 'If you can obtain a situation like Mary Brooke[7] you might do very well. But you could never live in an unruly, violent family of modern children, such, for instance, as those at Blake Hall.' Charlotte added that sickness and death prevailed at Haworth, and that the young curate who had proposed to her by letter after only one meeting had died. The second unexpected death of a young person of their own age in a short time must have made both the friends feel that life was very insecure. 'I felt both shocked and saddened', wrote Charlotte.

1840 was the year in which Queen Victoria and her Albert were married on the 10th February, and Ellen's brother John was appointed apothecary to the Prince Consort and to his household. John's practice included many of the nobility, and at some point the queen offered both him and Henry Holland (Mrs Gaskell's cousin, one of the queen's physicians) a baronetcy; they both refused. The queen did not realise what a difference marriage would make. Hardly had she been married a couple of days before she was importing numbers of friends to Windsor and having a party, dancing half the night. At that time she was still a typical, bouncing, hedonistic member of the House of Hanover.

In this joyful month of February 1840, when for three whole weeks Ellen was at Haworth, Branwell was safely away in the Lake District. 'Three happy weeks' Ellen called them afterwards, and indeed they were. William Weightman – nicknamed by Charlotte 'Celia Amelia' – was constantly in and out of the parsonage; even Emily liked him, better than she was ever to like any other curate. Accounts of that time come down to us: Charlotte drawing a portrait of Weightman; his sending valentines to each of them; his lecture and their attendance at it. Ellen recalled:

'. . . the taking of Mr Weightman's portrait by Charlotte. The sittings became alarming for length of time required, and the guest [Ellen] had to adopt the gown, which the owner was very proud to exhibit, amusing the party with his critical remarks on the materials used, and pointing out the adornments, silk, velvet, etc.'

Ellen in William Weightman's academic gown must indeed have been worth seeing, as he imitated a woman's discussion of fabric and ornament, and the three Brontë sisters laughed, Charlotte having to stop drawing until they had laughed themselves out.

Charlotte's portrait of William Weightman.

Ellen reminisced:

'There was also a little episode as to valentines. Mr Weightman discovered that none of the party had ever received a valentine – a great discovery! Whereupon he indited [sic] verses to each one, and walked ten miles to post them, lest Mr Brontë should discover his dedicatory nonsense, and the quiet liveliness going on under the sedate espionage of Miss Branwell and Mr Brontë himself.'

The girls were so delighted with the valentines that they wrote one to him in reply, and all four signed it. Ellen tells us of the lecture:

' "Celia Amelia" [was] Mr Brontë's curate, a lively, handsome young man fresh from Durham University, an excellent classical scholar. He gave a very good lecture on the Classics at Keighley. [Weightman had been taught by the classics don, as the divinity chair was empty at the time.] The young ladies at the Parsonage must hear his lecture, so he went off to a married clergyman to get him to write to Mr Brontë and invite the young ladies to tea, and offer his escort to the lecture, and back again to the Parsonage. Great fears were entertained that permission would not be given – it was a walk of four miles each way. The Parsonage was not reached till 12 p.m. [midnight], the two clergymen rushed in with their charges, deeply disturbing Miss Branwell, who had prepared hot coffee for the home party, which of course fell short when two more were to be supplied. Poor Miss Branwell lost her temper, Charlotte was troubled, and Mr Weightman, who enjoyed teasing the old lady, was very thirsty. The great spirits of the walking party had a trying suppression, but twinkling fun sustained some of them.'

There can be no doubt that Charlotte had been more than a little in love with Willie Weightman when they first knew one another, but as she realised that his charms were distributed generally and were not for her alone, she armoured herself against him. During Ellen's three weeks with them, Charlotte believed – or tried to believe – that he had fallen in love with her friend. Willie Weightman and his nonsense alone would have made this visit hilarious: he flirted with Ellen, and Emily gained her nickname 'The Major' for the military way in which she manoeuvred Ellen away from him during the walks on which he accompanied them. This was the holiday during which the incipient friendship between Ellen and Emily burgeoned. The only existing letters by Emily Brontë are three short ones she wrote to Ellen.

Ellen wanted Emily's friendship. She tells us of the time when Emily's dog Keeper pushed in between Charlotte and Emily as the four girls were sitting round the fire in the evening, climbed onto Emily's knee, then, finding that not big enough, overflowed onto Ellen's and lay across them both. Emily's friendship was won by Ellen's tolerance of the great dog. Ellen's tolerance was boundless because the remote Emily, who did not touch anyone except her sister Anne, with whom she was often entwined, was now sitting so close to herself, Ellen, that they were physically touching. The affectionate contact pleased Ellen and she would have withstood much more to gain it, because she loved to be one of the circle, accepted as family.

Charlotte wrote to Henry Nussey of this visit: 'her [Ellen's] company, when once obtained, is too valuable to be wasted for a moment. There is much, too, in that mild even temper and that placid equanimity which keeps the domestic hearth always bright and peaceful'. Around this time a new maturity shows in Charlotte's letters. She was too busy with her own writing, though, to do as Henry wished and exchange literary letters on set topics with him.

'We feel very dull without you; I wish those three weeks were to come over again', wrote Charlotte to Ellen, 'Aunt has been at times precious cross since you went, however she is rather better now'. After signing herself 'Charivari'[8] she added a postscript:

'To your hands and Martha Taylor's do I resign myself in a spirit worthy of a martyr that is to say with much the same feeling that I should experience if I were sitting down on the plat to have a tooth drawn; you have a peculiar fashion of your own of reporting a saying or a doing and Martha has a still more peculiar fashion of re-reporting it.'

In March, Anne Brontë went to her second post as governess, to the Robinson family who lived at Thorpe Green near York. It was to be her last employment, and to endure for a surprisingly long time.

The teasing, riotous humour continued at the beginning of Charlotte's next letter to Ellen on the 7th April, but she soon went on to more serious, stirring things:

'- little Haworth has been all in a bustle about Church-rates since you were here – we had a most stormy meeting in the Schoolroom – Papa took the chair and Mr Collins and Mr Weightman [Mr Brontë's curates] acted as his supporters one on each side – There was violent opposition which set Mr Collins' Irish blood in a ferment . . . He and Mr Weightman both bottled up their wrath for that time but it was only to explode with redoubled force at a future period – We had two sermons on dissent and its consequences preached last Sunday one in the afternoon by Mr Weightman and one in the evening by Mr Collins – all the dissenters were invited to come and hear and they actually shut up their chapels and came in a body; of course the church was crowded . . .'

Religious controversy was extremely important at that time and at the centre of life. Nationally, John Henry Newman and his *Tracts* were of vital interest. In Birstall Rev Heald, on receiving a copy of Newman's controversial *Tract 90*,[9] came searching for Ellen in the Sunday school to show it to her and discuss it. She liked and admired Newman, and even his later conversion to Rome did not lose him her good opinion.

In Haworth Charlotte respected Weightman's intellect and admired his good actions:

'There is one little trait respecting him which lately came to my knowledge, which gives a glimpse of the better side of his character. Last Saturday night he had been sitting an hour in the parlour with papa; and as he went away, I heard papa say to him – "What is the matter with you? You seem in very low spirits tonight?" "Oh, I don't know, I've been to see a poor young girl, who, I'm afraid, is dying." "Indeed, what is her name?" "Susan Bland, the daughter of John Bland, the Superintendant." Now Susan Bland is my oldest and best scholar in the Sunday-school; and, when I heard that, I thought I would go as soon as I could to see her. I did go on Monday afternoon, and found her very ill and weak, and seemingly far on her way to that bourne whence no traveller returns. After sitting with her some time, I happened to ask her mother if she thought a little port wine would do her good. She replied that the doctor had recommended it, and that when Mr Weightman was last there he had sent them a bottle of wine and a jar of preserves. She added that he was always good to poor folks, and seemed to have a deal of feeling and kind-heartedness about him. This proves that he is not all selfishness and vanity. No doubt there are defects in his character, but there are also good qualities. God bless him! I wonder who, with his advantages, would be without his faults.'

Away in the Lake District, Branwell was writing to Hartley Coleridge in this April of 1840 about creative writing, and was to meet him and correspond further. In May or June Charlotte wrote to Wordsworth using a pen-name, sending him some of her prose writing and asking for his opinion of it. There was quite a correspondence between Branwell and Charlotte and the group known as or connected with the Romantic poets. Hartley Coleridge was the son of the poet Coleridge and had been named in admiration after the philosopher David Hartley (whose career and family, with the relationship with Ellen's sister-in-law and influence on the Walker family are touched on elsewhere in this book), the very Hartley family whose name was also commemorated by Ellen's infant nephew, John Thomas Hartley Nussey.

Southey and Wordsworth were friends and mentioned this correspondence with the Brontës to each other – in spite of Charlotte's pen-name, her address, care of Rev Patrick Brontë, would connect her with her brother Patrick Branwell Brontë.

At the end of April, Ellen was writing reproachfully to Haworth. She had sent 'a very pretty Turkish-looking thing' as Charlotte's birthday gift, but no reply had arrived. She need not have worried. Charlotte had been busy working her a bag.

Ellen's sister Ann, now housekeeping for Henry in Earnley, Sussex, did not like Henry's fiancée, Miss Halkett, considering her bold and beneath Henry in social rank. She interfered, and it seemed that the match might be off. Charlotte commented tartly on the letter Ann had sent home:

'Ann's character is indeed developed, I fear she has done mischief, if Miss Halkett has any heart to break . . . I see something else too my *dear* Ellen in the whole spirit of that letter which makes me thankful you are not like some of your friends. [By 'friends' Charlotte here meant family.] Fashion, Wealth, Standing in Society seem to be her sole standards for measuring the worth of a character . . .'

Charlotte went on to query the mention of a Mr Vincent. Ellen had very much admired one John Bradbury,[10] but he had married someone else; she was not at all distressed. Then there had been the flirtation with William Weightman, and now there was this Mr Vincent.[11] Charlotte demanded to know more:

'If he's a decent fellow I hope something interesting may come of it – Don't blush he must be one of the right sort however or he shall not have you with my consent. I am afraid you are getting worked off your feet at Brookroyd – as Henry says take care of yourself and don't be over-anxious. Aunt was vastly pleased with the Knitting-needle case.'

By the middle of May the approaches of the Rev Osman Parke Vincent, who was four years older than Ellen, had become serious enough for Charlotte to refer to the matter again. Prophetically, she wrote:

'Do not be overpersuaded to marry a man you can never respect – I do not say *love*, because, I think, if you can respect a person before marriage, moderate love at least will come after; and as to intense *passion*, I am convinced that that is no desirable feeling. In the first place, it seldom or never meets with a requittal [sic]; and, in the second place, if it did, the feeling would be only temporary; it would last the honeymoon, and then, perhaps, give place to disgust, or indifference, worse perhaps than disgust. Certainly this would be the case on the man's part; and on the woman's – God help her, if she is left to love passionately and alone.'

One thing in Ellen's letter had nettled Charlotte and she responded to it in an indignant postscript: 'Don't talk any more of sending for me – when I come I will *send* myself.'

Eleven days later, Charlotte was still feeling so uneasy about Mr Vincent's courtship of Ellen, and about Ann's interference with Henry's love match with Miss Halkett, that she fished out an old letter of Henry's as an excuse to write to him.

In June 1840, Branwell returned home from his post as tutor at Broughton-in-Furness. He may well have been in a difficult mood. When Mary Taylor went later that month to Haworth, she went unknowingly to one of the turning points of her life. Branwell had always shown a particular interest in her; during this visit she allowed him to see that she was in love with him. At once he recoiled, his ardour cooled and he made her feel that he held her in contempt for displaying her emotions. It was a bitter blow to Mary. As far as we know, it was the only time she fell in love, and the rebuff may well have turned her against the idea of marriage for ever. The disappointment came during the year of her father's terminal illness, and the result of the experience was drastic; her character was ultimately strengthened and hardened, but at what a cost.

This event was not immediately obvious to their circle of friends; indeed, in her next letter to Ellen, Charlotte said nothing of it. The letter was filled by accounts of William Weightman's faithlessness, and telling Ellen to put no trust in him. 'Don't think of him – I am not afraid you will break your heart – but don't think about him', she wrote, trying to save Ellen from a similar experience to Mary's. Then on the 14th July the truth of the matter becomes clearer as Charlotte tried to get a letter to Martha without Mary's knowledge. 'Will you be so kind as to deliver the enclosed to Martha Taylor – do not go up to Gomersal on purpose with it and do not on any account send – but give it her yourself when you see her at Church –'.

In Charlotte's fierce protectiveness of Ellen, other things can be read. Was Charlotte heart-whole? Had not the handsome, prepossessing, good-humoured curate made inroads into her emotions? Now that she considered him faithless and liable to hurt as Branwell had hurt Mary, she was thrusting him from her, and desperately warning Ellen.

She need not have worried. Ellen was very ready to *almost* fall in love, very ready for laughing flirtations, but also very wary of the trap of seeming fond of a man before he became fond of her. She was inhibited and shy in sexual matters, and the innocence and naivety which she was never quite to lose protected her. William Weightman was a genuinely good-natured person and he was now on a shooting holiday. To all his friends and acquaintances he sent presents of game, including Ellen. She told Charlotte of the incident in a very amusing letter, which Charlotte enjoyed: but that letter also contained a cloud, no bigger than a man's hand, which was soon to cast a shadow over Ellen's sun. 'I hope [your brother] George will be better soon', wrote Charlotte.

By September Branwell had found employment nearer home, at Sowerby Bridge, as a clerk on the railway. Railway posts were prestigious in 1840, and there was a good chance of a lucrative and respectable career lying ahead of him.

The Taylors, with their part in the international trade in wool, had newspapers and books from France, and shared them with their friends. 'I have got another bale of French books from Gomersal –', wrote Charlotte, 'containing upwards of 40 volumes – I have read about half – they are like the rest clever wicked sophistical and immoral – the best of it is they give one a thorough idea of France and Paris – and are the best substitute for French conversation I have met with.' In view of Ellen's fluency to the end of her life in reading French, even though she was so unwilling to correspond in the language, there can be little doubt that she too read many of these 'wicked' French novels, and that they gave her a wider view than that of most provincial girls, without affecting that essential innocence.

Ellen was still being courted in a roundabout manner by the clergyman Osman Parke Vincent, but by the end of September the matter had progressed no farther. Charlotte discussed the subject in a long, whimsical letter which is very much in her brother's vein of frothiness, without the constant emphasis on sin, drink, drugs and immorality which makes his letters distasteful. While Henry Nussey was in Cambridge he had apparently become friendly with one or more of the three Vincent brothers. Henry tried to arrange for one of the Vincents a curacy near him in Sussex, but instead Osman Parke Vincent seems to have spent time in the Birstall district. It was, Ellen believed, 'a plot hatched in Earnley' – in other words an idea of Henry's – that Vincent should marry her. It is not surprising if he was attracted. There is a story that a curate in church was once so fascinated by Ellen's beauty that he sat staring at her and Charlotte remarked, 'What the dickens is he looking at?'

Vincent was very interested in Ellen, and Charlotte became annoyed by constantly hearing about the courtship. Instead of proposing, Vincent told Henry how he felt. On 20th November 1840 Charlotte condemned his 'writing sentimental and lovesick letters to Henry'. She wrote one intimate letter to Ellen, using 'thee' and 'thou', suggesting just how Vincent should approach things, how he should ride over and find her sitting sewing in the parlour one morning, and finally propose. But the sting of that letter was in the tail where Charlotte wrote as a postscript: 'I'll never come to see you after you are married'. That was enough for Ellen. Whatever she felt for Vincent, it was no proof against emotional blackmail from Charlotte; if she had to choose between them she chose Charlotte. The affair lingered on, and the actual proposal and refusal were months later. The fact that the choice was not easy is shown by the fact that to the end of her life Ellen cherished a little poem Vincent wrote to her;

'Ellen fair I love thee!
The Lord Almighty speed thee
Ellen dear, I leave thee!
And God be with thee.'[12]

On the surface Vincent was very suitable, an Anglican clergyman in the right age range, the eldest son of an eminent and wealthy surgeon. At the end of her life a neighbour said to Ellen, 'Doesn't it seem almost a pity that you did not marry and have someone to counsel you now?', to which she replied, 'Well, I don't know, but it was not the fault of the men!'

Among all this uncertainty of the heart at both Haworth and Brookroyd, this thinking of love and marriage, the one overriding certainty came again into the lives of the friends. At Christmas 1840 Joshua Taylor, Mary and Martha's father, died. He had been ill for over a year. He left his property to his wife with his sons Joshua and John as executors. His death meant the fragmentation of the family. Joshua Taylor junior and his wife took over the Red House, and shared it with Mrs Taylor until 1845. John and Joseph moved into the house attached to Hunsworth Mill, about a mile away. Mary had been deeply attached to her father and not cared much for her mother – all the children of the marriage found her difficult – and combined with Mary's unfortunate love for Branwell, 1840 must have been a traumatic year for her.[13] Charlotte commented:

'for my own part, I look forward to a dissolution and dispersion of the family, perhaps not immediately, but in the course of a year or two. It is true, causes may arise to keep them together awhile longer, but they are restless, active spirits, and will not be restrained always. Mary alone has more energy and power in her nature than any two men you can pick out in the united parishes of Birstall and Gomersal. It is vain to limit a character like hers within ordinary boundaries – she will overstep them. I am morally certain Mary will establish her own landmarks, so will the rest of them.'

After her own many efforts to find work – 'a world of trouble' – in 1841 Charlotte obtained a post as governess with the White family of Upperwood House, Rawdon, close to the school where her relatives the Fennells had lived. She went quickly and did not tell Ellen until the day after she was actually there, on the 3rd March, and then, as usual, wrote demanding an instant response, and, again as usual, deferring to Ellen in all matters of etiquette:

'Now can you tell me whether it is considered improper for governesses to ask their friends to come and see them. I do not mean, of course, to stay, but just for a call of an hour or two? If it is not absolute treason, I do fervently request that you will contrive, in some way or other, to let me have a sight of your face . . . Rawdon is only nine miles from Brookroyd.'

Ellen was depressed and unhappy, partly by the decision of Mary Taylor and her brother Waring to emigrate to New Zealand. 'You give me no further explanation of Mary's behavior', wrote Charlotte. In return for a long letter Ellen received a very short answer. Charlotte had to do a great deal of sewing for her employer, and was pressed for time. 'Take comfort, Nell', wrote Charlotte. 'Write to me often very long letters. It will do both of us good. This place is far better than Stonegappe, but, God knows, I have enough to do to keep a good heart in the matter . . .' Then again that fatal note: 'I like Mr White extremely. Respecting Mrs White I am for the present silent. I am trying hard to like her.' Again her longing for Ellen: *'Do, do, do* come to see me; if it be a breach of etiquette, never mind. If you can only stop an hour, come. Talk no more about my forsaking you; my dear Nell, I could not afford to do so. I find it is not in my nature to get on in this weary world without sympathy and attachment in some quarter; and seldom, indeed, do we find it. It is too great a treasure to be ever wantonly thrown away when once secured.'

Ellen arranged that her brother George's gig was to fetch Charlotte to Brookroyd one weekend. Charlotte replied:

'I don't quite know whether the offer about the gig is not entirely out of your own head – or if George *has* given his consent to it – whether the consent has not been wrung from him by the most persevering and irresistible teasing on the part of a certain young person of my acquaintance – I make no manner of doubt that if he does send the "conveyance" (as Miss Wooler used to denominate all wheeled vehicles) it will be to his own extreme detriment and inconvenience, but for once in my life I'll not mind this or bother my head about it – I'll come – God knows with what a thankful and joyful heart – glad of a day's reprieve from labour – if you don't send the gig I'll walk. Now mind Nell – I am not coming to Birstall with the idea of dissuading Mary Taylor from going to . . . New Zealand – I've said everything I mean to say on that subject – and she has a perfect right to decide for herself – I am coming to taste the pleasure – of liberty – a bit of pleasant congenial talk and a sight of two or three faces I like – God bless you – I want to see you again. Huzza

for Saturday afternoon after next! I'll snap my fingers at Mrs W and her imps.
Goodnight my lass!'

Charlotte had many reasons for cheerfulness. She was in work, however
uncongenial; her brother Branwell was progressing in his new employment
with the railways, and had been promoted from Sowerby Bridge to
Luddenden Foot, an area so pretty that it was known locally as Little
Switzerland; Anne seemed reasonably content with her post with the
Robinsons at Thorpe Green near York, and all was well in Haworth.
Charlotte's happiness is notable throughout the period, dating from the
holiday at Bridlington, and it is easy to believe that Weightman had much to
do with this. Like a warm fire or a glowing sun, he seemed to radiate happiness
to her.

Charlotte described her short visit to Brookroyd in a letter to Henry
Nussey:

'I had a most delightful holiday. I saw your mother, your sisters, Mercy,
Ellen, and poor Sarah, and your brothers Richard and George – all were well.
Ellen talked of endeavouring to get a situation somewhere. I did not encourage
the idea much. I advised her rather to go to Earnley for a while. I think she
wants a change, and I dare say you would be glad to have her as a companion
for a few months.'

Many of Ellen's friends from school were now engaged in teaching: the
Brontës themselves; Mary Brooke, who was happy in her post; and the Cockill
sisters, Sarah and Elizabeth, who with their mother and their elder sister
Hannah, were running a school for fifteen pupils at Oakwell Hall.

George took Charlotte back to Upperwood House, unfortunately giving
offence to Mrs White by driving away again without going in: 'She went quite
red in the face with vexation when she heard that the gentleman had just driven
within the gates and then driven back again . . . Mr White also seemed to
regret the circumstance from more hospitable and kindly motives.'

'Come and see me if you can anyway get', wrote Charlotte in May. She
wanted Ellen to see the 'exquisitely beautiful' house and grounds. Ellen
managed to visit, probably at the end of May, a visit during which Charlotte
expressed her affection and said how much she valued her. In spite of her large
family, Ellen felt that she had no one but Charlotte to share her thoughts. 'You
can tell as well as me the lonely feeling of being without a companion',
Charlotte wrote later. Ellen's idea of being a governess had been stamped on
by her brother George, who, like Mary Taylor's brothers, had 'a feeling of
pride that revolts at the thought of their Sister *"going out."* I hardly knew that
it was such a degradation till lately', commented Charlotte tartly. She had been
given the chance of a post in Ireland, had offered it to Mary Taylor, and now
had lost the chance of taking it herself.

During June, Charlotte was in charge while Mr and Mrs White were on
holiday. She longed for their return as she wanted to go on holiday herself to
Haworth, taking Ellen with her, while Anne was there. Anne was only
allowed three weeks because she was required to accompany the Robinsons to

Scarborough. On the Whites' return Charlotte stuck out for a holiday of three weeks, 'with a tenacity worthy of yourself, lassie', and next wrote to Ellen from Haworth, inviting her to come 'next Tuesday' and adding the postscript:

'I have lost the chance of seeing Anne. She is gone back to "the land of Egypt and the house of Bondage" . . . Also, little black Tom is dead;- every cup, however sweet, has its drop of bitterness in it. Probably you will be at a loss to ascertain the identity of black Tom, but don't fret about it, I'll tell you when you come. Keeper is well, big, and grim as ever. I'm too happy to write. Come, come, lassie.'

The invitation was quickly changed from Tuesday to Thursday, for Aunt Branwell was to be away and Ellen could have her room instead of 'being crowded into our little closet'. 'It will be a real pleasure both to Emily and myself to have you with us, and a great disappointment if you fail to come', wrote Charlotte, adding, 'Write by return of post'. Ellen promised to go, but outside forces were too strong for her. The girls expected Ellen's arrival at Haworth Parsonage. 'We waited long and anxiously for you on the Thursday that you promised to come', wrote Charlotte. 'I quite wearied my eyes with watching from the window, eyeglass in hand, and sometimes spectacles on nose.' The Brontë sisters had thought of starting a school, and were longing to talk over the project with Ellen.

Alas. The change in plan must have hurt Ellen as much as it hurt Emily and Charlotte Brontë, for she was breaking a promise, but there was no way of letting them know in time to stop them expecting her. Henry had come north to visit his mother and could escort her back with him to Earnley. The chance was too good to refuse. Charlotte herself had urged such a visit in her letter to Henry, so she could hardly complain when her advice was taken, but for some time this disappointment seemed to cool the friendship between the two girls. The happy confidence of Charlotte's affectionate recent letters, written in the same tone she used to Emily, was lessened. Writing on the 19th July, Charlotte said:

'However, you are not to blame; I believe you have done right in going to Earnley; and as to the disappointment, why, all must suffer disappointment at some period or other of their lives. But a hundred things I had to say to you will now be forgotten, and never said. There is a project hatching in this house, which both Emily and I anxiously wished to discuss with you . . . to come to the point, papa and aunt talk, by fits and starts, of our – id est, Emily, Anne, and myself – commencing a school.' Aunt Branwell was considering offering a loan, which Charlotte did not think would exceed £150. '. . . would it be possible to establish a respectable . . . school and to commence housekeeping with a capital of only that amount? Propound the question to your sister Ann, if you think she can answer it; if not, don't say a word on the subject.' Charlotte had thought of starting a school in the neighbourhood she had loved so much on her holiday with Ellen: 'Do you remember whether there was any other school there besides that of Miss J—?'

On the 7th August 1841, Charlotte was once more in charge while her employers were away. Guessing that Ellen was out of touch with home events whilst in Sussex, she wrote that Mary Taylor and her brother John were on the Continent for a tour of a month's duration. Mary had sent Charlotte an expensive present from Brussels (where the Taylors had deposited their younger sister Martha at school), 'a very handsome black silk scarf and a pair of beautiful kid gloves'. Mary's descriptions of the art and architecture she had seen aroused in Charlotte a great pang of desire 'to see – to know – to learn', followed by a collapse of the spirits:

'Dear Nell – I would hardly make that confession to any one but yourself – and to you rather in a letter than "viva voce" – these rebellious and absurd emotions were only momentary I quelled them in five minutes . . .' Later in the letter Charlotte says: 'On the whole I am glad you went with Henry to Sussex – our disappointment was bitter enough but that is gone by now – and it is as well you have got a change. You will not mention our School-Scheme to any one at present . . . Write to me often my dear Nell . . . Your loving child (as you choose to call me so) . . .'

The school scheme was not dropped by the Brontë sisters. It came within an ace of realisation, for Miss Eliza Wooler had given up the school at Dewsbury Moor formerly run by her elder sister, and Miss Wooler had suggested that Charlotte revive it. The use of furniture, which Miss Wooler owned, she offered in return for board and lodging for herself. Charlotte accepted this proposal. Having sent her letter of acceptance, she awaited further arrangements. No word came, and in the interval Charlotte could not help longing to visit the Continent, particularly Brussels of which Mary Taylor had written so enticingly. She discussed the matter with her employers, Mr and Mrs White, and they supported her feeling that six months spent in further education on the Continent would improve the chances of launching a successful school. Charlotte then wrote to her Aunt Branwell asking for a loan for this purpose. This was at the end of September; Charlotte's thoughts were taken up with it, all her time occupied with teaching and other work for Mrs White, so it is not surprising that she did not write to Ellen, or that Ellen felt neglected and said so.

On 17th October Charlotte wrote:

'Dear Nell,– It is a cruel thing of you to be always upbraiding me when I am a trifle remiss or so in writing a letter. I see I can't make you comprehend that I have not quite as much time on my hands as Miss Harris of S. Lane, or Mrs Mills. I never neglect you on purpose. I could not *do* it, you little teasing, faithless wretch . . . So you are coming home, are you? Then don't expect me to write a long letter. I am not going to Dewsbury Moor, as far as I can see at present. It was a decent friendly proposal on Miss Wooler's part, and cancels all or most of her little foibles, in my estimation; but Dewsbury Moor is a poisoned place to me; besides, I burn to go somewhere else. I think, Nell, I see a chance of going to Brussels. Mary Taylor advises me to this step. My own mind and feelings urge me. I can't write a word more. C B'

To Ellen in Sussex all this was a bitter pill, an intensely hurtful letter.

Vincent had at last proposed to her, she had refused him and told Charlotte of it, but there had been no reference to this in Charlotte's brief reply. She was far away from the scene of the action which really concerned her, and Mary Taylor's advice and opinion was shown as of weight with Charlotte when her own was not even sought. Charlotte was equally hurt by Ellen's reproaches, to which she replied in a long letter on the 2nd November 1841:

'. . . this appears strange conduct to a friend near and dear – long known and never found wanting – most true – I cannot give you my *excuses* for this behavior the word *excuse* implies confession of a fault and I do not feel that I have been in fault . . . If I could Ellen I would always work in silence and obscurity and let my efforts be known only by their results . . .' Commenting on Ellen's own affairs, she writes; 'You say Ellen you know my reasons for not alluding to the subject of Mr Vincent – the only reason for such neglect of which I am conscious is the extreme haste in which I wrote my last . . . I am glad that Mr Vincent has fairly proposed. I do not know what to say about your refusal if he is a good and clever man it seems a pity . . . Write to say all is forgiven. I'm fit to cry. C B'

In a later letter to Emily, Charlotte says: 'I shall probably take my leave of Upperwood about the 15th or 17th of December. When does Anne talk of returning? How is she? What does William Weightman say to these matters? How are papa and aunt, do they flag? How will Anne get on with Martha? Has William Weightman been seen or heard of lately?' The two references to William Weightman – as if she had forgotten the first when she wrote the second – show how much he was in Charlotte's thoughts. Branwell is not mentioned at all, although it is a letter about family concerns.[14]

Ellen, who had been ill again, returned to Yorkshire before Charlotte left Upperwood House. Feeling a little estranged from Charlotte, she did not at once inform her of the fact, which Charlotte heard through Mary Taylor. 'If you are able to write comfortably, let me know the feelings that preceded your illness and also its effects', wrote the medically inclined Charlotte on the 10th December, 'I wish to see you. Mary Taylor reports that your looks are much as usual. I expect to get back to Haworth in the course of a fortnight or three weeks . . .' Ellen obtained for her the address of Mr Jenkins, the English Episcopal clergyman in Brussels, and Charlotte comments:

'You always think of other people's convenience, however ill and afflicted you are yourself – how very much I wish to see you – you do not know – but if I were to go to Brookroyd now – it would deeply disappoint those at home. I have some hopes of seeing Branwell and when I should be able to see him afterwards I cannot tell he has never been at home for the last 5 months . . .'

The big guns of hospitality were brought to bear on Charlotte by a letter from Mercy Nussey inviting her to Brookroyd; but she withstood the attack. Determined on Brussels, not knowing that a period in her life had ended, Charlotte finished 1841 full of hope.

[1] Henry's second proposal to Margaret Ann was 18th February, the second refusal 26th February. He proposed to Charlotte 1st March and received her refusal 9th March. It is often stated that Henry Nussey proposed to his vicar's daughter, but this is impossible. Rev Lutwidge had only been married since 1831. The Lutwidge/Dodgson family was briefly as follows. Mr Charles Lutwidge of Holmrook Hall, Co Cumberland, and Shandon Hall, Tunbridge Wells, Major 1st Regt Royal Lancs Militia, was later head of Customs at Hull. He married Elizabeth Anne Dodgson, daughter of Bishop Dodgson of Elphin. His eldest son, Rev Charles Henry Lutwidge (1800-43), married Anne Louisa Raikes in 1831 and was Vicar of Burton Agnes 1833-9. Henry's *Journal* says that his refusal was from Mr Lutwidge senior, therefore a sister of his vicar is meant, and Margaret Ann Lutwidge had been baptised at Kirk Ella on 2nd June 1809. Another sister, Frances Jane Lutwidge, married a first cousin, Charles Dodgson, and one of their eleven children became the writer Lewis Carroll. Margaret Ann Lutwidge was therefore not only Lewis Carroll's aunt on his mother's side but also his half-cousin through his father. It is easy to see why Mr Lutwidge did not consider Henry Nussey, a poor curate in delicate health, a suitable match for his daughter, but Margaret Ann never did marry. She died in 1869.

[2] Henry Nussey had written a poem of 500 lines, and while in Burton Agnes had paid for publication of *An Address suitable for use on Sunday School Anniversaries*. Ellen's other clerical brother, Joshua, also published several small works during these years.

[3] Ellen's recollections from Shakespeare Head *The Brontës, Their Lives, Friendships and Correspondence*, vol I, p190.

[4] Letter 83 Shakespeare Head [ibid] 24th Oct 1839, vol I, p 190.

[5] The 1841 census shows three pupils aged fourteen and fifteen boarding at Earnley Vicarage and Henry's sister Ann also resident. The same census of Brookroyd shows two households, one of the agricultural labourer Thomas Wait, his wife, little son and baby, and the other of Mrs Ellen Nussey, age seventy, 'farmer', and her daughters Ellen, 20, Mercy 35, Sarah 30, and sons Joseph, 40, millowner, George, 25, commission agent, two female servants aged 15 and 14 and a living-in agricultural labourer aged 20.

[6] The *Bradford Observer* 17th Feb 1894.

[7] Mary Brooke was one of their school friends and the daughter of the Brooke who went bankrupt.

[8] Charivari means 'rough music', noises made by banging on various metallic objects, and Charlotte used it thus in *Jane Eyre*. But in view of her use of the names 'Charles' and 'Charles Thunder' for herself, she may have two things in mind here, the second being a play on words – 'Charley-varley'.

[9] John Henry Newman, later Cardinal Newman, 1801-1890, was a leader of the Oxford movement. His essay *Tract 90* (published 1841) was to test how far the articles of the Anglican church were compatible with the 'Via Media' of the Anglo-Catholics. It aroused much controversy.

[10] The Bradbury family, wool merchants, appear to have been neighbours of the Taylors at the Red House. Ellen was very friendly with the daughter.

[11] Osman Parke Vincent, BA 1839, MA 1842, Cantab. It is not known why he was in the Birstall/Batley area in 1840 but he may have had a temporary post as a curate. His career was; curate, Kingsdown, Kent, 1845, other parishes to 1872, then Rector of St Mildreds, Bread Street, with St Margaret Moses, London, until his death in 1875 aged seventy-two. He was the eldest son of John Painter Vincent, of Lincoln's Inn and Woodlands Manor, Sevenoaks, a notable surgeon.

[12] Ellen kept this little poem all her life and it is now in the Leeds Archive Office at Sheepscar, Hellewell and Sutton Deeds, envelope associated with bundle 117.

[13] The first marriage amongst Joshua Taylor's children was in 1838, when his eldest son married Jane Lister Charlesworth, a grocer's daughter from Hightown. The Charlesworths were a founder Moravian family – an ancestor of Jane's leased land to the Gomersal community on which they built their church.

Also see *Mary Taylor, Friend of Charlotte Brontë; Letters from New Zealand and Elsewhere* by Joan Stevens.

[14] J T Fowler's *Durham University; Early Foundations and Present Colleges*, pp 244, 245, shows that early students did not have to be resident for the whole of their years there. It seems likely that Weightman had come to Haworth before taking his finals. In addition to the Professor of Divinity, the Professor of Greek read with the divinity students during their whole period of study.

THE BRUSSELS YEARS, 1842-3

On the 10th January 1842, Charlotte was expecting Ellen to fix a day to come to Haworth, and wrote: 'Mr Weightman is still here, just the same as ever. I have a curiosity to see a meeting between you and him. He will be again desperately in love, I am convinced. *Come.*' January 1842 was full of hope, without warning of the experiences, the afflictions, the purging spiritual fires the girls were to undergo.

For some reason her family would not, or could not, let Ellen go to Haworth. She was no longer the more independent of the two girls. Charlotte, through working away from home, had become self-determining. Ellen, through staying at home or with her brothers, at the beck and call of her family, had become more dominated by them. Handicapped Sarah was a constant care, Henry needed one or other of his sisters at Earnley, George was suffering mysterious illnesses, Joseph was 'dissipated' – which means at the least that he was drinking heavily – and with this to cope with, ageing Mrs Nussey and her three daughters kept breaking down themselves. The Nussey family health was approaching crisis point. On the 8th February Charlotte and Emily Brontë were to leave England for a year, yet Ellen was not able to visit them.

Anxious to become better qualified to run their own school by perfecting their mastery of foreign languages, Charlotte and Emily had arranged through the Taylors to attend a boarding school in Brussels, and were meeting the cost through a loan from Aunt Branwell. They left in the company of Mary and Joe Taylor, and Ellen was afraid that they would all forget her. At first the deserted Ellen wrote the Brontës and the Taylors only short, scrappy letters with long intervals between. Cheerful letters came from Brussels once Charlotte and Emily had arrived there and settled in the school run by Mme Heger on the Rue d'Isabelle, even though the Brontës must have been dismayed to hear in April of Branwell's dismissal from the railway. He went home, and the thought that one at least of them was at Haworth may have compensated for their disappointment.

In August the Brussels schools were closed for the annual holiday, but the Brontës and their new friends the Wheelwright girls stayed on in the Rue d'Isabelle, while the Taylors, from their different school, travelled home.

On the 16th August 1842 the Yorkshire Plug Riots took place. In the early morning a large crowd attended a Chartist meeting in Dewsbury market place, and about 8 am they set off to march through Batley, Birstall,

Pensionnat Heger, viewed from the Rue D'Isabelle. Charlotte and Emily were pupils at the school run here by Mme Heger.

Littletown, Millbridge and Heckmondwike, before returning to Dewsbury. They called at mills and factories on the way and let the water out of the boilers by removing the drainage plugs. They would have passed through Brookroyd and Birstall Smithies, but no damage was reported there. Many mills shut down voluntarily before the crowd arrived. Both Ellen and the Taylors would be affected by this event, which was so near home, and might have damaged the businesses on which their families depended. The 16th August must have been an anxious, although exciting, day for them.

After their summer holiday at home, Mary and Martha Taylor returned to their school in Brussels. On the 6th September 1842 William Weightman died of cholera in Haworth at the age of twenty-six. Cholera is a water-borne disease and the water supplies to the village were becoming increasingly polluted. Just over a month later Martha Taylor died of the same disease in Brussels. 'They were ill the same length of time, with the same symptoms', Charlotte wrote. Charlotte and Emily were harrowed by losing boisterous, full-of-life Martha Taylor, and they walked six miles on a pilgrimage to visit her grave. Within days of Martha's death, Aunt Branwell became fatally ill at Haworth. As soon as the news reached them the two Brontë girls set off for home to comfort their father, and performed the journey in two days.

Branwell was the only one of the younger generation to be in Haworth through the agonising illnesses and deaths of his dear friend Willie Weightman, and of Aunt Branwell who had been a mother to him. He was emotionally and physically exhausted. 'Aunt, Martha Taylor and Mr Weightman are all gone; how dreary and void everything seems!', wrote Charlotte. She and Anne wanted Ellen to come to Haworth, but George had been ill and she was needed to nurse him – she could not come. Desperate to see her, Charlotte travelled with Anne as far as Bradford, then Anne returned to her post near York, and Charlotte went to Brookroyd and Ellen. George was by now improving, temporarily.

Mary Taylor had not returned to England after her sister's death. In the last eighteen months she had been disappointed in love and had lost the two members of her family who were most dear to her. She had to work through this period in her own fashion and decided to accept a governess post in Germany – to be alone among foreigners, far from everyone and everything she knew.

George was well enough in January 1843 for Ellen to visit Haworth. Branwell would be away; he went with Anne to the Robinson family, where he was to be tutor to their son. Far away in Germany, Mary knew just how her two friends would spend their time together: 'you would discuss all imaginable topics and all imaginable people all day and half the night'. In spite of her refusal Ellen was still being courted by the Rev O P Vincent, and both John and Joe Taylor were also showing a romantic interest in her. Emily Brontë refused to leave home again – and she never did, for more than a few days' holiday. The necessity to earn money had been removed by Aunt Branwell's will, which left each of the Brontë girls enough, if invested, to yield a small annual income, providing them for the first time with some security. Emily took on the management of the money and they bought railway shares. For some time these proved very lucrative.

Charlotte, however, could not settle. Perhaps she could have got over the death of Aunt Branwell without too much difficulty, for death was natural enough for an old woman. But Martha Taylor's youthful death had hit her hard and Willie Weightman's was even more devastating. She could not linger in the place where she had been used to seeing his bright face and to being warmed in spite of herself by his sunny personality.

In Brussels she and Emily had intensely enjoyed the intellectual challenges and stimulus which largely came through their contact with Monsieur Heger, who in addition to his duties at the nearby boys' college, spent some of his time tutoring his wife's pupils, and had become very interested in the two intelligent English girls. Charlotte had been offered a teaching post by Madame Heger, which she could combine with further studies; she would return to Brussels.

I would argue that Charlotte had loved Weightman deeply while refusing to acknowledge it even to herself. Those happy, light-hearted letters she wrote during his sojourn in Haworth were never to be equalled. She does not seem

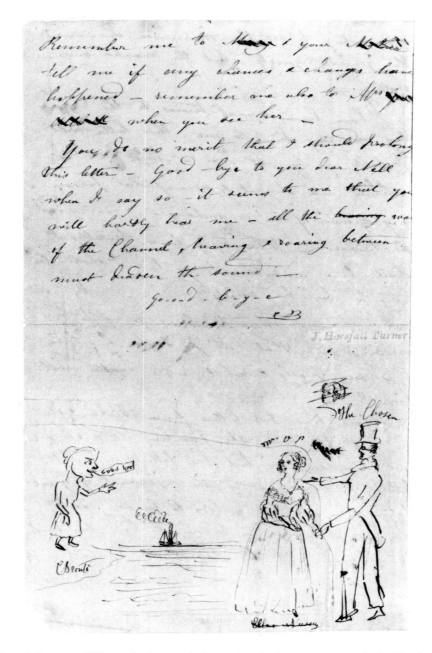

Charlotte's letter to Ellen referring to their parting in January 1843 when Charlotte left for Brussels for the second time.

to have realised how very different Brussels would seem without the presence of Emily and of Mary and Martha Taylor. She returned there in January 1843. There was talk of Ellen going with her, or joining her later, but this did not happen. Alone and emotionally bereft, Charlotte was in the right condition to be caught on the rebound.

Ellen had now begun to write long and much-cherished letters to her two friends. In February, Mary Taylor was replying from Germany that 'Your descriptions and opinions of the Miss Woolers etc. etc. are more interesting than you imagine. Why do you not write more of them?' And in April, Charlotte was writing from Brussels that Ellen's last letter was 'both long and interesting; send me quickly such another, longer still if possible . . .'

'Is there ever talk now of your coming to Brussels?', asked Charlotte. 'During the bitter cold weather we had through February and the principal part of March − I did not regret that you had not accompanied me − if I had seen you shivering as I shivered myself − if I had seen your hands and feet as red and swollen as mine were − my discomfort would just have been doubled − I can do very well under this sort of thing − it does not fret me − it only makes me numb and silent − but if you were to pass a winter in Belgium you would be ill − However, more genial weather is coming now and I wish you were here . . .'

Mary, 'resolute and intrepid', was teaching teenage boys in Germany. She wrote 'public letters' for general circulation with her main news, and Ellen saw these. When Mary had anything private to say she wrote to her separately. Emily Brontë wrote to Ellen in May, when the idea of Ellen joining Charlotte in Brussels was revived. But handicapped Sarah Nussey became ill so Ellen could not leave; and everything changed when on the 16th June 1843 Sarah died at Brookroyd at the age of thirty-three, from intestinal obstruction.

After her sister's death Ellen went to Harrogate to recover from the strain of nursing her, but she was hastily recalled to nurse her brother George who was not expected to live. Her brother Joseph was also ill periodically with a combination of tuberculosis and alcoholism; he was in the process of setting a terrible example for Branwell Brontë to follow. Most of the work caused by Joseph fell on Ann or Mercy, whichever was not away housekeeping for Henry, and most of the nursing of George fell on Ellen, who by now was worn out herself. Then Ann fell ill.

Isolated in Brussels, Charlotte had been lonely and homesick as early as April, and as the year wore on she sank into depression. Mary Dixon, who was the Taylors' cousin and Charlotte's friend, had also left Brussels, and when the summer holidays came round the Wheelwright girls departed too. Now there was not even an English acquaintance for Charlotte to turn to, and she dreaded the long summer holidays when she would be alone in the school. On her solitary wanderings through Brussels, she saw Queen Victoria, and wrote a description for Emily:

'I saw her for an instant flashing through the Rue Royale in a carriage and six, surrounded by soldiers. She was laughing and talking very gaily. She

The garden of the school at Brussels.

looked a little stout, vivacious lady, very plainly dressed, not much dignity or pretension about her. The Belgians liked her very well on the whole. They said she enlivened the sombre Court of King Leopold, which is usually as gloomy as a conventicle.'

Charlotte was gripped by the inertia of breakdown. She was miserable, but could not make herself change her condition. She had fallen into the old trap with regard to her employers, of admiring the husband and disliking the wife – she had always liked Monsieur Heger, now she was in love with him. She had intended to stay in Brussels until she had mastered the German language, but by October she felt she could stand it no longer. Endlessly she brooded over her love for Monsieur Heger and her dislike of his spying, underhand wife. At last she went to Mme Heger to resign; but M Heger came to her and persuaded her to stay on. Mme Heger had already realised that Charlotte's admiration for Monsieur and dislike and distrust of herself was dangerous, but either he did not see this, or he was attracted to Charlotte and overlooked the warning signals. Madame now made sure that Charlotte saw little of M Heger. Thus her life was still more solitary, and she placed increasing value on the few minutes when from time to time she enjoyed the intellectual stimulation of his presence. The fact that he was her 'master' and she his pupil provided an emotional situation needed by Charlotte's normally dominating temperament, and what came about was deep love and emotional dependence on her part, which he countered by striving to maintain the master/pupil relationship. It seems likely that had the situation been otherwise, had he not been a happily married man in a responsible position, he would have responded equally to her.

In Yorkshire Ellen was coping sturdily with the problems of her life. She was much attracted to Joe Taylor at this time, and this made her modestly unwilling to visit his home at Hunsworth. Charlotte told her not to be so silly. Ellen sent a portrait of her brother Henry over to Charlotte, perhaps hoping that she might change her mind about his proposal of marriage, which he had hinted that he was willing to renew. It was at this point that Henry, feeling he was making no progress in his profession, thought of being a missionary and thus diverted Charlotte. She wrote:

'His idea of being a missionary is amusing; he would not live a year in the climates of those countries where Missionaries are wanted. None of your family have much stamina in the constitution; on the contrary, all are delicate and he one of the most so.' To distract Henry from this missionary idea, his eldest brother John in London used his influence with the Duke of Devonshire to obtain for Henry the living of Hathersage in Derbyshire.

The approach of Christmas 1843 saw Charlotte jerking herself out of her inertia at last, into a resolve to escape. She returned to England at the beginning of 1844, after enduring a period in Brussels of such extreme isolation and depression that it scarred her deeply. Her emotions towards M Heger had become an obsession. But the trauma startled into life her mature talent. She must have begun working almost immediately on the story which was to become *The Professor*. She had counted on seeing Ellen 'SOON, as one of the great pleasures of my return', but Ellen was at Earnley with Henry. During her visits there she had made a new friend, Mary Gorham, from nearby Cakeham. Mary's mother came from the Spencer family, noted local Quakers. Her father was a farmer on a large scale and their home was within easy walking distance of the tiny hamlet of Earnley. Mary Gorham and her family were to be lifelong friends to Ellen.

The mental, spiritual, and emotional education of the Brontë sisters was complete. They had served their apprenticeship in writing, producing millions of words over the last years. The time was coming for the realisation of their genius, but it was not to come without more heartache and distress. For Charlotte her love for M Heger had to be a secret which gnawed at her vitals over the next few years and which was never to be forgotten, but which provided a driving power which she might never otherwise have had. Ellen always denied this love of Charlotte's, but she was so protective and defensive of her friend's posthumous reputation that this denial was clearly meant to disguise the facts. It is impossible to believe that when they met she did not intuitively sense Charlotte's emotional preoccupation, even if she had not guessed its depth from Charlotte's letter:

'I suffered much before I left Brussels. I think, however long I live, I shall not forget what the parting with M Heger cost me; it grieved me to grieve him, who has been so true, kind, and disinterested a friend . . .'

He had wanted her to take one of his daughters back with her to England as the first pupil in her own school, but Charlotte refused.

THE PROJECTED SCHOOL AND THE GENESIS OF
JANE EYRE, 1844-5

In Haworth at the beginning of 1844 the Brontë sisters decided that at last they felt ready to start the school which they had so eagerly discussed over two years before. It was to be in Haworth Parsonage, so that they could all be at home and care for their ageing father, who was losing his sight through the growth of cataracts. They had circulars printed advertising the projected school.

On Ellen's return from the south, the Nussey family health was good enough for the friends to have an exchange of visits at last. Ellen did her best to distribute the Brontës' circulars to people with daughters of school age. John Nussey in London was prospering, and had been able to pay off the mortgage of £5,000 which he had raised to buy the Rydings estate. George was still not very strong in March, but Sarah's death had eased the burden on the Nusseys.

Charlotte went to stay at Brookroyd, and took back to Haworth Ellen's gift of flower seeds to Emily, including Sicilian peas and crimson cornflowers. Mary Taylor was also in England at the beginning of April 1844, and stayed until the end of May, spending part of the time with her brothers at the house at Hunsworth Mill, only four miles from Ellen at Brookroyd. Mary found her home area in a whirl of social engagements, largely bride visits. On nearly every neighbourly call she made she found that Ellen was calling there too. Ellen also went to spend time with her at Hunsworth, so they saw one another often. During Mary's holiday Charlotte also stayed with her and on the 1st May, when the whole group of young people at Hunsworth were eagerly talking in the garden late at night, Ellen walked over to visit, escorted by her brother George. Ellen remembered: 'it was so dark when we joined them that we could distinguish nothing but figures approaching and so afraid were we of saluting a wrong individual that we cautiously peered into each other's faces. Then, all at once, a "Bless you" burst forth in all the power of friendship and affection.'

Unfortunately, the Taylor house at Hunsworth did not suit Charlotte's health. She said later that there was 'an abominable smell of gas' which she seemed to think was a malarial type of emanation from the ground, and which made her feel sick when she stayed there.

With the Brontës' own school in prospect, it seems likely that at this time Charlotte took advantage of being near to Ellen's friends and her own acquaintances, the Misses Cockill, and visited their girls' school at Oakwell

Hall, which they had opened in 1838 and were to run until 1853. On this and other visits to Oakwell, Charlotte fixed the old hall's character and appearance in her mind so carefully that, when her novel *Shirley* appeared, the people of Birstall recognised the fictional 'Fieldhead' of the novel as one and the same as their own Oakwell Hall.[1]

Ellen had hoped that her new friend Mary Gorham would come to see her during Mary Taylor's time at home, and with Charlotte Brontë 'make up a quartette'. Ellen had a passion for forming quartettes of friends. When at Haworth she, Charlotte, Emily and Anne had decided to call themselves 'the Quartette', no doubt at Ellen's instigation; it was not a typical Brontë idea.

At this time Henry Nussey was also at home at Brookroyd, organising himself for his new post in Hathersage. On the 4th May he took Ellen to spend three days there, and she was charmed, as people still are, by this area of the Peak District. This was the year when at nearby Chatsworth House, the home of Henry's patron the Duke of Devonshire, the Emperor Fountain was constructed to celebrate the expected visit of Tsar Nicholas.

The happy interlude of togetherness was shortlived for Charlotte, Ellen and Mary. On the 22nd May, Mary and Joe Taylor sailed from Hull to Germany, and for most of the time Charlotte had to be in Haworth and Ellen at Brookroyd. But at least now that they were both in England and expensive foreign postage was not a consideration, Ellen could write as often as she liked – she was afraid that Charlotte would swear at the postman when she saw yet another letter from her.

Throughout this spring, Ellen's diary tells us how she divided her time; a good many hours were taken up in dressmaking and other handicrafts;[2] she went visiting, usually on foot, and was busy in church affairs; but she also had a pony and rode quite often. There were, too, many letters to write and such domestic matters as washing, ironing, cleaning and cooking to superintend and help with.

On the 1st July Ellen went to Haworth and found all the family at home. On the 8th they went to Ponden Kirk and had 'plenty of fun and fatigue', and on the 10th they were at Oxenhope walking in a garden under 'umberellas'. Apart from this rain the weather was good, for on the 13th she went with Charlotte to Bradford, and on the 16th together with Charlotte and Emily she walked to Spinster Bridge. The weather seems to have broken the following day, when she and Charlotte had to turn back from an intended walk to the reservoir, and the next day they were confined to the house, but by the 21st they were enjoying the singing at Haworth School Festival. During this visit Ellen and the Brontë girls played 'High Water', which seems to have been a word game of the kind which was popular at the time. A cutting found in Emily's writing desk, probably from *Punch*, shows a drowning man with a punning reference underneath to 'High Water'. It was a game suitable for playing on journeys.[3]

Ellen returned from Haworth on the 22nd July with a bitch puppy from a litter sired by Flossy, one of the parsonage dogs. (Flossy seems to have been a male; there are no other references to puppies, and all the other parsonage dogs were males.) As puppies will, it had either chewed or dirtied Ellen's clothes and luggage on her journey home, and Charlotte called it 'the little varmint'. Although Charlotte referred to the puppy as 'he' at this point, by the end of the year, when it had ruined a book-muslin dress of Ellen's and a lace bertha,[4] she was calling it a bitch. Named Flossy after her parent, she seems to have been the same animal which later had puppies herself. Throughout Flossy's life she was to be an exceptionally troublesome pet, though much loved by Ellen. As far as we know Flossy was the only dog she ever owned, and we hear of no other dogs in the Nussey family. On the 29th September, still a puppy, Flossy junior was to eat one Mrs Browne's bonnet. About the destruction wrought Charlotte commented, 'the perfect serenity with which you endured the disaster – proved most fully to me that you would make the best wife, mother and mistress of a family in the world – you and Anne are a pair – for marvellous philosophical powers of endurance – no spoilt dinners – scorched linen, dirtied carpets – torn sofa-covers, squealing brats, cross husbands would ever discompose either of you –'. She and Emily wished that Ellen lived close enough to 'burst in upon us in an afternoon, and, being despoiled of her bonnet and shawl, be fixed in the rocking-chair for the evening once or twice every week'. It was the summer in which Charlotte had strained her eyes so much that she had to rest them, and only write one long letter or its equivalent each day.

The current curate in Haworth, Mr Smith, had paid some attention to Ellen while she was with them. Mr Brontë had become agitated about this and wanted Ellen to be warned of the curate's unsuitability. It was unusual for him to intervene in such a matter. By the end of the year 'Mr Lothario Lovelace Smith' as Charlotte called him, had left Haworth, and Ellen had never been interested. Arthur Bell Nicholls came to Haworth as a curate in his stead, went away for a time, and then returned. Curates moved frequently in most Church of England parishes at this period. Ellen saw in Nicholls 'interesting germs of goodness', but Charlotte thought him bigoted and narrow-minded. It was Nicholls who a little later banned the village women from hanging their washing out to dry in the Haworth churchyard. They put up a fight in defence of this old custom, but he won. Ellen wrote:

'From the Parsonage windows the first view was the plot of grass edged by a wall, a thorn tree or two, and a few shrubs and currant bushes that did not grow; next to these was the large and half-surrounding church yard, so full of gravestones that hardly a strip of grass could be seen in it; twice or thrice in the week there was a diversion from this saddening prospect, though in itself a very undesirable one, and one that proved as much as anything could do, HOW FAMILIAR to the villagers were the scenes of death and its accompaniments. The village housewives made the old Churchyard their general drying ground on washing days, but in process of time they were compelled to better arrangements. Great was Mr Brontë's amusement when the expulsion of the housewives was effected, and he commemorated the incident in [verse].'

One cannot help thinking that the band of talkative women hanging out their washing must have mitigated the effect of gloominess induced by the many burials, and regret Nicholls' stamping out of this cheerful custom.

Ellen attributed the high death rate in Haworth at this period – the average life expectancy in 1838 was nineteen years and six months – to the insanitary condition of the place, where many cottages would share a single earth closet and piles of 'night soil' were left standing in backyards and near alleyways. She tells us:

'Mr Brontë was frequently making efforts, and trying to stir up his Parishioners to efforts, for the sanitary improvement of the village, but for years all he could DO appeared to be unavailing . . . the Passing-bell was OFTEN a dreary accompaniment to the day's engagements, and must have been trying to the sensitive nervous temperaments of those who were always within sound of it as the Parsonage inmates were, but EVERYTHING around, and in IMMEDIATE VICINITY was a reminder of man's last bourne, as you issued from the Parsonage gate, you looked upon the stone-cutter's chipping shed which was piled with slabs ready for use, and to the ear there was the incessant sound of the CHIP, CHIP, of the recording chisel as it graved in the In Memoriams of the departed.'[5]

It was to be some years before Mr Brontë's efforts to improve the sanitary condition of his parish bore fruit.

By the 29th July, Henry Nussey had been confirmed as the next vicar in the living of Hathersage; he had had an interview with the Duke of Devonshire on the 22nd. Charlotte considered that he now had 'calm self-confidence' and perseverance. To his new affluence and responsibility more was to be added, for at the end of the year his engagement to Emily Prescott was announced, and she was a young lady with a handsome fortune. Charlotte, who 'did not advocate marrying for money in general', was pleased. 'I think in many cases (and this is one) money is a very desirable contingent of matrimony. In the second place I have a word to say in your private ear – Do your best to restrain Henry in the commencement of his career as Vicar of Hathersage – advise him not to launch out too much in the way of expenses – I always have a notion that the gentlemen of your family would be the better for a word of counsel from their sisters on this point – and you yourself often require a lesson in the art of saving – I have sometimes felt sorrowful when I see how easily money slips through your fingers – you like to give pleasure to others and I fear you sometimes do so at the expense of inconveniencing yourself –'. What excellent advice Charlotte's was, and how much better it would have been if Henry had heeded it!

Good fortune was thinner on the ground at Haworth, for by the end of 1844 no pupils had been found for the projected school. The idea was given up, so Charlotte had few distractions from brooding on her secret obsession with M Heger and from writing her novel with characters based on him and on herself. One of her few diversions came from her contact with Ellen. 'Your letters are a great comfort to me', she wrote.

Later in the century, old Haworth people could remember the Brontës as ordinary people, before fame touched them. In the *Bradford Observer*[6] we find a little known account by a man who had known the family well in his boyhood: 'Rev Brontë often took his family to concerts and other meetings of an elevated nature in Haworth, but always left at 9 pm . . . [During the day] Father and daughters used to be seen setting out for the moors with Keeper and Flossy running in front, a happy and joyous group, "carolling, light as lark at morn".' Mr Brontë's sermons impressed the lad because they were drawn from everyday life and events. 'When in Brussels he visited the field of Waterloo, and discussed this in his next sermon', and his delivery was described as 'steady as a gurgling rill.' We learn too that Rev Brontë often worshipped at the Methodist chapel on a Sunday evening when there was no service at the parish church, and he lent his newspapers to the Baptist minister. Haworth in those days was remarkable for the cultivation of music, and we learn that Mr Brontë was passionately fond of oratorio, and that at least one of Handel's works was given in the church.

The boy also remembered Branwell, who 'taught us in the Sunday School – he was rapid and impulsive in manner – could not bear slowness – one boy spelled every word and Branwell said, "Get on, or I'll turn you out of the class." The boy said angrily, "Tha' willn't, Tha' old Irish . . ." and took his cap and walked out'. After Sunday school the boys went in to church with Branwell and sat in the large square pew under the north aisle. Branwell sat in the back and read a book. If disturbed he was very cross: 'He would come to the interrupter and, twining a lock of the lad's hair round his finger, lift the offender from the floor and finish by giving him a sharp rap with his knuckles'.

About Charlotte, the boy remembered that she always stood up to teach in Sunday school, and sometimes walked round the class hearing every child read. The solid stoical manner of Emily made a lasting impression. He frequently saw the sisters trudging down to Keighley, where Charlotte 'procured books at a lending library kept by Mr Hudson, a bookseller and druggist in the High Street . . . Branwell went to Thomas Plummer in Keighley to learn drawing and painting'.

The trade directory of the time tells us of everyday life in the village. Cruel old entertainments were still taking place – bull-baiting, dog fighting, cockfighting, and fist fights. There were two annual cattle fairs, one on Easter Monday and one on the Monday after Old Michaelmas Day, and there was horse-racing.[7]

Another schoolboy who remembered the Brontës with devastating frankness and directness was Thomas Clifford Allbutt (a nephew of Miss Wooler), born at Dewsbury on the 20th July 1836, who was old enough to observe and remember by 1844–45. He gives us this little-known account:

'Am I the only person living who knew Charlotte and the rest? as well as a boy ever knows a grown-up, and not a very expansive grown-up at that.

Charlotte Brontë was a frequent and quite homely visitor at Dewsbury Vicarage in my father's time as Vicar, and my Aunt Miss Wooler was Charlotte's closest and dearest friend. I have heard and been familiar with the whole Brontë "atmosphere" all my life – or all of so much of it as was contemporary with my Aunts and oldest cousins. Charlotte was quite commonplace in conversation, one of those with the gift of genius attached to an insignificant personality, and as "the lamp-bracket which holds the light." Emily had probably more genius than Charlotte, but was self-centred and morose, and Anne tame and imitative. It was not Charlotte Brontë who was "Gey ill to live wi' " but EMILY. No human being – and she was surrounded by the kindest of folk – could get on with Emily Brontë, but Charlotte Brontë was quite liveable with if you didn't mind her being – to us boys – as dull as a "governess" ought to be . . . So far as I remember, I never saw Branwell Brontë, and he was rarely spoken of – just silence. Not merely because he was a bad egg – but because he was not credited with any of the family ability, or only some phosphorescence of it, he was just negligible, save as a thorn in other people's flesh. He seems to have been an irresponsible and boastful fellow.'

Allbutt described Dewsbury as the Brontës knew it well, 'with a beautiful little beck running through it past the vicarage gardens, where there were some stepping stones to the parish clerk's dairy farm on the other side, and so ran on to join the river Calder, where there was a pretty little strand of silver sand and shells'. The fifteenth century vicarage was built in a churchyard and prided itself over the countryside on the sparkling water of its well in the scullery. To this (probably polluted) water the boy ascribed the continued fever for which one of his five medical uncles treated him.[8]

Other children also remembered the Brontës. Charlotte's Sunday school pupils could recall her, as Branwell's had recalled him. Whiteley Turner interviewed them as old ladies, usually giving their initials only, and recorded the conversations. 'Mrs W' said of Charlotte, 'She was very sharp spoken'. As with all she undertook, Charlotte in school was 'strict to a degree. She always commanded attention, no matter who her company'. One Sunday morning, Mrs W recalls, 'the school . . . was in uproar. Miss Brontë appeared, and immediately there was peace. Mr Nicholls, the superintendent, was always punctual . . . After each service and every Sunday, Charlotte would wait at the foot of the pulpit stairs for her father, walk out by the west door of the tower arm-in-arm with him, and so forward through the churchyard, passing close to [where] Tabitha's grave [later was], and enter the Rectory garden by a gateway which . . . [now] is walled up'.

'Mrs T' said: 'Miss Brontë was very small-built. She was so much out of the ordinary from other women. Though hasty, she was a good teacher and kind in the extreme; one of the best of sick visitors, but rarely seen in the street except on errands of mercy or beneficience.' 'Miss L's most vivid recollection of Charlotte was of being helped out of a difficulty, when in the day school in 1847. She was ten years old and busy with sampler work, trying to depict the Nativity, and could not weave the arm of Joseph in the proper shade. She appealed to Charlotte, who, to her delight, showed her how to do it. Miss L was also in Charlotte's Sunday school class and remembered a careful lesson Charlotte gave them on "Jezebel", trying to instil into their minds something of the life of that wicked person. At the end of the lesson, she asked the children; "Have I been speaking about a man or a woman?" One of them answered, "A man!"; what was Charlotte's exact reply Miss L did not remember! 'There were no such things as class rooms then . . . The day school was the Sunday school, and the forms used during the week were re-arranged for classes on the Sabbath.'

Mrs Tempest (formerly Ann Hopkinson) also remembered Charlotte's visits to the day school, where she went twice a week to inspect work done by the girls. She would ask to see, say, a stocking a girl was knitting, 'insert her delicate hand, raise it near her large luminous eyes — she was very short sighted — slowly draw it up her arm, twisting it and exposing every round and stitch over her hidden fingers, then, apparently satisfied, she would turn to the knitter and in a somewhat mistrustful yet kindly tone would quietly inquire — Oh, so quietly', said Mrs Tempest — ' "And have you knit it all yourself, my dear?" '. Mrs Tempest considered herself greatly exalted when she was asked to knit Mr Nicholls a pair of socks.[9]

Now, to return from these sharp, clear, child's eye memories to the friends' direct story.

At the beginning of 1845, Mary Taylor was in England again and visiting Haworth, while Ellen was once more nursing her brother George. 'Poor Mr George!', sympathised Charlotte, 'What can be the cause of these severe attacks to which [he] . . . has been subjected?' Ellen took her brother to Harrogate, the favoured watering place for invalids, and in the second week of January he was strong enough to walk two miles. Then they went to Bridlington Quay, but by March he was finding his beloved sister an irritation and after a while Ellen left him there, and made the cold seventy mile journey home in an open gig. 'Don't do it again', scolded Charlotte. She considered George the best amongst Ellen's brothers, and thought that, when he was convalescing, the other brothers ought to see to it that he had a period of calm life before going back into business.

The name of Ringrose had entered the friends' letters for the first time not long before. The Ringroses were an East Riding family, long settled at Cottingham. Christopher Ringrose had married Mary Ann Boyes of Driffield. He was a merchant dealing with Holland and most of the couple's children were born in Rotterdam, hence the frequent references to them as 'Dutch'. On the family's return to England they lived at Tranby Lodge in the tiny hamlet of Tranby, Hessle, near Hull.[10]

Amelia Ringrose, engaged to be married to George Nussey, was the eldest of Christopher and Mary Ann's many children. She had been born in 1818: A younger sister was Margaret Rosita, known as 'Rosy', born in 1830. Charlotte Brontë met both these sisters, and Amelia figured considerably in her life and

Ellen's. Although Amelia was not happy at home, while George was ill she could not escape into marriage, which had to be postponed.

Joshua or Richard Nussey could certainly have supported George through a period of quiet retreat from life – neither of them had children and both were doing well. It was in this year that Joshua obtained the living of Oundle where he was to remain for the rest of his life, and Richard had allied himself to a sound business family, the Charnocks, and was trading satisfactorily in Leeds.

George, a young engaged man doing well in his career, was apparently suffering from temporary ill-health. At first thought to be physical, in March 1845 Charlotte referred to his illness as a 'diseased brain'. 'My dear Ellen', she wrote, 'I have often said and thought that you have had many and heavy trials to bear in your still short life. You have always borne them with great firmness and calm so far. . .yet there is something in your letter that makes me fear the present is the greatest trial of all, and the most severely felt by you . . .'

Charlotte herself had been going through the most profound misery because M Heger had ceased to write to her. Day after day for months she had expected a letter, but none had come. Both Mary and Joe Taylor had asked at the Rue d'Isabelle if there was a letter to bring, as they returned from the Continent in the previous December; but there was nothing.

March 1845 was the time when Mary Taylor set out for New Zealand. Quartettes including both her and Charlotte would never be possible again. Mary's brother Waring had already settled there and she was going out to him. 'It is as if a large comet had fallen out of the sky', commented Charlotte of Mary's departure. But by April an important parish event was under way in Haworth, to provide a new local interest. Mr Brontë was determined that the church should have a better peal of bells, and the inhabitants were more willing to support him in this than in his sanitary concerns. For a year, the life of the parsonage was to be dominated by the progress of the financial appeal for the bells. Perhaps his failing sight made the sense of hearing mean more than usual to the old man at this time.

Luckily for Ellen, she too had a distraction from the loss of Mary, in the preparations going forward for Henry's marriage to Emily Prescott of Eversley on the 22nd May at Everton, at which event Ellen was a bridesmaid. Henry and his new wife set out on a long honeymoon. With the security of his new post and the prospect of his wife's money, Henry had commissioned an extension to the vicarage at Hathersage – the very type of extravagance Charlotte had foreseen. The vicarage had originally been a small medieval thick-walled dwelling with one room up and one down, but as the centuries had gone by it had received additions until the original house was now embedded in a warren of later rooms. It was pleasantly situated near the church, a little way out of the village. Henry considered that it was not grand enough for his bride, and with the Duke of Devonshire's permission he built on a large new drawing-room with a master bedroom over.[11] This addition was designed by an architect and was a considerable undertaking.

We have Ellen's description of the nearby church:

Hathersage Vicarage. Charlotte Brontë spent three weeks here in 1845. Henry Nussey's extension to the vicarage is on the left, Charlotte's bedroom on the extreme right.

'The vicarage pew is elevated to a level with the reading desk, and is made the vestry – fancy yourself upstairs in a pew curtained round and both parson and sexton occasionally walking in and robing etc and besides that a lot of gentlemen in a neighbouring pew every now and then popping a hole and a pair of eyes between the curtains during singing. The church itself is very pretty, a good size and most enchantingly situated . . . The country is very, very beautiful . . .'[12]

While the young couple were on honeymoon, Henry's invaluable sisters lived in the vicarage to keep an eye on things. They were free to carry out this service because George was much better. He wrote a quantity of poetry to his fiancée, Amelia Ringrose, and Ellen sent copies of it to Charlotte, who liked the expression of George's affectionate nature in spite of the faults as poetry.

Ellen was in Hathersage for much of the summer, and for a while Mercy was with her. The curate, Mr Rooker,[13] who was carrying out the duties of the parish in Henry's place, called every day to see that the workmen were doing things properly. Often he stayed on, talking to Ellen and whoever was with her, long after the workmen had finished for the day. When Mercy went home, Ellen eagerly invited Charlotte to Hathersage. At first Charlotte refused to come, because her father's eyesight was deteriorating rapidly and she felt she could not leave home. The collection of money for the new peal of bells was going well – £230 had been raised by the 5th June. Mary Gorham, Ellen's friend from Sussex, came north to have a holiday and keep Ellen company at Hathersage. Ellen had very much wanted her to meet Charlotte, but it was not to be.

Then Anne Brontë, worried over Branwell's entanglement with the wife of his employer, decided to leave her post with the Robinson family. Once Anne was back in Haworth, Charlotte was free to travel. In June she said she would come by the new railway line, and Ellen went to Sheffield to meet her, but no Charlotte arrived. 'The opening of the railway is now postponed until July 7th', wrote Charlotte, but she was to come by horse omnibus instead.

When Charlotte at last arrived the friends had an idyllic time together. 'Of course when I come you will let me enjoy your own company and not drag me out a-visiting', Charlotte had written, but for the sake of her later work we must be glad that Charlotte was dragged out a-visiting, for the sights, happenings and people of Charlotte's visit to Hathersage were to be of vital importance in the creation of *Jane Eyre*. We hear of some of the events she witnessed, in a letter Ellen wrote to Mary Gorham. The 'we' means herself and Charlotte:

'Henry has been over from home and brought the architect to look at what the work people had done. The Archdeacon and rural dean also came to view the church the day that Henry was here, and Mr and Miss Rooker were here and accompanied the Archdeacon down to the village in order to make a call upon Mrs Shirley in her carriage, and to ask her to take tea with us, which in truth I hoped she and . . . hers would not do, for we had only the little room in use, Anne Allen the gardener's wife for servant and some very heavy bread of her making for tea. Fortunately . . . we had only the rural dean in addition to our party and his servant man in the kitchen. We have not taken tea at Thorpe since you left. At North Lees we have paid 2 or 3 visits. Miss Wright has been very good at calling. Mrs Shuttleworth did bring her cousins back with her and I have only seen her at church. The little girl has spent an afternoon here with her nurse, she was very amusing and very good; I wished we had her here when you were present. We have not daily visits from Mr Rooker. The work people don't require him now, so he has no pretence for coming so often. We have made more discoveries in his character and our opinion is rather favourable; he is only too frank. The Archdeacon told him of his odious aspirations[14] but not in our presence. He asked us if we had noticed it whereupon I could not help laughing and I said we had noticed something also . . . the church clock struck ten, the moon shone brilliantly into the room, and still his reverence stood with hat and whip in hand holding forth with much zeal. Miss Rooker is, we think, rather shy about coming here. Charlotte Brontë says I am to give her respects and say you are a subject of daily annoyance to her for I am so often talking of you. She has real regrets that she has not seen you. We have been to Castleton and the Miss Halls accompanied us through the caverns and were very lively and noisy; another party came in soon after, a gentleman and lady; they crossed the river Styx together to our great amusement. We could not discover whether they were brother and sister or what, but the lady was so very sweet looking and the gentleman twice addressed a word or two to me, once when we passed them in the caverns and to say good morning when they left. The [guide] said they were from Newark. Charlotte was very pleased with the caverns but the mirth of the Miss Halls was rather displeasing to her. We had Mrs Eyre's pony and we went a little way up Cave Dale. We shall not see Chatsworth again while Charlotte is here. Mrs Cave, the Vicar's lady from Hope, and a young lady have spent a day with us; they came by the onmibus in the morning and we have called there. They say they shall call when Henry and his bride come so I hope all unpleasantness will be forgotten. The plasterers have not yet finished their work; but the happy pair are to come next Thursday week whether we are ready or not for them. A new cook came today. The little dog is home, a most forward passionate little animal. Flossy is looking very pretty, we take her walks but do not allow her to visit us much in the room . . . My mother and sisters are quite charmed with Emily [Henry's bride, now visiting Brookroyd].'

There is much in this letter of Ellen's to amplify what was previously known about the genesis of *Jane Eyre*. Battlemented three-storeyed North Lees itself, with the remains of a small ruined church nearby, has long been regarded as one of the two chief inspirations for Thornfield in *Jane Eyre* and it corresponds in many respects to the descriptions in the book.[15] The letter tells us that Charlotte not only saw dramatic North Lees from the outside, but visited the Eyre family who lived there several times – two or three during the period covered by this letter alone, and probably more during the whole holiday. In the novel we have Charlotte's descriptions of the Eyre family's furniture. One piece in North Lees, the cabinet painted with the heads of apostles (now in the Brontë Parsonage Museum), is described in detail. Charlotte borrowed the Eyre family's name and their home for her novel, as well as in real life borrowing their pony. It was easy to gain access to the flat roof of North Lees, as Mrs Rochester does in the book. North Lees is said to have a legend of a mad woman shut in an attic, and a fire is said to have destroyed part of the building, but legends of mad women shut in attics were not infrequent at the time in Yorkshire and Derbyshire, when mental homes were few and expensive. (Many wills of earlier periods gave a widow the right to part of a building while leaving the remainder to the younger generation, and elderly women may often have seemed eccentric if nothing more.)

Together with the admitted resemblances to Rydings, and some interior details which may well have come from the White's 'exquisitely beautiful' home at Rawdon in which Charlotte had lived for ten months, we can reconstruct the inspiration for Thornfield with reasonable confidence.

It is also certain that Hathersage itself provided the inspiration for the

North Lees Hall, Hathersage; the inspiration for Thornfield in Jane Eyre.

village to which Jane Eyre travels from Thornfield and for the home of her cousins, the Rivers family. A number of the local descriptions can be identified. The surname Oliver, used in *Jane Eyre* for the rich and beautiful Rosamund Oliver, was that of the poorest family in the village. It probably amused Charlotte to make the first last and the last first, by calling her fictional rich residents by the name of the real-life poorest, and her poor and outcast heroine by the name of the ancient Eyres. It is interesting that Charlotte also met someone named Shirley, in view of her later use of this name. Three dogs died of rabies while Ellen was in Hathersage, including one of the vicarage dogs, and one belonging to the curate, which seized Miss Rooker by the arm. This, together with Emily Brontë's later experience, probably inspired the mad dog episode in *Shirley*.

The Apostle Cupboard, formerly of North Lees Hall and now at Haworth Parsonage.
Charlotte writes in Jane Eyre *of a 'great cabinet – whose front, divided into twelve*
panels, bore in grim design, the heads of the twelve Apostles'.

In this year of forty-five Charlotte wrote, in her friend Ellen's book, French verses entitled *Le Jeune Malade*, adding these remarks:

'Millevoye died young – a short time after having written these verses – in my opinion the French language does not possess anything more truly poetic than this effusion.'

It is pleasant to think of Charlotte's enjoyment of the caves at Castleton and her delight in this lovely region, particularly because she returned to

Haworth to find trouble. Branwell had been dismissed from his post with the Robinsons when his relationship with Mrs Robinson was discovered, and now was drowning his sorrows. Charlotte had reached Haworth at ten o'clock on the Saturday night, without visiting Brookroyd on her way as Mrs Nussey had invited her to do. She wrote to apologise and to tell the Nusseys that Ellen had been well during the time they were together in Hathersage, although rather anxious in case all was not ready for the arrival of the newly-weds.

Ellen was still very busy on the 8th August when she wrote to bring Mary Gorham up-to-date with the news. On the previous Thursday the bells had rung nearly all afternoon for the arrival of Henry and Emily, and all the people had turned out to see them drive through the village. The drawing-room carpet was still not down at four o'clock and the carpenters had been at work until the last minute, still hanging the door on its hinges a moment before Henry and Emily arrived. The plasterers were still working as Ellen wrote. For four days the inhabitants of the vicarage 'sat' in expectation of the neighbourhood paying bride visits, at which Ellen served the cake and wine.

At first Ellen was happy, but she soon found that the newly-married couple were not good company and made her embarrassed by their displays of affection. She began to miss Mary Gorham, who had walked so vigorously with her over the hills, and Charlotte Brontë, who had helped to give the curate good advice. Next Ellen discovered that her rich new sister-in-law was very mean with money. Although Ellen had worked hard to have the house ready and had looked after affairs in their absence, Emily wanted her to pay her own laundry bills and objected to her dog. Luckily Ellen was able to send Flossy home. By this time Flossy had had puppies, and one of her offspring was more welcome and remained at the vicarage. Dogs feature largely in the lives of the friends during this period. Flossy had another litter at the end of October, so large that Ellen thought some puppies should be destroyed to avoid the drain on their mother's physical strength of attempting to feed such a large number. Practical Charlotte agreed with her.

Ellen had followed Flossy back to Brookroyd as soon as she decently could, satisfying her conscience by writing a letter to Henry and Emily with suggestions about their conduct in the parish and towards the curate. (Henry had already managed to antagonise some of the local society and was irritated by Mr Rooker.) The letter only had the effect of annoying Henry's new wife.

By the end of 1845, men in general were causing a great deal of worry one way and another. Branwell, under the pain of his dismissal by Mr Robinson and the enforced separation from Mrs Robinson, was still drinking heavily. Ellen knew from her family's experiences with brother Joseph that 'no sufferings are so awful as those brought on by dissipation' and, speaking from her latest experiences with Branwell, Charlotte commented with fellow-feeling that 'Ann and Mercy must have had a weary and burdensome life of it in waiting upon their unhappy brother'. In both cases the problem was to continue. In addition, George Nussey had gone to York to a private mental home, Clifton House, to have his condition assessed by Dr H S Belcombe,

Clifton House, York. Believed to be a former private nursing home to which Ellen's brother George was admitted in 1845.

one of the foremost experts in mental health in the area at that time.[16] Ellen had to tread carefully, gradually revealing the truth to his fiancée Amelia Ringrose, without giving Amelia any reason to blame herself for the tragedy.

For a while Ellen lost one of her suitors. For months Joe Taylor had been paying attentions to her half-cousin, Isabel Nussey of White Lee. Isabel's sister Sarah had died in 1843 at the age of twenty-four, so Isabel was now the sole heiress to her father John, Ellen's cousin, who had done very well in business. Joe Taylor had disappointed Charlotte by becoming mercenary in his attitudes. The last time she was at Hunsworth, Charlotte could 'scarcely believe my ears when I heard the stress he laid on wealth'. His courtship of Isabel came to nothing, and by the end of 1845 Joe was visiting again at Brookroyd. His brother Joshua and wife in this year left Mrs Taylor senior's household at the Red House. Charlotte said of the old lady 'her unhappy disposition is preparing for her a most desolate old age'.

Charlotte was immersed in home problems and also in the vivid intellectual life she shared with her sisters. She had never made any secret of her own writing of poetry – Ellen had a copy of at least one poem Charlotte had written at school. After the accidental discovery of Emily's poems, Charlotte's conviction of their outstanding quality, and the later discovery that Anne also wrote poetry, the idea of publishing their poems themselves was born, and they had set about choosing and arranging the pieces to be included and enquiring about terms with publishers.

Ellen, not knowing of the project until years later, was distressed by her friend's unwillingness to visit Brookroyd, and did not write for three weeks, then sending a 'short and crusty' note. 'Do you scold me out of habit, Ellen, or are you really angry?' asked Charlotte. She said how very much she liked visiting Brookroyd and promised to come at the end of February or the beginning of March. 'I should like a long letter next time, with full particulars, and in the name of Common Sense, no more lovers quarrels . . .'

Like the Taylors and Brontës, Ellen was still reading a good deal of French. There were the newspapers and novels which were passed around the friends, and she had her own copy of *Rhin* by Victor Hugo, the most difficult French book she had read, but which she was enjoying. While staying in Leeds with her brother Richard's fiancée, Miss Charnock, Ellen looked at the recently published novel *Coningsby* by Disraeli, but she was not free to give her attention to it – the glimpse she had was disappointing. She read the whole of Mrs Trollope's *One Fault*, enjoying most of it and beginning to think the author's reputation for coarseness unjustified, but she was disgusted by the ending, where the heroine proposed to the hero. Her spiritual life continued to develop. She much enjoyed hearing Dr Hook preach in Leeds parish church, and did not agree with those who attacked his philosophies. Family life was a little better, because George, under the care of Dr Belcombe, now had a calm and tranquil mind.

1845 was the last year of the old private life; all was shortly to change.

[1] The circumstances of the visits have been mentioned in a paper published by a direct descendant of the Thomas Clapham who sub-let the hall to the Cockills at the period in question. Barbara Clapham, BST 1979 no. 3 of Vol 17, pp 210-213.

[2] Ellen Nussey's pocket diary for 1844 is at the Harry Ransom Research Center, Austin, Texas, USA. Apart from making dresses and a riding habit Ellen 'worked a mat' as a farewell gift for Mary Taylor, and also did some netting in the period covered.

[3] I am indebted to Sarah Fermi for her research on the subject of 'High Water', although we interpret her findings slightly differently.

[4] A large type of collar worn round the shoulders.

[5] Haymaking in the churchyard was possible after a new section was added. A photograph of Haworth churchyard – later than this period – shows haycocks and a considerable expanse of grass.

[6] The *Bradford Observer*, 17th Feb 1894.

[7] White's Directory for 1853, for the details of cattle fairs, horse omnibuses and carriers.

[8] From *Life of Sir Clifford Allbutt*, by Sir Humphry Rolleston (Macmillans 1929). Sir T Clifford Allbutt was the inspiration for Dr Lydgate in George Eliot's *Middlemarch*.

[9] From *A Spring-Time Saunter Round and About Brontëland* by Whiteley Turner.

[10] Tranby Lodge, a fine nineteenth century house, was built by Samuel Cooper, a Hull merchant, in about 1810 and sold to Christopher Ringrose in 1841, but sadly was demolished in 1985.

[11] The plans for the alterations to Hathersage Vicarage are among the archives at Chatsworth House.

[12] Ellen also visited Derwent, where Henry's other church was, and 'there, I *had* a treat in seeing Derwent Hall, it is most beautifully furnished with old black oak – the state back room exceeded anything I ever saw of the kind, it was really a room fit for a stately ghost to visit, if he had taste. Another room of tapestry pleased me very much, and also a library and some paintings . . .' Derwent Hall is now under the waters of a reservoir. Charlotte may have visited it. Ellen's letters to Mary Gorham are in the Brontë Parsonage Museum.

[13] From *Crockford*: Rooker, James Yates, Lower Gornal, Dudley. St Catherine's College, Cambridge. Deacon, 1845, Priest, 1846. P C of Lower Gornal, diocese of Lichfield, 1848. . .Formerly curate of Hathersage, Derbyshire, 1845-48.

[14] Rooker's breathing presumably.

[15] Both North Lees and Rydings had battlements but Rydings only had two storeys, whereas North Lees, like Thornfield, had three. North Lees was at one time larger than it is today, and had a ruined church at two fields' distance from the house. All trace of the church above-ground has now gone, but stones from the walls were still visible when Charlotte was there. Ellen picked out features of Rydings which are shared by Thornfield, such as the 'iron-girthed' tree which had been split by lightning, but said that the interior was different.

[16] Dr Henry Stephen Belcombe, son of Dr William Belcombe, owned Clifton Lunatic Asylum, the most prestigious of the eight small private mental homes in the York area in 1845. He was also the doctor at the Retreat, run by the Society of Friends, which pioneered humane treatment of the mentally ill. He lived first in Minster Yard and later in Grove Terrace, York, where he was said to be a neighbour of Charles Dickens' brother, and so became a friend of Dickens. George Nussey went to Dr Belcombe originally for assessment, but remained at the Clifton Asylum (now a hotel) on Clifton Green until it closed on Dr Belcombe's retirement in the 1850s. George then became one of the first four inmates of a private mental home at Lime Tree House, Front Street, Acomb, run first by Dr Samuel Nelson and later by Dr W J Nelson, and lived there for the rest of his long life. Patients at these small private asylums had the freedom to walk about the suburbs in which they lived if they were well enough. George certainly did this.

THE BELLS RING OUT FROM HAWORTH, 1846

Ellen's brother Joseph was now very ill as a result of his dissipated way of life and from tuberculosis; her mother was ill, and so were Mrs Walker at Rydings and Frances, one of her daughters – mother and sister of John Nussey's wife.[1] Charlotte wrote to Ellen that 'never a day passes, seldom an hour, that I do not think of you, and the scene of trial in which you have your being'.

The Brontë sisters had found the firm of Aylott and Jones, who were willing to publish their book of poems. Some of Aunt Branwell's money was to be used to pay for the publication. Aylott and Jones were a small publishing house who specialised in religious books and poetry, but not fiction. The exciting business of choosing and arranging the poems, and issuing instructions about type of paper and so on, kept Charlotte at home; but at last in February she felt that she could visit her friend. Once she was at Brookroyd, Ellen did not want to part with her, and wrote to Haworth for permission for Charlotte to stay a little longer. Emily Brontë replied saying that Charlotte could stay 'if you can persuade her to do so', and stay she did until the beginning of March.

On her return Charlotte made further arrangements about the poems, and at the same time the peal of bells for Haworth church was ready to be hung. For more than twelve months the lives of everyone in the parsonage had been dominated by the fundraising for the bells and the arrangements for them. On the 10th March the momentous ceremony took place, the work of bell-hanging being carried out by William Wood, who was Tabitha's nephew and the local joiner and cabinet maker. Joseph Redman was the architect for the project. There were general jollifications with prizes. The inscription on one of the bells reads: 'These bells were raised by subscription. Rev Patrick Brontë, Incumbent. Mr George Feather, Mr James Lambert, Churchwardens.'

Patrick Brontë was responsible for raising his daughters as well as for raising the money for the bells. What could be more natural than that they should take the name of Bell as their pen-name? They too were going to ring out from Haworth. The initial was the same as their own. When people change their name, they are noted for keeping the same initials, and this the Brontë girls were also anxious to do. Their grandmother Brontë's Christian name was sometimes spelt as Eilis[2] – it could be that Ellis Bell for Emily was a derivation of that. Charlotte took the name of Currer Bell, Anne took Acton Bell. By April Charlotte was offering three novels, not yet complete, to the publisher of their poetry, one from each of them, but Aylott and Jones were not interested in fiction. Charlotte's novel was *The Professor*, Emily's was *Wuthering Heights*, and Anne's was *Agnes Grey*. The excitement and thrill of all this did not make Charlotte forget Ellen; she sent letters and the French newspapers (circulated by the Taylors).

Joe Taylor had kindly made the arrangements for Ellen to visit George in York, and Ellen was also involved with George's fiancée, Amelia. 'Simple-hearted, sensible, but not brilliant', was Charlotte's impression from the letters of Amelia's which Ellen sent for her to see. Amelia had not yet met either Ellen or Charlotte.

On the 29th May 1846 Joseph Nussey died, and was buried on the 3rd June. The same cause of death was entered on his death certificate as was soon to be entered on Branwell's – 'phthisis', or tuberculosis. Brother Joshua came from Oundle and stayed a week with the devastated family at Brookroyd. On his way home he called at Hathersage to persuade Henry and his wife to visit their mother and sisters at this time, but, influenced by his economical new wife, Henry wrote to Brookroyd saying it was too expensive for them to travel, filling the rest of his letter with accounts of pleasure jaunts they were having.

By the 17th June, Charlotte felt that Ellen was beginning to recover a little from her sorrow and be more settled. 'These are not times of amusement', she commented from the depth of their own troubles with Branwell, who was distraught, after the death of his late employer Mr Robinson, to hear from Mrs Robinson that her husband's will forbade her to associate with Branwell, on pain of forfeiting her inheritance. There can be little doubt why in later years Ellen shied away from any discussion of Branwell's end – why she was so anxious to be seen as knowing nothing about his conduct. She was afraid that enquiries would uncover her own family's similar experience. Probably she felt upset at the bare memory of those years, particularly the last months, when she felt surrounded by horror and tragedy.

The Nussey problems were not over, for George's upkeep in York was very expensive, and Dr Belcombe did not feel he ought to return home.[3] Money was so desperately tight that Ellen again contemplated going out as a governess, but Charlotte counselled her to stay at home and sacrifice herself to her mother. Later in the year Brookroyd took in a paying guest, a Mrs Noble, to help make ends meet.[4]

In Haworth, Branwell had been applying for work without success. Charlotte longed to have enough money to spirit herself and Ellen, Emily and Anne to the seaside for a holiday, but instead the Brontë girls had to organise a cataract operation on Mr Brontë's eyes. Emily and Charlotte visited Manchester to make the arrangements, and on the 21st August Mr Brontë and Charlotte were established in lodgings there.

Now was the time when Charlotte could concentrate on writing her second novel, *Jane Eyre*. There were many hours when she had nothing to do, while her father lay in a darkened room looked after by a nurse.

Jane Eyre is written in the first person, as the experiences of an orphan girl

The earliest known photograph of Ellen Nussey.

rejected by her aunt and sent away to school – and here Charlotte portrayed her own bitter childhood experiences at Cowan Bridge School, and the deaths of her sisters. Then thoughts of Charlotte's weeks at Hathersage with Ellen surfaced, and the heroine's surname, the hero's home, and many other details reflect her recent holiday there. The whole treatment of the mad woman would be coloured by Charlotte's discussions with Ellen of mental illness and treatments for it. The possibility of George's comparatively mild illness developing into something more violent and extreme must have been Ellen's nightmare.

Rydings, too, was much in Charlotte's thoughts because it had been a place of great happiness for her, and now John Nussey was selling it to John Appleyard of Shaw Booth in Warley, who was interested in the coal seams under the estate. The Nussey family had been associated with the house since 1711 with only a short break. Now it finally passed out of their hands.[5] John's mother-in-law, Mrs Walker, continued to live there as Appleyard's tenant.

By the time Charlotte and Mr Brontë returned from Manchester – they were home by the 29th September – there was another money-making scheme afoot at Brookroyd. Ellen was planning to take two or three girls to live in the house as pupils, the same kind of scheme which had so occupied the hearts and minds of the Brontë girls during the previous year. Like their scheme, it came to nothing, although Ellen's brother Richard did his best to find pupils for her.

Rydings in 1956. The building has changed substantially since then.

'I do not know when you have been so long without writing to me before', Charlotte told Ellen on the 17th November, as Ellen was on the eve of departing to Oundle to stay with her brother Joshua. At least there would be one mouth less to feed at Brookroyd. But Ellen was miserable at Oundle; the weather was as intensely cold in December as it had been intensely hot in June, and her sister-in-law Anne went in for 'economical gentility' which was depressing after the more generous housekeeping at Brookroyd. She longed for her mother's warm room and the comfortable fireside of the Brookroyd drawing room. The year finished miserably for Ellen; it had been miserable throughout. She felt as lonely at Oundle as Charlotte had at Stonegappe or in Brussels, and longed to hear from Charlotte.

In spite of everything – Branwell and the whole Robinson debacle, Mr Brontë's operation, and a rumour during the summer that Charlotte was to marry Mr Nicholls, which made her furious – it had been a good year for Charlotte, Emily and Anne. At last they had found their purpose in life, even though the poor reception of their little volume of poetry, which sold only two copies, would have discouraged lesser talents, less stout hearts. There is no doubt of their unity, their exhilaration, their sense of purpose. The Bells had begun to ring.

[1] Mrs Mary Walker, who lived in Rydings after Mrs Nussey moved to Brookroyd House, had with her five unmarried daughters. These were: Elizabeth, 1800-75; Frances Foxcroft, 1807-48; Catherine, 1810-79; Charlotte, 1812-76; and Eleanor, Charlotte's twin, who later married Charles Carr, the local solicitor. Her daughter married the Rev Wm Margetson Heald jnr. Mrs Walker and Frances died at Rydings. Elizabeth, Catherine and Charlotte then moved to Spring Cottage, Dewsbury Moor, near to their cousin John Beswicke Greenwood, and lived there for the rest of their lives.
[2] This spelling is given by Rebecca Fraser in her biography *Charlotte Brontë* (Methuen 1988) p4.
[3] The Retreat Admissions Book (held at the Borthwick Institute of Historical Research, York) gives the Retreat's fees, which varied from 6/- to £3 per week. No records for the Belcombe family's Asylum have been found, but the fees were probably comparable. This was a great deal in 1845. George's brother Richard later bequeathed £100 a year for George's upkeep at the Nelson's Home at Acomb.
[4] Mentioned in Charlotte's letter of 21st September 1846. Ellen's annotation of the envelope shows that the paying guest was a 'Mrs Noble'. Grateful thanks to Margaret Smith for information about this annotation.
[5] The property was then described as 'The Rydings estate comprising the mansion house, farm house . . . the Grey Hound Inn, barns, cottages. and other buildings and about 76 acres of land . . . with the timber and other trees and fixtures': there was 'much fine oak panelling'. This oak panelling survived, at least in part, into the late 1940s.

THE YEAR OF FULFILMENT, 1847

Emily Brontë was insistent that no one outside the family should know about the publication of their book of poems in 1846, and there is no evidence that Ellen was aware of it at the time. Charlotte had said that she preferred to plan in secret; and paying for the publication of one's own work is something writers tend to be secretive about, although much non-commercial work well worth publishing sees the light in this way. What could be less likely to be profit-making than a slim volume of poetry by three unknown authors? Another factor would be the distress Ellen's family was going through. Sensitive Charlotte could hardly write joyously of the new Brontë venture to an unhappy friend, or mention the reckless expenditure of some £48 to one who was for the first time encountering serious financial trouble. When the volume failed to sell, she would be even less likely to speak of it.

The year 1847 opened for Ellen with her brother George's health still the main concern and the welfare of the Walker family at Rydings a close second. She had returned from Oundle by the end of January. On the 21st April Mrs Walker, who had lived so long at Rydings, died and was buried at Batley. Her daughters were soon to disperse. With Rydings owned and lived in by strangers, and Brookroyd inhabited only by Mrs Nussey and her three daughters, life was changed indeed.

Charlotte was reminded by a gift of 'wrist frills' from Ellen that they both had birthdays about this time, and she sent a present of a piece of lace 'made up into nothing' in return.[1] Now that no-one needed Ellen's personal care, Charlotte sent her several invitations to Haworth. In May she was writing that 'The railroad has been open some time but only comes as far as Keighley', but the carrier could bring Ellen's luggage from Keighley station if she came on a Wednesday. 'Emily, Anne and I will meet you at the station. We can take tea together jovially at the Devonshire Arms, and walk home in the cool of the evening.' What a happy picture is conjured up! Emily Brontë, Anne, Charlotte and Ellen, 'jovially' taking tea together at the Devonshire Arms![2] The jovial occasion was not to be, for Ellen did not come. At the last minute her sister Ann accepted an invitation from Mary Swaine of Brier Hall to go away with her, and therefore Ellen must remain at home.

The Brontës, preoccupied with their writing careers, would not miss her as much as they might otherwise have done. Emily's and Anne's books, *Wuthering Heights* and *Agnes Grey*, were accepted by the firm of Newby. Charlotte sent *The Professor* to a number of publishers who refused it, and at last to Smith, Elder on the 15th July.

Mary Walker of Rydings, wife of Richard Walker junior, who died in April 1847.

Ellen's normal social and domestic round continued, but she was at last free to go to Haworth at the end of July. (She was involved in a carriage accident, but without serious consequences, on her return journey.) Ellen was not told of the writing careers of her friends. Emily, with her horror of publicity, did not want any personal friend to know anything, and her wishes ruled Anne, who was at this time so habitually quiet that later, in October, even Charlotte was finding 'it is with difficulty one can prevail upon her to take a walk or induce her to converse'.

While Ellen was at Haworth, Charlotte was still collecting rejections, but

Branwell Brontë's portrait of his sisters (from left to right) Anne, Emily and Charlotte, circa 1834.

the guest was probably still in the house when the manuscript of *The Professor* arrived back accompanied by a very encouraging letter from Mr William Smith Williams of the firm of Smith, Elder and Co, a letter which Charlotte considered almost as good as an acceptance. Ellen would have seen the lift in her friend's spirits. She was too well-bred to make an outright enquiry if information was not forthcoming, but even if she had hinted at curiosity, the iron self-discipline under which Emily lived and of which all the family but Branwell were capable could hold out even against a 'teasing wretch', and an appeal to the tease's heart and good principles would be enough to make her refrain.

Although *The Professor*, a very autobiographically based story using Charlotte's experiences while teaching in Brussels, had been refused again, this time it was with expressed willingness to consider other work. Fortunately, on receiving this encouragement, Charlotte had her second novel, *Jane Eyre*, ready which she could send off to Smith, Elder immediately.

Ellen would have returned home by the time that Emily and Anne's novels were arriving in proof around the 24th August. The excitement of the three sisters when Charlotte had *Jane Eyre* accepted at about the same time must have been something to behold.

Charlotte went to see Ellen at Brookroyd in September, at the very time

Brookroyd, the house to which Ellen's family moved when they left Rydings in 1836. Behind the rooms on the left of the entrance is an attached cottage, and the buildings on the right formerly included stables and a farmhouse. The front faces south-west.

that proof sheets of *Jane Eyre* were already arriving in batches for correction. We know from Ellen's later statements that the two actually sat in the same room while Charlotte did her proof-reading, and that it was Ellen who posted the parcel back to Smith, Elder. She said that she honourably did not look to see to whom the parcel was addressed, and Charlotte was later to confess what a struggle it had been to keep silent, but she had promised her sisters to say nothing.

Charlotte was always happy at Brookroyd. It is through her that we have little glimpses of the activities of the household. We know that Mercy was the family poultry-keeper and had a collection of doves and hens and ducks, with sittings of eggs and little chicks to look after. We learn that Mercy was involved with a school, said by other sources to be a small school for poor children which she started at nearby Carlinghow. Neither Ann nor Ellen took an interest in this particular school. Ann Nussey is never recorded as teaching; she was in charge of the housekeeping, then a much more skilled occupation than today. Ellen was constantly teaching in various other schools.

Charlotte arrived back in Haworth on the 24th September. When her boxes came the next day she discovered that Ellen had secretly stuffed them with presents for everyone at Haworth – a cap for Tabby, a screen for Mr Brontë (probably to hold in the hand to protect the face from the heat of the fire), apples and a collar for Emily, and 'crab-cheese' for Anne.[3] 'You ought to be tenderly kissed, and then afterwards as tenderly whipped [for sending the presents]', wrote Charlotte to Ellen.

As if the Nusseys had not had enough trouble with Joseph's death and George's mental illness, Henry now gave them more. He and his wife Emily had not settled well at Hathersage. They could not get on with the local people or the curate. It seems too that Henry's health had deteriorated again. He and Emily decided that he must leave Hathersage and travel on the Continent until he was strong enough to take another post. Henry asked the Duke of Devonshire for reimbursement of the money spent on enlarging the vicarage, thus displeasing the duke so much that he cut John Nussey when they met in London, and this upset John – professionally such a slight was dangerous for him. He protested to their mother about Henry's conduct, but only his wife now influenced Henry. As far as we know he never took another post, or earned money in any way. Presumably he and Emily lived on her fortune.

Ellen made one more trip from home that year. She went to Tranby Lodge and stayed with the Ringrose family. Amelia travelled back to Brookroyd with her, to spend Christmas. These visits gave Ellen plenty of occupation, and much to fill her mind and heart. She took to Amelia and was afraid Charlotte might be jealous. While Amelia was at Brookroyd, Ellen persuaded her to write to Charlotte, and in the reply Charlotte expressed some of what Ellen meant to her:

'. . . it is much pleasanter to meet Ellen any day than to part with her. When she quits a place she generally leaves an uneasy vacuum behind her, for though not a rattling or dazzling, she is a very acceptable companion. I understand well the feeling you affectionately express, that when you are a little depressed it does you good to look at Ellen and know that she loves you. I am not acquainted with any one whose influence is at once so tranquil and so genial as hers. Faults she has because she is human, but I daresay in your pilgrimage through life, you will meet with few whose slight defects are counterbalanced by so many sterling excellencies.'

What remained of 1847 was filled for Charlotte by the reactions to *Jane Eyre*, which was published on the 16th October to become an immediate bestseller and the talking point of everyone with literary interests. Being new to the experience of public criticism, Charlotte was intensely hurt by the slightest unfavourable remark in reviews and equally elated by praise.

On seeing *Jane Eyre*'s success, Newby, the publisher who had still not brought out her sisters' novels although they had been in proof so long, now printed them both quickly. By mid-December *Wuthering Heights* and *Agnes Grey* were in print. Most of the corrections to the proof sheets which Emily and Anne had so laboriously made were ignored. Newby spread the rumour that these two books were also the work of the now talked-about Currer Bell.

1847: indeed a year of fulfillment, the year when *Jane Eyre*, *Wuthering Heights* and *Agnes Grey* were published, and when Charlotte's publisher began to press her for her next book and attempted to guide her writing, suggesting that she write a serial. She herself wanted to re-work *The Professor*.

About Branwell and his involvement in the books, I was convinced by the arguments of E F Benson, who did not accept Charlotte's statement that Branwell knew nothing of their publications. Benson pointed out:

'For the last two years of Branwell's life printed proofs were constantly arriving for the sisters, one packet of which was perhaps opened by Branwell himself by mistake; six presentation author's copies, Charlotte tells us, were sent to Emily and Anne on the publication of their books, and to her also, as well as multitudes of reviews which she always insisted on seeing. Mr Brontë, when *Jane Eyre* had begun to boom, was informed by Charlotte that she was the author; Charlotte and Anne went up to London more than a year before Branwell died, to disclose themselves to Smith, Elder and Co; Mrs Gaskell tells us how, when Charlotte had sent the manuscript of *The Professor* to a publisher, and had received no acknowledgement, she consulted Branwell himself as to the reason of his silence.'[4]

Benson also made out an excellent case for Branwell having not only known about *Wuthering Heights* but having had something to do with it. As a writer himself, Benson's comments deserve serious consideration. With that note of controversy – Ellen was to call *Wuthering Heights* 'that dreadful book' – we move on to consider the Brontës in their new role of published authors, which changed everything, and was so strongly to influence the rest of Ellen's life.

[1] The lace was given at the end of her life by Ellen to a Mrs Cameron, in whose family it has passed down to the present day. 'It is exquisite Bucks lace, could have been meant to be a veil, or one end of a long stole . . . The design is influenced by the 18th century but it is 19th century, probably made 1845-47.' This information forms part of an article *Laced with Literature*, by Jane Atkinson, which comments on Charlotte's frequent mention of lace in her novels. It has not been possible to discover in which publication this article was printed, although there is a photocopy of it at the Brontë Parsonage Museum.

[2] The Devonshire Arms still exists in Keighley. It is at the time of writing called the Grinning Rat and stands on the corner of Church Street and High Street. The facade looks as the Brontës would have known it, but recently modernisation of part of the building has taken place.

[3] This was regarded as a medicinal food for people with coughs, though it is not clear how it was used. Presumably it was made from crab-apples and sieved as one sieves damson cheese, producing a preserve with a cheese-like texture. Possibly a spoonful was dissolved in hot water and sipped slowly. A similar sounding quince cheese in Portugal is turned out of a mould like blancmange and eaten in slices.

[4] *Charlotte Brontë*, E F Benson (Longmans, Green and Co 1932).

TRIUMPH AND DISASTER, 1848-9

For the first time since their meeting seventeen years ago, Charlotte felt during much of 1848 that she could allow her relationship with Ellen to enter a more distant phase. By the end of March she was writing: '...if some kind, sensible man, with something competent to live on, would take a fancy to ask you to have him, and you could take a fancy to say yes, I should be glad to hear of the event . . .' The lines were almost a dismissal. The reference may have been to romantic possibilities between Ellen and the Rev Thomas Allbutt, Vicar of Dewsbury, who had become a widower on the death of his wife, Miss Wooler's sister Marianne. On the 24th May, Charlotte mentioned the attentions he was paying to Ellen, which Ellen did not think were serious.[1]

Becoming a published author brought Charlotte everything she had thought she wanted. She had gained more money than she could have earned in a lifetime of being a governess and knew that she could go on earning. She was corresponding with an intelligent man – Williams of Smith, Elder – who had known many great writers as a friend, and treated her with respect and consideration, discussing with her not only her writing but the affairs of the day. She felt herself on terms with Thackeray, her great hero among the writers of the time. He had written to her (via her publisher, and using her pen-name of Currer Bell) praising *Jane Eyre* with the most generous and obviously genuine admiration.

Her own father was proud of her when the publication of *Jane Eyre* was revealed to him. Her sisters had also published their books, although not to the same effect, but their publisher also wanted more, and in the future they too might enjoy her undoubted success. She was making new friendships among the writers of the day: G H Lewes and Miss Kavanagh were already corresponding with Currer Bell. By February *Jane Eyre* had been adapted as a play and a French translation was talked of.

The year had not long advanced when a second edition was printed. In gratitude to Thackeray, Charlotte dedicated this edition to him, not realising that his life had parallels with that of Rochester, in that Thackeray too had a mad wife. This was very embarrassing to Thackeray and created something of a scandal, it being surmised in London circles that 'Currer Bell' was an ex-governess of Thackeray's daughters.

The publishers were anxious that she should write a second novel at once, and Williams' advice and the opinions of the critics influenced her choice of subject. After many youthful years spent writing melodrama, she had matured

Hollows Mill in Shirley, *pictured here by Wimperis. The fictional mill was actually the Taylors' woollen mill at Hunsworth, built in 1788 by Mary Taylor's grandfather.*

to writing realistic fiction. But realistic *The Professor* earned rejections; when she wrote *Jane Eyre*, well imbued with melodrama, it was a great success. Now she was advised on all sides to eschew melodrama. After careful thought she chose her subject. At first she decided on the Chartist movement which she had lived through herself, but after discussion with a Mr Butterfield, in which he assured her that feelings still ran too high and people would be hurt or offended, she moved the scene back in time to the Luddites and the attack on Rawfolds Mill.

The discussion with Mr Butterfield may be apocryphal – it does not accord with Charlotte's own statement in her letter to Williams on the 17th September 1849 that she 'held no consultation about plan, subject, characters or incidents, asked and had no opinion from one living being, but fabricated it darkly in the silent workshop of [her] own brain', but it must be admitted that Charlotte was prepared to present to the world the picture she wished it to have. During the writing of about half of *Shirley* her sisters were alive, and we know that she discussed her work in progress with them, because she later lamented the loss of such constant consultation. Only the last chapters of volume two, and the whole of volume three, of *Shirley* were written after the death of Anne. Obviously she did not discuss with Mr Butterfield the plot of the novel or the characters; it is only the word 'subject' which is at issue here.

Birstall Old Church, the Briarfield Church of Shirley.

The surviving account of the incident has the ring of truth. Speight, in his *History of Bingley*, gives the episode:

'Mr Butterfield, though never a "physical-force" man, was in strong sympathy with the Chartists and there was no one in the neighbourhood of Bingley who entered with greater zest into the activities of their movement for the amelioration of the "poor factory slave" . . . Charlotte Brontë, with her famous dog "Floss", walked over from Haworth to Wilsden, the distinguished novelist desiring to consult Mr Butterfield with respect to a proposed story on the Chartist's agitation. She spent the best part of a long afternoon with him, taking tea at his house, and was dissuaded from engaging in the proposed work, which at that time would only have added a flame to the still-smouldering embers of discontent. In the evening Mr Butterfield accompanied Miss Brontë as far as Birchlands End, and for a moment they stood in rapt admiration of the magnificent scene around them, the sun at that hour lowering over the western moors; – presently they arrived at the old stone stile where the footpath leads down to Hallas Bridge, when the immortal authoress of *Shirley* and *Jane Eyre* said, "I will bring you no further; thank you for your company;" then offering her small white hand, she added, "I shall act upon your advice. Goodbye!" '

Wilsden is south of Bingley and when he left her she had three more miles to go. After walking half that distance she would be on top of the moors, with a view across the Worth Valley to Haworth on the next rise of hills.

Choosing the Luddite uprisings rather than the Chartists as her subject meant that Charlotte could use her knowledge of the Chartist movement to good effect, the two upheavals having much in common, but the Luddites were distant enough in time for memories to have softened and many of the protagonists to be dead. She could set the scene in the area she knew well from her schooldays, her time working for Miss Wooler, and her visits to Ellen and Mary. She could portray the society she had come to know there, and base the characters in the book on her friends and on her own sister Emily.

Emily Brontë, as she would have been, Charlotte thought, if born to wealth, was the model for the heroine, Shirley. Ellen Nussey was the model for the second heroine, Caroline Helstone, and the Rev Hammond Roberson for the fierce anti-Luddite Rev Helstone (Caroline's uncle in the book). Hunsworth Mill represented the real-life venue of the action, Rawfolds Mill. The whole family of the Red House Taylors, complete with house, were shown in Shirley as the Yorke family, and the descriptions were so good that, reading the book later in New Zealand, Mary Taylor was mentally transported back again to her childhood home and the family as they had been.

The year 1848 was a very different one for Ellen. Amelia Ringrose stayed with her until the end of February, and Ellen was sorry that she could not bring about a friendship between Amelia and Charlotte. Charlotte had no time for Amelia. She praised her to Ellen but had no desire to know her better or to correspond with her. It was only the pathetic circumstances in which Amelia was placed that made Charlotte take any interest in her at all. Amelia wanted the friendship. She wrote letters to which Charlotte could not be bothered to reply. She made three beaded watchguards as presents for the Brontë girls and they drew lots for them – perhaps a reminder of the old Moravian and Wesleyan custom, perhaps a mark of indifference. One remembers how as children they had fallen on the toy soldiers their father had brought from Leeds, which had been snatched up with the cry, 'this shall be mine!' They were controlled women now, and did not really care who had which watchguard.

The events which are to be the most important do not always announce themselves with a flourish of trumpets. The contact between Charlotte Brontë and Mrs Gaskell was to be important – and now it was foreshadowed.

The young Mrs Gaskell in Manchester had just sold her first book, Mary Barton – to many her finest work. It was in the press when she read Jane Eyre. She commanded her friend Anne Shaen:

'Read Jane Eyre, it is an uncommon book. I don't know if I like or dislike it. I take the opposite side to the person I am talking with always in order to hear some convincing arguments to clear up my opinions.'[2] The ambivalence which was to underlie the whole of her relationship with Charlotte Brontë was apparent from the outset.

Mrs Gaskell had reached a watershed with the selling of Mary Barton; it would make her into a famous writer. Her life so far had contained much loss and sorrow. Elizabeth Cleghorn Stephenson was born in 1810, six years before

Charlotte Brontë. Her mother died when she was a month old and her mother's sister brought her up. Her only brother disappeared at sea in 1827. Her father had remarried unhappily, and he too died in 1829. In spite of these and other traumas, Elizabeth grew up to be charming and beautiful, socially graceful, intelligent though not academic, bright-natured with a sense of humour, and fond of scribbling away at stories and letters. She had been brought up a Unitarian and met and in 1832 married a young, brilliant Unitarian minister, William Gaskell. They lived in Manchester, where William was on the staff of the Cross Street Chapel.

They had children as quickly as possible, a total of at least seven in twelve years. Elizabeth was well advanced in her pregnancy with the last, when at the age of ten months, her son Willie died of scarlet fever. There was barely time to adjust to this before the birth of Julia on the 3rd September 1844, and the result was that Elizabeth was thrown into a deep depression.[3]

She already had a short non-fiction piece of writing published, by the Howitts in 1840, and met this couple of professional writers in the following year while on a tour of the Rhine. She was impressed by their ability to make a great deal of money from writing and enjoy a luxurious lifestyle. Until then she had not thought of writing in a mercenary way – it had been a hobby which might produce a litte cash occasionally. Now, to help her conquer her misery after Willie's death, her husband suggested that she write a long story to distract her mind. He was a strong influence on the writing of *Mary Barton*. The book breathes of William Gaskell and his interests, his involvement with the poor of Manchester and his recording of their dialect.

Apart from being a city seething with vivid intellectual life – partly inspired by the colony of Germans who had settled there – Manchester was the centre of the social changes induced by the Industrial Revolution; its worst effects were first seen in Manchester's mills and overcrowded housing. Engels' book *The Condition of the Working-class in England in 1844* was based largely on his observations of Manchester, and was in its turn a foundation stone of Marx's economic theories.

Mary Barton was finished in 1847 and, like Charlotte's *The Professor*, went the rounds of the publishers. At last, early in 1848, Chapman and Hall bought the copyright outright for £100. Elizabeth Gaskell was in her thirty-eighth year. In view of her high fertility, it might be inferred that the Gaskells' most intimate relationship had come to an end in about 1844. The two seem never again to have displayed the closeness they had during the writing of *Mary Barton*, when William would read through what she had written each day, discuss it with her and correct it. By degrees during the remainder of their married life they became more detached, although always devoted to one another. The turning point of Elizabeth's life – after her children were born and *Mary Barton* written, and before she became famous as a professional writer – was the point at which she read *Jane Eyre*. From then on her future relationship with Charlotte and Ellen was waiting in the wings.

But if Elizabeth Gaskell had already felt the impact of Charlotte Brontë's personality, it was to be a few months before Charlotte was aware of Elizabeth's existence. Other things were occupying the Brontë family in the summer of 1848. By the beginning of June, Newby's suggestion that Currer Bell had written *Wuthering Heights* and *Agnes Grey* as well as *Jane Eyre* proved so irritating that Charlotte and Anne Brontë made their famous journey by rail to London, to demonstrate to Smith, Elder that there was more than one of them. Emily was still determined to remain anonymous. George Smith, who had been overwhelmed by *Jane Eyre*, was at first taken aback by these two quiet provincial ladies who appeared in his office bearing the letter he had written to his mysterious author Currer Bell, and was inclined to ask them sternly how it was that they had possession of it. Once he realised the true position, he wanted to inundate them with hospitality. It was their first taste of what it might be like to be famous authors.

Later in June, Ellen, who once again had not been well, went for a change of scene to stay with her brother John in Cleveland Row. As reported by Wise and Symington, she said:

'When I reached London I found there was quite a furore about the authorship of the new novel. The work was quickly obtained, and as soon as it arrived it was seized upon and the first half page read aloud. It was as though Charlotte Brontë herself was present in every word, her voice and spirit thrilling through and through, till a rapid escape was imperative for the outlet of feeling.'

Ellen knew at once that this was the book which Charlotte had had accepted. All afire to be allowed to tell her family that the author was her best friend, she wrote circumspectly to Charlotte, only to have her knuckles rapped and receive a stern refusal on Charlotte's part to acknowledge the book. She did not want her authorship to be known at Haworth or in Birstall, longing to walk invisible a little longer. Although she liked the praise, and had enjoyed the experience of overhearing a stranger commenting favourably on *Jane Eyre*, she dreaded the book being known and read in her own village. Emily would be distressed – and worse still there was the possible effect on Branwell. His health was now so poor that he could no longer drink as he used to. He had only to take a little alcohol for it to bring about a fainting fit.

Anne's second book, *The Tenant of Wildfell Hall*, was published in the summer and Anne was distressed by the adverse notices it received. She had set out earnestly to tell a moral tale which she felt was important, however distasteful it might be to dwell on the subject of drunkenness and mental cruelty, and was accused of revelling in coarse and unpleasant things.

Emily, in her turn, seems to have told her publishers that she had written a second book and was in the process of polishing it. Although she was so stoical, the bad notices and general disapproval of *Wuthering Heights* must have been agonising, even though it was selling well and the publisher was looking forward to another manuscript from her. Charlotte was later to say that her pleasure in her own success had been marred by witnessing Emily's silent suffering. Of the five reviews of *Wuthering Heights* which Emily preserved in her writing desk, only one was wholly favourable. The experience would not have been so painful had she been able to be objective and realise that this was good publicity, that bad notices are better than no notices and that the book was being very widely read.

Charlotte was well advanced with her next book, *Shirley*.

Branwell died at the end of September. Although his family knew that alcohol, opium and mental anguish had worn out his body and mind, his death still came as a shock to them. Mr Brontë, who forgave all his son's faults, gave way to a parent's normal sorrow. To Emily and Anne, sorrow was likewise straightforward although devastating. For Charlotte, remorse was added to sorrow – she felt that she had treated Branwell badly. After his death she took to her bed and stayed there for about a fortnight, unable to eat. Emily had borne up better and had attended the funeral, catching a chill in the process which exacerbated the tuberculosis from which she was already suffering.

In one way Branwell's death must have been a relief. Watching his constant downward slide and the extremity of his illness was a day-to-day purgatory for the three girls. The emotional strain was tremendous. There were also the practical problems of caring for a very ill yet obstinate person, which laid a burden on their physical endurance. Losing Branwell made the first break for many years in the magic circle of the family. Maria and Elizabeth had died so long before that to Emily and Anne they could only have been vague baby memories, but Branwell had been their adored brother and playmate, who shared every aspect of daily life.

Branwell's death came nearly a year after the publication of *Jane Eyre* and hardly a fortnight before the publication of Mrs Gaskell's *Mary Barton*, which had an electrifying effect on the reading public. As Charlotte had been the publishing sensation at the end of 1847, so Mrs Gaskell was at the end of 1848.

When the three Brontë girls were left together they might justifiably have looked forward, once the period of mourning was over, to a happy, settled and successful existence. They had proved themselves. They were now popular authors whose work was well paid and in demand, and they loved one another, helped and inspired one another and really needed no-one else. But the family ailment was to step in while their physical resistance was low, and demolish their dreams. By the end of October, Charlotte was telling Ellen in her letters – sparser and more formal during the whole year than ever before – that Emily was ill, and Anne in delicate health.

All this time Ellen was still away from home; after London she had visited her friends the Gorhams in Sussex and had been to Rye, perhaps in their company. She had not forgotten her friends at Haworth and had sent a biography of Simeon for Mr Brontë to read.

By November, Charlotte was frantic over Emily's illness. She wrote to Mr Williams of Smith, Elder asking his opinion about medical treatment, and suddenly her letters to Ellen became once again warm and natural. On the 23rd she was saying that there was no hope for Emily, and by the 10th December she was in torment over her sister's approaching death. Ellen, now back at

Brookroyd, sent some of her sovereign remedy, the crab-cheese, and Charlotte wondered if her presence would do Emily good, but it was obvious when she suggested it that Emily could no longer bear the slightest household disturbance, even the arrival of a friend as well-loved as Ellen. On 19th December Charlotte dashed off a brief note to say that Emily was worse, and two days later sought relief in writing for Ellen the well-known account of the horror of Emily's end, as she fought her illness to the last and only agreed to the doctor being sent for when she was within moments of death itself.[4]

The blow to both Charlotte and Anne was tremendous. It was harder to bear than the loss of Branwell, for he had courted his death by abusing his constitution and had left few achievements behind him. Emily, with her genius, her strong, powerful character, her willingness to be the homekeeping one of the sisters, was like a rock in their lives.

'Could you now come to us for a few days?', Charlotte begged Ellen. 'I would not ask you to stay long. Write and tell me if you could come next week, and by what train. I would try to send a gig for you to Keighley . . . I never so much needed the consolation of a friend's presence.' Ellen went as soon as she could and stayed for a fortnight. 'Your friendship is some comfort to me', Charlotte told her, 'I am thankful for it. I see few lights through the darkness of the present time; but amongst them the constancy of a kind heart attached to me is one of the most charming and serene.' On the other hand, she could not bear the idea of a visit from the Taylor family: 'I wrote to Hunsworth telling them candidly I would rather they did not come.'

Emily had died thinking that *Wuthering Heights* was misunderstood and undervalued, but Anne Brontë had the satisfaction of receiving an appreciative letter about *The Tenant* from the Rev David Thom of Liverpool, who divined her aim in writing it. On 30th December 1848, within days of Emily's death, Anne occupied and consoled herself by answering this letter, in so doing making a statement of her religious faith. We have so little first-hand evidence of Anne that this little-known letter is valuable, written as it was at this time of desolation, when Anne herself was in her last illness. Thinking of her religious torment at school and her discussion with the Moravian LaTrobe, we can see that the ideas she had then longed to hold, were now strong, giving her the serene faith which was to sustain her so remarkably:

'I have seen so little of controversial Theology that I was not aware the doctrine of Universal Salvation had so able and ardent an advocate as yourself; but I have cherished it from my very childhood – with a trembling hope at first, and afterwards with a firm and glad conviction of its truth. I drew it secretly from my own heart and from the Word of God before I knew that any others held it. And since then it has ever been a source of true delight to me to find the same views either timidly suggested or boldly advocated by benevolent and thoughtful minds; and I now believe there are many more believers than professors in that consoling creed . . . in my late novel TT of WH I have given as many hints in support of this doctrine as I could venture to introduce into a work of that description.'[5]

After Emily's death, the Brontës' writing was no longer secret from Ellen. She was given copies of *Jane Eyre*, *Agnes Grey*, *The Tenant of Wildfell Hall* and *Wuthering Heights* to take home on the 9th January 1849. When Ellen added the names of the books the Brontës had published to the list of her library, she did so in different ink. This enables us to know which books were available on loan from her to the Brontë sisters, up to the end of 1848. One wonders whether Ellen's copy of Ovid's *The Art of Love* ever went on loan to the parsonage at Haworth. (*See Appendix 3.*)

On the 11th January, Charlotte wrote reassuringly to Ellen that Anne was a little better, so Ellen did not reply until the 19th, being busy, during the dark winter days after her return to Brookroyd, knitting a pretty fringe to trim a shawl she had made for one of her sisters. We know that Charlotte often knitted by the fire in the evening. Perhaps Ellen had been making the shawl while she was at Haworth, and the two friends had talked as they worked, sitting without a candle and using the light of the fire to see by. How pleasant and soothing this would be.

From somewhere Charlotte had now bought, borrowed or been given a copy of *Mary Barton*, and she wrote to Williams of Smith, Elder at the beginning of February 1849 expressing her worry that *Shirley* had strong similarities to it. So that he could judge for himself she sent the first volume of the manuscript. No doubt this new anxiety would not help Charlotte's state of mind, as she realised from day to day how ill Anne was. As the weeks went by, Charlotte was so distressed that it was she who could not bear the thought of a visit, even from Ellen. In this situation Ellen did the only thing she could think of – on the 8th March she wrote directly to Anne, asking if she would come to Brookroyd to be nursed. Anne declined, but in reply asked Ellen to go with her to the seaside or some inland watering-place – she may have been thinking of Harrogate, as Ellen had taken George there. Charlotte in turn said that Anne might die while she and Ellen were away on such a visit; and she did not want Anne to leave home in any case until the summer weather in June. Ellen's mother and sisters now joined in the discussion. Alarmed by the idea of Ellen having to cope with Anne's death in a boarding house in some strange place on her own, they vetoed any idea of Ellen taking Anne away. This arguing took up the first two weeks of April. The result was an agreement between all parties that Charlotte and Ellen together should take Anne to Scarborough as soon as the weather was warm enough.

On the 12th May Ellen recorded in her diary that she had heard from her brother Henry at Pau of the fall and ruin of Mr Hudson, the 'Railway King'. The era of mad prosperity for investors in the railway was over. This would affect the investments of the two sisters at Haworth, but they had no thoughts to spare for such things. For Charlotte the writing of *Shirley* was almost at a standstill. Anne made valiant efforts to live: she bought a respirator through the agency of Ellen, and also some cork soles for inside her shoes. She took all the doctors' advice. In addition to the other suggested remedies and cures, she swallowed the crude, unrefined cod liver oil of the period, although it made

The pillar and first floor window are all that remain of the former George Hotel on Coney Street, York, where the Brontë/Nussey party stayed en route *to Scarborough.*

her retch. Everyone was concerned about her: Miss Wooler offered the use of a house she owned or leased in the North Bay at Scarborough, which would be empty as she would not be going there herself at this time, but Anne had decided that she wanted to go to stay at number 2 Cliff, where she had stayed whilst accompanying the Robinsons as their governess.

On Wednesday the 23rd May Ellen went to Leeds to meet her two friends at the railway station, where they expected to arrive soon after two o'clock. They did not come. She waited at the station for the rest of the day and then went home. The following morning she went back to Leeds station and waited again, and this time they arrived. She had been warned not to let her shock at Anne's appearance show in her face or manner, and she did not. Together they went to York, where they stayed overnight and Anne was able to fulfil her

Cliff Bridge and Woods Lodgings on St Nicholas' Cliff, Scarborough, around 1860. Charlotte, Ann and Ellen stayed at 2 The Cliff on Anne's final visit before her death in May 1849.

wish to see York Minster for one last time. The next day they travelled on to Scarborough. 'At the South Cliffe', wrote Ellen in her diary.

Charlotte had written earlier that they would travel light and 'buy gowns and bonnets in York or Scarborough'. They did buy bonnets, though their hearts could hardly have been in it. The purchase may have given distraction, even pleasure, to Anne, and was considered necessary before confronting the fashionable society of Scarborough. It must have been obvious to all of them that Anne could not live much longer.

'My friend Ellen is with us', Charlotte wrote to Williams after their arrival in Scarborough. 'I find her presence a solace. She is a calm, steady girl – not brilliant, but good and true. She suits and has always suited me well. I like her, with her phlegm, her repose, sense, and sincerity, better than I should like the most talent without those qualifications . . .'

Ellen's diary for 1849 survives. In it she made very brief notes, often one word, and she wrote things which had occurred during other years, so that it can be difficult to decide in which year something took place using the evidence of the diary alone. But for the events surrounding the death of Anne Brontë its guidance is clear.[6] When the death had only just occurred, Ellen dashed down in the diary this account of Anne's last days. It is not a polished and considered piece of work, but came straight from the heart. These broken lines were to form the basis of her later memoir of the event:

'A short account of the last days of dear A.B. She left her home 24th May –49, died May 28. Her life was calm, quiet, spiritual – such was her end – through the trials & fatigues of the journey she evinced the pious courage & fortitude of a martyr – dependance & helplessness were with her a far sorer trial than hard & racking endurance. Her visit to Y[ork] Minster was an overwhelming pleasure not for its own imposing & impressive grandeur only but because it brought to her susceptible nature a vital sense of the Greatness of our Divine Architect. Her weakness was great but her gratitude was greater after an exertion such as walking to her bedroom she would clasp her hands & raise her eyes in silent gratitude on reaching the side of her bed [deleted] ere

Minster Gate would in Charlotte and Ellen's day have been the approach to York Minster.

she prepared for rest & she did this not to the exclusion of wonted prayer for that too was performed on bended knee. On the 26 she drove on the sands for a hour & lest the poor donkey be urged by its driver to a greater speed than her tender heart thought right she took the reins and drove herself – when she was joined by a friend after bathing time she was charging the boy master of the donkey to treat the poor animal well She was (ever) fond of dumb things & would give up her own comfort for them – On Sunday she wished to go to the Church & her eye brightened with the thought of once more worshiping [sic] her God among her fellow creatures but her friends thought it prudent to dissuade her from the attempt – She submitted without an objection though it was plain her heart was longing for the performance of [such] worship. She walked a little in the Afternoon & meeting with a comfortable seat near the beach she begged her companions would leave her & enjoy the various scenes within their reach for the place & its attractions were new to them. The evening closed in with the most splendid sunset that was ever witnessed – The castle on the Cliff stood in proud glory gilded by the declining Luminary – the distant ships glittered like burnished gold & the little boats near the beach [heaved] with the ebbing tide waiting employment. The view was so grand so fine so far beyond any artistic imagination the dear Invalid was wheeled in her easy chair to the window to enjoy the scene with her friends – her face became illumed almost as much as the glorious scene she gazed upon. Little was said . . . for it was plain the dear invalid's thoughts were driven by the imposing view before them to penetrate onwards to the regions of unfading glory – She again thought of public worship and wished us to leave her and join those who were assembling at the House of God. We declined urging gently the duty and pleasure of staying with an invalid – on returning to her place near the fire she conversed with her sister on the propriety of returning to their home – she did not wish it for her own sake she said – she was fearing others might suffer more if her decease occurred where she was – she probably thought that the task of accompanying her lifeless remains on a long journey was more than her bereaved sister could bear – The night was passed without any apparent easing of illness – she rose at seven and performed most of her toilet herself by her expressed wish her sister always yielded such points as being the truest kindness and not to press inability where it was not acknowledged. Nothing occurred to excite alarm till about 11 a.m. The dear invalid then spoke of feeling a change she believed she had not long to live could she reach home alive if prepared immediately for departure – a physician was sent for – Her address to him was made with perfect composure – she begged him to say how long he thought she might live – not to fear speaking the truth for she was not afraid to die – The doctor being this urged reluctantly admitted that the angel of death was already arrived that life was ebbing fast – she thanked him for his truthfulness and he departed to come again very soon – she still occupied her easy chair looking so serene and reliant there was no opening for grief as yet though all knew the separation was at hand. She clasped her hands and reverently invoked a blessing from heaven upon her sister then upon her friend and thanked each for their kindness and attentions. Ere long the restlessness of death appeared and she was borne to the sofa she being asked if she were easier she looked gratefully at her questioners and said it is not *you* who can give me ease but soon all will be well through the merits of my Redeemer!

Shortly after this seeing that her sister could hardly restrain her grief she said "Take Courage, Charlotte. Take courage." Her faith never failed . . . about two o'clock her eye now dimmed when she calmly and without sigh breathed her last – so still and so hallowed were her last hours and moments there was no thought of assistance or of dread. The doctor came and went three times in the hours the hostess knew that death was near yet so little was the house disturbed by the presence of the dying – the second that dinner was announced as ready through the half opened door as the living sister was closing the eyes of the dying one. She could no more stay the [pent] up grief with her emphatic and dying "Take Courage" it burst forth in agonising strength – Affection had another channel – and there it turned, in thought, in

Anne Brontë's grave in St Marys Churchyard, Scarborough.

care, and in tenderness – there was not solitude though there was bereavement – sympathy was at hand, and it was accepted. Now came the function of removal home – this melancholy task was next performed for the afflicted sister decided to lay the flower in the place where it had fallen – she believed that to do so would [meet] with the wishes of the departed – she had no preference for place.'

Ellen arranged for the death certificate while Charlotte organised the tombstone, and Anne was buried within sight and sound of the sea she loved so much. Then Mr. Brontë wrote suggesting that Charlotte and Ellen stayed by the sea for a while, and they did so. On the 1st June they were at South Cliff. On the 7th they left Scarborough for Filey, and the following day walked to the end of Filey Brigg. They attended church on Sunday the 10th June at Muston, a little village near Filey. On Thursday the 14th they went to see their old friends at Easton and stayed with them until the 21st June. During this time, on Saturday the 16th, they visited the village of Boynton where Henry had friends. On Sunday the 17th they went to church at Bridlington and the following day they spent at Bridlington Quay. On Tuesday the 19th June they went to Boynton Hall. At the end of their visit to Easton the two friends returned to their respective homes.

Charlotte would not let Ellen go to Haworth with her. She felt the need to return alone and to endure the agony of loss and loneliness which she knew would await her. Ellen's presence was soothing and prevented the extremity of anguish. Once returned to the silent parsonage, the ordeal was all and more than she expected. 'I do hope and pray', she wrote to Ellen on the 14th July, 'that never may you, or anyone I love, be placed as I am . . .'

A little while after that bitter return to Haworth Charlotte decided to distract herself from the loneliness and grief she felt, alone for hours on end in the parsonage, by buying things that she had long wanted, and sent money to Ellen with a request that Ellen should purchase for her a shower bath and some furs.

Tabby was at this time still at the parsonage, but showing her age. Ellen tells us that 'in later days after she [Tabby] had been attacked with paralysis, she would anxiously look out for such duties as she was still capable of – the Post-man was her special point of attention, she did not approve of the inspection which the younger eyes of her fellow servant bestowed on his deliveries, she jealously seized them (when she could), and carried them off with hobbling step and shaking head and hand to the safe custody of Charlotte.'

Ann Nussey was going to be married, at the late age of fifty-three, to Robert Clapham, brother of the John Clapham who was a partner of the Nusseys in Brookroyd mill. He was a widower, the landagent for the manor of Batley, and had proposed to Ann on the 11th May. As has been noted earlier, Clapham, like Mr Brontë, had been much opposed to the Poor Law Amendment Act, and he was involved in the local uproar of 1838. Although Ann was happy, her snobbish attitudes were still in evidence; it bothered her that Robert sat down to his dinner in the jacket he had worn all day. 'Ann wants shaking to be put out about his appearance', commented Charlotte. 'What does it matter whether her husband dines in a dress-coat or a market coat, provided there be worth and honesty and a clean shirt underneath?' She and Ellen liked Robert Clapham very much. Ellen was commissioned by Charlotte to buy a pretty card-case as a wedding present to Ann, and asked to put the rest of the money towards her own bridesmaid's outfit. When Ellen married, Charlotte fantasised, she ought to wear silver-grey and white, or dove-colour and pale pink.

By now Charlotte had met Amelia and Rosita Ringrose. She had thought Amelia very plain – 'had I not known her amiable I should hardly have judged of her as favourably as she deserves' – and Rosita attractive – 'I shall not soon forget her face, so pretty, modest, SENSITIVE'.

Ellen now had leisure to read, and she finished reading *Jane Eyre* on the 15th July. As the first half page had moved her so much that she had had to leave the room and be alone to overcome her feelings, reading the whole book must have been a deep emotional experience.

Charlotte was filling her life with her work, and postponed seeing Ellen again until *Shirley* was written. She completed it at the end of August, and as Mr Taylor of Smith, Elder was in the north of England he arranged to call at Haworth and collect it. He called on the 8th September and fell in love with Charlotte. The firm were delighted with the book.

There was still no possibility of the friends being together. At Haworth, Charlotte did not feel she could leave her father. In Brookroyd, Ellen could not leave her mother, for they were in the middle of preparations for Ann's wedding – she was married on the 26th September 1849. Ann would soon be away on her honeymoon. Mercy's personality had become more difficult through the years, and she was not reliable enough to be left in charge of her ailing mother. Charlotte suggested that Mercy was jealous of Ann's marrying. Ellen had her own fears about the results of the marriage for herself, but in the event it turned out to be uniformly beneficial.

The two households shared roomy Brookroyd House, and life was brighter. A piano arrived on the 13th October and became Ellen's prized possession. It was a comfort to all four ladies to have a capable man under the roof. Once more they felt in the mainstream of life, with an active man coming and going. Clapham had property and business interests, so additional income was making a difference. Before this their financial position was precarious, and they had been assisted from London by John Nussey. John now offered to cancel the debt so that they might maintain their standard of living – their 'present comfort' – if they would bequeath whatever estates they might have at their deaths to John's children – their only nephews and nieces.

While the expectation that they would do so was reasonable, particularly in the cases of Ann and Mercy who stood no chance of having children, for Ellen, who might still marry and have a family, there could be weighty disadvantages. The suggested arrangement seems to have been complicated. Charlotte's comments indicate that if Ellen did not accept the proposal, this might prejudice its application to Ann and Mercy. Ellen, of the three, had least to leave. Charlotte did not mention the matter again after her letters of 4th and 14th July 1849, but what comment she does make seems fair – 'The scheme is worldly, but not inequitable'. Nothing more is known of the arrangement.

Money concerned Charlotte too. Her earnings from her books was invested and gave a return of about three per cent, which was standard for the time. The railway shares, in which the three sisters had sunk their inheritance from their aunt, had dropped in value after the Hudson débâcle. Whereas before, she had had enough income to live on with care, that was no longer so. She had wanted to sell out earlier and had not insisted because she feared to hurt Emily's feelings. Over the last months, since Emily's death, she had been too preoccupied first with Anne and then with finishing her book to think about such matters.

Shirley was published on the 26th October 1849 while Charlotte was staying at Brookroyd, having written on the 20th proposing a visit of a few days as she had to go to Leeds to the dentist. The friends met in Leeds and returned to Brookroyd together. Their social life during the visit is interesting because it is the only Brookroyd visit so documented.

On Friday 26th, they had Miss Wooler and Joe Taylor at Brookroyd to visit them. On Saturday they went to Leeds again. On Sunday they had the Rev Carter all day, probably taking services in their area. On Monday the two friends went to Dewsbury and Charlotte received a letter from Mary Taylor in New Zealand. The Carters called to see them on the Tuesday, and Ellen received a letter from her suitor, Rev O P Vincent. On Wednesday the 13th, the day Charlotte left Brookroyd, Joe Taylor called again, and then Ellen accompanied Charlotte to the railway station in Leeds.

A local family that Charlotte now grew to know well was the Fawcetts. George Fawcett was Robert Clapham's nephew, and the family tradition is that when Charlotte visited Ellen, he often drove his trap down to Brookroyd to fetch the two women to visit the Fawcetts. They proudly handed down through the generations the silver teaspoons Charlotte had used to stir her tea during these visits.

While at Brookroyd, Charlotte realised that everyone she knew there had by now read *Jane Eyre* and was aware that she was the author, although she was still using the pen-name Currer Bell and continued to do so. She was growing used to the mixed reactions the books evoked, but still found the situation uncomfortable.

Shirley arrived for the general readers of the Birstall area just after Charlotte left for Haworth. When she received her author's copies, one was dispatched for Ellen and a second for her to send to Mary Gorham. Charlotte felt the respect for Mary which she was never able to feel for Amelia. She sent a copy also to Harriet Martineau, and one to Mrs Gaskell, both authors she admired.

Charlotte desperately missed having someone with whom to discuss the reviews. She, Emily and Anne had always talked them over together and smiled at the absurdities of reviewers, which helped counter the pain caused by bad notices. She was amused by Ellen's partisan reaction to them:

'It is like you to pronounce the reviews not good enough – and belongs to the same part of your character which will not permit you to bestow unqualified approbation on any dress, decoration etc. belonging to you. Know that the reviews are superb . . .'

She tried to cheer herself in November by having new dresses made in preparation for a visit to London. She felt the need of Ellen's good taste:

'I wish you could have looked over them and given a dictum', and in one of her rare warm replies to Amelia Ringrose, who was then staying at Brookroyd, says:

'..in reading your little notes, I am at Brookroyd, I am with Ellen - I see her sewing, reading, writing, trying on her dresses, finding fault with them – (that of course – fastidious person as she is – I never knew her express full satisfaction with a garment) I see her cooking – and you kindly helping her –'

Ellen could not decide how to answer the letter from Vincent. She sent it to Haworth and asked Charlotte's opinion. It was obvious that by writing at all, he was hoping to begin a correspondence, which would enable him to renew his suit. Given a change of heart on Ellen's part, a marriage might result. Charlotte, needing Ellen now more than ever in the past, was dismissive, saying that there was nothing in the letter which needed answering apart from a slight enquiry after Ellen's sister Ann. Mr Vincent was not good with words. Presumably Ellen wrote a discouraging letter to him or did not reply at all. He does not seem to have approached her again, nor does he appear to have married.

Charlotte had the necessary change and break by visiting London for a fortnight in December as a guest in the house of George Smith. In her absence the new church at Oxenhope was consecrated; the money to build it had been raised by the untiring efforts of the curate there, Joseph Brett Grant, one of the curates she satirised in *Shirley*.

Charlotte's idol among the writers of the day was William Makepeace Thackeray. 'I have seen Thackeray', she wrote in December 1849, with the feeling of having encountered Everest. Thackeray's work she had read at this point was the early, quick, sketchlike pieces he dashed off by the thousand for periodicals, and *Vanity Fair*, his first full-length novel. This was being published in serial form as Charlotte was negotiating with Smith, Elder over *Jane Eyre*. She was very impressed by it. The success of *Vanity Fair* changed Thackeray from the rebel who rejoiced in the everyday life of servants, card-sharpers and artists in cafes and theatres and streets, to the conformist. He found himself a celebrity and he liked it. He liked good meals and fine houses and being sought after by aristocrats. His future novels were to be 'of higher tone'.

Charlotte Brontë appeared to Thackeray as a tiny walking conscience, telling him that he was not using his great powers to the best effect and suggesting how he could improve matters. He did not like this plain speaking but he liked Charlotte, even though she disturbed him. 'She wants [needs] a Tomkins to marry her', he commented. Tomkins was the name by which he sometimes referred to himself when writing to his friends. He was five years older than she; it would have been an interesting partnership, had it been possible. He ignored the call of conscience – she came too late, the decisions were already made. He must have money. He had two daughters and a mad wife to support, as well as needing to make provision for their futures. He wished to indulge his taste for fine food and wine, only partly satisfied by dining at the homes of the great.

During this visit to London Charlotte sought a meeting with Harriet Martineau. She was hoping for the society of 'clever people', and Miss Martineau, undoubtedly clever, had responded kindly to the gift of *Shirley*. On learning the real name of 'Currer Bell', Miss Martineau recognised it, for 'we had heard the name before, among others, in the way of conjecture'. At once Miss Martineau sent an account of the interview to Mrs Gaskell. In all the rush and hurry of her correspondence, Mrs Gaskell spread an account of this meeting, as full of errors and half-truths as if she were playing Chinese Whispers. Charlotte had refused an opportunity to meet Dickens, and was never enthusiastic about him, but almost revered Thackeray. Mrs Gaskell on the other hand became a friend of Dickens, who was to publish much of her work in *Household Words*, and does not seem to have taken to Thackeray – her references to him are usually casual. She had 'an extreme dislike' for writing for the magazine he was later to edit.

On the 28th December 1849, Ellen went to Haworth and stayed with Charlotte for almost three weeks. Ellen was to write:

'I realise . . . how useful I was to her in giving repose and sympathy. She used to say; "Oh Nell! Thy very nearness comforts me even when we do not speak." After talking sometimes vehemently she rested with loving confidence stroking my head and leaning over me. Once when doing this she said, "If I had but been a man, thou would have been the very ticket for me as a wife".'[7]

By the end of the year a worrying development had taken place among their friends: Joe Taylor and Amelia Ringrose were strongly and mutually attracted. Both Charlotte and Ellen thought them totally unsuited, and were concerned about the situation. 'I do not like to think about it [their marrying]; I shudder sometimes', said Charlotte.

[1] Letter 369 p 218, Shakespeare Head. The Rev Thomas Allbutt was later to marry a widow, Sarah Isabella Chadwick, and a brother of his, Dr George Allbutt, married a Miss Brook of Fall Lane, Dewsbury, one of the Batley Parish Dorcas Society which often met at Brookroyd. Information about the Dorcas Society from a newspaper article by Dr Erskine Stuart.

[2] Letter 25a, p57, *The Letters of Mrs Gaskell*, ed Chapple and Pollard (Manchester University Press 1966).

[3] My thanks to Mr J G Sharps, who kindly informed me of a Gaskell letter which reveals the existence of a first son, either stillborn or dying in earliest infancy. This explains their extreme joy when a second boy child, 'Willie', was healthy, and brings their total of known children to seven in twelve years. Since writing the above, an article on this has appeared in Vol 20 Part 4 of the Brontë Society *Transactions,* 'A Letter From Mrs Gaskell', by Sally Stonehouse.

Mr and Mrs Gaskell:

Married	30 August 1832
1st child stillborn daughter	July 1833
2nd child Marianne	12 Sept 1834
3rd child Margaret Emily (Meta)	5 Feb 1837
4th child first son, died an infant, presumably here	
5th child Florence Elizabeth	7 Oct 1842
6th child second son William	23 Oct 1843
7th child Julia Bradford	3 Sept 1844

[4] It is possible that Emily Brontë's consumption produced the difficult aspects of her character, for Ivy Compton Burnett's father, Dr James Compton Burnett, homeopath, wrote of consumptives that they 'are mum, taciturn, sulky, snappish, fretty, irritable, morose, depressed and melancholic, even to insanity'. That this picture is not necessarily true is shown by the contrast between Emily and Anne.

[5] Anne's letter was printed in *The Times Literary Supplement* 21st June 1923.

[6] The diary is written in *The Christian Remembrancer* for 1849, which was given to Ellen by one of her sisters. It is at the Brontë Parsonage Museum.

[7] In a letter from Ellen to Lady Morrison, in the possession of John Nussey.

CHARLOTTE THE LITERARY LION, 1850-2

By 1850 the atmosphere of the true Victorian period had developed. Between 1801 and 1851 the population of England and Wales doubled, from slightly under nine million in 1801 to eighteen million in 1851, and a very high proportion of the later population was young. There had been heavy immigration from Ireland in the wake of two years of dreadful famine. The railroads[1] had revolutionised transport. Jerry builders had rushed up acres of poor-quality housing. Concern for public health and knowledge of how to safeguard it were both in their infancy. Hypocrisy had grown out of all proportion. Tight lacing was narrowing waists and crinolines were widening skirts – they were to reach their zenith in 1860. The processes of production were becoming industrialised, yet this change was still far from universal. The over-riding sins of the era were drunkenness, fighting and sexual immorality. We have only recently surpassed the mid-Victorian high ratio of illegitimate to legitimate births in the population.

Charlotte was desperately lonely when she was at Haworth, and she was welcome wherever she wished to go. But she had a very strong sense of duty and had been brought up to put her father's welfare before her own wishes. Also, she could only concentrate on writing at home. So that was where she spent most of her time.

In January 1850, while Ellen was in Haworth, the two talked all day and half the night:

'Just now I am enjoying the treat of my friend Ellen's society and she makes me indolent and negligent – I am too busy talking to her all day to do anything else', she wrote to Williams. 'Single women often like each other much and derive great solace from their mutual regard. Friendship however is a plant which cannot be forced – true friendship is no gourd springing in a night and withering in a day. When I first saw Ellen I did not care for her – we were schoolfellows – in the course of time we learnt each others faults and good points – we were contrasts – still we suited – affection was first a germ, then a sapling – then a strong tree; now – no new friend, however lofty or profound in intellect – not even Miss Martineau herself could be to me what Ellen is, yet she is no more than a conscientious, observant, calm, well-bred Yorkshire girl. She is without romance - if she attempts to read poetry – or poetic prose aloud – I am irritated and deprive her of her book – if she talks of it I stop my ears – but she is good – she is true – she is faithful and I love her.'

This visit was a respite in a weary solitude.

Charlotte had decided to spend some of her capital on improving her home. She had now earned money from *Shirley* and felt more secure. Probably some of her sisters' money had also devolved to her. In addition, the shortness of earthly life had been demonstrated in no uncertain manner, and the immediate benefits of increased elegance and comfort gained precedence over providing for her future. Probably she was putting into operation plans which she and her sisters had discussed. She bought curtains dyed a cheerful red (though the quality of the dyeing did not satisfy her), wallpapers, carpets, new furniture. The furniture was made by Tabitha's nephew, William Wood. More books appeared on the shelves; gifts from her publishers, presents from other authors, or books she had chosen and bought for herself.

The knowledge of her writing had spread to Haworth. Mrs Ratcliffe, the younger sister of Martha Brown, who '. . . well remembered her father had been to Halifax one day on business, and on returning home said that he had heard who was the real author of *Jane Eyre*. If that which had reached his ears was correct, "Currer Bell" was none other, he exclaimed, than the parson's daughter, Charlotte'.

The news was too good and startling to be confined within the walls of the house. First it was told to Martha, who, at the earliest opportunity, and with elation, 'plumped' Miss Brontë. She was quietly and mildly put off with 'Hush, Martha, you should not talk so very much'. Some time prior to this, their father had sat up all night, fascinated by the novel.[2] Charlotte gave Ellen her version of this event:

'Martha came in yesterday, puffing and blowing, and much excited. "I've heard such news," she began. "What about?" "Please ma'am, you've been and written two books, the grandest books that ever was seen . . ." "Hold your tongue, Martha, and be off." I fell into a cold sweat. *Jane Eyre* will be read by John Brown, by Mrs Taylor, and Betty. God help, keep and deliver me . . .'

Shirley had a mixed reception. It proved to the public that Charlotte was not a one-book author, and that she was one of the foremost writers of the age, but it did not have the popularity of *Jane Eyre* except in Yorkshire, where it was very popular indeed. Charlotte, consciously or not, based many of her characters almost photographically on people she knew and a good many individuals living in the parishes of Birstall and Batley found that they appeared in *Shirley*.

'The Haworth people are making fools of themselves about *Shirley*', Charlotte told Ellen, 'They take it in an enthusiastic light'. The theme was popular in Yorkshire, and all the little details of place and of the type of life, as well as the typical regional characters, were revelled in. Even Mr Nicholls roared aloud with delighted laughter when he read the scenes with the curates. He had become an accepted part of Charlotte's life, much as Martha Brown was. Charlotte referred to him now with more geniality, although only a year or two before she had been comparing him most unfavourably with Willie Weightman.

Ellen said, at the time of publication of *Shirley*, that she could not

Oakwell Hall, Birstall. In Shirley *Charlotte renamed it Fieldhead and made it the home of the heroine Shirley Keeldar.*

recognise either of the heroines, although she recognised other characters, and liked the book very much as a whole. Later in her life she was to agree that in some respects Caroline Helstone was like herself. Mary Taylor in far-off New Zealand was enthusiastic - her family were portrayed in detail - but her brothers were not altogether pleased. Mr Brontë was one of the enthusiasts. He revelled in his daughter's success and wanted her to write more books as quickly as possible. He was delighted when the celebrated social reformer Sir James Kay-Shuttleworth and his wife, the heiress whose name he had added to his own, came to call and when they invited Charlotte to stay with them.[3] Much against her will, for Sir James was bossy and didactic, Charlotte had to accept the invitation. Charlotte visited the Kay-Shuttleworths for the first time at Gawthorpe Hall, Lancashire, and the sofa on which she sat is still displayed there.

The roof of Haworth Parsonage was leaking, and it had been arranged that repairs were to take place during the summer of 1850. Charlotte decided to undertake an interesting and sweeping action – the remodelling of the house, while the great weight of the stone slab roofing was removed from the structure. She had the internal wall between the entrance hall and the dining room moved and made thinner, so that the dining room was three feet wider and better for entertaining. The hall was then much narrower. This alteration gave her extra space in her bedroom over the dining-room, but it made the small bedroom over the hall, where once Emily had had her bed under the window, eighteen inches shorter and too small for further use as a bedroom. It was probably at this time that the alcoves were made in her father's study, and an internal door pierced through from the landing into Tabitha's bedroom, so that the old woman did not have to use the outside stairs.[4] All these alterations were to take place during the summer, and after organising her own part of the project Charlotte planned to be away from home while the work was done.

In April Ellen had carried out another of Charlotte's shopping commissions, which was to buy her a silk plait of artificial hair so that she could make the fashionable coiffure; the plait was sharply criticised later by the smart London ladies who saw it. At the end of May Charlotte went to stay again with her publisher. There were many things in the visit which she enjoyed, but she had the unpleasant experience of being 'lionised' in various ways.

Miss Martineau gives an idea of what it was to be 'lionised' in the London of the time:

'It is somewhat new to see the place of cards, music, masks, my lord's fool, and my lady's monkey, supplied by authors in virtue of their authorship . . . The lady of the house devotes herself to "drawing out" the guest, asks for her opinion of this, that, and the other book . . . Authors would like to know why they must receive flattery as if it were welcome, and be made subject to fine speeches, which presuppose a disgusting degree of vanity in the listener . . . it may be questionable whether it is equally necessary for him to acquiesce in being the show and attraction of an assemblage to which he is invited as a guest, if not as a friend . . . The crowning evil which arises from the system of "lionism" is, that it cuts off the retreat of literary persons into the great body of human beings . . .'[5]

Reading this, one can realise why Charlotte, when she discovered that her dinner at Thackeray's house was not to be an intimate evening with a good discussion of value to both of them, but that a number of unknown society and literary people had been invited to come in after the meal, entered 'in mittens, in silence, in seriousness', and there was no persuading her to speak all evening. It had not taken her long to revolt against the system of 'lionising'.

It is not altogether clear, but Thackeray seems to have given two parties for Charlotte, with a good many guests of both sexes in the first, then, realising that this was too much for her, a select group of literary women in the second. This was also too much. He disappointed her by deferring to 'the duchesses and marchionesses' when he dashed off early from a meeting with her to visit various aristocratic ladies, who, as the custom was, displayed themselves to callers in the costumes they were to wear for that evening's fancy dress ball. Later he postponed the third of his lectures for a week because it clashed with Ascot.

'I think I should scarcely like to live in London – and were I obliged to live there, I should certainly go little into company - especially I should eschew the literary coteries', was Charlotte's opinion. After her June visit she spent a

George Richmond's portrait of Charlotte Brontë from 1850.

week at Brookroyd with Ellen before her most enjoyable experience of the year, her visit to Edinburgh with George Smith and his sister. They went in July to fetch the younger Smith brother from his school there. Charlotte loved the dramatic city. It must have reminded her of the John Martin engravings in her father's room, for Edinburgh is as reminiscent of John Martin's cityscapes as any city is ever likely to be. It is also fresh and open with endlessly varying weather, an atmosphere of intelligence and culture, and many romantic associations.

Ellen Nussey always said that the much younger George Smith proposed marriage to Charlotte. If he did, she refused him. She would have seen what he did not see, that the literary life of London would not suit her, and that not only their lifestyles but their life experiences unfitted them for one another. Charlotte stayed with Ellen for a while in July on her way home from Edinburgh and they set off from Brookroyd together – Charlotte back to Haworth where most of the disturbance of the renovations was now over, and Ellen to Tranby near Hull to visit the Ringrose family again.

Later, in August, Charlotte went to stay with the Kay-Shuttleworths for three days at a house they rented in the Lake District. Mrs Gaskell was also invited. Charlotte was delighted to meet her and form a friendship.

Elizabeth Gaskell, by Richmond.

Mrs Gaskell and Charlotte's hostess at this time, Lady Kay-Shuttleworth, displayed a somewhat patronising attitude towards the authoress from Haworth. Phrases from the two ladies' letters about wanting to 'do her good' and 'be of great use' – a desire to meddle in her life and rearrange it – would have infuriated her if she had known of them. One remembers the indignant postcript she once added to a letter to Ellen, that she would not be 'sent for' – when she wished to make the journey to see her friend, she would arrange it herself. Charlotte was an extremely independent person, holding the position of teacher and benefactress in Haworth, capable of sharpness, and would hardly have liked Lady Kay-Shuttleworth and Mrs Gaskell to discuss between them 'how to do her good'. What she wanted and needed were relationships of equality with other gifted women.

There appears also to have been an attitude among society and literary people that Charlotte was something weird and strange. This is demonstrated by Lady Kay-Shuttleworth's eager retailing of all the melodramatic gossip about the Brontë family which she gleaned from a woman who had been dismissed from their service, and by Mrs Gaskell's unquestioning acceptance of these stories as true, and later use of them in the biography. In the delightful personality of Elizabeth Gaskell, the author of socially aware books which can be both moving and charming, I find her attitude to Charlotte Brontë to be her least attractive aspect.

Many people see the relationship as all respect, warmth, graciousness and delicate helpfulness on Mrs Gaskell's part. I see it as patronising, manipulative, and lacking in the respect due from one human being to another.

The three days in the Lake District were strange ones. Lady Kay-Shuttleworth was indisposed and hardly appeared. Sir James offered to take his guests to meet Tennyson, but when it rained on the journey he instantly turned back, to their disappointment. Charlotte had a severe headache for the whole of one day and was in a state of depression and low spirits for all three. The only bright spot for her and for Mrs Gaskell was getting to know one another.

As soon as Mrs Gaskell reached home she began writing excited and highly-coloured accounts of Charlotte to all her friends. One of them, Emily Winkworth, wrote to her sister after reading one of the letters of description of Charlotte, 'Poor Miss Brontë . . . one feels as if one ought to do something for her˙. . . One feels that her life at least almost makes one like her books, though one does not want there to be any more Miss Brontës . . .' Mrs Gaskell did not allow her daughters to read *Jane Eyre* for a considerable time, although Thackeray's daughters had long since fallen on it and devoured it, only half-understanding what it was about.

Later in the year Charlotte felt threatened by an invitation to stay with the Kay-Shuttleworths in London, and was relieved when she was there at a different time to her would-be hosts. She enjoyed some of her new contacts, and exchanged a number of letters with Sydney Dobell, an intelligent and sympathetic young journalist and poet.

Harriet Martineau drawn by Richmond.

As the anniversary of Emily's death drew near, Charlotte could not bear to remain in the parsonage. Miss Martineau invited her to the Lakes and she accepted. Once there she got on well with her unusual hostess and found her highly individual lifestyle fascinating. Then she went to Brookroyd and Ellen, and did not venture home again until the dreaded Christmas was over.

Among their friends, other events had happened during this year of 1850. Mary Taylor in New Zealand set up shop and entered into trade, with her cousin Ellen Taylor; her brother Joe courted Amelia Ringrose and married her in the December; Ellen's brother Henry and his wife travelled in Italy; Ellen's mother had been frequently ill; and a working man in Haworth had written an appreciation of *Jane Eyre* which Charlotte thought so good that she sent it both to her publishers and to Ellen, for them to read.

The only new writing of Charlotte's during the year seems to have been the *Biographical Notice* of her sisters, which was attached to a new edition of their works. Looking through their papers and re-reading their books made her ill with sorrow. E F Benson wrote of her account of Emily's last weeks:

'Truly, if Charlotte was reaping the hardness she had sown, she made expiation in that bitter harvesting . . . She missed all that *Wuthering Heights* stands for; she shuddered at its "horror of great darkness", she wished to cease "to breathe lightning", not knowing that the darkness and the lightning are It; . . . when it came to the true genius of the book she was blind . . . As in her portrait of her sister in *Shirley*, as in her Preface, [these notes] are mere external observations; Emily was beyond her.'[6]

Emily's genius was also beyond many other people at that period, one of them being Ellen, even though she had loved Emily and had longed to be close to her.

It must have been about 1850 that the events took place which John Greenwood's daughter recounted to Whiteley Turner. Her husband's mother, Mrs Widdop, used to wash for the Brontës and took her children:

'An infant brother of Mr Widdop's was often fondled by Charlotte while the washing proceeded. Plato, a big, brown, curly-haired retriever, successor to Emily's Keeper, was one washing day ranging the kitchen, the while switching his long tail, signifying friendship when alas! he lashed it with dire results. A terrible howl rent the air. The toiler at the wash-tub was too intent on her work to notice she was twining into the machine [presumably an early type of mangle] the dog's hind appendage. Mrs Widdop junior remembers many a time being ridden on the back of Plato along Parson's Fields with Mr Nicholls as driver.'[7]

Ellen and Charlotte were closer than ever after the tragic experiences they had shared, but circumstances often kept them physically apart. They were no longer enthusiastic girls, but sadder, wiser women in their thirties. When they did meet, they had plenty to talk about.

1851 was in many ways a repetition of 1850: the same type of experiences, the same friends, filled it. Charlotte's father and Ellen's mother respectively took up a great deal of their attention. But Ellen was able to visit Haworth during March: she was there on the night of the 30th, when the 1851 census was taken. Pets were significant; Flossy junior, the puppy given to Ellen by Anne Brontë, a pup one of whose parents was Anne's own dog Flossy, had always been a troublesome although much-loved animal – 'little hapless plague!' Charlotte called her. In April she was burrowing into a portmanteau of Ellen's to have the latest batch of her own pups, and in May she met a tragic death. Charlotte hardly dared to tell her father of it.

Amelia became pregnant soon after she and Joe Taylor were married, and the ups and downs of the pregnancy were closely followed by the friends. Ellen gave the Taylors a present in advance, of a bassinet, a wicker cradle. 'Has anything tumbled into the bassinet at Hunsworth yet?' asked Charlotte. In 1851 Amelia gave birth to a sickly daughter. This poor creature, nicknamed Tim, was to cause everyone connected with the little family unending concern.

Ellen's sister Mercy, once a favourite of Charlotte's for her warm-heartedness, was still difficult and often ill. It is likely that she had a bad menopause. Charlotte said that Mercy '. . . draws very heavily on good-nature and forbearance, she must be looked upon in the light of a "cross to take up". Comfort, or pleasure even, I fear, peace and safety will never be had out of

A photograph of Mercy Mary Nussey, Ellen's older sister.

her; of ordeal and discipline she had given plenty, and will give yet more. I suppose that is her use – to test and try others like a fiery furnace.'

1851 was the year of the Great Exhibition. Charlotte spent most of June in London, at the home of her publisher. Ellen imagined her having a splendid time, but it was a very mixed experience. Charlotte hated the exhibition, which she visited, due to her host's insistence, on five occasions. The only thing that pleased her was seeing the exiled French royal family walk through one of the transepts of the Crystal Palace. For a moment her old illusions, her youth's dreams of life in the capital, must have revived. She also found interesting a visit she made with an eminent scientist, who explained the industrial exhibits.

On her way home in June, Charlotte stayed for some days with Mrs Gaskell at Plymouth Grove in Manchester. An episode during this visit seems to have given rise to one of the incidents in Mrs Gaskell's *Cranford* – it is that of the green tea:

'As may be imagined Miss Brontë was none too easy a visitor. This was the occasion on which she was asked if she preferred tea or coffee. "Tea" was the reply, "but please see that there is no green tea mixed with it, as I am never able to sleep after partaking of a cup of tea that has the least particle of green leaf." Mrs Gaskell in vain recommended a mixture of green and black blended, which in fact was the tea she was making use of. Besides, it was too late to make a change, and the ordinary tea was used. Next morning the guest was asked how she had slept. There was a general smile when she said, "Splendidly", and a similar tea was used to the end of the visit!'

The parallel incident in *Cranford* runs:

'If she [Miss Matty] was made aware that she had been drinking green tea at any time, she always thought it her duty to lie awake half through the night afterward (I have known her take it in ignorance many a time without such effects), and consequently green tea was prohibited the house . . .'

Green tea was considered a powerful stimulant. Charlotte spent the whole of this visit in a state of exceptional nervous tension, unable even to brace herself to visit someone she wished to see again. When she said that she slept splendidly it may have been merely good manners. On her next visit to Mrs Gaskell in April 1853 she lay awake every single night.[8]

Charlotte and Ellen had been together at Brookroyd in January and in Haworth in March. Ellen visited Haworth in July, a time when Charlotte was writing to Williams that 'she had learned not to take at their face value expressions of partiality for herself.' A bitter learning process seems to lie behind this; does she refer to George Smith or James Taylor, both of the firm of Smith, Elder? Although in the abstract Charlotte liked the idea of marrying James Taylor, who paid her court persistently, whenever she was close to him she felt great physical repulsion and knew that she could not marry him. Her father was surprisingly in favour of an engagement, perhaps because Taylor was on the point of going to India for five years to represent Smith, Elder who had a large connection there, and so an early marriage would not have been possible.

In her turn Ellen visited London, to stay with her brother John and his large family.[9] His daughters were growing up; Georgiana, who had been such a baby favourite, was rather spoiled and Charlotte thought it would do her good 'to go out for a year as a maid-of-all-work, or as a plain cook in a respectable family'.

In September, Charlotte, overcome by loneliness and with Ellen out of reach, urgently begged Miss Wooler to visit her. The ten days her old teacher spent at Haworth were much enjoyed. Mr Brontë and Miss Wooler took to one another particularly well.

Cheered by this company, Charlotte at last began work on a new novel,

Villette. Once more she returned to her old theme, which she had used in *The Professor*, of the time she had spent in Belgium at the school run by Mme Heger in the Rue d'Isabelle. This time she took a different angle on the subject and produced a much stronger book, but one which was bitter and caustic in its strength. She included recognisable portraits of George Smith and his mother, also of M and Mme Heger, their pupils and staff, in addition to describing the Belgian school and its garden minutely.

She was working at *Villette* during November, perhaps as early as October, but physical illness began to bother her and once more she was slipping into depression. Probably the subject, bringing back in full force the memory of Brussels and her obsession for M Heger, had a depressing effect. She could conjure up her story so vividly in her mind's eye that she seemed to be living there again, and in the quiet of the parsonage there was nothing to stop her moving into this trance-like experience. Almost any other story would have been better for her mental, and therefore her physical, health; but she had an inner compulsion to rid herself of her experiences by writing them and re-living them, which could not be denied; and as *The Professor* had not found favour she recast and rethought the whole thing and started again.

By January 1852, Charlotte was in such a low state of mind and body that she sent hurriedly for Ellen, who came at once for the few days that her friend had requested. While she was there, Charlotte felt better, but as soon as she went back home Charlotte became severely ill. Whatever the underlying physical malady, the worst thing was the medical treatment. Dr Ruddock gave her 'blue pills' which were a standard medicine at the time containing mercury, and Charlotte developed severe mercury poisoning. Her mouth and tongue were ulcerated, and for days on end she could only take sips of water and no food. She became rapidly thinner. If she had continued with the pills, she would have died. Mr Brontë, much concerned, was all for sending for Dr Teale, in whom both of them had much faith, but Dr Ruddock realised what was happening in time to save her. He said indignantly that even a child should not react as she had done to the quantity he gave her and that she must be unusually sensitive.

As soon as she felt well enough to travel, Charlotte went to Ellen at Brookroyd for a fortnight to recuperate. She recovered within a few weeks, in spite of the quinine Mr Ruddock gave her as a tonic, which also disagreed with her, and by March she was writing again. It was towards the end of April that news arrived from Mary Taylor in New Zealand of the death of her cousin Ellen, who had gone out less than two years before and had joined Mary in starting her shop. Ellen died of tuberculosis and Mary was devastated. Charlotte, reading of the event, was reminded in full force of everything her brother and sisters had undergone.

Ellen Nussey had planned a long holiday with her friends the Gorhams in Sussex, beginning in May and lasting for two or three months, and she wanted Charlotte to accompany her, but was refused. Instead Charlotte went on her own to Filey for the month of June, possibly writing hard all the time.

In a letter to Ellen, Charlotte said: 'How sorely my heart longs for you I need not say'. When she wrote to her father, she asked to be remembered to Mr Nicholls, Tabby and Martha. Nicholls had at least acquired the standing of household staff, and she felt friendly enough towards him to say that she would like him to see a little church that she had visited.

By July, Charlotte was home again. Ellen's letters kept her up with events such as Mary Gorham's marriage to the Rev Thomas Swinton Hewitt and public reaction to the death of the Duke of Wellington. Wellington had always been Charlotte's hero. She saw him in the flesh on one visit to London, and the sight had shattered none of her illusions; he looked noble and impressive.

Ellen's return home meant that when Charlotte became depressed again in September, she was at hand to be sent for and could spend a week in Haworth. A new money-making scheme had been promoted. From somewhere the suggestion had come that Ellen should go to live with a middle-aged couple called Upjohn at Gorleston near Yarmouth as a companion cum housekeeper, and in return they would leave her something in their wills. This extraordinary and parsimonious arrangement was being seriously considered. Ellen was intending to go as soon as it could be arranged, to see how she got on with them. Charlotte, Mr Brontë and Mary Taylor in faraway New Zealand were all against the scheme.

Desperately in need of Ellen's company, Charlotte was yet afraid of going to Brookroyd too often. She needed to work on her novel and to feel that she was not neglecting her father. By October she was writing again: 'Let me see your dear face just for one reviving week'. When Ellen was there to share her bed she had that blessed calm sleep. Alone, she would wake, sit up in bed, and long for Ellen.

After all the agony involved in its composition, *Villette* was finished and with her publishers in October. She then felt free to seek congenial society and have a holiday. She visited both Brookroyd and Miss Martineau, and planned to visit London also.

For the best part of two years her strange, mainly long-distance courtship by James Taylor had kept her on tenterhooks. Now there was to be another challenge to her spinster peace in the shape of a proposal of marriage from her father's curate, Mr Nicholls.

---

[1] It was the track, not the train, which made such a difference. Previously there had been experiments with steam coaches, but the roads were too bad for them to be a success.

[2] Whiteley Turner's *A Spring-Time Saunter Round and About Brontëland*.

[3] Sir James was a doctor, and also a social reformer who almost single-handed created the form taken by mass education in the nineteenth century. He wrote two novels, and enjoyed the company of writers. Some of his theories on social reorganisation seem to modern ideas unfortunate if not callous.

[4] *Haworth Parsonage, the home of the Brontës* by Jocelyn Kellett (Brontë Society 1977), is an excellent study of the architecture and history of the parsonage building.

[5] Harriet Martineau's article 'Literary Lionism' appeared in the *London and Westmister Review*, April 1839. It includes also: '. . . the author has to do with those two things . . . which are common to the whole race, – with living and thinking . . . The very first necessity of his vocation is to live as others live, in order to see and feel, and to sympathise in human thought'.

[6] *Charlotte Brontë* by E F Benson.

[7] As note 2. Many of the mementos purchased by the Greenwood family found their way to the Brontë museum, such as the boots in which Charlotte 'tripped noiselessly to school'. The uppers are of silk rep, hail-stone pattern, and side laced. Mrs Greenwood said, 'Her hands and feet were the smallest I ever saw,' and the soles, no thicker than a florin, are 9" long and 2" broad. There was also a brass-mounted mahogany writing desk, and an original photograph of Charlotte.

[8] *Mrs Gaskell's Observation and Invention*, J G Sharps, p128-9 (Linden Press 1970); also Haldane, *Mrs Gaskell and her Friends*, pp 133-4. Green tea was used by many hack writers to enable them to stay awake to pour out more words – Miss Martineau comments on the practice. George Smith could work continuously for thirty-six hours on a diet of green tea and pork chops, and pork chops are not noted for their stimulating or insomniac qualities.

[9] John Nussey had taken a lease of the Ivy House at Chislehurst as a country home, but 4 Cleveland Row was still the London base of the family.

CHARLOTTE'S COURTSHIP, 1853-4

Charlotte wrote at once to tell Ellen of Nicholls' proposal and her reception of it. Her tone was calm, as if the events were happening to someone else. She had refused him in a note, he had replied in writing, and his note was sent for Ellen to see. There had been indications, which Charlotte had ignored, that he was in love with her. When he at length spoke out, his emotion 'made me for the first time feel what it costs a man to declare affection where he doubts response'. She immediately told her father, who almost had an apoplectic fit in his anger. Charlotte hated injustice, and her 'blood boiled' to hear the epithets used of the hapless curate. She did not want his love, and was annoyed that pity should enter her mind and bother her, when she had so much else to think of.

Villette was now coming through in batches of proof sheets for correction and Ellen was told of the progress; she was now the closest to Charlotte, the one in whom she confided. All Ellen's activities were of interest to her friend: the great New Year's tea-drinking which she helped with, the sewing she was engaged on, the prospect of her going to live with the Upjohns. Ellen in her turn was longing to hear more of Nicholls' proposal and to read *Villette*. 'Don't you think you have been shamefully impatient about *Villette*?', asked Charlotte.

Mrs Gaskell was about to publish *Ruth*, and she made an extraordinary request of Charlotte, namely, that the publication of *Villette* be delayed so that it would not coincide and therefore compete with *Ruth*. Charlotte wrote: 'Mrs Gaskell wrote so pitifully to beg that it should not clash with her *Ruth* that it was impossible to refuse to defer the publication a week or two'. It says a great deal for Charlotte that she agreed, and with courtesy.

She was now realising to the full her position as celebrated authoress and the last thing she wanted was trouble in the household and among the staff – Nicholls was staff, employed by her father. As a consequence of the curate's daring in proposing to Charlotte, Mr Brontë was behaving very coldly to him and so were the family of the sexton, John Brown, with whom he lodged. Charlotte was the only one who pitied him. He had resigned his post and gone off his food. She 'wished devoutly that Papa would resume his tranquillity and Mr N his beef and pudding'.

She decided to get away from the 'atmosphere' at Haworth and in January stayed again with her publisher. The Smiths, mother and son, had been faced by the fact that she had portrayed them recognisably in *Villette* as Dr John

Brandon and Mrs Brandon. The whole relationship was changed on their side, but it had already become different for Charlotte, who saw behind their facade. She remarked how sweet Mrs Smith's kindness had been to her once – it was no longer sweet, though the kindness was unvarying. Without more evidence, one can only suggest that Charlotte had realised how much of business was in this friendliness from the Smiths. The possibility of romantic involvement between herself and George Smith was over – he was paying attentions to someone else. Charlotte realised that Smith, Elder were paying her less than the market value for her work; she and her father had expected her to receive £700 for *Villette*, but the payment was £500. She knew that they paid other authors more generously.

For perhaps the first time, Charlotte met Ellen's London relatives. First, niece Georgiana and nephew Edward (whom she may have met when he was at school in Liversedge) brought round a parcel of books to be taken back to Yorkshire. Georgiana had a striking appearance, but Charlotte thought Edward had more of 'the Nussey goodness – for there *is* a goodness I like in the better members of your family'. Then Ellen's sister-in-law Mary Nussey called 'very stately in her carriage' when Charlotte was out and left an invitation to dinner at 4 Cleveland Row. This Charlotte declined but she paid a morning call, and presumably met the rest of the family. This visit to London was the one she appreciated most, for no social life was pressed on her by her hosts. She was allowed to do what she chose, and to see the real world; two prisons, the Bank, the Exchange, and the Foundling Hospital.

Ellen's brother John and his wife Mary, whom Charlotte met in London during January 1853.

Villette was published on the 28th January 1853 while Charlotte was still in London. She sent off presentation copies to Ellen and Miss Wooler, and planned to meet Ellen on her way home so that they could go to Haworth together, where a 'nice piece of cold boiled ham' was awaiting them. What they did not eat 'came in for breakfast in the morning'. Reviews of *Villette* were very mixed, which worried Ellen more than it did Charlotte, who had become philosophical about reviews; but her armour was penetrated when Miss Martineau, whom she had prized as a friend, attacked the importance given in the book to love. This published criticism broke off the friendship.

Ellen stayed at the parsonage for a fortnight, during which the two women enjoyed going out in the crackling snow, and in the evenings walked round the table with arms entwined, or sat over the glowing peat fire with their feet on the fender and talked to their hearts' content while they put their hair in curl, before sleeping their calm sleep in the same bed. The Upjohn affair was annoying to Charlotte. She wished her friend could get the whole thing over, but Mrs Upjohn did nothing but prevaricate. Ellen in her turn was worried by Nicholls' proposal and expressed her emotions in a letter to Mary Taylor in far-away New Zealand.

Bishop Longley[1] came to stay overnight at Haworth – Ellen shopped in Leeds for the dessert to be offered him, and had the mysterious comestible sent. Presumably he enjoyed it. Ellen also had commissions from Charlotte about this time for the purchase in Leeds of favourite biscuits, which were bought by the pound and for which Ellen tried to avoid taking the money. Charlotte regarded the bishop's visit as a success, but she wished Ellen could have been present. Nicholls' behaviour was annoying: 'I thought he made no effort to struggle with his dejection . . . he showed temper once or twice when speaking to Papa . . . I shall be most thankful when he is well away. I pity him, but I don't like that dark gloom of his . . . If Nicholls be a good man at bottom, it is a sad thing that nature has not given him the faculty to put goodness into a more attractive form.' He had started a needless argument, which revived all her old unfavourable impressions.

1853 was a year of postponements and delayed decisions. Charlotte's visit to Mrs Gaskell had been postponed, but took place at last from the 22nd to the 29th April. Small Julia Gaskell captivated her as few children did. It was on this visit that Charlotte records her sleep as restless, unrefreshing and full of dreams. She put it down to a story Ellen told her in a letter, but one cannot help concluding that it was the green tea which was to blame. Mrs Gaskell's description of Charlotte was '. . . pleasant countenance, sweet voice, gentle timid manners, very attractive to gentlemen . . . I thoroughly loved her before she left', she added, 'She has had so little kindness and affection shown her . . . everything does prey on her mind in the solitude in which she lives . . . she is thoroughly good, only made bitter by some deep mortifications – and feeling her plainness as "something repulsive.".'

But Charlotte had grown up in a singularly loving and united family. She had many friends who loved her; contacts such as her godmothers, her aunt, her teachers, her publishers had all shown kindness to her, and several men had proposed to her. Her distresses – and they were deep, her loneliness was desperate – arose from the death of much loved siblings and her obsession with a married man, and the fact that a home which had once held ten happy and united beings now held four, two of them very old and the third a young servant-girl, so that for the first time she spent hours alone at home. Elizabeth Gaskell must have experienced a much lonelier childhood. She had shared little of it with her father and brother, having been brought up like an only child, once her cousin had died, by her widowed aunt, sharing the quiet life amongst the ladies of Knutsford; whereas Charlotte had had the constant mental stimulus of her family.

Mrs Gaskell's dramatic account of Charlotte's time in Manchester contrasts with Charlotte's cool remark to Ellen; 'I have had a very pleasant visit here, but we shall chat about it anon'. The chat took place when Charlotte broke her home journey at Brookroyd, arriving about five on the Thursday and leaving 'on Saturday or Monday, as we shall decide when we meet'.

One of the subjects of the chat was the postponement of Ellen's visit to the Upjohns. Robert Clapham, Ellen's resident brother-in-law, teased her by saying he believed Mrs Upjohn's house was haunted. It was not until the end of May that Ellen went to Gorleston near Yarmouth to spend a month with the Upjohns to see how they got on together. In spite of the postponements made by Mrs Upjohn to suit her own convenience, when Ellen arrived her hostess was away from home.

During the six months since Nicholls' proposal, he and Charlotte had not seen much of one another. He was away from time to time having interviews for new posts, and he avoided taking the Haworth Sunday services, arranging for other clergymen to officiate. She had also been away and no doubt avoided him when at home. But his leavetaking proved a turning point. Earlier in May he was almost overcome when she was at a communion service he was taking. His lack of self-control aroused Mr Brontë's scorn. Now at the end of the month she was to find her suitor in tears after he said goodbye officially and left the parsonage. He had found a post at Kirk Smeaton, south-east of Pontefract.

There can be no doubt of the emotional effect of this event on Charlotte. She was in future times to call him 'my boy'; now it was the revelation of the depth of his feeling for her in the 'weakness' of tears, and her own role as a comforter, which transformed the situation. She became over the next months his defender and protector in this state of emotional vulnerability.

Ellen had 'a hard time of it and some rough experience' with the Upjohns, 'those strange unhappy people'. The Rev Francis Upjohn MA was incumbent of the living of Gorleston,[2] which brought in £381 a year. Before taking Holy Orders he was a captain in a dragoon regiment. Gorleston itself was a big handsome village close to the sea, and the church, a large ancient structure built of flint, was thatched. We do not know why the Upjohns and Ellen did not get on together, but she soon left them and went to her brother Joshua's at Oundle before returning home.

Emotional stress resulted in a septic throat for Charlotte. When it was better, Mrs Gaskell was to visit Haworth. She would not have been flattered if she could have read Charlotte's letter to Ellen: 'I now long to be better, to get her visit over if possible, and then to ask you'.

Needing a holiday at the seaside, Charlotte set off instead on a visit to Scotland with Joe Taylor, his wife Amelia and their little daughter, nicknamed Tim, but it was a fiasco. The child developed some trifling ailment and the anxious parents insisted on turning back. They decided to have a holiday at Ilkley instead but, as Charlotte's box containing changes of clothing was mislaid on the railway, she could only stay there three days. Mr Brontë was not in good health and Charlotte was reluctant to leave him again, so she did not have a real break from home that summer.

Since the revelation of the depth of Nicholls' feeling and his departure from the parish, she had been receiving letters from him, unknown to her father. For some time she had not replied to them, but at last she did, and on several occasions Nicholls visited Haworth and they met. Pity being akin to love, she was beginning to consider as a possibility what had at first been dismissed out of hand. Her father suspected her of weakness where Nicholls was concerned. The situation in the parsonage between the two passionate Brontë personalities was very embattled when Mrs Gaskell finally made her first visit to Haworth from the 19th to the 23rd September 1853. Charlotte was pleased to have the opportunity of asking the advice of a married woman whom she respected and whose experience would, she thought, be of help to her in deciding what to do.

Mrs Gaskell was impressed by the scrupulous cleanliness which prevailed everywhere in the parsonage, the tidiness and the comfort:

'The room looked the perfection of warmth, snugness . . . crimson predominating in the furniture . . . everything, furniture, appointments, etc . . . is admirable for its consistency. All simple, good, sufficient for every possible reasonable want.'

The fires on the hearths created 'a pretty warm dancing light all over the house' and the view was 'really beautiful in certain lights'. There were things the visitor did not like, such as the strange sounds the winds made round the exposed house, and the illimitable rolling moorland which seemed to go on for ever and where the heather had been prematurely browned by a thunderstorm instead of showing its annual purple glory.

In the mornings they had breakfast with Mr Brontë in his room but he dined alone as he had done for decades. He joined them for tea and talk in the afternoon, which was his normal custom. At this period tea seems to have been taken in the parlour, Mr Brontë's room, although the names for the rooms seem to vary. At half past eight they went into his room again for family prayers, then back into the dining room where the two women sat and talked until about ten o'clock. After Mrs Gaskell was in bed, Charlotte came down

The dining room at the parsonage. 'Everything fits into, and is in keeping with the idea of a country parsonage possessed by people of very moderate means', wrote Mrs Gaskell.

again and spent some time walking round the table, composing her thoughts for rest.

Mr Brontë no longer preached sermons. He was in his late seventies and his health had needed care for a long time. He felt harassed by Charlotte's attitude to Mr Nicholls and still more by the lack of the one curate on whom he had learned to depend. His eyesight was poor. He was clinging desperately to his authority and pride, insisting on taking walks alone and then acting like a hurt child when he lost his way and arrived home exhausted. (He may have refused Charlotte's company on these walks to free her to enjoy the companionship of her guest; he was always the most courteous of men.)

Charlotte entertained Mrs Gaskell with stories of the isolated inhabitants of the moorland farms, and with reminiscences of her sisters and the household pets. Whereas Ellen's record of a visit to the parsonage shows a good deal of social life, and it cannot be doubted that if Ellen had become a permanent resident, there would have been many pleasant little events to bring sunny enjoyment – Mrs Gaskell was impressed by the extreme monotony, solitude and silence.

It is obvious that by now Charlotte was seriously considering Nicholls as a husband. If she could bring her father round to the idea it seemed to offer the perfect solution to her problems. She would secure a live-in lieutenant for him in the parish who, as his son-in-law, could take the whole burden from his shoulders. She did not feel physical repugnance to Nicholls as she had to the publisher, James Taylor.

Although she had said to Ellen that her initial refusal was based on a sense of 'incongruity and uncongeniality in feelings, tastes, principles', she respected Nicholls in many ways, knowing him to be reliable, capable, gentlemanly (extremely important to her), whole-heartedly a Church of England man even if rigid and High Church, and high-principled. They had known one another for years and gradually he had won a place in her life. She was accustomed to seeing him in the parsonage. He had known her sisters and brother. The routine of the house was familiar to him and he did not view the life there as strange or eccentric. He admired her writing and had taken the satire in *Shirley* in good part. The more she considered the matter, the more advantages such a marriage presented. Above all, strong-willed and independent though she was, she was tired, deadly tired, of having the whole responsibility of the household on her shoulders and having no companion with whom to discuss daily events. If Ellen had been free to share a life with her it would have been different. The events of May would not have happened as they did, for the friends could have been together had it not been for those troublesome Upjohns. The two women might have been eagerly planning a sea-side holiday to watch the 'vast brewing-tub' of Bridlington Bay, or a long visit to Edinburgh. But Ellen had not been and was not free. Upjohns apart, she had her ageing mother who relied on her without giving many thanks for her devotion. Charlotte had told her to sacrifice herself for her mother and Ellen had done so.

As young women long ago they had talked of living in a cottage, just the two of them; but how many years might it be before such a situation was possible, and how many crises might Charlotte have to face alone before then? Besides, the love of a man, a strong capable man, and the fulfillment of marriage, was a lure that could not be denied.

So if only Mr Brontë would agree, many desirable consequences would result from a marriage with Nicholls. Mr Brontë's greatest and most rooted objection was that Nicholls was only a poor curate, and Charlotte was a successful authoress, with a financial competence, worldwide fame and the friendship of the great. The problem came down to the obstacle of Nicholls' poverty, and her discussions with Mrs Gaskell resulted in this conclusion.

Mrs Gaskell was a believer in marriage and wanted to help. The most obvious thing was to bring influence to bear to obtain preferment for Nicholls in the Church of England. Had Mr Gaskell been a Church of England minister, she would have been able to achieve this; they would have had the connections and knowledge required. But a minister of the Unitarian church could do nothing, and a famous novelist could do nothing, even though she approached people of prominence in the Church of England who were known to her. Dr Hook in Leeds 'had just filled up his staff of curates'. Reluctantly, after a short while, Mrs Gaskell had to acknowledge failure. Her next idea was to make the couple independent of a church salary by obtaining for them the annual payment of a pension from the Civil List. This was more within her power because she was on friendly terms with influential Monkton Milnes, who was later to become Lord Houghton. Monkton Milnes had a family seat in Yorkshire, Fryston Hall (where later the Gaskells were to be his guests), only about five miles from Kirk Smeaton where Nicholls was working, and he admired the Brontës' writing greatly. He had gone so far as to introduce himself to Charlotte while she was in London.

Mrs Gaskell was aware that what she was doing would not meet with her friend's approval. She herself called it 'well-meant treachery' and asked Monkton Milnes to keep her intervention a secret. While she was at Haworth it seems as though she had suggested the idea of a Civil List pension to Charlotte, who was averse to the idea of receiving one. She was proud, and knew herself capable of earning enough money for her needs. Mrs Gaskell gave it as her own opinion to Monkton Milnes that Charlotte would not object if Nicholls were given such a pension 'as an acknowledgement of his merits as a good and faithful clergyman', but there is no evidence that she suggested this to Charlotte herself or that Charlotte agreed with the idea. This was not the purpose for which this type of state pension was designed; it was assumed that a young, vigorous and capable clergyman could make his own way in the world. Civil List pensions were intended to reward outstanding merit which had not been commercially successful, and to helping people of great talent to avoid the miseries of poverty in old age.

Charlotte had stated her own views on money and marriage in a letter to Ellen in 1846. Henry Nussey's marriage to a rich wife occasioned her remarks, and they are apposite. She said:

'There is a defect in your reasoning about the feelings a wife ought to experience in paying money for her husband. Who holds the purse will wish to be Master, Ellen; depend upon it whether man or woman – who provides the cash will now and then value himself (or herself) upon it – and even in the case of ordinary minds, reproach the less wealthy partner – besides no husband ought to be an object of charity to his wife – as no wife to her husband. Sisterly affection makes you partial and misleads your usually correct judgement – no dear Nell – it is doubtless pleasant to marry "well" as they say – but with all pleasures are mixed bitters – I do not wish for you a very rich husband – I should not like you to be regarded by any man even as "a sweet object of charity".'

Charlotte's thinking was modern. She was not taking the mid-Victorian view which Mrs Gaskell held, but instead wished both marriage partners to have an income of their own. Most women today will agree with her. To have to beg and plead for money is degrading. To be always the benefactor has bad results on the character of the benefactor him or herself. Applying this to

Charlotte and Nicholls, her income from investments was not as great as his could be from a decent post as curate, but she would have that vital independence. If he had a permanent post as secure and well paid as Mr Brontë's, Mr Brontë would probably have felt happy with the financial situation. That would not have solved all Charlotte's problems because there would then have been another parish to serve and the relief to her father would not be as great.

Mrs Gaskell, however excellently she pleaded the cause of women in her novels was, by her own statements, against their liberation and equality although she was for fair treatment. She was against their becoming members of the medical profession, in spite of her hero-worship of Florence Nightingale. She wrote to an unknown correspondent on the 31st October 1856:

'. . . I would not trust a mouse to a woman if a man's judgement was to be had. Women have no judgement. They've tact, and sensitiveness and genius, and hundreds of fine and lovely qualities, but are at best angelic geese as to matter requiring serious and long scientific consideration. I'm NOT a friend of Female Medical Education.'

According to her lights Mrs Gaskell thought that she was now doing a good deed and Monkton Milnes was ready to be guided by her. She said a pension of £100 a year to Nicholls was what was needed, making this suggestion at the end of October 1853. Nicholls was living near Pontefract; Milnes' father had been the MP for Pontefract and the family home was not far away. Milnes did not arrange a Civil List pension; at least, Nicholls' name does not appear in the lists of beneficiaries for the next few years. But Milnes may have obtained other financial support for him, and certainly they met and talked.

During the autumn Charlotte spent a week with Miss Wooler at Hornsea and some time with Ellen at Brookroyd, arriving home on the 7th October with a good many purchases, some of which she showed to her father and some she hid away to produce later. Up to this point the relationship between Charlotte and Ellen seems unchanged. Then Charlotte planned a visit to London, booking lodgings instead of staying with her publisher, but at the last minute – the 24th November 1853 – she changed her plans.

This abrupt change is mysterious. Later, in February 1854, she told Sydney Dobell that his previous letter to her had arrived while her father was very ill and she could not leave his bedside. Yet in March she was writing to Ellen: 'so far Papa has borne the winter surprisingly well on the whole'. What was it that had produced such a change between the 23rd November and the 6th December? On the 6th December 1853, Charlotte sent a curt note to Williams of Smith, Elder asking them not to select or send to her any more books. In view of the delight the books sent by Cornhill[3] had been to her, and the need she had of the interest, variety and excitement the parcels gave, this abrupt decision is very significant and deserves more discussion and consideration than it has received.

It is possible that this change, the abrupt turning away from literary

The poet Sydney Dobell, a correspondent of Charlotte's.

London and her accustomed interests, was a reaction to the news that George Smith was engaged to be married, which appears to have reached her at this time. She had urged this course of action upon him herself, describing the kind of woman who would suit him, but it might be that she subconsciously hoped that a marriage between author and publisher might yet come about. This could have been the case, in spite of her refusal when he proposed, the opposition of his mother, and the fact that neither George nor Mrs Smith had enjoyed becoming characters in one of her novels.

It seems to be at this point, during this mysterious but crucial fortnight, that she decided to marry Nicholls, although it was some months before the official engagement. She intended to continue writing and publishing, whether married or not. Did a possessive Nicholls express dislike of her being beholden to Smith, Elder by accepting loans of books? This seems likely, though indefensible. Or was it during this short space of time that Charlotte heard of some financial benefit he was to reap through Mrs Gaskell's interference?

It is at this point, after the 7th October 1853 and before the beginning of 1854, that her emotional movement away from Ellen becomes so clear. During an illness of Ellen's, Charlotte appeared indifferent and Ellen was distressed. There had been similar hiatuses before, and Charlotte may have learned to disregard what panic-stricken Ellen wrote when feeling ill. In those days when an apparently slight illness could suddenly take away one's life, fear could easily become irrational.

It seems that Ellen had written to Charlotte appalled at the trend of events towards a marriage between her friend and Arthur Bell Nicholls, and Charlotte had replied very tartly. In this crisis Ellen confided in Mary Hewitt (née Gorham) and it is from their correspondence that our knowledge of Ellen's feelings at this period comes; also from Mary Taylor, for at length a reply arrived from New Zealand:

'You talk wonderful nonsense about Charlotte Brontë in your letter. What do you mean about "bearing her position so long, and enduring to the end"? and still better, "bearing our lot, whatever it is." If it's Charlotte's lot to be married, shouldn't she bear that too? . . . It is an outrageous exaction to expect her to give up her choice in a matter so important, and I think her to blame in having been hitherto so yielding that her friends can think of making such an impudent demand . . .'[4]

Once again we have a reference to the old Moravian habit of the lot, and abiding by that declaration of the will of God. If Ellen had asked that Charlotte give up thoughts of marrying Nicholls, was this not exactly what Charlotte had asked of her when Ellen was being courted by Vincent, and Ellen had complied? Ellen must have thought bitterly of her own obedient rejection of her suitor. And had not Ellen been exhorted by Charlotte to go on bearing her own position, and enduring to the end? The situation between Charlotte and Ellen at this point has been compared to the ending of a marriage.[5] In some ways the comparison with divorce is a valid one.

Nicholls visited Charlotte at Haworth for ten days in January 1854. He was admitted to the parsonage and to Mr Brontë's grumpy presence and tolerated by him. Charlotte was now determined that her friendship with Ellen would continue. By March she was writing in quite the old way, full of concern because she heard that Richard Nussey's wife had had a stroke,[6] and she tried to invite Ellen and Nicholls to Haworth together around Easter time, but it was not possible to arrange this.

The April visit by Nicholls resulted in the couple becoming officially engaged, and Ellen must endure the situation as best she could. Charlotte felt very calm, and said she had many times wished that Ellen was with them, during the week Nicholls spent in Haworth. He had wished for no such thing. On the 11th April Charlotte was asking Ellen to be her bridesmaid and giving her a résumé of the progress of the courtship.

The breach between the two friends had caused concern among their circle, demonstrating the closeness of the bonding between them and the acknowledgement of this by other people. Miss Wooler seems to have interceded. Charlotte wrote to her also on the 11th April:

'Ellen and I are – I think – quite friends again – thanks, in a great measure to the kind mediating word which "turned away wrath", Blessed are the peace-makers!'

Reverend Arthur Bell Nicholls, circa 1854.

Mary Hewitt wrote: 'I congratulate you and Miss Brontë especially on the at length happy conclusion . . . I am so glad of your reconcilement'. Mrs Gaskell thanked Monkton Milnes for his exertions and for the 'kind words' he had given Nicholls, when in April she wrote to say that she had heard from Charlotte and that she was engaged. Milnes may then have talked again with Nicholls, as on the 17th May 1854 Charlotte was telling Mrs Gaskell in a letter of such an interview and that Mr Nicholls had been puzzled to arouse such interest.

By early June Mrs Gaskell was writing to Milnes thanking him 'most truly about Mr Nicholls', being sure that he would keep the secret of her own intervention, and playfully offering to get him a steam engine or a thousand yards of calico in return, if he should want such articles. Whatever Monkton Milnes had done it may have turned the scales; it could explain Mr Brontë's sudden change from intense opposition to acquiescence.

¹ Charles Thomas Longley, formerly headmaster of Harrow, Bishop of Ripon 1836–56. Then Bishop of Durham, Archbishop of York, and finally Archbishop of Canterbury

² Upjohn is a common Welsh name coming from Ap John, or son of John. Francis Upjohn was born about 1808 in London and was captain of a dragoon regiment before taking holy orders (Forbes Alexander Phillips *Gorleston and its Parish Church*, London 1894, p 51). Fellow of Queens, Cantab 1826, deacon 1830, BA 1833, priest 1831, curate of Gorleston, Suffolk 1841. Gorleston is now in Norfolk. In the same year, 1841, he became Vicar of Gorleston. Upjohn disappears from *Crockford* in 1875. It is believed that his wife's maiden name was Gorham. Unsuccessful efforts have been made to connect her with Mary Gorham's family.

³ Smith, Elder and Co's offices were at Cornhill, London. They later published a magazine called the *Cornhill* and were often referred to as 'Cornhill'.

⁴ Joan Stevens; *Mary Taylor, Friend of Charlotte Brontë; Letters from New Zealand and Elsewhere*.

⁵ By Rebecca Fraser in *Charlotte Brontë* (Methuen 1988).

⁶ After a long engagement the marriage had been a happy but childless one, although Charlotte thought the couple's treatment of Ellen cold and unsympathetic. Although she recovered on this occasion, Mrs Richard Nussey died long before her husband, who never remarried.

CHARLOTTE'S MARRIAGE AND DEATH, 1854-5

Ellen resigned herself to the marriage and invited Arthur Bell Nicholls to accompany Charlotte to Brookroyd on her visit in May 1854. Charlotte was grateful to her friend for bowing to the inevitable, and looked forward to her help in choosing wedding clothes in Leeds. Nicholls said he was on duty in his parish and could not accompany her. Mrs Gaskell also invited him and was refused. Charlotte's journey was to begin in Manchester, go on to Hunsworth to stay with Joe and Amelia Taylor, and end at Brookroyd with Ellen. Such a visit would have been good for Nicholls, it might have broadened his narrow outlook.

Charlotte's state of mind before her marriage is portrayed by Catherine Winkworth, a friend of Mrs Gaskell's:

'I began; "I was very glad to hear something Mrs Gaskell told me about you." "What was it?" "That you are not going to be alone any more." She leant her head on her hand and said very quickly, "Yes, I am going to be married in June." "It will be a great happiness for you to have someone to care for, and make happy." "Yes; and it is a great thing to be the first object with anyone." "And you must be very sure of that with Mr Nicholls; he has known you and wished for this so long, I hear." "Yes, he has more than once refused preferment since he left my father, because he knew he never could marry me unless he could return to Haworth; he knew I could not leave my father." She stopped, and then went on, "But Katie, it has cost me a good deal to come to this." "You will have to care for his things instead of his caring for yours, is that it?" "Yes, I can see that beforehand." "But you have been together so long already that you know what his things are, very well. He is very devoted to his duties, is he not? – and you can and would like to help him in those?" "I have always been used to those, and it is one great pleasure to me that he is so much beloved by all the parish; there is quite a rejoicing over his return. But those are not everything, and I cannot conceal from myself that he is *not* intellectual; there are many places into which he could not follow me intellectually." '[1]

Charlotte was still so unsure of the whole matter that she made a legal settlement excluding Nicholls from participation in the money she had earned; this was very sensible in view of the importance she placed on each partner having an income of their own.

Ellen's persistent cough worried even Charlotte, and as usual her mother and Mercy needed care, but she was able to organise Charlotte's wedding clothes and order the wedding cards. Meanwhile at Haworth, Charlotte was having the old storeroom, which once had only an outside entrance, altered, turned out, cleaned, and made into a study for her husband-to-be. A new doorway was made into the hall of the house, and a new chimney built so that Nicholls could have a fire. She had the room wallpapered and stitched the curtains for the windows herself. The storeroom became a very acceptable little workplace.

The wedding dress was white embroidered muslin, worn with a lace mantle and a white bonnet which was trimmed with green leaves. The going-away dress was shot-silk with narrow stripes in a colour which is now light brown, but at an angle shades to silver-grey. The bodice was decorated by fringed scalloping. All was both elegant and suitable.

Miss Wooler and Ellen travelled to Haworth together on the day before the wedding, which was at the earliest legal hour, eight o'clock in the morning, on the 29th June 1854. Mr Brontë was not well enough to give his daughter away, so Miss Wooler carried out the office. The ceremony was followed by a small wedding breakfast, to which Rev and Mrs Grant had been invited. Martha collected a basket of flowers from the village gardens and Ellen decorated the table for the celebration. Then the newly-married couple set out for Ireland, breaking their journey in Wales on the way. It speaks volumes for Charlotte and Ellen's relationship that Charlotte spent part of the evening of her wedding day writing to Ellen and suggesting that she replied quickly: 'If you get this scrawl tomorrow, and write by return, direct me at the Post Office, Bangor, and I may get it on Monday . . .' A change, though, is soon apparent. A few days later when they had reached Banagher, Charlotte was writing to Miss Wooler and asking her to share the letter with Ellen, but still with the insistence that Ellen write soon.

Charlotte had a cold on her wedding day which grew steadily worse, and the excitement and fatigue of constant change and travel over the next few days resulted in her being, in her own words, 'nearly knocked up' by the time they arrived at Banagher, where Nicholls had lived in his uncle's household. His aunt sick-nursed Charlotte and she soon felt better. The couple then went to Kilkee in County Clare, a little seaside place, and there her delight in the magnificent ocean and the grand coastline were extreme. Nicholls wrapped her in a rug and left her to enjoy the scene in her own way, showing sensitivity to her emotion.

An accident happened one day as they went on horseback with a guide through the Gap of Dunloe. It says much for the confidence marriage had given her that Charlotte was not only willing to ride on a large animal, but insisted on remaining on the mare when the guide suggested getting off as the pass was difficult. When the mare was unruly after the real danger was over, Nicholls went to hold the animal's head, and 'suddenly without any apparent cause – she seemed to go mad –'. Charlotte was thrown to the ground and was amongst the plunging hoofs without Nicholls realising what had happened. 'My husband did not see that I had fallen – he still held her –'. It seems miraculous that she was not hurt.

Mr Brontë was ailing in Charlotte's absence and after only a fortnight she was so anxious about him that she wanted to go home. After a month's more or less constant travel they did go back, rather earlier than they had intended. A tea and supper were arranged in the schoolroom for 500 Haworth people, to which Sunday and day scholars, church bell-ringers and singers were invited. Charlotte appeared for a short while, then went home to her father, leaving Nicholls doing the honours.

Ellen was invited for the 6th September: 'I want to see you again, dear Nell', but could not get away so soon because of a constant stream of visitors at Brookroyd. At last she went to Haworth on the 21st: 'We shall be very, very glad to see you, dear Nell, and I want the day to come'. The marriage had made Charlotte radiantly happy. The glow of physical joy and fulfilment surrounded her like a halo and pervaded her with a kind of 'holy calm' when Ellen first saw her after the marriage. Ellen was pleased to see this but feared that such perfect happiness could not last except in heaven.

Many years later Ellen spoke to Wemyss Reid of this visit. She found 'somewhat to her surprise, that [Charlotte] had also become the model clergyman's helpmeet, busying herself in the affairs of the parish in a way that she had never done before. Charlotte and her husband went for a walk on the moors with their guest. "Are you not going to write anything more?" asked Miss Nussey of Charlotte. "Oh," was the reply, "I have got a story in my head, but Arthur does not wish me to write it. He thinks I should attend to other things now." Then, according to her statement, Ellen Nussey waxed valiant on her friend's behalf, and contended with Nicholls against his idea that a clergyman's wife ought not to engage in literary work. "I married Charlotte Brontë, not Currer Bell," was the husband's rejoinder.'

Although Nicholls had always liked Ellen, he now showed a strong desire to have her 'well settled', in other words married and less close to his wife, whom he kept constantly busy, doing parish work, entertaining visitors, or walking with him. He did not like Amelia Taylor, and 'threatened to bolt' when she came, but when Amelia and Joe arrived for a short visit it did not pass off too badly. Charlotte in her turn did not like 'the Mrs Parsons'- she had little in common with other clergy wives – and decided not to go to the consecration of Heptonstall church, not wishing to be thrown into their company. 'If you were here I should go', she told Ellen in a letter.

It was this letter – written on the 20th October 1854 – which Nicholls read before it was posted, and disapproved of. 'He thinks I have written too freely about Amelia, etc . . . you must BURN it, when read . . . Arthur says such letters as mine ought never to be kept . . . "fire them," or "there will be no more," such is his resolve. I can't help laughing, this seems to me so funny. Arthur, however, says he is quite "serious" and looks it . . . I am now desired to "have done with it".' Here, although Charlotte laughed it off, was a very serious problem rearing its head, which would surely have led to conflicts between them had the marriage lasted longer than it did. Nicholls' voice seems to have held an unpleasant harsh note of command, as if Charlotte was indeed a chattel, a being inferior to himself. The problem continued. On the 31st October Nicholls was saying that unless Ellen promised to burn Charlotte's letters he would censor them. Charlotte was conciliatory and asked Ellen to write out the required promise on a separate slip of paper and enclose it in her next letter. Ellen gave the promise on condition that he did not censor the letters, but did not keep it because she averred that Nicholls *had* censored them.

Charlotte wanted to visit Brookroyd, but again and again events foiled her, often guests coming to stay. Even Sir James Kay-Shuttleworth came with a friend for a weekend in order to appraise Nicholls. Liking him, and liking the idea of having Charlotte settled near Gawthorpe Hall even more, he offered the living of Padiham in Lancashire, which was in his gift, but Nicholls had to refuse. He could not leave Haworth while Mr Brontë was alive. On the 14th November Charlotte was still hoping to get to Brookroyd 'before Christmas'. She could have gone the following week, but Amelia begged her to wait until she, Joe and Tim got back from a fortnight's holiday in Scarborough (Joe was ill and they were hoping the change would do him good), so that Charlotte could also visit them at Hunsworth. This unlucky and selfish request of Amelia's meant that Ellen never saw Charlotte alive again.

In retrospect it is sad that when she began to think herself pregnant, Charlotte turned for advice and support to Amelia in a way she never had before – Amelia who she had never truly liked, but who could discuss marriage and pregnancy. For the first time in her life Charlotte said critical things of Ellen, in response to ungrateful Amelia's complaints. Amelia must have been delighted – she had always wanted to be close to Charlotte and had never succeeded in being more than tolerated. Now she thought she was going to supersede Ellen with Charlotte, as she had superseded her with Joe – Ellen having introduced her to both. Amelia was ready to kick away the ladder by which she had climbed. Ellen's years of loving kindness to her, when Amelia needed a friend, were forgotten. The praise Amelia used to heap on Ellen when writing to Charlotte was now replaced by unpleasant sniping. Amelia comes out badly from any examination of her character. She was made of inferior stuff.

At least at the end Charlotte's old love of Ellen was to be as unclouded and strong as it had been for so many years.

It was on the 29th November 1854 that Nicholls and Charlotte went a long walk to see the waterfall swollen with melted snow. It began to rain and they became very wet. At the same time at Brookroyd a visitor had brought in an infection, Mercy was feverishly ill and there was the risk of it spreading to others in the house. Miss Wooler wrote to say that Mercy had typhus and Nicholls became very set against Charlotte risking a visit to Brookroyd. 'It pains me to disappoint Ellen and nearly as much to disappoint myself', wrote Charlotte. 'I still hope to go to Brookroyd soon after Christmas.'

'Arthur is sorry to disappoint both you and me', Charlotte wrote to Ellen in December, 'but it is his fixed wish that a few weeks should be allowed to elapse before we meet. Probably he is confirmed in his desire by my having a cold at present. I did not achieve the walk to the waterfall with impunity, though I changed my wet things immediately on returning home, yet I felt a chill afterwards, and the same night had sore throat and cold; however, I am better now, but not quite well.'

Ellen must have heard warning bells when reading this. How often had Charlotte exhorted her to take care, not to expose herself to cold, to wrap up well and keep dry, not to take risks of chills, to put a fur boa over her mouth in cold weather, to avoid night air! In letter after letter over the years the commands had come. She would also remember how Emily Brontë had gone to Branwell's funeral and caught a chill which had accelerated her fatal disease. Now Charlotte said she was 'not quite well', those ominous words, and that 'when Arthur is in, I must have occupations in which he can share, or which will not at least divert my attention from him; thus a multitude of little matters get put off till he goes out, and then I am quite busy'. This is a common problem of wives with husbands at home. In Charlotte's case, she was robbed of her hours of quiet and repose, and of the time she would normally have spent writing.

Joe Taylor was seriously ill, in fact dying. Charlotte had 'known Joe above twenty years and differed from him and been enraged with him and liked him and cared for him as long'. 'I hope to visit Brookroyd about the beginning of February', she wrote to Ellen's sister Ann. 'Give my love to Mercy. I hope she will be a very good girl'. Although Nicholls set his face so sternly against Charlotte going to Ellen at Brookroyd, he took her in the month of January to Gawthorpe Hall to stay with the Kay-Shuttleworths. He wanted to wean her from Ellen and he was as much a social snob as was Mr Brontë.

It does appear, throughout the marriage, that Nicholls never realised how extremely delicate Charlotte was. The exhilaration of marriage had masked this to a certain extent – she said she had never been so well as since their wedding – but he had known and observed her for eight years before that. In Hathersage, Ellen had noticed that Charlotte could not walk nearly as far as Mary Gorham could; she had frequent migraine headaches during her adult life and journeys exhausted her. Yet her husband, thoughtful though he intended to be, gave her a month of constant travel for a honeymoon, took her on long walks in bad weather, kept her on the go hour after hour, invited many visitors, and did not allow her the long periods of peaceful sedentary occupation which she had been used to for a lifetime.

Soon after the winter trail to Gawthorpe – Charlotte disliked the Kay-Shuttleworths and would certainly have refused to go if left to herself, but Nicholls insisted – she began to be ill with perpetual nausea and faintness. The doctor thought that it was pregnancy sickness. A cousin of Nicholls' arrived on a visit, and needed looking after. Tabby, who had cared for Charlotte for so long, became ill. Martha, young and willing but quite inexperienced as a sick-nurse, did her best. Nicholls did his best, but he too had no experience of nursing. 'I very much wish to come to Brookroyd', wrote Charlotte on the 19th January 1855.[2]

On the 23rd and 29th January and again on the 14th February, Arthur Bell Nicholls wrote notes to Ellen saying that Charlotte was too ill to write herself. She was 'completely prostrated with weakness and sickness and frequent fever'. On the 17th February Tabby died. On the 21st Charlotte managed to write to Ellen herself, saying how tender a nurse her husband was. She wrote again soon after, and at the same time to Amelia, saying plainly to her what she shielded Ellen from knowing, just how ill she really was. Joe Taylor was dying more slowly. A shock for Charlotte was hearing of the unexpected death of Ellen's brother-in-law (Mr Clapham, who everyone had liked so much) in the middle of March. Nicholls wrote to Ellen in sympathy on the 15th. On the 30th Mr Brontë himself wrote to Ellen, telling her that Charlotte was 'on the verge of the grave' – she died during that very night.

As soon as she received Mr Brontë's letter on the 31st Ellen set off for Haworth and reached the parsonage the same day, but she was too late to see Charlotte alive. Nicholls had already written to tell her of the death and his letter was in the post as she was on her journey. Charlotte had died on the Saturday and was to be buried on the Wednesday.

Ellen was kindly received by the bereaved father and husband, and they asked her to stay until after the funeral. Martha went out and gathered a basketful of evergreens and such flowers as were available and silently gave them to Ellen, indicating that she might like to use them to deck Charlotte's corpse as it lay in the coffin. The memory rushed over Ellen of the flowers Martha had gathered to deck out the table at the wedding-breakfast, and at first she felt that she could not do what she was asked. But she overcame the emotion and carried out this last office for her friend.

No doubt having a capable woman like Ellen in the house was a great help to Arthur Bell Nicholls and Mr Brontë at this time. Ellen had a good deal of experience of deaths and funerals and the work which they entail. The two men treated her with every consideration as one who had loved Charlotte faithfully for twenty-four years.

After the funeral Ellen went home, to her difficult aged mother who was nearly eighty, widowed invalid sister Ann who was fifty-eight, and ailing Mercy who was fifty-four. Nicholls and Mr Brontë were left alone in the parsonage with Martha to look after them. Amelia's husband Joe Taylor did not long survive his friend Charlotte, his clever little daughter Tim did not see her seventh birthday and Amelia herself is said to have died in 1860.[3] Life was indeed black for this group of people whose hopes had been so bright not long before. 1855, it transpired, had been a year for dying.

[1] This quotation from the Shakespeare Head edition of *The Brontës; their Lives, Friendships and Correspondence* letter 896.

[2] Edward Bickell, who knew Charlotte, left Haworth in 1855 to become a school master in Winteringham, Lincolnshire. He had a signed photograph of Charlotte, which she is said to have given him as a leaving present. He became sub-postmaster instead of schoolmaster in Winteringham, where he remained for fifty-eight years, retiring in 1917 and dying aged ninety-two on 17th January 1925.

[3] Joseph Taylor 1816-57, described as Martin Yorke in *Shirley*, married Amelia Ringrose in 1850. Their child Emily Martha (Tim) lived from 1851-8 and died of dysentery. Joe died of a liver complaint. Mrs Gaskell relates a story Charlotte told her which might refer to Joe and his daughter, in letter 192 of *The Letters of Mrs Gaskell* ed J A V Chapple and Arthur Pollard (Manchester University Press 1966).

MRS GASKELL'S BIOGRAPHY, 1855-6

Charlotte died on the 31st March 1855, and on the 4th April Mrs Gaskell received a letter telling her the news. It was from John Greenwood, the Haworth stationer, whom she had met when she visited Charlotte. Mrs Gaskell was shocked. She wrote in reply: '. . . My dear dear friend that I shall never see again on earth! I did not even know she was ill . . . You may well say you have lost your best friend; strangers might know her by her great fame, but we loved her dearly for her goodness, truth, and kindness, and those lovely qualities she carried with her where she is gone. I want to know EVERY particular. Has she been long ill? What was her illness? You would oblige me EXTREMELY if you would, at your earliest leisure, send me every detail . . .'

She had not heard from Charlotte since October of the previous year when, worried that the friendship would be ended by Charlotte's religious bigot of a husband, Mrs Gaskell had written carefully explaining the Unitarian religious position she held. Now, nervous of writing to him, she wrote her letter of condolence only to Mr Brontë.

John Greenwood complied at once with Mrs Gaskell's request for more information, and expressed his own prejudices. In reply she wrote in a friendly, even fulsome letter on the 12th April:

'I shall be very much obliged to you, dear Sir, if from time to time you will let me know how Mr Brontë and Mr Nicholls go on and are in health; and I shall also always take a great interest in all your own personal concerns . . . I almost think I shall try and come over for a day to Haworth this summer, and see Mr Brontë . . . I need hardly say how completely confidential I consider your most interesting letter. ANYTHING else you can ever remember to tell me about her will be most valuable.'

Greenwood was pleased and flattered. He wrote a number of times, and Mrs Gaskell replied at length. For example, on the 5th May:

'EVERY[thing] you can tell me about her and her sisters – of HER especially is most valuable. I wish they would allow her portrait to be daguerreotyped for her friends. But I am sure it is too soon to name or propose it to them as yet. Was there a new study built at Haworth Parsonage last summer? One of the newspapers says there was. When did YOU first know of CURRER BELL?'[1]

Matthew Arnold, who had met Charlotte only once and briefly, now published his poem, *Haworth Churchyard*. It seemed all her acquaintances were publishing homage to Charlotte.

It was obvious where the correspondence was leading, even more so when Mrs Gaskell wrote to George Smith on 31st May: 'Sometime, it may be years hence – but if I live long enough, and no one is living whom such a publication would hurt, I will publish what I know of her . . .' In writing thus to Charlotte Brontë's publisher, there can be little doubt that Mrs Gaskell was hoping he would ask her to write a memoir. As an enticement, in June she sent him one of John Greenwood's letters to see.

'. . . I determined that in our country-leisure this summer I would put down every thing I remembered about this dear friend and noble woman, before its vividness had faded from my mind; but I KNOW that Mr Brontë, and I FEAR that Mr Nicholls, would not like this made public . . . Still my children, who all loved her would like to have what I could write about her; and the time may come when her wild sad life, and the beautiful character that grew out of it may be made public. I thought that I would simply write down my own personal recollections of her, from the time we first met at Sir J K Shuttleworth's . . . here and there copying out characteristic extracts from her letters . . . [describing] the wild bleakness of Haworth.'[2]

In this same month of June, Sharpe's *London Magazine of Entertainment and Instruction* published the anonymous article 'A few words about *Jane Eyre*'. Ellen was distressed by this article, which is written in an unpleasantly half-joking tone unsuitable for an obituary notice. It quotes a description of Charlotte's appearance, from one of Mrs Gaskell's letters to her friend Catherine Winkworth, which reads like a caricature. Apart from this quotation, which is indubitably Mrs Gaskell's, the article is not in her style of writing. The writer of the article has not been identified. It contains a number of inaccuracies: for example, it says that Patrick Brontë never taught his children anything; that Maria Branwell's family refused to have anything to do with her after her marriage; that Charlotte asked her father's permission to go to Cowan Bridge school; that Adele in *Villette* is drawn from life (but Adele is in *Jane Eyre*); that the parsonage 'until a few months since' had not a touch of paint or any new furniture for thirty years.

Mr Sharps regards this as an ironic beginning to the famous biography.[3] It is indeed ironic that it should be this article which provoked Ellen into suggesting Mrs Gaskell as Charlotte Brontë's biographer, when part of it consists of Mrs Gaskell's own, if out-of-date, words. On the 6th June Ellen wrote from Brookroyd to Nicholls:

'Dear Mr Nicholls, I have been much hurt and pained by the perusal of an article in Sharpe (for this month) entitled 'A few words about Jane Eyre'. You will be certain to see the article and I am sure both you and Mr Brontë will feel acutely the misrepresentations and the malignant spirit which characterises them. Shall you suffer the article to pass current without any refutation? The writer merits the severest contempt (even that of silence) but there will be readers and ignorant believers, shall such be left to imbibe a tissue of malign falsehoods or shall an attempt be made to do justice to one who so highly deserved justice (whose very NAME we speak, those who had known

Reverend Patrick Brontë.

her, but with reverence and affection) and shall not her aged father be defended from the reproach the writer coarsely attempts to fix upon him . . . I wish Mrs Gaskell who is every way capable would undertake a reply and give moral castigation to the writer. Her personal acquaintance with Haworth, the Parsonage and its inmates, fits her for the task and if on other subjects she lacks information I would gladly supply her with facts sufficient to set aside much that is asserted . . . Will you ask Mrs Gaskell to undertake this just and honourable defence . . . I hope you and Mr Brontë are well – My kind regards to both – Believe me, yours sincerely, E. Nussey.'

Nicholls replied saying that he thought the article harmless and that Mr Brontë had been very amused by the remarks about him. Mr Brontë, when further erroneous notices appeared, reconsidered the matter, decided to follow Ellen's suggestion, and wrote to Mrs Gaskell asking her to produce an official biography. On the 18th June Mrs Gaskell told George Smith of this request, and that she had agreed: 'Of course it becomes a more serious task than the one which, as you know, I was proposing to myself, to put down my personal recollections etc . . .'

Smith naturally wished to publish the biography, so Mrs Gaskell began her research. Unfortunately she had, from first hearing of Charlotte's identity, begun to jump to exaggerated conclusions and to form vivid but erroneous impressions. Once formed, nothing could efface them. She was a very good writer and a charming woman who had known Charlotte. But as Charlotte's biographer, it is unfortunate that although they were together for at least seventeen days, she never saw Charlotte well and happy. They did not meet until Emily, Anne and Branwell were dead, leaving Charlotte lonely and depressed. For the first three days of the friendship, in the Lake District, Charlotte felt ill throughout and had a severe headache on one day. In Plymouth Grove for a few days in 1851, Charlotte was nervous in the extreme – partly, it has been suggested here, through drinking green tea. In Plymouth Grove again, in 1853, for seven days she said that she could not sleep, was restless and had dreadful dreams, which may have been the green tea once more. When Mrs Gaskell visited Haworth in 1854 for four days, she stayed with an embattled pair, locked in the dispute over Nicholls. As far as we know it is the only occasion apart from his reported tempers during his wife's lifetime that Mr Brontë was seriously at odds with his family; normally they were happy together. So Mrs Gaskell had a distorted picture of her subject and envisaged the Brontës' lives as miserable and gloomy, when among themselves they had normally been deeply happy, even joyful.

After Mrs Gaskell had visited Haworth, Nicholls asked Ellen to let them have any letters from Charlotte that she still had, for loan to Mrs Gaskell, not for publication. He did not want a biography himself, but did not think it right to oppose Mr Brontë.[4] On the same day Mrs Gaskell wrote direct to Ellen, asking for her help and saying she wished to meet her and Miss Wooler. Nicholls had already shown her '. . . about a dozen letters addressed principally to her sister Emily; one or two to her father and her brother; and one to her aunt. The dates extend from 1839 to 1843. But Nicholls said that he thought that you were the person of all others to apply to; that you had been a friend of his wife's ever since she was 15; and that he would write to you today, to ask if you would allow me to see as much of her correspondence with you as you might feel inclined to trust me with.'

Here we have the beginnings of the occupation and the trouble which was to be one of the chief factors in Ellen's life over the next forty-two years. The request reached her while she was staying at Ilkley on holiday with Miss Wooler, who did not want to meet Mrs Gaskell or to be involved. It should be noticed that while Nicholls had asked Ellen to send Charlotte's letters to Haworth, so that he and Mr Brontë could select some to show to Mrs Gaskell, Mrs Gaskell's request was for Ellen to let her – Mrs Gaskell – see the letters. This direct method was the one Ellen chose, no doubt thinking, because of Nicholls' previous desire to have the letters burned, that if once her precious letters went to Haworth she would never see them again.

Mrs Gaskell had not seen John Greenwood when she was in Haworth, and now that she had official access to the parsonage, to Ellen, and to all Charlotte's other friends, she hardly needed him. 'It was a most painful visit. Both Mr Brontë and Nicholls cried sadly. I like Nicholls', she wrote to her daughter.

Bereaved Ellen, eager to help, suggested that it would be better to talk about Charlotte while walking on the moors in the free open air than in a room. Mrs Gaskell visited on the 14th August, travelling by 'the train that leaves Manchester at 8.50 and arrives at Birstal[5] at 10.55 . . . I should leave at 4.5 that afternoon . . .' They quite liked one another. Ellen lent Mrs Gaskell some of Charlotte's letters to take home to read, and sent others on later. 'I like the one you sent today much. I shall be glad to see any others you will allow me to see.' In all, Mrs Gaskell told George Smith, she borrowed 350 letters from Ellen.

No control over Mrs Gaskell's researches was now being exercised by Charlotte's father or husband, although Nicholls had wished to have such control. The subject was being pursued in all directions, to Brussels and the Hegers and everyone else Mrs Gaskell could think of. To an unknown correspondent she made this request: '. . .I want to know all I can respecting the character of the population she lived amongst . . . are there any local publications giving an idea of the peculiar (customs etc) character of the population towards Keighley, Howarth, etc . . .'

When she met the Rev Dr William Scoresby[6], who had been Vicar of Bradford for some years and knew Mr Brontë well in those days, 'he told me many curious anecdotes about the extraordinary character of the people round Haworth'. There was nothing Mrs Gaskell loved as much as curious anecdotes about extraordinary characters.

On her second visit to Ellen in early October, Mrs Gaskell was able to meet Miss Wooler and visit Oakwell Hall. Ellen was delighted with the course events were taking, and that she was recognised as having the best information on her beloved friend. 'Does Mr S[mith] know that you are in a better position for the work you have undertaken than any other person ever can be, that you already have the longest history and the best authenticated?', she wrote to Mrs Gaskell. She sympathised over George Smith's slowness to lend *his* letters, realising there were things which might be causing him unease:

'It is possible Mr S may be looking over the letters before sending them or perhaps he dislikes the aspect of himself therein. I dare say there is a tolerable portrait given in some of [the] letters of him to whom they were addressed.'

Ellen's emotional state, so soon after the sudden and unexpected bereavement, was still very unsettled. She was much inclined to play down all Charlotte's relationships except that with herself – the tendency to possessiveness shown by so many human beings towards their loved ones. It hurt Ellen that Charlotte's writings had caused the assertion that the author was unladylike and, like Mrs Gaskell, she was anxious that a portrait of Charlotte be included in the biography, saying, 'It has been a surprise to every stranger . . . that she was so gentle and lady like to look upon'. She was in awe of Mrs Gaskell, this great authoress, who at the same time was a busy wife and mother. 'What a clever person you are to get through so much labour and so varied as it must be, perhaps though the variety enables you to sustain it all.' Her own concerns seemed trifling in comparison, though important to her; she was rushing to dress a doll as a parting gift for a child.

George Smith did lend Mrs Gaskell his letters from Charlotte, as did Miss Wooler, and in December so also did Williams of Smith, Elder. Of all the letters, Mrs Gaskell preferred those to Miss Wooler and to Williams, the two series which were the most formal, showing least of the real natural woman. On the 20th December she wrote to Ellen: 'Miss Brontë's letters to Mr Williams ARE very fine and genial. She seems heartily at her ease with him; which I don't think she does in those I have seen to Mr Smith.' Ellen intended to call at Manchester on her way to see her family in the south, thinking that some of the memoir would be ready, and that she would be able to read it; but it was not even begun.

The year ended with an exchange of letters between Ellen and Nicholls. Neither she nor Mrs Gaskell had heard from him for months. On the 22nd December Ellen wrote, stiffly, for she resented him bitterly, probably blamed him for Charlotte's death, and could not be at ease with him:

'It cannot but be a source of satisfaction to me to hear from time to time of those who were the nearest and dearest of my oldest and most valued friend. Your protracted silence seems to indicate something amiss and how or in what way I cannot imagine . . . She [Mrs Gaskell] has not made the progress in her precious work which she promised herself at the commencement and I can well imagine that the delay is very trying to Mr Brontë but I believe in the end the result will be the more satisfactory. Mrs G is taking infinite pains to do her work perfectly which is essential to her own reputation and due to the valued subject. There are very important reasons why Mrs Gaskell's work should be as perfect a biography as it is possible to make it and every facility should be given to Mrs Gaskell for the purpose – Her judgement and taste may be fully relied upon and I feel sure the day will come when you will be thankful that her able pen undertook the task of telling the truth and vindicating the memory of the dead. Do you think Mr Brontë would allow Mrs Gaskell to peruse the packet of letters addressed to himself by Mrs Brontë before their marriage he once gave them to Charlotte in my presence and we read them together they made a most pleasing and lasting impression on both our minds the tone of them was so good so pure and so refined . . . Mrs Gaskell told me if she had not undertaken to write a life there were those who would . . . My relations unite with me in kind regards to yourself and Mr Brontë.'[7]

Ellen mentioned Charlotte's mother's letters in her *Reminiscences*: 'After Charlotte became the solitary survivor of brother and sisters, one day Mr Brontë placed a packet of letters yellowed with age, in the hands of Charlotte as she was standing by the sitting room fire along with her friend, saying, "These are your mother's letters, perhaps you and Miss [Nussey] will be interested in reading them." [As Charlotte told Ellen of her mother's letters in a letter of her own, perhaps she had asked her father to produce them again when Ellen was staying with them.] Interested indeed they were; the readers experienced a heartache of sympathy with the writer. Her gentleness and lovingness, her purity and refinement, her goodness and modesty, all shone forth forcibly, they could not help thinking and feeling how hard her lot had been, torn from her children ere she could reap for herself any of that sweetness and goodness which they had derived from her, and long ere she could have the gratifications and joys her mother's heart would feel in the unusual talent and gifts of her children. Her intelligence and cultivation were such, there can be no doubt that the Brontë family were, as is usually the case, eminently indebted to their mother for their manifold excellencies if not for their talents likewise. Miss Branwell's letters shewed that her engagement though not a prolonged one, was not as happy as it ought to have been – there was a pathos of apprehension (though gently expressed) in part of the correspondence, lest Mr Brontë should cool in his affections towards her, and the readers perceived with some indignation, that there had been some just cause given for this apprehension.

Mr Brontë, with all his iron strengths and power of will, had his weaknesses, and one which, wherever it exists, spoils and debases the character – he had personal vanity. Miss Branwell's finer nature rose above such weakness, but she suffered all the more from evidences of it in one to whom she had given her affections, and whom she was longing to look up to in all things.

Charlotte was sometimes stirred into avenging her mother, for when her father boasted, as he did occasionally, of the conquests made in his earlier days, she put his self-complacency down with a strong emphasis of disapproval.

This fragile delicate little woman [Mrs Brontë] found time in the midst of her young family and busy household to write poetry and small articles for a Cottage Magazine which her husband was interested and also a contributor.

Mrs Brontë had the inestimable blessing of a well-balanced mind, yet she was imbued with a degree of superstition, and Charlotte inherited its influence, presentiments made deep impressions upon her, she gave the rein to herself in this respect when she wrote *Jane Eyre*: its escape seemed to have done her good, as if she had braced herself up for ever after.'

Nicholls replied politely on the 24th, reporting that they were both well, although Mr Brontë had a cough. They had heard nothing from Mrs Gaskell, but felt sure that she would do justice to Charlotte. Nicholls thought the biography would be a difficult task. About Miss Martineau he remarked on the high opinion she held of Charlotte's abilities. His tone was more easy and friendly than Ellen's was; but he had not been supplanted, as she had, and he was a busy, if sorrowing, man with the added responsibility of ageing Mr Brontë.

Ellen, on the other hand, had been harbouring a grievance for some time, and although she had the care of her mother, and was working for the church and helping friends and neighbours as she always did, her mind was free to dwell on her past and present pain.

Mrs Gaskell would have written a memoir without Ellen's intervention. She wanted to do so from first hearing of her friend's death. Had she carried out her original intention, it is doubtful whether she would have become the official biographer. It would have been seen that she let her novelist's imagination run away with her, and accepted distorted accounts as true, painting a melodramatic picture instead of 'something real, cool, and solid . . . something unromantic as Monday morning'.[8] As it was, with her powerful storytelling ability, she was to create a myth, and to write one of the most influential biographies in the language.

At the beginning of 1856, Mrs Gaskell told Ellen that the form of the biography was now quite clear in her head. By the 22nd February only about twenty pages had been written, but the American rights were under negotiation and had been sold by mid-March.

Mrs Gaskell's daughters always took up a great deal of her time and thoughts, and between their concerns and the biography she was very rushed. She made visits to as many as possible of the places Charlotte had known. Mr Nicholls was refusing to have Charlotte's portrait copied, or to lend the manuscript of *The Professor* and other papers.

Mrs Gaskell in July brought Ellen up to date with her adventures:

'. . . Brussels, where Mme Heger, understanding that I was a friend of Miss Brontë's, refused to see me; but I made M Heger's acquaintance, and very much indeed I both like and respect him. Mr and Mrs Smith, Junr, and Mrs Smith Snr, (EXACTLY like Mrs Bretton) Mr Smith said (half suspiciously, having an eye to Dr John, I FANCIED) "Do you know, I sometimes think Miss Brontë had my mother in her mind when she wrote Mrs Bretton in VILLETTE?" As I had not then seen Mrs Smith I could only answer, "Do you?" a very safe reply . . . I still want one or two things to complete my materials, and I am very doubtful if I can get them – at any rate, I think they will necessitate my going to Haworth again, and I am literally AFRAID of that. I will tell you the things I should LIKE to have, and shall be glad if, knowing the parties, you could give me advice. First of all, I promised M Heger to ask to see his letters to her; he is sure she would keep them, as they contained advice about her character, studies, mode of life. I doubt much if Mr Nicholls has not destroyed them . . . Mr Smith says that her letters to her father from London, giving an account of places and persons she saw, were long, constant, and minute . . . Now for questions I should be much obliged to you if you would answer – I am afraid to say by return of post, but I should LIKE that . . . I thought that I carefully preserved the reader's respect for Mr Brontë, while truth and the desire of doing justice to her compelled me to state the domestic peculiarities of her childhood, which . . . contributed so much to make her what she was . . . May I call you simply "Ellen" in the book? . . .'9

Ellen, shrinking from prominence, did not wish her name to appear. In this she was concurring with the mores of her time which held that ladies avoided publicity; the strength of this taboo can be seen in Emily Brontë's attitude over her writing, though Emily was, in any case, a very private person.10

When Sir James Kay-Shuttleworth went with Mrs Gaskell to Haworth he was able to overbear both Mr Brontë and Mr Nicholls, who were in awe of him, and carry off the manuscript of 'The Professor, Emma, and a packet of the tiny books'. These tiny books, the juvenilia which now arouse so much interest, were described by Mrs Gaskell as 'the wildest and most incoherent things . . . all purporting to be written, or addressed to some member of the Wellesley family. They give one the idea of creative power carried to the verge of insanity . . .'

Sir James arranged for the photographing of the Richmond portrait. 'Mr Nicholls . . . and Mr Brontë declared that all her letters were destroyed.' With hindsight we know that this was untrue. A year or two later Mr Brontë is described as sitting in bed cutting up Charlotte's letters to send the pieces to people who asked for samples of her handwriting.11

Of Mrs Gaskell's admiration of Charlotte as a writer there is no doubt. She told George Smith: '. . . as to its genius [The Professor] she hardly writes 2 lines on the commonest subject, in the most hasty manner, but what there is a felicity of expression, or a deep insight into the very heart of things quite separate and apart from anybody else.' But she thought The Professor inferior to all the published works, and that parts needed deleting, '. . . disfigured by more coarseness – and profanity in quoting texts of Scripture disagreeably than in any of her other works . . .'

This is a very interesting remark of Mrs Gaskell's about profanity, because in our own day it would not apply. Charlotte was so saturated with knowledge of the Bible that Biblical references and assonances abound in her writing. Ellen regarded this as evidence of Charlotte's faith. Mrs Gaskell's emphasis is perhaps on the word 'disagreeably', but to modern eyes this is no more apparent than it was to Ellen or to Nicholls.

Coarseness was a bogy in this period; Ellen had accused the anonymous author of the Sharpe's article of it; Charlotte, Emily and Anne had been constantly beaten by this stick. Said of men it was a shaming indictment, of women even more shaming. The times were struggling to rise above the brutal basic truths of life. Polite behaviour and achieving a pleasant surface were of great importance, a shield against a world which held slums, starvation, twelve-hour days and families of over twenty children without social security or health care.

In August 1856, Mrs Gaskell was telling George Smith that she thought she was halfway through the biography:

'. . . the remainder will consist so very much of letters, involving merely copying, that I do not fancy it will take me very long. I do not wish the letters to assume a prominent form in the title or printing; as Mr Nicholls has a strong objection to letters being printed at all; and wished to have all her letters (to Miss Nussey and every one else) burned. Now I am very careful what extracts I make; but still her language, where it can be used, is so powerful and living, that it would be a shame not to express everything that can be, in her own words. And yet I don't want to alarm Mr Nicholls' prejudices . . .'

By September Mrs Gaskell was looking forward to finishing the book by February 1857. Nicholls' prejudices about the publication of any letters, and most particularly his wife's, were a matter of deep concern to Mrs Gaskell, as they were later to prove a nightmare to Ellen. She appealed for George Smith's help:

'Remember correspondent's permission to publish goes for nothing; the legal power over an deceased person's papers lies with the executors; . . . and thus Mr Nicholls MAY, if he likes turn sharp round on you, and not merely protest, but PROHIBIT. Now I did NOT know all this, and Mr Nicholls is a terribly tickle person to have to do with; . . . I foresaw some difficulties certainly, as Miss Nussey evidently expects to see the extracts I have made from Miss B's correspondence with her – interwoven as those extracts were into the Life – while Mr Brontë and Mr Nicholls write to desire I will let NO ONE but Mr Gaskell see the MS before it is given up into your hands . . .'[12]

Smith sent Nicholls a business form of application, which produced a more generous permission than Mrs Gaskell had dared to hope, and more generous than Nicholls had meant to grant. Another problem was under discussion in December:

'There is some little jealousy (the nearest word, but not the right one) of Miss Nussey on Mr Brontë's part, and he especially forbids my showing the MS of my biography to her. Now she is about the only person who would care to see it in MS, because she wants to know what extracts I have taken from all her letters; and she has a right to know this, if she wishes. So, after some consideration, I find I must READ it to her – all where her letters are quoted from at any rate; and today I have written to ask her to come here, and be read to about January 10th. I hope you will have it by about the end of January . . .'

It seems strange that Mr Brontë now had this attitude to Ellen, who had always been a favourite of his. Probably he was influenced by Nicholls' attitude. As Mrs Gaskell was asking Ellen questions about the Brontë family which she did not dare to put to him, he may have sensed this and felt justifiably resentful.

By the end of December Mrs Gaskell was sending the first hundred pages of the biography to George Smith so that he could begin the printing, and she had asked Ellen to visit Manchester to have the part containing extracts from

Charlotte's letters read aloud to her. The plan was that, after Ellen's approval, the remainder of the manuscript should go at once to Smith, Elder by the end of January. Mrs Gaskell always ran away if she could when a book of hers came out; she found the time of publication very trying, so she planned to be on holiday in February. She was anxious to know how much money she would make out of the book and the position about copyright, pointing out that she had received £600 for *North and South* and had retained the copyright; the result of this was that Smith increased his offer for the biography to £800. She received in addition £75 from the American rights, and more from translation rights; the circulation on the continent of the English version brought her £50. She thought of sending £100 to Mr Nicholls to provide a village pump for Haworth.

Of Ellen's visit, she said 'I don't mind if she does not come'; but to Ellen 'I shall be delighted to see you', and to George Smith that Miss Nussey 'comes here to be read to' on the 12th January. When Smith received the first hundred pages he foreshadowed the whole future of the biography by at once asking for changes. She had indicated Mrs Robinson too clearly as the cause of Branwell's misfortunes, and he wanted the passage dealing with his acceptance of *Jane Eyre* deleting, and also personal passages referring to himself and to Williams.

[1] Letters 232, 233 and 238 in *The Letters of Mrs Gaskell* ed J A V Chapple and A Pollard (Manchester University Press 1966).

[2] *The Letters of Mrs Gaskell* 239, 242 and, below, 245, 257, 259, 275a. Ibid.

[3] *Mrs Gaskell's Observation and Invention*, J G Sharps (Linden Press 1970).

[4] The Rev A B Nicholls' letters to Ellen Nussey are in the Brotherton Collection, the Brotherton Library, Leeds University.

[5] Birstall has been spelt both with and without the second l. When the modern postal services were introduced they used the spelling Birstal for their cancellation stamps, but it tended to be confused with Bristol. After some years the Post Office reverted to the historic spelling with two ls, which then became standard.

[6] The Rev Dr William Scoresby, 1789-1857, wrote a biography of his father, Captain William Scoresby, the famous Whitby Arctic navigator. A copy of this letter belongs to Mr J G Sharps quoted on p 387 of his book (*note 3*). Another copy was used by Chapple and Pollard (*note 1*) letter 267a.

[7] Ellen's letters to Nicholls, Cadman Collection, Brontë Parsonage Museum.

[8] Charlotte Brontë, the first page of *Shirley*.

[9] Gaskell Letters (*note 1*), 294 and later in this chapter, 297, 299, 303, 318, 322.

[10] This attitude was shown earlier by the Austens. Jane Austen's books were published anonymously, and after her death her sister Cassandra destroyed any of Jane's letters which, she thought, might interest the public or posterity.

[11] The albums into which these pieces of Charlotte's letters were pasted have no doubt been thrown away long ago. If any survive, Brontë scholars would be grateful for a sight of them.

[12] Original letter in the possession of Mr J G Sharps.

THE PUBLICATION OF THE BIOGRAPHY, AND 1857-65

Ellen had, as far as we can tell, a quietly domestic year during 1856.

The year 1857 began with her visit to Manchester, 'to be read to' as Mrs Gaskell put it. The first section of the biography which described the Yorkshire background, and was to cause such indignation amongst Yorkshire readers, was already at the printers and Ellen saw nothing of that, although Mrs Gaskell seems to have read sections to her during a previous meeting. Although Mrs Gaskell had promised Mr Brontë that Ellen would not see the manuscript, she was ill in bed for part of Ellen's visit and according to Catherine Winkworth 'Miss Nussey was there all last week reading through the "Life", and says it is excessively interesting, and seems to approve it altogether'.[1] Ellen was reading almost entirely excerpts from Charlotte's letters to herself, and she was under a good deal of constraint – scanning hastily, a guest in a strange household with her hostess ill in bed, and shown only parts of the whole.

Miss Winkworth went on to describe Ellen:

'I . . . wished much I could have seen more of her. She must have been very pretty once, not a sparkling beauty at all, but a quiet one, tolerably regular features, large eyes, soft complexion, and thick wavy brown hair.'

'Dear good little lady', Mrs Gaskell called her.[2] To Mrs Gaskell Ellen said 'how completely the life at the Parsonage appeared to her reproduced. Much of this was owing to the remarkable extracts from letters; but she said several times how exactly and acurately I had written about the life and characters.'[3] The biography was finished on the 7th February and with the £250 advance Mrs Gaskell and her daughters set out for Rome, leaving instructions that those who had helped her by lending their letters from Charlotte should be thanked by being sent a copy of *The Life of Charlotte Brontë*. By the time Ellen received her copy in April her mother was very ill. The holidaymakers did not return until the very end of May.

Mrs Gaskell received great initial acclaim. Lewes wrote warmly. He saw that much of the *Life* consisted of Charlotte's own words: 'The early part is a triumph for you; the rest a monument for your friend', and of Mrs Gaskell's own part, 'it also, thanks to its artistic power, makes us familiar inmates of an interior so strange, so original . . . so picturesque . . . that fiction has nothing more wild touching and heart-strengthening to place above it.'[4]

The 'wasp's nest', which Mary Taylor had predicted would be pulled about Mrs Gaskell's ears if she wrote about living people, then descended in the shape of numerous accusations that what was presented as fact was fiction, and usually libellous fiction. For example, a young woman from Haworth was described as having been seduced, and Mrs Robinson was implicated in Branwell's downfall. Mrs Gaskell had to retract; the revised third edition omitted long passages, had minor amendments, and new parts were added. At home again in June she wrote, 'I hate the whole affair, and everything connected with it'.[5]

The large exhibition in Manchester, opened by the queen, inundated her with guests, including Ellen, who presumably wanted to talk the book over as well as seeing the exhibition. She and Miss Wooler had amendments which they desired Mrs Gaskell to make to any new edition of the Life, and in July Meta wrote asking Ellen to put these into a formal note which could be passed to the publishers. In addition to the fatigue of constant guests to see the exhibition, Mrs Gaskell was much occupied by her daughter's intended wedding. During this busy year the famous authoress also stayed at Chatsworth, and with various other aristocratic families.

Although she repeatedly said that she would never write another biography, Mrs Gaskell was already considering writing another by August, when Smith, Elder suggested that she write about Sir George Saville, who had been the friend of Priestley, and of the Nussey/Walker relative David Hartley and his brother Winchcombe.[6] She was interested and made enquiries, but decided not to proceed when she found that the theme would be mainly political. George Smith, not daunted by the criticisms of the biography of Charlotte (which was selling well), did some research for her, and was told, '. . . for the life of a great Yorkshire Squire of the last century, I think I could have done pretty well; but I cannot manage politics'.[7]

Nicholls at Haworth was very distressed by the biography, so much so that Mrs Gaskell told him that any further letters on the subject would be referred to her solicitor. She came to the conclusion that he had kept letters which he had said were burnt.[8] He had seen, more clearly than anyone, the kind of detail and revelations which the public would want and with which they had now been supplied. He had to bear the brunt of the whispers behind the hands of his congregation and neighbours, and the reactions of Mr Brontë.

Throughout 1857, Ellen's mother was increasingly frail, but events in the lives of relatives and neighbours would interest her. Her son John's family moved permanently to the Ivy House in Chislehurst, Kent, keeping 4 Cleveland Row in London only as a surgery and a place where John lived during the week.

Ellen's correspondence with Mary Taylor, still in New Zealand, was a slow process taking months, but on request Ellen sent her such things as clothes and dressmaking patterns, taking a good deal of trouble over their selection. Both friends had followed with fascination the progress of Joe Taylor's marriage; now it had ended with his death. Ellen felt this as a deep personal blow, for Joe had been a part of her daily life for as long as she could remember.

The impact of the furore around the biography was dulled for Ellen by her day-to-day task of caring for her dying mother. In spite of short breaks away from home, it was customary for her to be the main person at her mother's service. On the 2nd December 1857, Ellen (*née* Wade), widow of John Nussey and mother of twelve children of whom Ellen was the youngest, died aged eighty-six. She was buried in the family tomb in Birstall churchyard.

In her grief Ellen's religion was her solace. Years later, in a letter of condolence to her friend Lady Morrison, she wrote: 'You will have the comfort and trust of thinking of your dear husband as now in God's light seeing the light of Life which is eternal and knows no dimness. This was my abiding solace when I lost my dear Mother.' She also wrote, 'I know my devotion to my aged mother was always a delight though it cost much personally as to advancement in life – but then what is life but a schooling for a *higher* and more blessed existence hereafter – it will not matter when that time arrives whether we have been among the great ones of the earth.'[9]

At the end of December Mrs Gaskell wrote her a long and helpful letter. It seems that Ellen had confided some of the troubles of the end of her mother's life, including her own feelings of not being loved or appreciated. 'I feel sure that love for them [her children] lives as long as the mother lives, whatever failures of nature and mind come on in extreme old age. And oh! dear Miss Nussey faithful love is, I do think, the greatest of earthly goods! Besides you will love the object of daily thought and care, and that alone is enough to make a terrible blank in your life. I am sorry you are to leave Brookroyd, and it was so very "homey" looking a place.'[10]

After Mrs Nussey's death the three sisters – widow Ann Clapham and unmarried Mercy and Ellen Nussey – had to uproot themselves from the house which had been their home for some twenty years. Although it had been built by their uncle Richard Nussey, Brookroyd House was owned by the manor of Batley. The three women went to live in a dwelling which was part of the old Gomersal Cloth Hall[11] and were there for two or three years. They found a home that suited them better by about 1860. This was Laneside, on Church Lane, Gomersal.

The Life of Charlotte Brontë shows all Mrs Gaskell's virtues and all her weaknesses – weaknesses which can go unnoticed in her fiction. She was neither an academic nor a scholar. She was a compulsive teller of good stories with a vivid imagination, an excellent evoker of character and place. She loved the curious and strange and did not much care how factual a story was if it was a good one. This can pass in fiction. It did not greatly matter that in *The Heart of John Middleton*, a Lancashire story, she used a Yorkshire folktale from Haworth which Charlotte had told her.[12] In the allegedly true story *The Mystery of Owen Parfitt*, William Maskell said that in Mrs Gaskell's account 'guarded as it claims to be by so much of corroborative proof, almost every particular rests on imagination'.[13] Yvonne French mentions a 'certain lack of integrity', and that 'on every occasion that Mrs Gaskell indulges in subjects involving the extraordinary, the inexplicable, or the marvellous, there is a careless abandonment of historical accuracy in favour of purely sensational effect'. On the gossip in Mrs Gaskell's character Yvonne French says: 'In *Cranford*, this was an asset; in the *Life* a liability'. She had a careless attitude towards years, names and ages.[14] It seems likely that Mr Gaskell, who had vetted her writing so carefully in the early days and put right the Lancashire dialect, was by now confident of his wife's abilities and too busy to interfere, although he is said to have done her proofreading. Ellen was much in awe of her and too much involved emotionally to act as a corrective.

Opinions varied about the *Life*, as they have continued to vary ever since. 'Libellous or not', wrote Mary Taylor from New Zealand, 'the first edition was all true'. Miss Wooler wrote, 'The third edition has now ventured out. Our curate tells me he is assured it is quite inferior to the former ones. So you see Mrs Gaskell displayed worldly wisdom in going out of her way to furnish gossip for the discerning public'. The *Life* was not the only Brontë publishing event of 1857, for George Smith had succeeded in publishing *The Professor*. Mrs Gaskell considered it much inferior to Charlotte's work published in her lifetime.

For Ellen the next few years continued a gradual progression: people were born, married or died, and work of various kinds continued. The many years during which she had served and looked after her mother were over. Had the release come earlier, she and Charlotte might have shared the last years of their lives together. As it was, the part of Ellen's personality which had responded so deeply to Charlotte was unfulfilled and bereft until at the end of her life she met Lady Morrison, and that could only be a sparse friendship compared with the wealth which she and Charlotte had shared.

Even Mary Taylor could not provide compensation for the loss of Charlotte. During 1859 Mary returned to England and built herself a house called High Royd on Spen Lane, Gomersal, where she was to live for the rest of her life. She was now close to Ellen once more. Mary wrote very warmly the previous June on hearing that Mrs Nussey had died: 'Keep yourself well, dear Ellen, and gather round you as much happiness and interest as you can, and let me find you cheery and thriving when I come.' Once back in England, Mary was to continue striking out in individualistic ways, later taking groups of young ladies on Alpine holidays.[15] Ellen was still in touch with the Gaskells. Meta Gaskell had broken off her engagement, and in a long and pleasant letter Mrs Gaskell told Ellen all about it.

It is easy for us to forget that *Jane Eyre* had a profound practical influence on young women. Mrs Teresa Earle wrote of 1859:

'The winter was an eventful one for me, as I was very near marrying some one who was introduced to us in Paris, and who travelled with us to Nice. I was not very gracious, as I was absorbed in one of the most remarkable books of my time, *Jane Eyre*. I had not been allowed to read it before . . . I consider it one of the [most] strengthening and powerful novels in the English language. Seeing more of this man during the early part of the winter, I felt I never could

Ferndean Manor, drawn by Wimperis for the illustrated edition of Jane Eyre.

care enough for him to marry him . . . so I refused him, greatly to his indignation.'

The implication that *Jane Eyre* influenced her against this marriage is very clear.[16]

The shock waves of the biography were still in motion, for in April 1859 Ellen was writing to tell Mrs Gaskell that 'some of the West Ridingers are very angry [about the biography] and declare they are half a century in civilisation before some of the Lancashire folk, and that the neighbourhood is a paradise compared with some districts not far from Manchester' – a rather belated protest.[17] In his old age Sir T Clifford Allbutt insisted that 'Mrs Gaskell in her life of Charlotte Brontë had been misled by someone's account of the West Riding as a semi-savage region in which these clever girls were marooned, and so gave an exaggerated impression of the isolation of the Brontës, who in reality were much in touch with cultivated neighbours'.

Ellen's nephews and nieces at Chislehurst were growing up and as usual providing interest for their three Nussey aunts at Gomersal. The eldest boy, Edward, was a curate. His youngest brother Antony Foxcroft trained in law.[18] Things had not gone so smoothly for John Thomas Hartley, the second son. He qualified as an apothecary and GP in 1858, and was intended to carry on the medical practice. Unfortunately Thomas hated the profession; it contained too much humbug for him. He ran away to Australia, very poor, and for a

Dr Nelson's nursing home Lime Tree House at Acomb near York, where George Nussey lived.

long time his disappointed father refused to give him financial help. Tom became a schoolmaster. At last the ladies of the family persuaded his father to give Tom some capital, and he then became a sheep farmer. His fate was much on Ellen's mind.[19]

Deeply disappointed by Tom's defection, with no one to continue the practice, and in ill-health, John Nussey retired to Chislehurst in 1860 and parted with the premises at 4 Cleveland Row in 1861, when in June a sale was held of the collection of paintings there. The association of the Walker/Nussey families with the firm which was originally John Truesdale and Joseph Partridge, royal apothecaries, ended after almost ninety years. John Nussey died on the 14th April 1862 aged sixty-eight. It was written of him, 'he was a man deservedly esteemed; he had that gracious manner which comes often from enjoying the confidence of the great.'[20]

With John's death, Ellen, Ann and Mercy had only four brothers left to them: Richard, prosperous and living in Woodhouse Lane, Leeds; Joshua, prosperous and living in Oundle; Henry, who was presumably still abroad with his wife Emily, living on her income (the last material relic of Henry is a notebook dated 1857 which was in Ellen's possession when she died); and George, who was living in Dr Nelson's nursing home near York.

Ellen had some contact with George Smith during 1860, when she wrote to him of a friend of hers who wished to do translation work; it is conceivable that this was Mary Taylor. Ellen also sent some verses – the assumption is that they were by the same friend – but they were not good enough for the *Cornhill* magazine.

Mrs Gaskell paid her last visit to Haworth Parsonage in December 1860, finding Mr Brontë failing in health and Mr Nicholls 'more unpopular in the village than ever'. On this occasion she was able to fit in a visit to John Greenwood. Mr Brontë died some six months later on the 7th June 1861 aged eighty-four, and John Greenwood followed him on the 25th March 1863, aged only fifty-six. After Mr Brontë's death Nicholls considered his duty done. He resigned his post and sold most of the Brontës' possessions, keeping only manuscripts and paintings and personal mementos of the four creative young people he had loved and admired. He gave Mr Brontë's copy of Mrs Gaskell's *Life* to Mrs Wood, a friend of Martha's. (It was Mrs Wood who said that

Ellen and her sisters Anne and Mercy moved to Laneside, Gomersal, in 1861.

Charlotte liked high game and that Martha had to prepare hares with a handkerchief over her nose.)

Then, having organised everything, Nicholls went back to Ireland to his home area and apparently led a quiet country life. Possibly his inherited capital from the Brontë sisters' books enabled him to do this. He was married again, to his cousin, who Charlotte had met on her honeymoon in Ireland. As far as is recorded Nicholls did not benefit Mr Brontë's sisters and brothers financially, but he may have been more generous to them than we know.

By the spring of 1861 Ellen and her sisters were established in their new home, Laneside, with one live-in servant. It is a pleasant stonebuilt house which stands end-on to the road, looking down through its garden to the view spread out before it.

During 1861 Mrs Gaskell planned to continue her career as a biographer with a life of Mme de Sevigne and was finding out what research she needed to do. She was always willing to contribute to a worthy cause and these contributions sometimes took the form of letters she had received, including Charlotte's: 'Here comes another note, to beg you to accept the accompanying autographs, to be sold for the benefit of the Sanitary Commission. I give them with all my heart – and I trust they will do some of the good anticipated. They are . . . [list which includes] Letter from Miss Brontë (this is, and ought to be very valuable – it is a very rare autograph.)'[21] Soon she had only 'a very few scraps' of Charlotte's handwriting left.

---

[1] *Memorials of Two Sisters* by Margaret J Shaen (Longmans, Green and Co, London 1908).
[2] *The Letters of Mrs Gaskell* ed J A V Chapple and Arthur Pollard (Manchester University Press 1966), letter 352.
[3] Ibid. Gaskell letter 335.
[4] 15th April, Lewes letter to Mrs Gaskell.
[5] *The Letters of Mrs Gaskell* (note 2), letter 348.
[6] The Hartleys were trustees under Sir George Saville's will.
[7] *The Letters of Mrs Gaskell* (note 2), letter 370.
[8] *The Letters of Mrs Gaskell* (note 2), letters 379 and 381.
[9] *The Letters of Mrs Gaskell* (note 2), letter 385a, also letters from Ellen to Mrs Nussey of Potternewton Hall, February 1885 and to Mrs Cortazzo 7th September 1889, Cadman collection, Brontë Parsonage Museum.
     Samuel Leathley Nussey, a descendant of George Nussey of Hunslet, married Agnes Clark, who became very interested in the history of the Nussey family, collected data on them, and corresponded with Ellen.
[10] Brookroyd House was later lived in by Michael Sheard, the local historian. He was the agent for Lord Wilton's Batley estate, the post once held by Robert Clapham. Sheard wrote (or compiled) the *Records of the Parish of Batley,* and also had the Batley parish register transcribed to about 1775. His copy was presented to the British Museum MSS Room. A similar, looseleaf version is in the Leeds City Library.
[11] Information from H A Cadman, of the solicitors who were Ellen's executors (and earlier, under the Carrs, had looked after the affairs of the Nusseys). Gomersal Cloth Hall office buildings were, at the time of his writing (1930), in use as offices and stores.

[12] *Mrs Gaskell's Observation and Invention,* J G Sharps (Linden Press 1970), p110.

[13] William Maskell, in 'The Mystery of Owen Parfitt', *Odds and Ends* (James Toovey London 1872), p78.

[14] *Mrs Gaskell* by Yvonne French (Home and Von Thal 1949).

[15] Mary Taylor had begun to write a novel while she was in New Zealand. This became *Miss Miles, or a tale of Yorkshire Life* (Remington and Co, London 1890). She also wrote or compiled *Swiss Notes by Five Ladies* (Leeds 1875), and her articles for the *Victoria* magazine were collected in book form.

[16] Mrs Maria Theresa Earle, *Memoirs and Memories* (Smith, Elder and Co London 1911).

[17] *Charlotte Brontë and her Circle,* Clement Shorter. 16th April letter of Ellen to Mrs Gaskell.

[18] Edward Nussey was a curate at Whiston, Yorkshire 1853–8, Euston with Barnham, Suffolk 1858–60, Ware, Hertfordshire 1860–65. In 1865 he became Vicar of Longney, Gloucestershire.

[19] Only in quite recent years did Thomas Nussey's descendants leave the old homestead. His descendants are well-established and one of his great-grandsons is a doctor.

[20] *Memoirs of 80 years,* Thomas Gordon Hake (Richard Bentley and Son, London 1892), p52. John Nussey's will showed effects under £35,000. One of the executors, a first cousin of John Nussey's wife, was John Beswicke Greenwood (previously mentioned). He was a barrister in London, and in 1864 when his aunt Elizabeth Foxcroft Taylor of Purlwell Hall, Batley, died, inherited that property.

[21] *The Letters of Mrs Gaskell* (note 2), letter 552. In letter 646, undated, Mrs Gaskell to 'Mary' says about autographs: 'I enclose a note from Dickens, Holman Hunt, Lord Wrottesley, late P R S, and one of a very few scraps I have left of Miss Brontë's handwriting on an envelope. I am sorry it is not her signature, but here is MINE'.

ELLEN, WEMYSS REID, AND 1866-76

Mrs Gaskell's sudden death in November 1865 was the end of a significant era in Ellen's life. The biography of Charlotte must now stand as Mrs Gaskell had left it in the revised third edition. It was a finished thing, no longer developing or capable of being influenced.

The household at Laneside continued on its tranquil way. Ann had become an old lady and we hear nothing of her activities outside the home. Mercy too was ageing, but she had always been given to good works and it was she who concerned herself most with visiting their brother George in York. Ellen was by the nature of things the most active of the three. She was in 1866 nearing fifty years of age and, apart from domestic duties, sewing, and the social life of the neighbourhood, went on long visits to different parts of the country to stay with family and friends.

She was also doing a certain amount of teaching. Teaching was not a new activity for Ellen. She had taught in Sunday schools at least since 1841 and probably longer. When Ellen's acquaintances the Miss Carters, Miss Wooler's

Oakwell Hall, Birstall. Ellen taught at the Misses Carters' school here.

nieces, set up school at Oakwell Hall she did some teaching for them. They were there by 1871, when they appear in the census with their school, and we know from the testimony of a girl who was a pupil that Ellen used to drive over each week with her 'very nice black pony' and trap to teach scripture. Miss Wooler visited the school frequently, and Mary Taylor used to go to give talks on her travels and life in other countries.

Ellen also taught elsewhere: 'Miss Nussey was very well thought of in Birstall. She went to the village school to read scripture to the children, and was busy with benevolent projects. She loved animals, and was devoted to the pony and to the donkey sometimes driven in the trap.'[1] How much of her time was taken up by teaching it is difficult to tell. As far as we know Ellen always taught scripture in day schools, but she had been teaching for years in Sunday schools, which gave a good deal of general teaching before the Education Acts of the 1870s brought in elementary education for all during the ensuing decade. It is likely that she had taught the three Rs and needlework. This part of Sunday school teaching faded out as Board schools became established.

During these ten years there were a number of significant family events. Of all Mrs Ellen Nussey's large family, the only one to have children had been John, and a good deal of the interest of the three sisters at Laneside centred on these nephews and nieces. Ellen often travelled down to the Ivy House at Chislehurst. As Napoleon III and his queen, Eugenie, were living in Chislehurst in exile there was still a slight royalist frisson about visiting the Nusseys in the south of England.

Ellen's nephew Antony Foxcroft Nussey was by 1866 enrolled as a solicitor and had set up in partnership with a Mr Fellowes. Antony married the beautiful Marianne Charrington (of the coal-merchanting branch of the family better known as brewers) in 1870, at a choral wedding in Chislehurst with twelve bridesmaids, then went to live in Richmond, Surrey.

Nieces Rachael Elizabeth and Frances Booth married into the sugar-rich Booker family,[2] and Tom in Queensland, Australia married a girl called Janet Wilson.

These ten years were to see the deaths of three of Ellen's brothers. Henry died first in 1867. His widow, Emily, continued to live abroad and survived Ellen. John Nussey's widow, Mary, died at Chislehurst in 1868. It is likely to have been as a result of this that the lease of the Ivy House was given up. Mary had been Ellen's second cousin as well as her sister-in-law, and her link with many West Riding notables. The unmarried daughters lived on at Chislehurst, in Church Row, across the road from the common.

It was in 1868 that Ellen began to think seriously of writing something about Charlotte. Her friends pressed her to defend Charlotte's memory from 'the charge of irreligion'. She had already determined that after her death her collection of Charlotte's letters should be Charlotte's defence, 'after, so I thought, my own web of life should have run its course'. Pressure increased:

letters from Brontë fans in America, and promised visits from them, were pushing her in the direction of publishing more of the letters.

Ellen had a friendly correspondence with George Smith in 1868. She began copying out parts of the letters for possible publication, but Smith explained to her that the copyright belonged to Nicholls, although the letters themselves belonged to her. Ellen sent Smith her suggested excerpts, but after all the bad feeling that had ensued between herself and Nicholls since Charlotte's death she was frightened by this question of copyright and began to retreat from her intention, saying that she was very busy preparing for a sale of work in aid of the rebuilding of Birstall Church.[3]

She felt doubtful of her ability to write publishable memoirs, and asked Smith if he could find out if Nicholls still had letters written by herself. It appears that about a month after Charlotte's death Nicholls, in the course of sorting out papers, had discovered something that told him of the courtship of Charlotte by James Taylor of Smith, Elder. Very upset, he had travelled to Birstall to ask Ellen about it. She was pleased to have been away from home, and so avoided the encounter. This and the distress over the biography – where she had communicated far more to Mrs Gaskell than Nicholls approved of – had produced a coolness. He had not written the chatty letters about Haworth which would have brought her round in no time – he had not written at all. She unfortunately bore him a grudge, and had become afraid of his reactions to events. Had she been able after Charlotte's death to continue as a family friend of Haworth Parsonage, given a little importance there because of her long association with the Brontë family, this would have made Ellen happy. Instead Nicholls, with his proprietorial attitude to 'my wife', made her feel cut off from what had been so valued by her.

George Smith suggested that she take passages from the Letters and 'incorporate them in a brief and simple narrative of your friendship with Charlotte Brontë giving also your impressions of her and her family . . .' and offered publication in the *Cornhill* magazine. Ellen prevaricated, asked for contributions to the church bazaar and wrote with bitterness about Nicholls. George Smith then said there was no hurry, that she would have to get copyright permission herself, and the firm did not contribute to bazaars. So in March 1869 this phase of the affair ended in an impasse.

A year later, in March 1870, Scribners of New York were interested in publishing the letters in their monthly magazine *Hours at Home*. They suggested printing them at the rate of six or eight pages a month, with a possible total payment of £100, in spite of the intensive use Mrs Gaskell had made of the material. They were also willing to consider book publication if the letters were popular. In May 1871 *Scribners Magazine* published an article by Ellen, 'Reminiscences of Charlotte Brontë'. In the previous volume they had published Ellen's selection of passages from Charlotte's letters. Unfortunately Scribners could not find an interested publisher for a new book on Charlotte, and they were not able to use the last article and photographs Ellen sent to them. It appeared that general American interest in the Brontës was

Ellen's brother the Reverend Joshua Nussey of Oundle.

too low at this time for successful commercial publication, although individuals were still ardently interested. Ellen had been hoping to raise enough money for a memorial window to the Brontës in Haworth Church, and Watson Gilder of Scribners was willing to collect towards this if the project went ahead. When the church at Haworth was rebuilt, descriptions of the old church mention a stained-glass window to the memory of the Brontës, so this idea seems to have reached fulfilment.

In 1871 the Rev Joshua Nussey died at Oundle, where Ellen had visited him and his wife Anne so often. He left some £5,000, part of which came to his three sisters in the form of annuities. He left money to Brownhill Church in Brookroyd Lane, which he benefited altogether through the years to the tune of £1,000. He had also in his lifetime spent a great deal of money on the church at Oundle.

The next of the siblings to die was the last surviving brother, Richard, who fell ill at the beginning of 1872. Ann and Ellen went to Leeds to see him during his illness. He died on the 23rd February, and the executors of his will were the Nussey half-cousin, William Carr, and George Clapham, a Leeds solicitor and a connection of the Birstall Claphams. It would be a great relief for the sisters that Richard left £100 per annum for the upkeep of their brother George in York. The bulk of the rest of the estate was divided between Ann,

Richard Nussey, Ellen's brother.

Mercy and Ellen. In spite of their grief at Richard's death, they must have felt pleased and grateful at the freedom this promised from financial worries. From now on they should be in easy circumstances. Little did they realise how William Carr's trusteeship was to affect them. Ellen thought that as Richard's sister and the most capable of the survivors she should have some say in the affairs of Richard's estate, but William Carr was determined that she should not. His attitude to women as a whole was antagonistic; exceptions were few. Legally he was in the right. Executors need take no heed of the wishes of the beneficiaries.[4]

One of Ellen's unmarried nieces, Georgiana Mary, living in Church Row, Chislehurst, unexpectedly at the age of forty-three, married Capt Tremlett of the Madras Army. When she was a baby Charlotte Brontë had sent kisses to her, in letters to Ellen.

In Mary Taylor's family, marriages were also taking place; in May 1872 one of her nephews, Edward Taylor, married Teresa Madeleine Hasse, a teacher in the Moravian School – 'a love match', the mercenary William Carr noted in his diary. Her father had been a Moravian minister and her grandfather a noted teacher of music. Later, in 1874, another of Mary's nephews, Richard Taylor, married his cousin Annie, a daughter of William Waring Taylor of New Zealand, who had come to England on a visit. The marriage was a very happy one.

Ellen was still fruitfully busy with Brontë affairs. In March 1872 George Smith had asked for her help in identifying places mentioned in the novels under fictitious names, as he was planning an illustrated edition. The artist Wimperis visited Yorkshire and Ellen showed him various places, which he sketched. As a thankyou gift Ellen received copies of the books, *The Life and Works of Charlotte Brontë and her sisters*. Wanting to be sure that Charlotte's letters went ultimately into the safe keeping of the British Museum, Ellen asked Smith how much he thought the trustees would pay her for them, but he replied that as she did not own the copyright she could not sell them. In this he was mistaken, as physical ownership of a manuscript, and copyright, are two different things. Some of Charlotte's letters had been sold already – Mrs Gaskell had given letters from Charlotte to be sold for charity, and Ellen had herself sold one to a friend to raise money for a local charity.

In 1873 Ellen's nephew Edward visited Yorkshire, and went to see rich old John Beswicke Greenwood, to whom he was closely related through his mother. He saw William Carr, too, in the hope that after the deaths of Ann, Mercy and Ellen he could arrange for the remainder of their brother Richard's estate to revert to him and his siblings.

By the following year, 1874, William Carr was recording in his diary the trouble he was having with Mercy and Ellen. He had arranged to have Richard's residual estate invested in Pennsylvanian Railway Bonds. Unfortunately Mercy and Ellen did not like this investment, probably influenced by the collapse of British railway shares. He over-ruled them. The sisters would certainly have preferred local house property, which they understood.

Money troubles now hit the Wooler family. In August 1874 Miss Wooler's youngest brother James Wooler, nineteen years her junior, failed in business with liabilities of £15,000. It may have been in some way connected with this that in October 1874 William Carr was arranging (through a Wooler nephew, Dr T Clifford Allbutt, then in medical practice in Leeds) to let a house to the three ladies, Miss Wooler, her sister, and niece Marianne. This was 'the middle house' of the three terrace houses which were originally built for the Moravian Sisters at Little Gomersal. As usual in his dealings with women, William Carr was soon complaining about the three ladies in his diary, finding their tenancy a great bother.

Smithies Mill, so intimately connected with Ellen's family memories, was partly destroyed by fire in 1874 and its owner Mr Chapman sold it and its freehold out of the family. One by one old ties were going. In September 1875 the Vicar of Birstall, the Rev W M Heald, died. He and his father had inspired one of the pleasantest characters in *Shirley* and he had married, late in life, the sister-in-law of a second cousin of Ellen's; the Heald family were among the Nusseys' lifelong friends.

The Nussey sisters at Laneside probably saw their nephew Edward quite

An early photograph of the Moravian Sisters' houses at Little Gomersal. Miss Wooler, her sister and niece rented the middle house.

often during the late seventies, for like various other relatives, he made several visits to ageing J Beswicke Greenwood. Although he was still acting as a magistrate, Greenwood was no longer capable and William Carr was taking his notes for him. Carr was pleased when Greenwood resigned. 'It will . . . be the last time I shall have this disagreeable duty [of taking notes]', he told his diary. Carr grumbled to his diary every time he was called upon to help anyone, particularly women. Ellen had written to him twice about the affairs of Richard's estate. At last in 1877 he had to call at Laneside to see Ann, as she had applied for money. It was now five years since Richard had died, and the sisters do not yet appear to have gained any benefit from his will. Carr encountered Ellen on his visit to Laneside and she told him exactly what she thought of him. He referred in his diary to her 'bitter tongue'. It may not have been Carr's fault that the estate took so long to settle.

A pleasanter side of William Carr was that although he had retired from medical practice, he treated poor patients free before church on Sunday mornings, continuing the tradition Richard Walker had begun so many years before. He was interested in antiquarian matters, and took an active part in the cultural side of the community.

A more gratifying relationship for Ellen was that with Wemyss Reid, editor of the *Leeds Mercury*.[5] He gave a lecture on the subject of the Brontës and Ellen, hearing of it, asked if she might read it. She then asked him to visit

her. He found 'a cheerful, neat, and well-preserved woman, who, though she
was well advanced in middle life, retained a good deal of the charm of manner
with which Caroline Helstone, in the delightful story of *Shirley*, is endowed'.
Later, in an obituary of Ellen, he was to write: 'Ellen Nussey when I first knew
her was a singularly beautiful woman, who certainly gave no one the idea that
she was approaching her sixtieth year. She had regular and pleasing features,
keen intelligence, and an oldfashioned precision of manner, which alone
seemed to associate her with the era to which she really belonged'.

Almost Ellen's first words to Wemyss Reid expressed her regret that Mrs
Gaskell had not done justice to Charlotte. Later she asked Reid if he would
write a book to tone down the over-colouring of Mrs Gaskell's narrative, and
offered him the loan of Charlotte's letters, including some which Mrs Gaskell
had not seen, about Charlotte's courtship and marriage. 'They are charming!',
wrote Reid, 'the day will come when these letters will be given to the world,
almost without the omission of a single word, and "Charlotte B[ronte] and
her Friends" will become as well known as Dr Johnson and his friends now
are. But that will not be in your time, or mine. I have put aside a certain
number of letters (about 100) from which I propose to make extracts'. Reid
planned three articles and hoped that they would appear in *Macmillan's
Magazine* in August, September and October. Later they were enlarged to
form a small book. Reid told Ellen that his payment from Macmillan was to
be £100, and offered her and Miss Wooler £33 between them for his use of
their letters. Their co-operation was all sweetness and light, but a 'peremptory'
letter to Reid arrived from Nicholls, 'desiring me to inform you [Ellen] of his
displeasure'. Reid's soft answer turned away wrath, and, like Ellen, Nicholls
was to approve of Reid's work. He wrote again, 'thanking me very sincerely
for all I have written about his wife! . . .' The small book which resulted from
this, *Charlotte Brontë – a Monograph*, published in 1877, pleased Ellen. It earned
general appreciation, and Swinburne much liked it. Ellen gave Wemyss Reid
a pen and ink sketch which Charlotte had drawn of her, but which he no longer
possessed in 1897.

Among the memories of Ellen which Wemyss Reid recorded, he tells us
how when she and Miss Wooler were together they talked constantly of
Charlotte and of the old days:

'When one talked to her the three Brontë sisters seemed to live again . . .
She could tell of Anne, gentle and pretty, sweet and dutiful as Charlotte
herself, without any of the slight asperities of character that appeared in her
two sisters. She had, even to the last, a vivid sense of the strangeness of Emily
– her aloofness from human society, her wayward eccentricity. Charlotte was
herself amazed when one day, during one of Miss Nussey's visits to Haworth,
Emily volunteered to accompany the visitor on a ramble over the moors. Such
favours she had never been known before to bestow upon anyone not of her
own family.'

It is obvious that by this time Ellen was, on occasions, allowing wishful
thinking to cloud her judgement. She suggested to Wemyss Reid that her

brother Richard was the original of Rochester in his 'unpolished force and dogged egotism' which Charlotte idealised into the character in *Jane Eyre*. Ellen apparently also suggested that her brother Henry was the original of St John Rivers. Although when *Shirley* was first published Ellen said she did not recognise the heroines, Shirley and Caroline, she now acquiesced in the usual identification of herself as Caroline. All this is unsupported by the facts, apart from the identification of Ellen as Caroline Helstone which seems almost certain.

[1] Memories of the school at Oakwell, Ellen's transport and her teaching at the village school, were passed down in the family of Mary Ellen Critchley and told by her grand-daughter, Mrs Stenning, to John Nussey. A slight confusion arose in these memories between Miss Wooler and Mary Taylor, but it has been corrected in this text. The 1871 census for Oakwell Hall gives: Ellen M Carter, unmarried, 36, schoolmistress, Catherine Carter, unmarried, 31, schoolmistress, two assistants, domestic staff, eighteen pupils, all girls, including Mary Ellen Critchley.

[2] Josias Booker, of a Lancashire family, founded a successful business in the sugar plantations of British Guiana. His eldest son, also Josias, married the daughter of the Bishop of Guiana in 1862. Another son, George, married Rachael Elizabeth Nussey in 1864. A third son, Arthur W Booker, a vicar in England, married Frances Booth Nussey in 1877.

[3] Birstall Church was extensively repaired and extended. Ellen was to record: 'Workmen destroyed the oldest Nussey tombstone during alterations to Birstall church, by using it for a table to polish stones on, and it was either broken up or built into the church'.

[4] Richard Nussey's will shows effects under £4,000. After bequests and provision for his brother George, the 'residue of said trust money and premises to be equally divided between my three sisters Ann Clapham Mercy Mary Nussey and Ellen Nussey for their own and absolutely'.

[5] Later Sir Thomas Wemyss Reid (1842-1905); living at this time at Thorn Lea, Cardigan Road, Leeds, he moved to London in 1887, and became a very influential writer, editor, and supporter of Gladstone.
His other biographical works and two novels were also successful. His memories of Ellen quoted here have been seen only in photocopy but appear to have been first published in the *Speaker* and reprinted, possibly in the *Bradford Observer*, on 11th December 1897.

ELLEN AND BIDDELL, SCRUTON, AND WILKES, 1877-85

Ellen's sixtieth year opened with her still in the thick of the trouble over her brother Richard's will. She requested a statement of accounts since his death, objected to the investment in Pennsylvanian Railway Bonds, and wanted to be able to bequeath the capital tied up in George's maintenance, should he pre-decease her. All she had for her pains was abuse recorded in the trustee's diary, where William Carr called her insolent, foolish, mischievous and bad; and his traducing of her to her nephew Antony, prejudicing one of her nearest male relatives against her for years to come, the one who might have been the most helpful in the trials of her later existence.

William Carr was also unpopular with his uncle at White Lee because of financial matters. John Nussey of White Lee severed the social relationship, and only later on his deathbed in 1879 aged ninety-three, about to meet his maker, did he make peace with William Carr. John was the last of Ellen's first cousins. His surviving daughter Isabel (once courted by Joe Taylor) had married the Rev George Richardson, vicar of Kilburn, and he died only days after her father. Later, in January 1880, Ellen saw Isabel at White Lee sorting out and packing 'for a final departure from the home of her childhood', and then the place to which Charlotte and Ellen had so often walked was no longer a home of the Nussey family.

J Beswicke Greenwood of Dewsbury Moor was now drawing towards the end of his life, and relatives from all parts of the country hoped to inherit a share of his vast property. William Carr listened to their outpourings about their poverty and their hopes. As he was a more remote connection, he was not regarded as a rival, but when Greenwood died in 1880 William Carr was the major beneficiary, and was able to become a landed gentleman. He began to look for a country estate.

Fortunately for Ellen, her other concerns were turning out more happily than her inheritance from Richard. Wemyss Reid's book was soon to be published by Macmillan. Reid was the only one, of all the people who Ellen helped in their work on the Brontës, to share the money earned with her. He was also trying to negotiate the sale of Charlotte's letters to the British Museum on Ellen's behalf – the one thing she wanted so much, the action which, she was convinced, would ensure the letters' safekeeping for the nation.

In 1878 a clergyman called Altheus Wilkes, of New Walsingham, Norfolk,[1] contacted Ellen. He wanted to write a book about the Brontës and

Ellen Nussey in her middle years.

visited her at Easter. He also saw Mary Taylor, who was kind and helpful to him and willing to talk about the Brontë family. During Wilkes's correspondence with Ellen, he asked her a host of questions about the Brontës but her answers, as far as is known, have not survived. She lent him letters and other things. At the end of the year he pressed her to visit Norfolk and stay with him, saying that the weather was too cold for him to visit Yorkshire! He sent a portion of his manuscript and invited criticism. Ellen read it aloud to her friends Miss Brown and Miss Wooler. When Ellen told him that his manuscript was verbose and repetitive, he was disheartened and gave up the project. Ellen said that it took her a year to recover the letters she had lent to Wilkes.

It was in these last peaceful years at Laneside that Ellen's elder sister, Ann, dictated reminiscences of their ancestors to Ellen. The communal life of the three sisters was drawing to an end. Ann died on the 24th April 1878 aged eighty-two, and Mercy, now seventy-seven, was in poor health. Although Ellen struggled on for a while, she could not cope alone with Mercy's infirmities, so it was arranged that Mercy should move into lodgings at Acomb, York, close to the small mental home where their brother George was

Ellen's eldest sister Ann Clapham in old age.

living, so that she could be looked after by his doctor, whom she liked. Mentally Mercy was sound, but she had always been a fussy, worrity person. Even when she was living at Acomb, she still relied on Ellen to bring over money when their rents on house property fell due, and organise her clothes.

Mary Taylor's life was about to be ruined by another family tragedy. We have Wilkes's word for it that in 1878 she was friendly, approachable, and willing to talk about the Brontës, but over the next years this was to change. In 1879 two of her nephews who ran the firm T C and E Taylor of Birstall were in trading difficulties and their father, Mary's wealthy elder brother Joshua, refused to help them. Joshua was living in London. He had become involved with bogus spiritualists who had spirited money out of him which he spent the rest of his life trying to recover, becoming as time passed more and more eccentric. Mary and the wife of one of her nephews travelled to London but they could not influence him. Mary became one of the five guarantors in her nephews' bankruptcy in July.

September 1879 saw the last service in the old church at Haworth, the building the Brontës had known, before it was pulled down except for the tower, and rebuilt. The clergyman, Rev Wade, felt that the church should be

for God and not a shrine to the Brontës, and he found the literary pilgrims to
Haworth an irritation. The protests by Brontë admirers were not able to stop
the demolition – they probably made it more certain. The church was crowded
for the last service and people who could not get in stood outside in the
churchyard. Nicholls had written from Ireland giving his approval to the
rebuilding.

Ellen was packing up her family home. The death of her uncle Richard
Nussey had brought about the move from Rydings, her mother's death had
produced the move from Brookroyd, now her sister Ann's death had as its
consequence her move from Laneside. She had decided to share a house with
her friend Annie Bradbury, and at some time between August 1880 and
February 1881 she moved into North Terrace, Birstall, almost certainly into
Ingwell House. The arrangement proved a temporary one. By the autumn of
1881 Ellen had moved to Fieldhead, a hamlet on the side of the moor higher
than Birstall but within easy walking distance. For the rest of her life, Ellen
was to live alone apart from servants – she usually had one servant living in.
The Fieldhead house was one of a recently erected stone-built row of four, and
Ellen lived there for the next nine years.[2]

She continued to live the double life she had lived since Charlotte's death.
The greater part of every day was occupied by domesticity, local social life,
and her faith which was embodied in practical help for the poor and work for

The terrace at Fieldhead, where Ellen lived in one of the two centre houses.

the parish church of Birstall. Her other life was her continued devotion to Charlotte, her determination to defend her from vulgar defamation, her willingness to help anyone who was, she thought, trying to do justice to her friend; and her guardianship of her letters. Her position as Charlotte's closest friend brought her interesting and sympathetic visitors, but it also brought exploitation, deception and finally heartbreak. She had to contend with this side of her life alone. At times friends helped her but they were busy with their own lives, and their tragedies had to take precedence over hers.

After the tremendous financial problems surfaced in the Taylor family of the Red House, Mary Taylor, who alone could have understood, was, as far as we know, never so close to Ellen again. For a while the Taylors 'professed annoyance' with Ellen, though we do not know why. By the autumn of 1882 they were 'amiable' with her once more. Mary became increasingly eccentric during the next years and although she would still talk to some people about the Brontës, she refused to discuss them with others and seems to have wished to push her early life and its connections out of mind. It must have been bitter instead of sweet for her to look back and remember those early hopeful days, when so much had ended in death and disillusion.

One of Ellen's pleasant friendships started during 1881. She met one Sydney Biddell when staying with mutual friends at Eastbourne and they began a correspondence, exchanging opinions of the books they were reading and lending them to one another by post. Biddell wanted to erect a memorial to the Brontë family in the new parish church at Haworth: 'Mr Nicholls I believe, contemplates erecting a memorial to his wife ONLY, but probably he would not object to this being a memorial to the THREE sisters so that the outside public might take a part in it.' As the project developed Biddell found it very troublesome. 'I have not the heart to do much in reply to Mr Wade's letters', he wrote. Among others, Biddell approached George Smith of Smith, Elder, but over the years the firm's attitude to charity requests had not changed and he would have nothing to do with the scheme. Biddell sent Ellen a copy of the proposed words of the memorial.

In 1882 Ellen was trying to raise money towards this memorial in Haworth Church. She attempted to sell an oil painting of Rydings to a Mr A Hopps of Birkenhead, who had been a pupil there when Rydings was a boys' school: 'How well I remember the old place', he wrote. 'Its battlemented front – the large entrance hall with glass doors (our school room) and the long dark corridors leading to the bedrooms etc – the steep slope at the back under the rookery and the brook across which we had many a pitched battle with the village boys. In my time there was on the lawn near to the iron gates a young Siberian crab tree . . . the park in front enclosed on two sides with plantations . . .' Ellen told Hopps that Rydings was the original of Thornfield in *Jane Eyre*, that the illustration in that book did not do it justice, and sent a photograph of the oil painting, but he did not buy.

Ellen asked Sydney Biddell about selling some of Charlotte's letters, intending to put the money towards the memorial, which seemed important enough to justify this action. He agreed to select two or three letters which were suitable, but they were never sold. Biddell criticised writers on the Brontës: 'Mrs Gaskell's and Mr Wemyss Reid's books on the Brontës are both failures – they do not show home life'. He was later to urge Ellen to write on the family herself.

In 1882 Ellen was approached by Miss Mary Robinson who had been commissioned to write a book on Emily Brontë as one of a series of primers on 'Representative Women'. Ellen met Mary Robinson with friendship and co-operation, answered lists of questions, offered to correct her manuscript, and lent her some of the letters. When she read the manuscript Ellen was disappointed with it. She insisted on references to herself being cut out, did not want it dedicated to her, and said that she 'did not recognise' the portrait given of Emily.

Among the close female friends of her last years was Madame Cortazzo, an American admirer of the Brontës who spent a lot of time travelling in Europe with her daughter Catherine (Catrine). The Cortazzos stayed with Ellen in August 1882 while she was at Fieldhead, and for the rest of her life the friendship was of mutual delight and help. Mme Cortazzo suggested that Ellen bought a stove to heat the house, sent her corsets and garments to keep her warm and bought her pre-prepared soups and tinned meats. In return Ellen sent gingerbread and other locally baked cakes, and even bread. 'Your sweet daughter made me long again as I have often done for a younger sister', wrote Ellen. She told them of Birstall Feast Week, when the road through Fieldhead 'teamed with pedestrians all afternoon' and flower shows and open air concerts were held in the grounds of Rydings. The Cortazzos wanted to rent Oakwell Hall for a winter, but it was not available at a convenient time. This made Ellen think how nice her chairs, which she was having recovered, would look in the Oak Room at Oakwell. She might have been gratified to know that after her death her writing bureau went there, and was displayed for years in the pink-painted drawing room.

From the Cortazzo letters and from other chatty ones to Annie Atkinson of Laneside House, Churwell, Mrs Nussey of Potternewton Hall, and finally Lady Morrison, we can learn of Ellen's life, and of herself. 'I have had long schooling in the habits of self-denial so it comes easy now', said Ellen when she decided that she could not afford velvet for her new chaircovers.

Needing a servant she went to the Servants' Home and chose Hannah, a lame woman of forty who was not strong enough to take a post in a large family. 'A good cook, trustworthy and clean.' At one point Hannah fell down the steps to the kitchen and sprained her ankle badly. While she was in bed, Ellen herself 'bundled out of bed at seven' and by doing so caught a chill. With both of them in bed they had to rely on kind neighbours to fetch the doctor's prescriptions and help generally.

Despite dull, misty, rainy weather at the end of 1882, Ellen enveloped herself in shawls and persisted in her regular church-going, once having a bronchial attack warded off only by a glass of hot port at the vicarage. Ellen

The only known photograph of Charlotte and Ellen's friend Mary Taylor.

was starved of intellectual company and found that exposed Fieldhead was colder than Birstall village which nestled near the valley bottom. The previous winter had been mild, but as the winter of 1882 set in, the wind seemed even to blow up through the floors and Ellen was wadding the windows and having 'lats'[3] nailed round the doors, before she settled down to her plan of reading through the remainder of Scott's novels that winter – she had previously only read half of them.

Mary Taylor was having new troubles with her family. By the turn of the year her brother Joshua had died and in January 1883 her nephew Richard also died.[4] Mary's sorrows would be felt by Ellen, but not as keenly as they would have been years before. Ellen was living her own life now with her own circle of friends for the first time, and good and bad were mingled in it.

In April 1883 Ellen had two pleasant and affectionate letters. Wemyss Reid wrote to tell her of the publication of his novel *Gladys Fane*, and Mary Robinson sent her a copy of the biography of Emily and offered to send one also to Sydney Biddell. The biography was a success, although it disappointed

Ellen. When Mary Robinson saw her about this time, she thought her looking 'more tired and delicate than when I stayed with you . . .'

An old sore was now reopened. A letter from Leyland in the *Athenaeum* blamed Ellen for divulging confidential details of Branwell's conduct from Charlotte's letters. 'This I never did', countered Ellen, 'she was always reticent of details concerning him'. Knowing that her own brother had gone the same way as Branwell, we can understand the distress she felt whenever it was suggested that knowledge of Branwell's behaviour had come through her. She may have feared publicity about Joseph; in any case she was hypersensitive on the topic. These family tragedies were better hidden and one tried to forget. She cannot have realised how revealing were the few remarks which Charlotte had made. Leyland went on to write a biography of Branwell.

In the hope of defending her reputation in America, Ellen made a few notes for Mme Cortazzo to use in a letter to the American press:

'Could the Brontë's friend have had her will, the record of the sisters' lives should have been as pure and high in standard as their noble and self-denying lives – such a record as any child might have read and profit thereby – a thousand pities that the great trouble and shadow on their lives was not suffered to rest as the sisters would have had it – a shadow indeed, and a trouble indeed, but not a burden that they would ever have shown of their own wish to the public, or given sign of, if they could have helped it.'

She could not resist adding that 'Without this friend's aid so generously given without any recompense (except in one instance) what truth, what accuracy, could we have had in the records given?'. In this affair Ellen showed her dual attitude: on the one hand, she made writers cut acknowledgements to her out of their works; on the other hand she longed to be credited with being the source of knowledge of 'what is *good* of the Brontë sisters'. She had blamed Nicholls for making money out of Charlotte by allowing Smith, Elder to publish *The Professor* in 1857, yet Ellen was distressed when authors made money out of the information she gave them and did not make the gesture of sharing it with her. She wrote to Biddell that 'I have been the mine whence writers on the Brontës have drawn their ore', and he agreed: 'what would we have known of the sisters but for you?'.

Yet even in her distress over Leyland's letter, Ellen could be detached enough to find the reaction of local people amusing, when she had a glance from Miss Carter which said louder than words, 'There now, you have your extinguisher'. Ellen could always laugh at herself, and was never pompous, but she was vexed by the friction in the parish – 'the scheming twaddle and gossip is hateful as it sometimes creeps into view' – and rose above it; 'Silly body!' she exclaimed of Miss Carter.

In 1883 Ellen's enjoyment of the best of English writing was as keen as ever. She recalled the time she sat up until midnight completely fascinated by reading Macaulay. She looked forward eagerly to the loan of the recently published letters of Jane Carlyle. When she read the letters, Ellen's reaction was eminently sensible: 'They are interesting and good, but much of a sameness, and both husband and wife are dreadfully afflicted with egotism. Their temperaments were so much alike, they were unfit to mate, each should have had an opposite.'

The writing aspirations of Rev Wilkes were not yet over. Having once had the loan of Charlotte's letters, he seems to have proposed issuing a garbled version of them. In response to this threat Biddell suggested to Ellen, when he returned eleven letters she had loaned to him, 'Why not prepare a little volume containing nothing but her letters to you?'. He offered his help, and the loan of R D Blackmore's novel *Lorna Doone*, which she had been longing to read. As the winter of 1883 approached, Ellen was continuing her project of reading the whole of Scott. She was charmed by the style of *Waverley*. She liked and admired a biography *The Life of the Prince Consort* and read a book called *Elaine* – which 'is interesting to me as a view of French life but it is not original'.

Ellen was busy seeing to her sister's wraps and bonnet for the winter, going to York for two days for the purpose in November 1883 and buying herself a bonnet at the same time. Mercy at eighty years of age 'is stronger than I am and sees very well without glasses'. George was also well. 'My dear brother I found looking better and stronger, he was at my sister's lodgings before I was downstairs in the morning, so we had a great deal of time together and I am comforted by the knowledge of their welfare . . . You would admire my dear brother! He is such a thorough gentleman, and so handsome, though thin and feeble in health.'

The coldness of the house at Fieldhead was still bothersome, she had to wear a shawl over her head indoors, the weather was miserable and she began to have rheumatism, but a carpenter made the doors fit better, and she was as always made happy by the minor pleasures of life; 'It is so cheery by a blazing fire!'. Fortunately her servant the 'old-fashioned maiden, manages the cooking so well, and takes care of me as an invalid'. Winter always brought Ellen illness. From now on it took the form of sore throats and rheumatism as well as her usual bronchitis, so she was often confined to the house. Port wine helped the throat, but was bad for the rheumatism. She was an active woman, and without daily exercise in the open air her 'liver went wrong'.

Gifts from Mme Cortazzo included 'the pen-nibs which I like so much' – they were broad-nibbed J pens – and fur with which Ellen retrimmed her velvet jacket. The Cortazzos were in Italy, and Ellen hoped they would meet Mary Robinson who was also there, but warned them that they might not like the friend Mary was visiting - 'Vernon Lee', the lesbian Violet Paget, a writer and lifelong friend of the painter Sargent and his family.

As always Ellen spent a lot of her time assisting the poor. Her 'dear old Lady friend in London, a niece of Lord Chatham, whose Pitt blood can boil on occasion', sent her parcels of books, tracts, and flannel, which she distributed in addition to her own efforts. If the Cortazzos could be with her for Christmas, Ellen promised them beef tea and the old traditional dish of furmety.[5] She had found the tinned meats they gave her indigestible, and recommended strong beef tea properly made; 'or a shin of beef for soups done gently for hours in the oven – we leave it all night as well as day and it is strong jelly'.

The year 1884 was to bring fresh trouble to Mary Taylor, when her brother Waring went bankrupt in New Zealand. For Ellen, the involvement with Brontë matters went on. Wemyss Reid told Ellen that he had spoken to Lord Houghton (formerly Monkton Milnes), a trustee of the British Museum, about the letters, but Lord Houghton did not think the British Museum would buy them.

In January 1885 Biddell said he was enjoying Cross's life of George Eliot, and Ellen read it too. She differed from Biddell's assessment of it; Wemyss Reid also found it disappointing. Then in February Biddell suggested Ellen treat Charlotte's letters as Cross treated George Eliot's, and here he was unknowingly paving the way for the next stage in the saga of the letters. In the same month, Ellen received a letter from William Scruton,[6] who introduced himself as a Moravian with a collection of Brontë memorabilia who would like to buy an autograph letter of Charlotte's. In March Ellen offered to give him a short letter in Charlotte's hand if she could find one, as a thank you for a copy of his 'little work on CB's birthplace.' Then in April she offered him a lock of Charlotte's hair. Ellen must have taken a great fancy to Scruton to indulge him in this way.[7]

'Mr J Horsfall Turner who wrote the "History of Haworth" is a very dear old friend of mine', Scruton had written when he introduced himself: the first mention of Horsfall Turner in the surviving correspondence. At that stage Ellen did not know who Horsfall Turner was, and asked Wemyss Reid for information. Scruton also mentioned that he knew the Taylors of Gomersal, through the Moravian church. During the year Ellen's friendship with Scruton flowered, and he has left delightful reminiscences of her.

In the autumn of 1885 Ellen had the grief of the death of her only surviving brother. George died on the 24th October, aged seventy-one. Ellen had admired, loved and cared for George, and Charlotte had always mentioned him in her letters with liking, even affection.

At the end of the year Biddell was writing to tell Ellen of the publication of Leyland's two volume biography of Branwell Brontë: '. . . as a literary work, not to be mentioned with Mrs Gaskell's, Mr Reid's, or Miss Robinson's'. Ellen hated volume one of Leyland's book – and like Charlotte, if Ellen disapproved, she said so. It was with some trepidation that Biddell[8] posted the second volume to her, hoping 'he did not vex her by sending Vol. II', and adding that he would like to ask her about Branwell.

Meanwhile Ellen was seeing J Horsfall Turner. 'I often hear of you through my dear friend Turner', wrote William Scruton. As always, Ellen could not help being generous with Charlotte's letters, lending them to Horsfall Turner. Writing to her in December 1885, he said that after reading the letters he had quite a new view of *Shirley*.

The very end of the year saw the realisation of Ellen's half-cousin William

Carr's ambition. With Ellen's nephew Antony Nussey as his solicitor, he purchased the mansion Ditchingham Hall and the Norfolk estates of the Bedingfield family, at a cost of £32,500.

[1] Altheus Wilkes, BA London, deacon 1868, priest 1869, curate of Stowmarket 1868-70, Titchwell near Lyme Regis 1870-73, then New Walsingham, Norfolk.

[2] The row of houses at Fieldhead was built by one of the Claphams (Ellen's connections by her sister Ann's marriage), who bequeathed them to his daughter. By 1880 the ownership had passed to the daughter's husband, J William Priestley, whose tenant Ellen became.

[3] 'Lats' is a dialect word for laths, thin strips of wood. When I was a child in Sheffield the word lats was always used, and like Ellen, we had them nailed round the doors to stop the draughts, and very effective they were.

[4] Richard Taylor had a weak heart through diptheria, but he had commercial ability. He was in partnership with his eldest brother Joshua, as J and R Taylor of Hunsworth Mill. He married his cousin Annie from New Zealand and had a son. His wife's death after three or four years was a great shock to him. The failure of the firm and his father's eccentricities depressed him and his health gave way.

[5] Usually called frumety or frumenty, this was a porridge made of cracked wheat from the recent harvest, cooked very slowly in milk, enriched with eggs, sometimes coloured with saffron, sometimes spiced, served with sugar. The long slow gentle cooking was the essential part, to avoid burning.

[6] William Scruton of 35 Clough St, West Bowling, Bradford.

[7] The two letters to William Scruton making these offers are in the library of the University of Texas.

[8] Sidney Biddell, or Biddle, attended Trinity College, Cambridge in 1848 aged nineteen. BA 1853, MA 1856, entered Lincoln's Inn 1853, called to the Bar 1856. Of Farmhill House, Stroud, Gloucestershire.

ELLEN AND HORSFALL TURNER, 1886-92

As 1886 opened, Ellen and J Horsfall Turner[1] were in constant contact by letter and visits. She lent him without stint her Brontë papers, including the valentine sent so long ago by William Weightman. It was, Horsfall Turner said, 'too sacred for eyes apart from the most trustworthy'. Ellen, like Charlotte, could never really comprehend the repressive moral mood of the high Victorian era. They were Regency-born and reared in the earlier traditions. The attitude which covered up evils with a cloak of gentility was foreign to their natural, commonsensical approach. They were delicate, reserved and ladylike, but they did not perceive coarseness where there was none, or read double meanings where none were intended. They could enjoy fun, games, love and affection, without suspecting anything prurient or immoral.

Ellen's life was still an active one. She went to a lecture on Dante, a very grand dinner party, an amateur concert, a ball, and was expecting two daughters of Mary Hewitt's to stay, all in the first weeks of 1886. Unfortunately she had to part with her crippled servant, who had come under the subversive influence of the servant next door, but the new servant was trustworthy and a good cook.

The *Yorkshire Post* published a list of the Brontë relics which were being gathered as the nucleus of a museum. 'It makes me feel sick', wrote Ellen. 'How dreadfully shocked dear C would be could she see it. To me it is a vulgar desecration and insult to everything that was precious in her'. She had also been dismayed to find that someone was 'actually publishing what I have SPOKEN of the Brontës to very few indeed . . . It is too bad. We are losing our English reserve sadly too much'.

An example of Ellen's practical approach to life was the dossall curtain for Birstall Church. Miss Carter was making a fuss about decorations, and a curtain would stop that. Ellen decided to employ a clergyman's daughter from Leeds, who supported herself by ecclesiastical embroidery, to do the work, and pay for the whole out of some compensation money she had received from the railways. So the money was of benefit to the church, the community and a needy woman, all at the same time.

Although not very interested in politics, she was asked to support the new Primrose League, a Tory organisation, and threw herself into writing letters for the cause. She was a Tory – several remarks attest to this.

At some time in 1886 Ellen was returning to Fieldhead on foot from Batley accompanied for part of her route by the Rev W Matthews. He referred to Dr Priestley, the great scientist and Unitarian, saying what a great work Priestley had done for England, and Ellen rejoined, 'Well, you know, sir, he *rejected* the Way, the Truth, and the Life – our Lord'. The New Connection minister, whose path was then parting from hers, bid her goodday and added the remark, 'Madam, I believe that even *he* found the right way and now lives with the Father of all'.[2] The Unitarian belief was that Christ was sent by God but was not himself divine; this was the rock which Mrs Gaskell thought would shipwreck her friendship with Charlotte, after she married the rigid Nicholls.

Mercy now came to the end of her life, dying in Acomb aged eighty-six, in September 1886. As Mercy Mary Nussey, she was buried in the same churchyard, St Stephen's, as her brother George. Although Mercy was a demanding sister, she was a well-meaning woman, a kind and loving one. As Ellen stood by the graveside she must have been overwhelmed by sorrow at losing the last of her immediate family. Now she was truly alone. For the first time in her life no-one was dependent on her, no family duty must take precedence over her own desires. Alone she could take charge of her own life, but alone she must face old age and infirmity. Luckily, she had causes about which she cared deeply, to distract her from grief.

By September of this year Horsfall Turner was suggesting to Ellen a private printing of the letters. He gave her to understand that to print a handful of copies would in some way prevent unauthorised pirate editions. The agreement was that although a printer was to be employed to set the type, and an edition prepared which she would correct and annotate, the printing of all but the necessary few copies would not take place until after her death, when the full edition would be published and the original letters deposited with the British Museum.

She became completely absorbed by the work of preparing this edition. By January 1887 Horsfall Turner was saying that 'another proof will be ready soon' and these may have been the proofs which in March he was asking her to return. She had objected to the quality of the paper.

A new correspondent had come into Ellen's life – Erskine Stuart, who had begun to write articles about the Brontës. He was a local medical man and she liked the 'new and intelligent view you are taking'.[3] In his turn he was astounded by her store of Brontë information, and grateful to be allowed to quote her. When she mentioned Erskine Stuart to Horsfall Turner he was derisive, but Ellen was capable of making up her own mind.

Another and more significant new correspondent from the point of view of Ellen's inner life was Lady Morrison (*née* Tatham)[4], a Leeds woman, the daughter of a Quaker lord mayor. She married the Leeds town clerk, an able young lawyer who had risen rapidly in his profession and was knighted. It was as a true lover of good literature, and an admirer of the Brontë sisters, that Lady Morrison ventured to contact Ellen, and she received a kind welcome.

Ellen was seventy years old when she wrote in a letter of the 10th May 1887: 'Your intense interest (and Miss Morrison's) are an affectionate link to dear C's memory. I cannot help loving and appreciating those who love her and her sisters'. The friendship with Lady Morrison was to delight her in her last decade of life. Lady Morrison visited Fieldhead, and they took to one another even more when meeting in the flesh. Ellen was eager for further visits; 'I have another life of CB to shew you – and well written too – by a Mr Birrell – it will interest you'.[5]

Ellen sent a set of the proofs of Charlotte's letters to Sydney Biddell for his comments. He wrote 'how charming, how delightful they are, how brimful they are of humour and fun . . . she is such a perfect letter writer – the letters were not for the public eye'. Was he warning her of what she was unable to see for herself – how very revealing the letters were, and how they might be interpreted by a censorious public?

Replying to Erskine Stuart's questions in June 1887, Ellen said she could not help him over localities with which Emily and Anne were familiar, as she had never visited the places. She warned him against identifying the scenery of Anne Brontë's novels, as Anne had been a governess at Blake Hall and the surviving family might be hurt or offended by such identification. 'I am deficient in prying curiosity and never desired to have it', and she often praises those who do not enquire into 'other people's business'. Erskine Stuart found her letters kind and encouraging, and she liked his writing. When his book *The Story of The Brontë Country* was published, she called him 'the Boswell of the neighbourhood'.

It was in her letters to Lady Morrison that Ellen revealed herself more fully than to anyone else. When Lady Morrison sent photographs which Ellen had framed to hang in her drawing room, she wrote: 'When I take my lonely walks round the room in the winter evenings I shall have the happy consciousness of having through you three living friends not very distant, and there to look at.'

This relationship was very precious. 'I miss you more and more each time we are together when you leave me – you comfort and soothe a sore place in my heart and I feel that we are in unison on higher ground than the world's standard', wrote Ellen. She prepared for Lady Morrison's visits with happy anticipation. In the summer of 1887 she wrote, 'Could your sisters accompany you with the children? The paeonies will be quite out next week, and I have *Hoops* ready for them . . .' Watching children at play was a great pleasure to Ellen and she always provided amusements when she had the happiness of their presence. Lady Morrison and the other women of her family were educated, literary people, and soon they and Ellen were discussing books and lending them to one another. One longs to know which book it was that made Ellen write – 'I am interested and excited by the book you kindly sent. Oh! the presumptious men and women who dare to analyse a being like CB through their own stupid souls! I am eager to get through it . . .'

It is in 1887 that we get the first hint from the Graham family that the interior of Norton Conyers might have been the model for the interior of Thornfield in Jane Eyre. Ellen believed Rydings exterior and park to be the main original of the outside of Thornfield. Now Sir Reginald Graham, saying that Norton Conyers was uninhabited in his father's time and Charlotte *might* have visited it, asked Erskine Stuart to go to see it. Ellen thought the suggested inspiration provided by Norton Conyers was merely Sir Reginald's fancy.

Trouble was beginning in the relationship between Ellen and Horsfall Turner. She became anxious that no outside person should see the proofs of the letters as they were prepared. 'Mr John Harrison is the only person that sees a line of MSS or a line of print', Horsfall Turner assured her. By January of 1888 Horsfall Turner was telling Ellen that more proofs of the letters would be ready soon. He seems to have had a few at a time to be set in type. As she had been ill as usual in winter and was going to recuperate at Harrogate, he sent proofs to her there. Meanwhile Ellen offered the letters covering the first nine or ten years of the friendship on loan to Lady Morrison, probably those which had already been typeset. Horsfall Turner wanted her to add notes. She could not see the need, but if Lady Morrison felt any passages needed elucidating, she was willing to do that. 'I laughed many times as I read', said Ellen, 'the fun sparkled as of old; and then the sad sigh – it had lived but not the writer.' In the event, she did annotate at least two copies.

Ellen had recently taken an orphan child as help for her current maid, Anne. This aroused her interest in the fate of children in the society of the time and she became the local secretary for the Diocesan Association for Waifs and Strays. 'Since I took the little orphan girl I have learnt a good deal respecting the need for Homes', she wrote. 'She is such a clever child and so very full of energy – she is too much for my old servant – so she is going to a Home by my request. She is the very child for emigration, so ready and alert and capable although so young. I am sorry to let her go, but for the child's sake she must be away from Anne who does not like children.'

By 1889 the rumblings of trouble between Ellen and Horsfall Turner had become an outright break. The full correspondence is not available to the public,[6] but it is easy enough to discern what happened. Ellen had always been adamant that the edition of the letters, prepared during her lifetime, was only to be printed after her death, apart from a few copies to prevent pirated unauthorised editions. Now she discovered that Horsfall Turner had printed an edition of a thousand or so copies. She regarded this as a betrayal and him as a traitor. He presumably regarded his action as justified and sanctioned. She appealed to her solicitor nephew, Antony Nussey, for help and he contacted Augustine Birrell for legal advice on how to recover the printed books from Horsfall Turner. It was Augustine Birrell who had written the book, *Charlotte Brontë*, published in 1887, which Ellen had praised to Lady Morrison. He came from the good old Nonconformist liberal tradition, had become a lawyer and was to become a statesman. It was his legal opinion which Antony asked for, but obviously his interest in Charlotte and his literary ability made him an appropriate choice.

Ellen still wanted an edition of the letters to be prepared, and Birrell was asked whether he would be interested in editing them. He refused, but gave

his legal advice, and Horsfall Turner was served with a writ. The ins and outs
of the affair are singularly tedious, but they were an agonisingly painful series
of events to Ellen. At last she was able to take possession of the edition on
payment of £100. The printed sheets were in twelve large parcels, and some
of these Ellen fetched herself. William Scruton persuaded her not to charge up
to Horsfall Turner's house, as she had at various times intended to do. It must
have been a very painful time for Scruton, who was the friend of both the
disputants. After taking possession of the twelve parcels, Ellen asked her friend
John Ridley, Vicar of Brownhill Church,[7] to help her. Together they had a
bonfire and the offending edition was reduced to ash. Some twelve bound
copies survived, plus either one or two interleaved copies, and Ellen was to
make good use of them in the subsequent years. Augustine Birrell told her that
she could publish in America without worrying about copyright, but until
Nicholls' death she needed his permission to publish in the British Isles. George
Smith, when approached for advice, was crusty and unco-operative, nor did
Ellen obtain much help from a correspondence with M Heger.

Ellen had experienced fierce joy when burning the Horsfall Turner
edition; from henceforth she felt an enmity towards him so bitter that for any
of her friends to associate with him was to place themselves beyond the pale.
She sent Augustine Birrell a Yorkshire ham for Christmas, which hung, 'a
splendid subject for a Dutch painting, in his kitchen'. His opinion on the letters
– he was allowed to see one of the unburnt copies – was that all the best parts
had already been published by Mrs Gaskell and Wemyss Reid. Of those letters
in which Charlotte criticised her future husband, he said: 'How disagreeable a
map do they present of the Rev A N! But it would be unfair on Miss Brontë
to make her dislike of her husband public'. What remained 'are either of no
interest or else of a kind which could not with propriety be published'. There
was the rub. To Ellen everything which had touched Charlotte was holy. To
commentators of the time, their friendship may have seemed to have lesbian
overtones which were not acceptable. To the seventy-two year old who had
been reared in the breezy youth of the century, this interpretation was so
unthinkable as to be invisible.

Ellen had her little vanities. When her nephew Edward obtained a grant
of arms for the family, she put the design on her writing paper. She also used
the lion of Nassau, in the vague belief that in some way the Nusseys were a
bastard line of the House of Nassau. 'But these things are best not enquired
into', she told Erskine Stuart. The suppositions seem to have been based on a
name-change adopted many years before by Joseph Nussey of Thornhill, an
active Moravian. Ellen really had – as she claimed - little curiosity about
anything she regarded as private business and although she always lived in a
cloud of family connections, she was not the stuff of which genealogists are
made.

She lent the Horsfall Turner edition of the letters to friends. 'I have not
been so genuinely interested for a long time. To be brought so closely in
contact with a mind so strong and vigorous and honest does one good – its

perfect candour is so manifest one longs to have shared such a friendship', said Ridley. Ellen had been busy writing her own reminiscences of her association with the Brontës, and reading them aloud to Ridley and his wife. They felt, as did all her friends, that they ought to be published.

By the summer of 1890 the friendship between Ellen and Lady Morrison had reached the point where Ellen began her letters 'My dearest Friend', and ended them 'Your loving "E"'. 'You have been constantly in my mind since we parted', she wrote, very moved that Lady Morrison was taking the step of baptism into the Church of England. 'I can only wish that the ordinance may bring you all the blessing I have been conscious of through life – I mean the grace given at Holy Baptism and its constantly renewing power . . . I cannot tell you how much I feel this closer bond of friendship and affection between us.' In this state of emotion she told Lady Morrison, 'You supply to me better than any one the loss of dear CB'.

The summer of 1890 was so busy that Ellen did not manage to read the copies of the *Spectator* which Lady Morrison sent her. She had been trying to work through a backlog of sewing, and 'I wanted to set my house in order, and gain the sense of repose which order always conveys to my mind and feelings. Housekeeping is not nice at all unless you have someone to fall back on in business matters – all sorts of things turn up about property, rates, etc.'

At a dinner party at Mr Brown's[8] where Wemyss Reid was also a guest, Reid told her of his theory that Charlotte had been in love with M Heger, and he later published an article on the subject. Ellen was very hurt and angered. 'I disclaimed his notion as a great insult to Charlotte and now I am sorely wounded by the mischief he has effected.' Ellen was never to feel as friendly to Wemyss Reid again. She could not bear anyone to publish anything which might be taken to be derogatory about Charlotte, whether it was true or not.

Cardinal Newman's death in this year was a sorrow to Ellen: 'I remember Tract 90 and the wrong things said about it. Canon Heald brought it to me in Sunday School, there was nothing to make so much noise about, and he liked it – so did I. I wish I had a copy of it now to compare past and present judgement. I feel all the poorer for Newman's death – with all that was amiss he has been a type of goodness and intellect to me through life'. Here we have the two things that mattered most in life to Ellen, and the order in which they mattered – *goodness* and *intellect*. And – how few seventy-three year olds are willing to reconsider and change their opinions!

Unusually for Ellen, she had a summer attack of bronchitis, and she recuperated in Saltburn during August. Lady Morrison's husband, Sir George, was going to America and was willing to take a copy of the Horsfall Turner edition of the letters personally to Scribners. Ellen stated her motive for publication – a desire to defend Charlotte against the slanderous accusations made against her, and Scribners expressed a keen interest. The stage was set for a successful publication of the letters in America, but waiting in the wings was someone who was to upset the whole project.

Ellen had repudiated Wemyss Reid's suggestion that Charlotte had been in love with M Heger as a calumny, but it seems to have been this suggestion that had changed her mind about immediate publication of the letters.

Dr William Wright, who worked for the British and Foreign Bible Society, had already become one of Ellen's correspondents. Now, in February 1891, he advised delay in agreeing terms with Scribners. He offered to be joint editor of the letters and believed that the book should make a steady income, telling Ellen how much his own book royalties were. He said he had taken the opinion of an able (but unnamed) barrister on the publication of the letters. If he had indeed taken this action, it was without a shadow of authority, but this did not seem to occur to Ellen. She had already had the best advice in the country on the legal position. But she was taken in by smooth-tongued Wright.

His remarks that the Nicholls 'grabbed up everything at Haworth whether it belonged to him or not', and that Mr Brontë's sister Alice had written to himself saying 'we were wronged of all my Brother's property', were bound to impress Ellen, with her nice sense of family decency, who considered herself wronged of her own brother's property and who had been unable to co-operate happily with her supplanter in Charlotte's affections. Wright played on Ellen's susceptibilities, saying that she should have received at least £300 from Mrs Gaskell alone, and telling hard luck stories of Charlotte's relatives in Ireland.

Scribners were disappointed that so much material had already been used, but offered Ellen a very fair deal of 15% of the retail price as royalty and an advance of £50 on a complete and consecutive edition. At Easter, in bitter weather, Wright visited Ellen at Fieldhead. 'A clever, genial, Christian man', she described him. She went to visit him in London, where he suggested she also met a man named Clement Shorter. As it turned out, Wright was away, or unavailable, and 'did not know where West Ham was', and they did not meet. What did happen is a mystery. In a surviving draft letter Ellen wrote:

'You never TOLD ME of your decision which you allowed Mr Shorter to make, so it was a great shock to learn it in a public manner and on Mr S's part there was an infinity of spite in making it . . . You have told me nothing of your communications with Mr N[icholls]. I went into the South AS I BELIEVED for the convenience of your consulting with me on the preparation required for the publication of the letters − otherwise I should not have gone at all, for the seeing of relatives and friends was merely an accident of vicinity . . . You came to me as a help to pilot me through the difficult waves of a publishing business and I gave you my sincere faith and confidence in the matter. The object is just where it was − with painful additions.'

She may not have sent this letter. Wright certainly managed to wriggle back into her good graces and explain away Shorter's *faux pas*, whatever it was. Ellen sent him photographs of both herself and Charlotte, and locks of their hair, all of which he intended to have mounted in one frame. Wright tried to buy Charlotte's letters, offering her £50, which he said was well over the market price, and assuring her that after her death and his own the letters would go to a national repository − Ellen had obviously told him this was her hope for them. 'I so wish it were possible to get the E J B [Emily Jane Brontë] letters back again. It was mean and wicked taking them from you. I think you have nothing of the other sister's', wrote Wright, fishing to discover just what manuscripts Ellen was holding. It is interesting that this reference suggests that originally Ellen had more letters from Emily than we now know of.

Ellen enlisted the help of her American friend Mme Cortazzo in the matter, and Mme Cortazzo did call at Scribners. By now, largely through Wright's influence, Scribner was finding Ellen no longer amenable to his requests. As far as Ellen could make out, not even a third of the letters had already appeared in print. 'There has been so much BOTHERATION in one way or another for these many years, I often wish I had persisted in my desire not to let anything appear in my life time – and I very much fear that remuneration will never repay, though friends think differently.' Mme Cortazzo was brushed off by Scribners and did not see Scribner himself.

'I fear Dr Wright who came with such a flourish of friendship last Spring has done more harm than good by talking – time reveals him as a great egotist – given to promises but not performances . . . Tomorrow I am going to Kirklees, invited for Luncheon [with the Armytage family] . . it is a long drive . . .' wrote Ellen on the 24th September 1891. Wright said that he had spent thirty years gathering material for a book on the Irish background of the Brontë family. He wanted Ellen to tell him about Patrick's storytelling; 'I am inclined to think that his narratives largely influenced his daughters. Don't you

Haworth Parsonage, taken around the turn of the century.

think so? I think you told me that Emily hung on his lips when he was telling his strange tales.'

Ellen was now seventy-four. The mass of newspaper cuttings and other papers she had accumulated was becoming a burden. She was growing fatter – the corsets Mme Cortazzo sent her were too small. This year she had had her bronchitis summer as well as winter, and holidays had not really helped. She was constantly inundated with correspondence, and spent hours each day writing letters.

Scribner at length answered Ellen's repeated letters, pointing out that she had not responded to the editing suggestions made in August, and that the photographs she had sent were not suitable for illustrations. She did have profound self-doubts whenever she was asked to edit. Wright's assurances that Scribner was only going through the motions of asking her to do it and that really he wished to edit himself, hardly assisted matters. Now Wright assured Ellen that the firm of Scribners could not get out of their contract. 'Some time ago I had almost come to the conclusion to throw all my notes and photos regarding the Brontës into the fire', he wrote encouragingly. Ellen ended the year with influenza and doubts of Wright. Although there was henceforward a coolness between them, he had succeeded in sabotaging her deal with Scribners. In the following June, 1892, they posted everything back to her on the steamer, because she had been unable or unwilling to edit as they suggested, and was no longer happy with their terms.

[1] J Horsfall Turner of Idle was a noted antiquary. His many publications, from local histories, notes and queries, etc, to transcriptions of parish registers and manor court rolls, made a valuable contribution to local historical knowledge. It was a tragedy that he became involved with the Brontë letters. Information from John Nussey. Another informant, Chris Sumner, stated that the letters Horsfall Turner wrote to Ellen were so insulting that she was totally justified in regarding him thereafter as she did.

[2] This little episode was remembered and published in obituaries of Ellen.

[3] Dr J A Erskine Stuart was a Scottish surgeon. He settled in Yorkshire, and became interested in the area and its connections with the Brontës. His best known book is *The Brontë Country; Its Topography, Antiquities, and History*. After Ellen's death he contributed good articles about her to local papers, including the *Halifax Courier*, and recognised how well she expressed herself on paper. He believed that Ellen should have published a follow-up to Mrs Gaskell's biography. He was one of the most pleasant and well-meaning of the Brontë enthusiasts who met Ellen in her old age.

[4] For an obituary of Mr Tatham, see the *Yorkshire Post*, Monday 28th September 1896.

[5] Of Birrell's writing, the *Dictionary of National Biography* says that he was 'one of that happy fellowship who, by recording good lives of the past, and adorning their tale with scintillant wit and kindly humour, have helped to make goodness attractive to the less gifted of their own and future generations'.

[6] The correspondence is in the care of the Brontë Society.

[7] Rev John Ridley, London College of Divinity 1875, deacon 1875, priest 1876, Vicar of Brownhill from 1880.

[8] Presumably the father of Ellen's friend Miss Janie Brown of Barden Grange, Weetwood, Leeds.

THE OLD LIONESS DEFRAUDED, 1892-5

In the summer of 1892 Ellen left the house at Fieldhead to move back into the centre of Birstall. Fieldhead, with its good views and airy situation, had been a pleasant if cold home, but it was time to make a change.

She took Ingwell House on North Terrace, which was probably the house she had previously shared with a friend in the spring and summer of 1881. Now she was back closely in touch with her roots in the heart of the community:

'You can't think how often I am reminded of the long residence of the Nusseys in this immediate neighbourhood – the aged people who claim acquaintance as I chance to move among them, and the personal respect which is quite touching – the anecdotes they tell me of old times, of my father and my uncles . . .'

Ingwell House, on North Terrace in Birstall, was Ellen's home from the summer of 1892.

Ingwell House is a stone-built house, as were all Ellen's homes. It has a blue-slated roof and is separated from the road only by a narrow strip of garden. The view at the back in Ellen's day was of thickly wooded country; there were many footpaths through woods and fields. The road slopes steeply, so under the lower half of the house are good cellars, containing a large stone table. Viewed a few years ago, there was a pleasant central entrance hall stretching back to a pretty staircase lit by a tall window of the 'Oxford' type, the type of window which now lights the staircase at Haworth parsonage. There is an Oxford window also at Brookroyd House, where Ellen had lived for so long. Many of the windows of Ingwell House had small panes, a Georgian appearance, and their original shutters. On the right of the entrance hall was a large dining-room, with a white marble fireplace, and behind it a large kitchen. The sitting-room on the left of the entrance had a slate fireplace and doors through to the bay-windowed room at the back; it was this bay-windowed room which was photographed during Ellen's tenancy of the house. Upstairs leading from a charming landing were five bedrooms and a bathroom. One room had a built-in cupboard with carved wooden Gothick mouldings, and the large back bedroom had a pretty plaster lattice moulding round the ceiling, a wide bay window, and splendid views. It seemed a most pleasant and convenient house. Ellen lived at Ingwell House from at least October 1892 to April 1895, but age and worry and T J Wise spoilt it for her. The stage was set for her final betrayal, but luckily she was not yet aware of that.

Thomas James Wise, 1859-1937, was a criminal and his crimes were carried out in conspiracy with others. Literary forgery, fraud and deceit were the game. He began book collecting seriously in 1877 with first editions. Later he became friendly with H Buxton Forman, who liked to embellish first editions with letters, autographs, bits of the original manuscript or even relics. Soon after their first meeting in 1886 they combined to produce forgeries of alleged 'private editions' of poems, and this was done mainly between 1887 and 1897. The two had also discovered how to make use of literary societies. Forman began with the Villon Society founded in 1877, followed by the Browning Society founded in 1881, and the Shelley Society first mooted in 1885. Ellen was to refer to Wise as 'the Shelley man', and his position at the head of the Shelley Society gave him credence in the London literary and antiquarian book worlds, and also cover and finance for the printing of forgeries. He bankrupted the society, but avoided the blame.

In addition, Forman had discovered the value of buying the remaining papers of writers from surviving friends and relatives. Before 1878, he had acquired from Fanny Brawne's children (by a marriage ten years after Keats's death) the letters and books Fanny had from Keats, and had been able to produce a volume of letters. In 1879 after the death of Shelley's natural daughter, Forman bought from her niece many letters, manuscripts and relics, for £150 cash.

Ellen was to be the third, but not the last, of the victims of this kind of legal theft.

It was easy, for she had already told Wright, a friend of Clement Shorter, who was a friend of Wise, what her ambitions were for the letters. Wise had only to represent himself as an undercover agent for the British Museum, or the 'museum at Kensington' as the V & A and other museums there, founded from the proceeds of the 1851 exhibition, were then referred to. Sly hints would be enough to convince her, because this was what she had always wanted. Once convinced, she agreed to sell him a number of the letters. She consulted John Ridley and together they chose a hundred. The deal was to be kept secret during Ellen's lifetime and the letters deposited with a museum after her death. Wise paid her £125 for a hundred, according to his statement. Later, he said, Ellen decided to let him have a few more, and he paid her *pro rata*.

Shorter, who was a journalist, took this opportunity of seeing and using the letters as the basis for a new book on the Brontës. Ellen wrote to Wise, when she received a payment on the 18th November 1892: 'the enclosure, for which you have my thanks – especially for the *promise* you give in connection with your possession of my dear Friend's letters . . . I anticipate with considerable emotion Mr Shorter's coming work and shall be glad to give every further aid in my power . . . I hope to hear from Mr Shorter very soon. It is no doubt wise to part with the Letters as I have now done – but can you imagine what it has cost? A second parting as it were . . .' She believed that her dream for their safety had come true.

Wise always had a few irons in the fire. At this same time he was also 'editing' – publishing J P Smart's edition of a bibliography of Ruskin, but adding new material including some Wise/Forman forgeries, thus giving them apparent authenticity.[1] For the moment, as far as Ellen was concerned, Wise was satisfied.

As always, Ellen was busy sewing for her poorer neighbours, and grateful when her friends assisted her. 'I am going to make up a white frock for a cantata, and the grey petticoat will . . . protect the child from cold'. 'My poor people', Ellen called them and always spent a tenth of her income on loving help, saying that this blessed the remainder and made it go twice as far. She was tireless in her concern and generous with her time, taking endless trouble to ensure that the things given were what was really wanted. Her particular interests were the children and the old. 'Some aged pensioners who look so thinly clad' worried her in the winter of 1892 and she was planning cosy petticoats for them, wanting to quilt them using an old marseilles quilt for warmth, but she could not get used to the new sewing machines and the rheumatism in her hands was also a problem.

Erskine Stuart's friendship still meant a great deal to Ellen; she told him he was 'lucky to have missed' Wright when that gentleman was visiting Morley.

During 1893 Mary Taylor, the closest living link between Ellen and Charlotte, died. To the end she had lived in High Royd, the house she had built for herself on her return from New Zealand; a house considered delightful, where in summer the chairs were set facing the window so that the superb view could be enjoyed. Mary and Ellen had known one another all their lives, and their families had been as close in friendship as if they were one. Mary was survived by two of her brothers, John, who never married and died in 1901, and William Waring in New Zealand, who died in 1903. Only two of the six siblings who had made up that ebullient, intellectual household left children; William Waring had twelve, and the eldest brother, Joshua, had six. Shorter wrote an obituary article on Mary which upset Ellen considerably; she had asked him not to mention some of the information he gave in it. In spite of her annoyance with him previously, when she had met him on the abortive visit to London to gain Wright's help, and now on this further occasion, she was won over sufficiently by Shorter's undoubted charm to continue the acquaintance.

In 1893 the next phase of the defrauding of Ellen began. She was already committed to co-operating on a Brontë book with Shorter. It was to be a book superior to anything that had gone before. 'Mr Shorter is fully imbued with the right spirit', she wrote to Lady Morrison, 'and in due course you will see such a result as even *you* will deem well worth the waiting for! . . . The Work . . . will be full and instructive. It will expose all errors which from time to time have crept in and at last the Brontë story will be told in all its truth to the end'.

Shorter warned her not to put any more memories on paper in letters to friends, but to save them for inclusion, so in response to enquiries about the Brontës she could only talk her sparkling talk. Shorter asked – demanded – to see the more intimate letters, which she had kept back from Wise, and all else that she was still holding, saying that he needed to read everything, however personal, and convinced her that he would need to keep them until the book was finished. Gradually he managed to get the remaining letters into his hands, from whence they passed to Wise. Ellen had earlier estimated that she still had about 330, and Wise had bought, according to his own statement, not many more than 100. Wise was to carry out several other coups of this nature 'in conjunction with Clement Shorter, the genial irresponsible editor of various literary journals. "Clem" and "Tommy" . . . were on the best of terms'.[2]

As usual Ellen was taking part in all the intellectual life she could, attending lectures (Charles Dickens was one of the speakers she heard) and planning holidays. She longed to go for a month to Aix-les-Bains but was not able to organise the necessary party of friends. Her new servant, a Scotswoman, asked for high wages but was very satisfactory. When Ellen could not understand her accent, they both laughed and started again.

'Flowers are a double treat to me now I have no garden', she wrote in thanks for a gift of snowdrops. 'How delightful the sunshine but how cold it is! This is my 6th epistle today, and I want to go out while the brightness is on . . .' Ellen exemplified what so many modern exponents of Zen are seeking. She combined a strong spiritual life with a delight in the moment, an ability to live in the flying minute and to take joy in a flower, her friends, an animal or a child, the fresh air and the brightness of the sun. She mentioned her increasing infirmities without moaning, always finding some alleviation – a good pen nib, a cheery fire, a gift of cream cheese . . .

By August she was showing disillusion with Shorter and his friend Wise. 'They are not showing themselves gentlemen.' Indeed Wise was not a gentleman. She little knew into what hands she had fallen, through her trust in Wright which had led her directly to them. To the conventional society of the day Wise seemed beyond reproach, while Ellen was merely an old spinster in Yorkshire, easily abused. Her family were far off in Chislehurst and London, and the baleful influence of William Carr had left its mark on her nephews' attitude. Her great-nieces and great-nephews came to stay with her but their visits were fleeting, and they had no real interest in her relationship with Charlotte. They were young with their own lives to lead.

Ellen was placing her faith in the fact that she had letters from Shorter and Wise which would, she thought, enable her to make them keep their pledges: '. . . Lady Morrison promised to see Mr S[horter] for me and learn what he is intending by the delay being so long in fulfilling his own promises. I fear there is some shirking of trust and faith like all the rest – but I have HIS, and his friend's letters'.

At Ingwell House, Ellen had a constant stream of visitors – 'often I can't snatch time for looking at the daily papers'. One fine December day she managed to walk as far as Drighlington to see her friends the Hammonds,[3] and in the evening of the same day the governess from the Moravian school, a frequent visitor, came to see her. The next day Lady Morrison came, and the following one Ellen went to Leeds to see Lady Morrison and her sisters. It is not surprising that she was often still at her 'pen duties' until after ten at night. 'The gaiety of last week has been too much', she wrote – for her friend Mrs Ridley, wife of the vicar of Brownhill, was tireless in arranging musical evenings and theatrical productions.

In September 1893 she was made unhappy by the results of a strike in the area; suffering, distress, and starvation were around her. She was grateful for the gift of a brace of pheasants, for she could not bring herself to spend money on luxuries when there was such an urgent need of her financial help. She was again oppressed during the winter by the plight of the poor: 'Think of AGED and INFIRM couples subsisting on 5/-per week for everything a home needs yet these houses are palaces to them for they can be together which they cannot be in a [work]HOUSE . . .'

At one point, she was sent for urgently to Chislehurst, now once again the family home of her nephew Antony Nussey, who had taken the opportunity of buying the Ivy House a few years earlier. He and his wife were keen to support the artist Fred Yates and wanted him to paint Ellen's portrait, so she must needs be asked to come down from Yorkshire to sit.[4]

In 1894 a new irritation arose for Ellen – the formation of the Brontë Society. She was against it. Dr Erskine Stuart declined the secretaryship, and came to talk it over with her. 'The museum question which you have taken up HAS BEEN and is likely to be no *small trouble* to me', she told Mme Cortazzo. Wright's book had been published, and he was active in the Brontë Society. 'His book is perfectly odious for its fictions and vulgarity', was Ellen's opinion.

Ellen had troubles both of health and money: there was a deep-seated abcess in her unusually slender jawbone, and the cost of repairs to her cottage property had used up two whole years' rents. Her injured leg, believed to be sprained, was now diagnosed as a ruptured Achilles tendon. Even these troubles did not make her despair. 'You and my many friends are very good in making life sweet and interesting', she told Mrs Nussey of Potternewton Hall. But by the summer of 1894 a seventy-seven year old Ellen was to find fault with the situation of Ingwell House, and the landlord wanted to put up the rent.

Ellen liked some of the new foodstuffs which were coming onto the market. Some tomatoes had been 'so fresh and nice', and cream cheese sent by a friend, Mrs Atkinson,[5] was 'beautiful'. Other changes earned less approval. About the results of the Education Acts of the 1870s, which brought universal elementary education for the first time, she said: 'What is gained in knowledge seems to be lost in principle and honour'. The nostalgia of old age is apparent in this remark. The errors being printed about the Brontës and their friends irked her. 'The account in the Cleckheaton Guardian on the Red House full of èrrors', and the *Woman at Home* pen portrait of Emily 'perfectly ridiculous'. Her interest in literature was unchanged, and she was looking forward to reading Stopford Brooke's *Tennyson – his art and relation to Modern Life.*

All through the summer of 1894 Ellen was ill, and she began to conclude that Ingwell House was not healthy for her. In an effort to recuperate she went on holiday with Janie Brown, her friend from Weetwood. She enjoyed the change, but soon after her return had a nasty accident when driving to Kirklees Hall for an overnight visit to the Armytages. A lively pony caused a wheel of the trap to hit a gatepost, Ellen's wrist was broken and her face badly bruised. The love and concern of her friends and neighbours were almost over-whelming. 'Rich and poor are constantly coming'. It was the end of December before she was again able to attend church. 'I was obliged to give myself up to negative existence', said the active Ellen. 'A lesson in patience!'

By February 1895 she was still having constant feverish colds and bouts of bronchitis, and when the hot water pipes froze and in consequence they dare not light the kitchen fire, she resolved to leave 'this cold draughty house' in the summer. Even troubled and incapacitated, she could still identify with the joys of others. 'How the skaters are enjoying themselves, especially while the moonlight nights lasted', she exclaimed. It was clear that her ill health was becoming chronic, but in spite of it, she visited the Moravian chapel to hear 'some charming sacred music'.

The interior of Ingwell House, taken by Annie Atkinson in March 1895.

It was in March 1895 that Annie Atkinson, caught up in the newest hobby, came to photograph Ellen's home. 'The Bay window room is lightest in the afternoon', said Ellen. Shown in the resulting photograph is family furniture which Charlotte had known so well, chairs, table, bookcase, piano. A vase of snowdrops stands near Ellen's pen and ink, reminding us of Charlotte's wine glass which always held a wild flower. The grand piano is noticeable. The bookshelves are much used, and around are paintings and photographs of beloved people and places. It is a charming, gracious room. 'Quaint', was Lady Morrison's word, but one could move happily into this room today, and can imagine Ellen's old friend Mary Hewitt sitting here on her visit from Herefordshire, talking, and enjoying tea from Ellen's small Georgian silver teapot. The friendship had been an important part of the two old ladies' lives since they first met as girls, when Henry Nussey was a young curate at Earnley proposing marriage by post to Charlotte.

On the 31st March 1895, forty years to the day since Charlotte Brontë died, Shorter arrived at Banagher to meet Nicholls who gave him access to Charlotte's letters from Brussels, the Brontë childhood manuscripts, Maria Branwell's letters to Patrick Brontë – in fact everything. Shorter must indeed have been a charming and persuasive man. Nicholls allowed him to buy and take away almost the whole. It was a further coup for Wise. Shorter also managed to obtain Charlotte's letters to William Smith Williams of Smith, Elder and Co's publishing house, via one of Williams' daughters.

On top of all her other troubles Ellen had another bad fall, tripping over her hall carpet. She sprained and bruised herself. Then Mary, the Scots servant, gave notice, because her mother needed a daughter at home. By May Ellen was feeling a little better, and Shorter was again requesting her help with his book. But the shocks in that direction were about to begin. She heard that some letters to herself from Charlotte were on show at the Brontë Museum at Haworth. These letters were owned by a Mr Waugh, from Stackhouse near Settle. She wrote to ask where he obtained the letters, jumping to the conclusion that the source was Horsfall Turner, and that he must have kept back some of the originals when he was setting up type for the now-destroyed editon of the letters. (So strong was her dislike of Horsfall Turner that she broke off her longstanding friendship with Erskine Stuart because he had attended a lecture by Turner in Heckmondwike and proposed the vote of thanks.)

For two whole months, June and July 1895, Ellen was in a ferment of distress over these letters bought by Waugh. Again and again she protested that she had only sold a single letter, and that to an un-named friend, who still had it and refused to part with it. But gradually enquiries by the solicitors involved discovered the source of the letters: it was Wise, who Ellen had believed had taken them in trust for the nation, to be deposited after her death, the deal to be completely secret while she lived, and the money not a sale, but a thank-you from the country. A letter of hers held by Texas University, dated 25th July 1895, refers to the letters as a sacred deposit with Wise which were ultimately to be deposited in the museum at Kensington.

Barker and Collins say of Wise in a later episode with the Swinburne manuscripts: 'when his rights, real or supposed, were threatened, he reacted with a characteristic mixture of bullying and deception which would scare off those less sure of themselves'. And again, when he had been caught out in simple theft, he 'combined brutal bullying with discreet blackmail, a characteristic and remarkably effective strategy which he was to pursue again when threatened'. This brutal bullying attitude was exactly what Wise adopted towards Ellen. He wrote, showing himself in his true colours, 'The only mercenary person concerned was Miss Ellen Nussey, who sold the letters which had cost her nothing, and haggled over the price!' Wise, on the committees of literary societies and founding a notable library, pillar of the establishment, conman and fraudster, was pitted against a seventy-eight year old lady, frail, constantly ailing, alone, the old lioness, brave still and devoted to the memory of her friend. It was no sort of a contest.

Wise wrote to Waugh telling him that Ellen had sold hundreds of Charlotte's letters and boasting of the extent of the Brontë manuscripts he then held. Waugh heard that Pearsons, dealers in manuscripts, were 'hawking 300 letters round the country'. Ellen's name was besmirched for ever as a seller of

Charlotte's letters, although of everyone concerned with the Brontës, she had given most and gained least.

Nicholls, who fell heir to everything the sisters had worked for, who sold *The Professor* and almost all his manuscripts as well as the contents of the parsonage, never had a breath of blame for taking the money, except from Wright. Mrs Gaskell allegedly made £2,000 from the biography, which was largely made up of extracts from Charlotte's letters to Ellen, and had no compunction in doing so.

Ellen, who would have used the money for the church and the poor, spent £100 on buying in the Horsfall Turner edition which she destroyed, and gained less than this by, as she believed, depositing the letters with the nation for posterity. What she received from other sources amounted to less than £100 altogether. She gave unceasingly of her time, spent endlessly on travel and postage as she visited and loaned her letters to writers on the Brontës, and she came out in every conceivable way the loser. It was a complete betrayal of everything Ellen had tried to do in the forty years since Charlotte's death, a defeat of reticence, probity and honour. Ellen was forced to apologise to Waugh through her solicitors, and she did so freely. Fortunately the full horror was only revealed to her gradually.

'I was so ill and everything went so strangely wrong I had to turn my back on all cares for a week to get round again. It really seemed as if an evil spirit were let loose in the place', she said of this time.

[1] Quotes and information on Wise, Buxton Forman and Shorter from *A Sequel to an Enquiry; the Forgeries of Buxton Forman and Wise Re-examined*, Nicolas Barker and John Collins, pub London and Berkeley by the Scolar Press 1983. The original being *An Enquiry into the Nature of Certain Nineteenth Century Pamphlets*, by John Carter and Graham Pollard, 1934, re-issue by Haskell House, USA, 1969.
   Wise published Charlotte Brontë's *The Adventures of Ernest Alembert* in 1896, and Anne Brontë's *Self Communion* in 1900, as separate booklets. He was responsible for the scattering throughout the world of the letters he sold, for the direct theft and later sale of material lent to Shorter for study during the writing of his book, and for much adulteration of the Brontë texts he purchased. Later Wise took to tearing pages out of rare books in the British Museum and stealing them. Although discredited, he died worth £130,000, a fortune in 1937.
[2] Earlier in 1893, the *Bookman* called him 'Mr Thomas J Wise, the well-known collector and bibliographer' when he began to edit their 'Notes on Recent Book Sales'. He used this position to describe and authenticate several forgeries.
[3] Vavasor Fitz-Hammond Hammond was vicar of Drighlington from 1869 to at least 1875.
[4] This is almost certainly the portrait in the Brontë Parsonage Museum.
[5] Mrs Atkinson (*née* Crowther), a close friend of Ellen's last years, was the wife of Samuel Atkinson, of Laneside House, Churwell. She had distant links with Ellen via the Crowthers of Gomersal and Ellen's connections the Claphams, and a similar remote connection with the Red House Taylors.

ELLEN AT MOOR LANE HOUSE, 1895-7

Unable to bear Ingwell House with its reminders of the deception practised upon her, Ellen found another dwelling, a large house. Birstall society thought she moved there out of social pride and Ellen was aware of their opinion, but she was attracted by the airy, sunny rooms looking out onto a delightful garden, the seclusion, the view, the fresh air, and the quietness. It was the very place she had suggested to Mme Cortazzo, some years before – Moor Lane House.[1] The rent was high, but she was becoming crippled by rheumatism and her chances of pleasure were few. Warmth – apart from its sunniness, the house had central heating – space inside to move about in bad weather, and the pleasant lawns when it was fine, were uppermost in her thoughts. She missed her garden terribly while living in Ingwell House. At seventy-eight moving house was heavy work and a great worry, but she coped with the preparations at the end of August 1895.

The owner, Mr Wormald, was abroad which delayed the tenancy agreement and she finally moved in during the second week in September on a beautiful day. The gardener already *in situ* was in the landlord's service, partly paid by him and partly by the tenant. 'Old MacLean's a terrible scrub', thought Ellen. At once she was inviting friends to visit, explaining how to reach her by train and tram. She was anxious to see them individually, so that she could enjoy each in turn without over-excitement. Lady Armytage, her very first visitor at Moor Lane House, came while she was still all in confusion, and then Rev Ridley and his wife came to help her arrange her books. Lady Morrison came for a few hours soon after the move.

Ellen still believed in Shorter's promises, although she now knew what sort of man Wise was. Shorter was making demands on her time, asking for more and more information, promising to come to see her without actually doing so. Mary Hewitt was coming to stay for at least a week, and Ellen hoped that she would be a help in sorting papers out for Shorter.

In spite of visitors, attendances at church when she was able to go, central heating and open fires, the winter was a hard one for Ellen. She was often 'frozen' with cold, sitting by the window to make the most of the daylight when writing to her numerous correspondents. In February 1896 her great-niece Mary was with her. Mary was to be trained to work among the poor, and Ellen wished she would take up work in Birstall and live at Moor Lane House.

'Old ties are slipping away', wrote Ellen, and 'old property crumbling to

Ellen's last home, Moor Lane House.

nothing that used to bring in a nice little rental'. She was lucky in having many visits from dear old friends and relations, but in common with most of Victorian England, she had a servant problem. What Ellen needed was a relative to look after her, or, failing that, a companion who was at the same time a lady, a friend and a housekeeper, and such a treasure was not to be found.

When the summer of 1896 came and with it the long-promised visit from Shorter, it made Ellen ill with shock and disappointment. She said, 'The interpretation given of literary law was utterly unprincipled and unscrupulous'. As his hostess, Ellen felt unable to tell him what she thought, but she wrote afterwards, and asked for the return of letters she had lent him. His reply was another shock. In fact these most precious and private letters, on loan only, were never returned to her but joined the others being hawked for sale around the world.

'I have been shamefully treated by the greed and grab of these two men [Shorter and Wise] they have cheated and deceived me over and over again . . . They have KEPT what was only lent for perusal and defy my demands for the return of what was most precious to me', she was to write. 'After the most serious pledges of secrecy now and deposit for the future they lyingly appropriated everything – they knocked me up with worry and distress'.

She still had a touching faith in the outcome of Shorter's writing. She had been promised two-thirds of all the profits, but now Shorter was only offering her £50. 'It is not the loss of money to be spent to CB's memory which grieves me so much as the treachery practiced – the friend [Wise] sold twelve letters for £50 unknown to me! . . .'

With this worry, the intense heat of summer and 'flocks' of visitors who took advantage of the good weather, Ellen was exhausted.

With the autumn two more great-nieces came from the south, and enjoyed themselves so much that they did not want to leave. Many of the people who visited Moor Lane House have recorded their memories. Children found a cupboard in which fascinating toys resided, and remembered long afterwards playing diabolo and other games. The coach-house had an outside stair which led to a large upper room, where Ellen allowed the local children to have their dancing classes. In late September, early October 1896 Ellen went to stay with Mary Hewitt in Herefordshire, a complicated journey by train. She asked Annie Atkinson to meet her in Leeds and return to Moor Lane House with her, as long ago she herself had met Charlotte and gone with her to Haworth. 'Dearest Annie', now fifty-six, was invited about once a month. Ellen saved things to tell her instead of putting them in letters. 'I have not time now to tell you all adventures, they have been many', she wrote once when anticipating a visit from Annie. 'Come for two nights if you can . . .'

In February 1897 Ellen went again to the Hewitts at the Homestead in Tenbury, Herefordshire, and once more Annie Atkinson helped her on her journey. One of Mary Hewitt's daughters was always referred to by Ellen as 'the doctor daughter' who took special care of her. There was music twice a day which Ellen revelled in and the gardens were 'quite gay with flowers'.

In this last year of Ellen's life she had to bear the bitter disappointment of her treatment by Wise and Shorter. The promised book, *Charlotte Brontë and her Circle*, was published at last and caused her intense distress. Relatives and friends, who knew how earnestly Ellen had helped all she could, were alienated by revelations of matters which she had told Shorter were on no account to be mentioned. Her eightieth birthday was soured by the knowledge that an interleaved copy of the suppressed edition of the letters, with her written comments, which she had only lent, had been sold.

To escape from her distress she went for a holiday to Grange-over-Sands in April. While there her thoughts were with the poor families she tried so hard to help. One woman who told Ellen all her troubles had said to her, 'I'm no scholard, so you mun guide me a bit wi' your judgement, he [her husband] said ye'll tell me right'.

Birstall was busy that summer of 1897. Amongst other things, it was Queen Victoria's jubilee. Fifty years before when Victoria had come to the throne, the Brontë girls, Ellen, and Mary Taylor had all been excited at the idea of a girl like themselves on the throne of England, a fairytale come true. To mark this jubilee, Ellen gave every employee of the local tramway a Testament.

As her health gradually failed Ellen found running Moor Lane House a trouble to her, although it was so pleasant. The old gardener was 'unbearable' and he and his wife 'corrupt every domestic that comes'. Even 'old Mrs Dunn' to whom Ellen had been so kind was discovered to be a pilferer.

In the midst of her troubles when it seemed too much effort to housekeep, Ellen could still be taken out of herself by little things. She delighted in lying awake on a warm August night with the window open and seeing four or five watchman's fires burning on the high embankment being built for a branch line of the railway, their golden glow piercing the darkness. She still took a keen interest in literature: 'Have you seen the new book on Lady Novelists of the Victorian Age – some extracts I have seen are very interesting . . .', but 'two more Brontë books are forthcoming from very incompetent writers'.

A West Riding lady set down her experience:

'Miss Nussey had been waited upon by many persons for literary purposes, but I believe an interview I had with her during the autumn just past was the last she was able to grant. It was in a state of great nervousness that I found myself at the inner door of Moor Lane House, Gomersal. With my heart in my mouth I saw Miss Nussey come forward to the door. All nervousness, however, vanished under the charming manners of this gracious old lady. Taking me into the drawing-room, I noticed she wore an old-fashioned brown silk dress and a rather modish cap of black and white silk over her thick white hair. A noticeable feature was her bright eyes when she removed her spectacles. One of the first questions Miss Nussey asked was, "What religion are you?" "Church of England, and from a long line of Church-people," I replied. My answer gratified her, and I soon found that she was an ardent, nay a passionate Churchwoman. One of the chief objects of my visit was to obtain her opinion on a portion of a letter said to be written by Charlotte Brontë to a correspondent unknown to me and all others to whom the document had been shown. What I had with me was a photograph. On inspecting it she said, "Undoubtedly the original is in Charlotte's handwriting." She soon decided to whom the letter had been addressed – Miss Leah Brooke, of Aldams House, Dewsbury, a former schoolfellow. Miss Nussey gave some interesting particulars about the then girl and her relatives. This led to a chat about Charlotte's god-parents, the Rev Thomas Atkinson and his wife . . . The shy schoolgirl became teacher, then novelist, and Miss Nussey informed me that a distinct coldness arose between Mrs Atkinson and Charlotte. It grieved Mrs Atkinson keenly that the daughter of a clergyman should hold up in a contemptuous light any clergyman. It was a regret, she said, of Charlotte's that Mrs Atkinson took umbrage at her novel-writing, for she felt her

Ellen Nussey in old age.

indebtedness to her god-parents in the matter of education. Speaking of the Rev P Brontë, Miss Nussey said he was very fond of horses and dogs, but not to the extent his girls were; also that in his later years he became rather boastful of his conquests with ladies, a failing which much annoyed Charlotte and which she always tried to check. He was a high-spirited man, full of courage. In connection with her correspondence with Charlotte, Miss Nussey said she had often been badly treated, and I quite agreed with her when she informed me of the circumstances. This led me to tell her that I had heard something of the kind before, and that I had felt diffident about seeking an interview, but that at last I had yielded, the suggestion being that I should "beard the lioness in her den." She laughed heartily and exclaimed, "That's exactly what I am, a lioness. I have to be, because of the way I have been treated." To me she was all kindness, and the interview throughout seemed mutatally satisfactory. We parted, but she called me again to the house door, and then with a serious air said, "Remember! All who have had anything to do with the Brontës have had great trouble." I parted from the venerable lady with much admiration for her mental powers and gracious manners.'[2]

In the stormy weather of September 1897, Ellen realised that she had not much longer to live and wished that she had family living nearby. The friends she loved most were in Leeds and Tenbury. In any case, friends can rarely serve the needs of a dying person as a relative can. Ellen was a realist: 'People rather look forward to the change you may cause when removed and speculate on what they should like when a sale has to take place . . .' But always her faith sustained her: 'It is nice to look forward to the eternal and higher scenes of the coming future in another state of existence, where [there is] no doubt employment too for the highest and very best that is within us – soul satisfying delights', she wrote to her American friends. Her current servant could not cook good bread, beef tea or anything else but as always 'the lovely sunshine is my cheerer'.

After a long and severe illness with pleurisy she was sitting up and writing to friends early in November, in beautiful clear writing with a fine nib and blue ink. On the 14th she wrote a little note to Lady Morrison, 'my dearest Friend', with her 'dearest and best love'. In addition to the endless flow of letter-writing she was planning decorations for the church at Christmas.

It is good to be able to record that Mary Hewitt's daughter came to stay with Ellen at the end of October and was 'exceedingly kind'. This pleasant young woman, seeing how ill Ellen was, sent for her mother and they both stayed until Ellen died on the 26th November. 'Up to the very end Miss Nussey retained possession of her intellectual faculties . . . She was conversing quietly with her lady companion when the end came . . . A sudden spasm, and the long life was over.'[3]

A few days before, on the 22nd, William Carr, who happened to be over from Norfolk, had called for the first time in years. Ellen was too ill to see him.

When she died Ellen had long been the last of her immediate family in the district. The Brontës had vanished many years before. Even the Taylors, established at Gomersal since at least Tudor times, were to leave the area soon afterwards. The song was over.

A *Yorkshire Post* reporter spoke to a working man on the high road to Gomersal:

' "Do you know Miss Nussey, of Moor Lane House?" The man's face brightened immediately. "Oh, yes, sir!" was his response; "she sends me and my mate the *Evangelist* paper regular. She's a very kind lady is Miss Nussey." And when told – what he evidently did not know – that his aged friend had suddenly passed away the honest fellow's concern was unmistakeable. He had not seen her in her usual haunts for some time; but then, she was such a very old lady, and could not be expected to go about as in former days; she had always taken an interest in poor people, and he was genuinely sorry to think she had gone. A homely matron, trudging home from market . . . regarded her neighbour's death as a distinct loss to Birstall. "There will indeed be a great many who will miss her," was how she put it. And this would seem to be the general feeling of the district . . . Crotchety she may have seemed to some – she had strong likes and dislikes – yet she preserved the amiable disposition and equable temper which so distinguished her early relationships, and those who knew her best found her ever a true friend . . . She tried to be helpful whenever help was wanted.'

The funeral took place on a pouring wet day with the weather so extreme that people were deterred from attending, but it was noticed that many of Ellen's humble neighbours were present. The hymns intended to be sung by the graveside were abandoned and only the briefest ceremony could be held in the torrential downpour. Lady Morrison had come from Leeds despite everything the climate could do, and there was a representative from the Brontë Society which Ellen had disapproved of so powerfully. Ellen was buried in the family grave, and the stone above her is still to be seen in Birstall churchyard.[4]

Mrs Ridley, the clergyman's wife who was so fond of amateur theatricals, wrote to tell the Cortazzos in America of the event. 'I really think she worried herself to death over those "letters" ', she said, and stated that Ellen had consulted a lawyer over suing Shorter. 'People will be astonished to find she has so little to leave!' The Pennsylvanian Railway Bonds, in which William Carr had invested the sisters' inheritance from their brother Richard, were left to their nephew John Thomas Hartley Nussey in Australia. Her furniture was in trust to go to increase the stipend of the curate at Birstall Church, and after bequests and expenses had been met, the residue of her estate was to be used by the vicar and curate for the benefit of the poor of the parish.[5]

The Nussey family in the south would be sorry to be having no more visits from Ellen, mysteriously light in luggage because when travelling she filled the framework of her bustle with her rolled-up clothes and personal possessions. It would hardly affect them that the last link with their homeland was severed. Their life was in Kent and London now. Ellen was the last of her generation.[6]

Lady Morrison's tribute to her 'loving E' was printed in the *Bookman* of January 1898:

'On the morning of Friday, the 26th of November 1897, there passed away, in the seclusion of her quiet Yorkshire home, Miss Ellen Nussey, the life-long friend of Charlotte Brontë, and the chief, if not sole, personal link existing in connection with that gifted family . . . Charlotte Brontë died at the age of 38 – Ellen Nussey had completed her 80th year. And, not in frailty of feebleness has she departed now. Her spirit was strong within her; her name was honoured and revered – especially in those districts surrounding her home, where it was loved and known – and her heart, with unfaltering affection and deep love for the friends of her youth, beat, up to the last, with a loyal devotion that knew no diminution and no change.

. . . I recall . . . her quaint old-fashioned home. In the hall, as I enter, I see her coming to meet me, gracious . . . who, with the simple courtliness which was always hers, draws me, not only into the warmth and cosiness of her sunny drawingroom, but also into the sympathy and the sanctuary of her own heart. In person Ellen Nussey was not striking, but she was sprightly, attractive – coquettish, no doubt, in her younger days – and intelligent; her manners charming; every word and gesture bearing emphatically the stamp of truth; while her voice, mellowed and modulated to a peculiarly gentle cadence, was exceedingly pleasant to hear.

I have often sat beside her, and heard with unfeigned interest her sparkling talk about the Brontë family; have heard her relate incidents and anecdotes in the lives of the sisters, which seemed to me better than any information to be gathered from books; and I recall the unabated affection and zest with which she dwelt upon the ways and merits of her gifted friends, while the indignation with which she denounced any aspersion cast upon the memory of Charlotte Brontë and her sisters was, in its righteousness, beautiful to see.

Miss Nussey told me that she considered Branwell, the brother, the cleverest and most talented of the whole family, and, but for his misused powers, he could, had he chosen, have outstripped his sisters in literature. Many of the incidents which she related go far to prove that Charlotte Brontë was keenly alive to humour, fun, and all the brighter aspects of life; that she eagerly enjoyed and participated in a joke; and that, until grave and distressing sorrows visited and clouded her life, she was at all times open to, and rejoiced in, its gaiety and sunshine.

That Ellen Nussey is the prototype of "Caroline Helstone" in "Shirley" cannot for a moment be doubted. It may be remembered that in one part of the book Caroline is described as wearing a brown dress with a pink bow. When I enquired of Miss Nussey if this also was taken from herself, she said that she WAS wearing that particular kind of attire at the time "Shirley" was written. It is to Ellen Nussey that the public is, and will ever be, indebted for authentic information with regard to the Brontë family. But for her, no history of these remarkable people could have gone forth to the world in a truthful and reliable form; while, be it said, to her everlasting honour and credit, she ever kept HERSELF in the background – she, a living and no ordinary personality – in order that the crown of glory should rest in its entirety upon her gifted friends. In this respect her loyalty and unselfishness were remarkable. Not her own, but THEIR exaltation was her aim, her hope, her endeavour. She was content to remain comparatively unknown so her great friends should be honoured and acknowledged before the world.

It is to be regretted that Miss Nussey not infrequently found herself at variance with the different writers of Brontë history and that she occasionally involved herself in small disputes and antagonisms, which, it is to be feared, disturbed the serenity of her declining years. But to me – as I knew and loved her – Ellen Nussey was a sweet and gracious being, true and steadfast in her heart's affections and in her large-hearted loyalty to those who had gone before; a patron saint to the poor, whose blessing followed her; living her life full of gentle deeds and kindnesses, and whose memory in the many hearts which loved and revered her will remain green and fragrant for ever. Fortified with the Christian's courage she met the approach of death without fear and when death itself came it found her "Quiet, confident, unbewildered".'

It was the poor of Birstall who would miss her most in their daily lives, for her practical help, kindness and sympathy had meant much to them. The middling folk, as she knew, were more concerned with her possessions and what they might buy of the same. Due to a problem with her will – she had struck out a clause and signed the document without the presence of her solicitors – there was delay in proving it and carrying out its conditions, but at last on the 18th and 19th May 1898 the sale of effects was held at Moor Lane House. A report appeared in the *Bradford Observer* of the 19th under the heading 'The Late Miss Nussey; Sale of Brontë Relics'. Family bequests of paintings and so on had been removed and were not included:

'The effects of the late Miss Ellen Nussey, of Moor Lane House, Gomersal, were offered for sale by auction yesterday by Messrs. Firth and Wright, auctioneers, Cleckheaton. The fact that Miss Nussey was for many years intimate with Charlotte Brontë, and other members of that illustrious family, lent unusual interest to the sale, as it was known that Miss Nussey had been the recipient of many presents from the gifted authoress, and was one of her most cherished correspondents . . .'

The Brontë Society was represented and 'secured several of the most coveted relics offered. Lady Morrison, a great friend of the late Miss Nussey, attended in person, and made some purchases. The attendance of the general public was very large . . .'. A gun and two swords said to have been used in the defence of Rawfolds Mill, Liversedge, were among the effects. Thomas Nussey of Bramley Grange bought a button and a brooch. The button was from one of George III's coats, and the brooch the king had worn on his shirt front.

It is strange how Ellen's will and her sale brought out once again so many interlinked threads: the royal connection of part of the family; the religious connection and her own deep faith, through her books and her bequests; the longest connection of all, with the woollen trade and its evolution, through the link with Rawfolds Mill; the long-forgotten connection with the Hartley family who had once been influential in world affairs, through her nephew's name; her concern for the poor around her; and over-riding all other threads, her bond with Charlotte and through her with the other Brontës, and her loyalty to them. She deserved the tribute, 'Well done, thou good and faithful servant'.

¹ Now a hotel.

² After Ellen's death this lady sent her notes of the visit to the *Yorkshire Post*. They were also printed in the *Cleckheaton Guardian* of the 4th December 1897. The newspaper cutting quoted here is annotated *Yorkshire Post* without a date.

³ The sentence describing Ellen's death is from an unidentified newspaper cutting in the possession of John Nussey.

⁴ Inscribed as follows: 'Beneath this tombstone lie the mortal remains of John Nussey of Birstall Smithies, third son of the adjoining Joshua and Mercy Nussey, who in the enjoyment of the goodwill and esteem of all who knew him departed this life on the 14th day of July 1826 in the 66th year of his age. Also of George, fifth son of the above John Nussey, who died October 7th 1812 age 8 years. Also of Sarah Walker, third daughter of the above John Nussey, who died June 16 1843 age 33 years. Also of Joseph, second son of the above John Nussey, who died May 29 1849 age 49 years. Also of Ellen relict of the above John Nussey, who departed this life 2 December 1857 in the 86th year of her age. Also of Ann, widow of Robert Clapham, eldest daughter of the above John Nussey, who died April 24 1878 aged 82 years. Also of Ellen, youngest daughter of the above John Nussey, who died November 26th 1897 aged 80 years.'

⁵ In the last years of Ellen's life her income was about £300 pa. Much of it was from annuities, which died with her, and property in trust, which passed on automatically.

⁶ Ellen's remaining family consisted only of her eldest brother's descendants. Her nephew Edward retired in 1904 as Vicar of Longney in Gloucestershire and went to live at Rose Cottage, Chislehurst, near his brother Antony, dying unmarried in 1911.

APPENDIX ONE:
THE INGHAMS OF BLAKE HALL
based on information from John Nussey

Because Anne Brontë used her experiences as governess to the Ingham family as the foundation for part of her novel *Agnes Grey*, 1837, the place, people and period are of abiding interest. The Inghams lived in Blake Hall, which then stood in its own grounds of over thirty acres, some 370 yards to the south of Mirfield parish church, with extensive views of the wooded hills on the Hopton side of the river Calder. It had been an ancient building but was rebuilt, the new Blake Hall being 'topped-out' in October 1747. It was bought by the Inghams as a property investment in 1784, and they also bought the home farm of twelve acres and the pews or 'sittings' in the parish church which went with the hall.

The Ingham family were then cloth merchants of Huddersfield and successful businessmen. In 1801 they took over the Huddersfield Commercial Bank, better known as Inghams Bank, and about that time Joshua senior moved into one of their investments, Blake Hall, to live. This first Joshua Ingham at Blake Hall gained, presumably by some arrogance, the nickname of 'Lord' Ingham. He died in 1814; his son Joshua, a compulsive hunter and gambler whom it was unwise to cross, saw the financial blow of 1815 when, due to the failure of their London agents, Inghams Bank had to stop payments. The following year he died young leaving his wife Martha (who was also his second cousin) widowed, and his two young sons fatherless.

It was this Martha, *née* Taylor of Purlwell Hall and second cousin of Ellen Nussey's sister-in-law, who had been kind to Ellen at Roe Head in 1831 and who also seems to have been reasonably considerate to Anne Brontë during her brief time as governess at Blake Hall in service to Martha's elder son, Joshua Ingham, and his wife Mary, *née* Cunliffe Lister. In addition to being one of the Dewsbury Board of Poor Law Guardians, Joshua Ingham was also deputy lieutenant for the West Riding and chairman of the Dewsbury Magistrates Bench. Joshua's record of support to the Poor Law Amendment Act substantiates the picture of him given by Anne Brontë, and he seemed to owe more of his character to his father and grandfather than to his mother.

By the time Anne Brontë arrived at Blake Hall in 1839, travelling alone, 'as she thought she could manage better and summon more courage if thrown entirely upon her own resources,'[1] the young Inghams had four children and a baby. Mrs Mary Ingham was only eight years older than Anne. She had been married aged about nineteen, and Anne Brontë is believed to have been her first governess. Anne's initial reaction was not unfavourable: 'We have had one letter from her since she went', wrote Charlotte, 'she expresses herself very well satisfied, and says that Mrs Ingham is extremely kind; the two eldest children alone are under her care, the rest are confined to the nursery – with which and its occupants she has nothing to do. Both her pupils are desperate little dunces – neither of them can read and sometimes they even profess a profound ignorance of their alphabet, the worst of it is the little monkies are excessively indulged and she is not empowered to inflict any punishment – she is requested when they misbehave to inform their Mamma – which she says is utterly out of the question as in that case she might be making complaints from morning till night – "So she alternately scolds, coaxes and threatens – sticks always to her first word and gets on as well as she can" – I hope she'll do, you would be astonished to see what a sensible, clever letter she writes – it is only the talking part that I fear – but I do seriously apprehend that Mrs Ingham will sometimes consider that she has a natural impediment of speech.'

Anne was the first of the Brontë sisters to work as a governess in a private household, although both her sisters had taught in private schools and Charlotte sometimes referred to this school experience as 'governessing'. We have Anne's own authority in her preface to the second edition of *Agnes Grey* for stating that an account of her experiences at Blake Hall is contained in the book. Blake Hall and the Inghams appear disguised as Wellwood House and the Bloomfields.

The Yorkshire Archaeological Journal (vol 55, 1983) contains an article by John Nussey entitled 'Blake Hall in Mirfield, and its occupants during the 18th and 19th centuries', from which the following is an extract:

'Anne [Brontë] was determined to do her best and make a success of her first job, but conditions, though probably normal enough in the local society of the rapidly developing period, were much beyond anything she had imagined. After persevering courageously for nearly nine months and having at last begun to make some progress with her unruly charges, she was unexpectedly dismissed. Her own comments, delivered by Agnes Grey, when she decided to try for a further post, were: "I knew that all parents were not like Mr and Mrs Bloomfield, and I was certain all children were not like theirs. The next family must be different, and any change must be for the better."

Among the minor characters in *Agnes Grey*, Mr Bloomfield's mother must be suspected of portraying Martha Ingham . . . The name of the Bloomfield's mansion – "Wellwood" – however, seems so far to have escaped notice . . . Anne Brontë had made some acquaintance with Mirfield earlier, when she was a pupil at Roe Head. During that time she had been rescued from acute spiritual doubts and depression by the understanding counsel of the Minister of the Moravian chapel in Mirfield, to whom as a last resort she had applied. The Moravians' premises in Mirfield were situated at Wellhouse, which had earlier belonged to Joshua Ingham I's brother-in-law Daniel Shepley, who himself became one of the Moravian Brethren. This experience of Anne's was of great significance to her, and she undoubtedly had Wellhouse in mind when she gave the name "Wellwood" to the scene of Agnes Grey's first attempt to earn her living.

Something of Blake Hall's influence may even have extended to Anne Brontë's second novel, *The Tenant of Wildfell Hall*, one theme of which is concerned with the gradual degeneration of a promising but self-indulgent young man, and the effects of this on his family; his final illness is the result of a fall from his horse while hunting. Just as from time to time old "Mrs Bloomfield" would chat in a friendly manner to Agnes Grey, so very likely old Mrs Ingham chatted to Anne. She may very well have confided to Anne, and exaggerated, her sufferings caused by Joshua II's hunting and gambling mania. She may, too, have retold tales heard from Joshua I, her father-in-law, of William Turner (a previous owner of Blake Hall) and the miserable end to which *his* excesses had led him and his family. In the four years which elapsed between Anne's start on *Agnes Grey* and her start on *The Tenant of Wildfell Hall* her experiences of life had admittedly widened a great deal, but what she had heard of Blake Hall could well have prepared the ground for some of her writing in the later novel.'

The YAJ article contains a map of Blake Hall, details of the household and staff given in censuses, and a photograph of Mrs Mary Ingham, Anne's employer, at a later stage of her life. Charlotte put the end of the episode like this: 'Mrs Ingham is a placid, mild woman; but as for the children, it was one struggle of life-wearing exertion to keep them in anything like decent order'. (*The Brontës, their lives, friendships and Correspondence*, the Shakespeare Head Press, vol I, letter 88)

Apart from the general interest of any Brontë experience and source material, this episode in Anne's life was bound to affect Ellen. Her sister-in-law Mary was close to the Ingham family and stayed at Blake Hall on occasions, Ellen herself knew the family, and many years later, after the publication of Anne's books, Ellen was to be uncomfortably conscious of the opprobrium heaped on the Inghams. In view of the distress caused to the family by Anne's portrayal of them, Mrs Ingham seems remarkably restrained in her only reported remark on the subject, that she 'had once employed a very unsuitable governess called Miss Brontë'.

Blake Hall was pulled down in 1954.

' Charlotte, in a letter to Ellen.

APPENDIX TWO:
THE *SHIRLEY* COUNTRY
From the unpublished work of John Nussey.

The Five Parishes
The district which was the homeland of the families of Ellen Nussey and Mary Taylor, and provided temporary sojourn for the Brontë family, comprised the five parishes of Birstall, Batley, Mirfield, Dewsbury and Hartshead. These parishes were contiguous and formed together a block roughly square in shape with sides of eight miles long, lying at the centre of the countryside encircled by the market towns of Leeds, Wakefield, Huddersfield, Halifax and Bradford. Away to the west rises the great backbone of the Pennine Chain, and the five parishes occupy a pleasant part of its eastern foothills among the last tumble of smaller hills and ridges before they sink into the eastern plain.

These five parishes are watered by two streams which flow south-eastwards in parallel valleys and drain into the River Calder, which forms the southern boundary of the district. The larger of the two streams is the River Spen, and its valley is comparatively wide and spacious. It was on the upper stretches of the River Spen, at Hunsworth, that the Taylors built their woollen mill. The other stream, to the eastward, runs through the parishes of Birstall, Batley and Dewsbury in a generally narrower valley. It carries less water than the Spen River and has different names in different reaches, of which the chief are Birstall Beck, Batley Beck and Dewsbury Beck. It was on the banks of this lesser stream that the Nusseys and their partners the Claphams built their mills, one at Brookroyd and one at Birstall Smithies.

The parishes have much in common and are a recogniseable entity, part of what was the 'Heavy Woollen District of the West Riding of Yorkshire'. Since 1974 the effects of the Maud Act which destroyed ancient administrative areas, and the destruction of the industrial base of the economy, have made this description no longer applicable. A more appropriate name would be 'The *Shirley* Country', for it is in these parishes that Charlotte Brontë set her novel *Shirley*.

The village of Birstall gave its name to a large parish which was divided into eight townships. Birstall church and village formed part of the largest of these townships, that of Gomersal, for there was no township of Birstall. Brookroyd was historically in Batley parish but was nearer to Birstall than were many places in Birstall parish. Particularly from the later part of the eighteenth century and the ensuing increase in population and building,

Brookroyd became scarcely distinguishable from Birstall. The common ties were given some recognition in 1871 when a new church, St Saviours, was built and consecrated on land between Brookroyd and Birstall.

Batley, Dewsbury and Mirfield were conventional parishes, whilst Hartshead-cum-Clifton, to give it its full name, was a curacy under the vicarage of Dewsbury. Composed partly of high moorland, Hartshead remains today a country parish free from industrial development except where it borders on the River Calder and the Clifton Brook, and in the north-west at Bailiff Bridge. Hartshead parish is chiefly known for Kirklees Hall, the home of the Armytage family from about 1560 until recently, which with its extensive grounds is situated between Clifton and Hartshead villages. In the Brontë connection Dewsbury is remembered as Rev Patrick Brontë's first curacy in Yorkshire. He was soon promoted to take charge at Hartshead, the former incumbent of which had died. It was while he was at Hartshead that he married and had his first two children.

Land of Content

The wealth of the West Riding of Yorkshire was founded on wool. From the late fourteenth century, there had been a growing trade both in wool from the north-west of England to Halifax, and in woollen manufactured goods from Halifax to the cloth fairs of London.

After the end of the Wars of the Roses in 1485 Halifax and the upper Calder Valley became populous, and by the middle of the sixteenth century some clothiers were prosperous enough to buy up the ecclesiastical estates then coming on to the property market after Henry VIII dissolved the monasteries. Prosperity continued and there was a wave of building throughout the district, many clothiers building themselves substantial houses of stone. The export trade developed.

This busy prosperity spread out from the Halifax area, when that became overpopulated, across the *Shirley* country as well as other districts. One example of such immigration is provided by the family of Ellen Nussey's great-grandmother Hannah Oldroyd, which settled in Heckmondwike in about 1610 and appears to have come from the Elland district.

The general contentment had much to do with the fact that many of the inhabitants were their own masters. With the exception of the Armytages at Hartshead, no one of over-riding authority was in residence. (At the time of the Luddite troubles, Sir George Armytage commanded the local volunteer militia.) The Batte family, who had settled in Birstall as lords of the manor of Oakwell, Gomersal and Heckmondwike in 1565, had departed by 1707, and thereafter Oakwell Hall was let to tenants. Where any part of the district remained a lordship the influence of the lord of the manor was little different from that of any other absentee landlord. Local government was in the hands of the ratepayers, who elected their representatives to the parish vestry (or council) concerned, which in turn appointed men to fill, often in rotation, the various offices of the parish: constable, surveyor of the highways, and overseer of the poor.

The clothmakers often combined their cloth-making with farming a little land, so that they were not totally dependent on the one activity or the other. The whole family was normally involved as an economic unit, with hours of work and type of work dictated by the season of the year and the demands of trade. It was this domesticity and family unity which were looked back on with such infinite regret when towards the end of the eighteenth century the 'domestic system' was threatened and at length destroyed by the 'factory system'.

The Evils of War and Industrialisation

The American War of Independence (1780) and the wars with France (1793-1815) had disastrous effects on overseas trade, and the application of new mechanical inventions to the manufacture of woollens took place without thought or provision for the skilled manual workers displaced by them. The famine years of the end of the eighteenth century and immediately after the wars with France added to the distress. The Luddite riots of 1812 which feature in Charlotte Brontë's novel *Shirley* were one symptom of the unrest. The Chartist movement, the Plug Riots, and the agitation against the Amendments to the Poor Law Acts of 1834, also marked the clash between the old and the new order.

The inadequacy of the old road system for the needs of increasing population and the demands of the manufacturers, to whom time was money, resulted during the 1820s in the construction of turnpike roads. The old road from Leeds to Huddersfield had wound its way through the centre of Birstall village and twisted itself up Smithies Moor to White Lee and down the other side to Millbridge. Along the valley of the Birstall, Batley and Dewsbury Beck there was no road at all, only a bridle path. To deal with this situation two new turnpike roads were constructed, each as straight as possible and necessitating compulsory purchase of land. Rydings, in addition to losing part of its park also lost a section of the beck where formerly 'grottoes, waterfalls and fish ponds were constructed'. (J A Erskine Stuart, *The Brontë Country*.)

Apart from these new roads, by 1831, when Charlotte Brontë, Mary Taylor and Ellen Nussey were preparing for their first term at Roe Head School, the appearance of the countryside had on the whole not greatly changed. Mill chimneys were not as rare as formerly and new buildings were gradually spreading along the lanesides between one hamlet and the next. But the hillsides, the woodlands and the cultivated fields remained much as they had always been. It comes as something of a surprise to note that on the first of the Ordnance Survey maps, surveyed in 1847, the new turnpike roads above-mentioned, then already some twenty years old, are depicted as virtually free of new building. Writers later in the century recalling their childhood in the area were at pains to record how beautiful it was between 1830 and 1850, with pure air and clean trout streams, yellow gorse colouring the hillsides and walks through quiet woodland carpeted in spring with bluebells.

There was good reason for the Batley men to turn their thoughts to the earlier times, for by the 1880s (well after the period in which the novel *Shirley* was set) the valley was quite ruined, its beck channelled underground, its beckside meadows covered with bricks and mortar, and its hillsides obscured with smoke or poisoned with sulphurous fumes. This martyrdom of Batley was due to the pioneering spirit and commercial enterprise of its own sons, who invented ways of making cloth from discarded rags and clippings. The two varieties of cloth so manufactured were termed shoddy and mungo. The narrow valley became the focus of attention for buyers and sellers from all over the world, and Batley was served by a railway as early as 1847.

Fortunately, perhaps, Batley was the exception in the *Shirley* country in the extreme degree of its industrialisation. Lower down the valley, Dewsbury remained essentially a small market town, though the water meadows alongside the River Calder and what little space there was between town and river were given over to woollen mills. At least in the earlier part of the nineteenth century, the slopes round the town were densely populated by handloom weavers, an important feature when it fell to the lot of the guardians of the Dewsbury Union (which roughly corresponded with the *Shirley* country) to enforce the new Poor Law Amendments in the years after 1834.

The upper end of the Batley valley remained comparatively little changed. Even today, the ancient triangular outline of Birstall village formed by Church Street, Low Lane and High Street embraces the essential parts of the village, most of the small modern housing estates having been added between the village and the valley road, and between the village and Fieldhead. Here, in peaceful and pleasant conditions, the names Brontë, Shirley, Lowood, Briarmains, Rawfolds, and others of the kind, can be found commemorating the still-valued links with the past, as names for the small interconnecting roads and avenues. Oakwell Hall and its former farmlands are well preserved and accessible. Little imagination is needed to view the scene as Ellen Nussey must have known it from the different aspects of her successive dwellings, Laneside, Fieldhead, Ingwell House and Moor Lane House.

A Stroll through Birstall Parish in Search of a Bygone Age

Travelling south-westwards from Oakwell Hall (in Gomersal township), we climb the ridge separating the two valleys on the top of which we come to the road joining Great and Little Gomersal. It is a pleasant stroll of about a mile, through fields shaded now and then by trees, reminding us of the aptness of the comment; 'Great Gomersal is without doubt the most unlike a manufacturing village of any within the radius of Bradford; it abounds in vegetation'. (H A Cadman, *Gomersal Past and Present*.) Its staple trade was the manufacture and merchandising of army cloth. In the earlier part of the nineteenth century there were dozens of manufacturing families who made their cloth in premises attached to their houses, some of which were very fine buildings.

Descending the further southwestern slopes of the Gomersal ridge, we come down after another mile to the River Spen, having just passed the hamlet of Spen after which it was named. Across on the further side of the stream is the small town of Cleckheaton. If we were to turn upstream, we would in little over a mile reach the site of the Taylor's mill at Hunsworth, the Hollows Mill of *Shirley*. But we turn instead downstream and in slightly less than half a mile come to the site of Rawfolds Mill, the actual mill attacked by the Luddites in 1812 and successfully defended by its owner, William Cartwright. Looking south-west across the stream and beyond the present railway, we see Primrose Hill Lane, down which the Luddites marched to the attack after leaving the Shears Inn on the Hightown ridge. Beyond this ridge is the further small valley of Clough Beck, after which the main slope of Liversedge Moorside sweeps up towards Hartshead Moor Top.

From Spen to the vicinity of Rawfolds the stream has formed the township boundary between Gomersal on the one hand and Cleckheaton and Liversedge on the other; but as we proceed beyond Rawfolds we find ourselves passing through Liversedge land on both sides of the stream. Between Rawfolds and Littletown we notice, two fields away to our left, a pleasant-looking though isolated dwelling known as Eddercliff. This was the temporary residence of Joseph Bilton, a newcomer to the district, pending completion (in 1766) of his building of Healds Hall, of which more, presently. Soon we reach Littletown, which more than once in the past suffered serious flooding after heavy rains had caused the Spen to overflow its banks.

As we approach Millbridge the most striking feature is now Healds Hall, standing away to the left on a bank high enough to keep it safely above all floods. At the time of the Luddites this hall was occupied by Rev Hammond Roberson, who had moved there in 1795 as suiting the purpose of his boys' school a great deal better than the accommodation he had had to make do with at Dewsbury. In 1812 he had been instrumental in arranging for a detachment of military to be sent to Millbridge to keep order in the district, and the story of how he and the soldiers, aroused by the distant alarm bell at Rawfolds Mill when the rioters made their attack, arrived at the mill just as the defeated Luddites were in headlong retreat may be read in Charlotte Brontë's dramatic, if strictly speaking fictional, account in *Shirley*. According to a subsequent letter of his, Mr Roberson's own account of the events of that night was published in the *Leeds Intelligencer* of the 19th April 1812.

Roberson had taken a lease of Healds Hall following the death in early 1795 of a Mrs Bilton, widow, whose husband had built the hall in 1766, two years after his marriage. In 1810 the hall was put on the market and Roberson bought it. Failing health in later years caused the Rev Roberson to hand over his school to his nephew, Henry Roberson, who continued to run it until 1856. The hall was then bought by Samuel Cooke of Millbridge. Cooke had been born at Bridge House, just down the road from Healds Hall and opposite the carpet mill built by his father about 1795, and was only eleven years old in 1812. He remembered all his life the excitement and terror of the comings and goings on the night of the Luddites' attack on Rawfolds Mill, when windows in his father's mill just across the road had been broken, although it was not the planned target for an attack. It appears that the soldiers stationed in the area as a precaution had been billeted at the mill and, having been called out, had left the mill almost defenceless, a circumstance taken advantage of by a few stragglers to mark their resentment.[1]

Millbridge was a place of importance from quite early times. The corn mill, a little upstream of the bridge, appears to have been the *soke* mill of the manor of Liversedge, at which all tenants of the manor were obliged to have their corn ground. When the valley was subject to serious flooding, the safe river crossing provided by the bridge, the only substantial one in the neighbourhood, was also vital, all the more so because Millbridge lay centrally in the *Shirley* Country at the point where the major highways crossed. A traveller to Huddersfield would, at about a mile and three-quarters after leaving Millbridge, having passed through Roberttown, be able to look to his right and see the house called Roe Head, the school where Charlotte and Ellen first met. Here, where the road runs alongside the garden wall, Ellen's brother George, on his way to Huddersfield market, used to deliver the packets that Ellen had made up for Charlotte's delight by tossing them over the wall as he whirled past in his gig. The time when Charlotte returned to Roe Head as a teacher was an unhappy one for her, and any such small comfort that Ellen could provide for her was most welcome.

Our walk from Oakwell Hall to Millbridge has amounted to slightly over three miles. If we still feel like walking we can continue in the same direction as before towards Heckmondwike, across the marketplace there and up past the Upper Independent chapel to Staincliffe, or Kilpin Hill, from either of which it is barely half a mile to Healds House (not to be confused with Healds Hall), to which Miss Wooler moved her school in 1837. We can most pleasantly return to Birstall by retracing our steps to the top of Heckmondwike, and then taking the righthand turn into White Lee Road instead of continuing down past the Upper Chapel, and finally taking either Smithies Moor Lane or the Leeds road to Birstall Smithies.

Apart from the extensions to see Roe Head and Healds Hall, this walk has taken place entirely within the former parish of Birstall. Even Roe Head and Healds Hall are no more than 300 yards and 515 yards respectively beyond the old parish boundary.

[1] Family papers of the Cooke family, in possession of Mrs A W Hall of Burnley.

APPENDIX THREE:
CATALOGUE OF BOOKS,
ELLEN NUSSEY, BIRSTALL

Catalogue of books, Ellen Nussey, Birstall. In Ellen Nussey's hand. Small sheets approx 3" x 3" folded together. No watermark. Leeds Archive Office, Sheepscar, Hellewell and Sutton Deeds, envelope with bundle 117, item four.

As the books to which Charlotte, Branwell, Emily and Anne Brontë had access is a matter much discussed, this list of books in Ellen Nussey's personal possession during the lifetime of the Brontës is of interest and significance. After Emily Brontë's death in December 1848, Charlotte and Anne gave Ellen copies of all the sisters' novels then published. She added their titles in darker ink to her list, so those entries provide a closing date.

Many of the books were available in the lifetime of Ellen's great-uncle Richard Walker, and his own publication *Memoirs of Medicine* is included among them, so a considerable number of books from his library may have persisted in the related Walker and Nussey families living at Rydings and Brookroyd during the time that Charlotte Brontë was a regular visitor there, and some of these have come to Ellen. We know that she and Charlotte lent books to one another, and some of the works on this list are mentioned in their surviving correspondence. It is noticeable that Ellen's books include many of the standard eighteenth century authors. Most, though not all, of her own additions to this presumably largely inherited library are religious in nature.

Any of these books could have been borrowed and taken to Haworth by Charlotte Brontë and there read by her sisters and brother. Later when postage was cheaper we know that they did post books to one another.

The list of Ellen Nussey's books is here transcribed as exactly as possible; in some places a lack of legibility has been indicated. The list is annotated by identification and notes on the books, almost entirely taken from the British Library's *Index of Printed Books* and from the *Dictionary of National Biography*.

The envelope with Bundle 117 also includes:

1) One of Mrs T Swinton Hewitt's printed visiting cards, in an envelope addressed to Mr and Mrs Nicholl and family in Ellen Nussey's hand. Also visiting card of Rev T Swinton Hewitt. Names only on cards. Delightful tiny envelope.

2) One of Mr John Taylor's visiting cards. On reverse: 'Dear Mrs. Clapham, Amelia has written to say that you might wish to have the carriage

some day – I called to say that it was at your disposal whenever you wish – it would be as well to let me know the day before.' Small beautiful handwriting, similar in style to Mary Taylor's.

3) Little card 'pocket'. One side says STAMPS with wreath of flowers, on other side gypsies round a camp fire with back of reclining donkey. Both sides hand painted. Inside folder for stamps, partly made from card advertising 'H——Ladies Outfitters Wa——6 Bruns——(near the Crystal Palace)——'.

Bundle 117 is entitled: *Ellen Nussey dec. Miss Nussey's collection of Charlotte Brontë relics etc.* It includes:

1) Notebook with embossed border, inside front cover 'Henry Nussey 1847'.

2) Blue covered notebook, Henry and Emily Nussey 1857.

3) Pages stitched together. In Memoriam Nov 18th 1852, verses by Ellen (Rickman?) Postlethwaite, possibly on the death of Wellington.

4) Single greenish sheet:

> 'Ellen fair I love thee!
> The Lord Almighty speed Thee
> Ellen dear, I leave thee!
> And God be with Thee.'

Initialled O P V [Osman Parke Vincent].

5) Folded sheet. 'Inscription on a Monument in Hathersage Church.' Probably Ellen Nussey's hand.

6) Folded sheets stitched together headed 'Whit Sunday St John: 14: 16, 17'. On back, 'W Wg Whit Sunday 1847'. (Sermon.)

7) Folded sheet with poem 'My Birthday' on a 23rd birthday, by R H Chapman. 20th April 1837. (Hard to read, very faded.)

8) Letter from Ellen Nussey at Moor Lane House, Gomersal, 31st March 1897, about an exhibition of Brontë relics.

9) Two newspaper cuttings of obituaries, one of Charlotte Brontë. Also obituary of Dr Bennett (Joseph Blacker) of Cleckheaton.

10) Four sheets stitched together, with verses initialled WN and a poem translated from the German.

11) Two sketches.

CATALOGUE OF BOOKS, ELLEN NUSSEY, BIRSTALL

LIST	NOTES
A	
Addison, Anecdotes	Privately printed London 1794-7. Interesting anecdotes, memoirs, allegories, essays, and poetical fragments tending to amuse the fancy and inculcate morality. Compiled by Mr Addison.
Aitkin, Chase	Anna Laetitia Aikin, later Mrs Barbould. *A summer evening's Meditation.* In *The hunting of Chevy Chase* published 1795 in Roach's *Beauties of the Poets.*
Alexandre Dr Advice Young Xtians	There are several possibilities for this title.
Adam, Modern Travel [added in darker ink]	Not identified.
Acton Bell, Agnes Grey I vol.	Given to Ellen 9th Jan 1849.
Acton Bell, Wild Fell Hall 3 vols.	Given to Ellen 9th Jan 1849.
B	
Beveredges, Thoughts	Wm Beveridge, Bishop of St Asaph. *Private Thoughts upon Religion and a Christian Life; To which is added, the Necessity and advantages of frequent communion.* With introductory essays by Rev Henry Stebbing 2 vol with portrait. J Hatchard and Son, London 1834 (Sacred Classics vol 10 and 11).
Buffon, 2 vol Nat. History	Georges Louis le Clerk, Count de Buffon; other details not identified.
Bibles [faint illegible word]	
Bridges Revd, CXIX Psalm	Rev Charles Bridges; *Exposition of Psalm CXIX, as illustrative of the character of Christian experience* [with the text] ppxi. 474 published 1827.
Bonar, Night of weeping	Horatius Bonar, published Nesbit, London, 1846.
Baxter's, Saint's Rest	Rev Richard Baxter; *The Saint's Everlasting Rest.* The 9th edition of 'The Saint's Rest' under that abbreviated title was published in 1662. Constantly re-issued, including one edition by John Wesley. It is not possible to know which edition Ellen owned.
Batty's abridged Practical Sabbatarian	Not identified.
C	
Chamuys Essays, 2 vol.	Not identified.
Churchill's, Poems	Charles Churchill. Numerous editions 1763-1933.

Churchmans, Magazine	Periodical, London, 1838-43.
Christian Ladies Magazine	Periodical, London 1834-40
Chambers, Magazine	Periodical, presumably *Chambers Edinburgh Journal,* pub London 1832-44.
Collins, Poems	Almost certainly William Collins, whose *Poems* were published in several editions from 1765, London. Alternativly John Collins *Scripscrapologea, or Collins doggerel dish of all sorts* Birmingham, 1804.
Christ Our Example	Not identified.
Christian Pattern, T A Kempis	*Companion to the Christian Pattern by Thomas a Kempis; or; a selection of spiritual thoughts from the other works ascribed to that writer, with an account of his life.* Translated from the German by S Jackson, published in London by J Mason 1831.
Chapone and Gregory	*Letters on the Improvement of the Mind* by Mrs Chapone and *A Father's Legacy to his Daughters* by Dr Gregory. Published London 1810 by J Walker. Later editions.
Christian Family Library	Not identified.
Churton Early English Church	Edward Churton, Archdeacon of Cleveland. *The Early English Church* with maps, published by James Burns, London, 1840, vol 8 of Englishman's Library.
[Addition in darker ink] Currer Bell, Jane Eyre 3 vol 2 vol	One copy given to Ellen 9th January 1849, the other later.

D

Dodridges Rise and Progress	Philip Doddridge; *The rise and Progress of Religion in the Soul, illustrated in a course of serious and practical addresses,* with a devout meditation, or prayer, added to each chapter. Originally published London 1745, many later editions.
Duncan Mrs M L, Memoir	Memoir of Mrs M L Duncan (Mary Lundie Duncan) Edinburgh 3rd ed. 1843.

E

English Dictionary hard words	Not identified.
[Addition in darker ink] Ellis Bell, Wuthering Heights En [nothing else that line]	Given to Ellen 9th Jan 1849.

F

Fenelon, Telemaque — Salignac de la Mothe Fanelon, Archbishop of Cambrai. *Les Aventures de Telemaque* many editions. Ellen's copy almost certainly in French.

G

Gardners Chemical Lectures — John Gardner M D *Familiar Letters on Chemistry* 1843.

Guardian — Possibly *An address to the Guardians and Overseers of the Poor of the Parish of Birmingham on the subject of Parochial Infant Schools* signed A Guardian, 1835 pub H C Langbridge, Birmingham; or, *Remarks on the Opposition to the Poor Law Amendment Bill,* by a Guardian (ie William Senior Nassau) published by John Murray, London, 1841. Another possibility is a reprint or bound copies of Steele's periodical, *The Guardian,* c 1713.

Gregory's Legacy — John Gregory MD; *A Father's Legacy to his Daughters,* London 1774; constantly reprinted for more than a hundred years.

Goldsmith's, History of Rome 2 vol — Dr Goldsmith; *The History of Rome,* 2 vol, eleventh edition, Leigh and Sotheby, London 1812, or a later edition.

Goldsmith's, History of England 4 vol — Dr Goldsmith; *The History of England from the earliest times to the death of George II,* 4 vol, T Davies London 1771, or 5th ed, 1787, or one of later 4 vol editions.

Goldsmith's, History of Greece — Dr Goldsmith; *The History of Greece.* If in one volume, presumably one of the abridged editions such as that published by J F & C Rivington, London 1787.

H

Hook Dr, Lectures Advent to Lent — Probably part of Dr W F Hook's *Short Meditations for Every Day in the Year,* issued in parts, 1-3 1846-8-7.

Hearts ease — *The Heart's Ease,* a religious tract, ?London ?1844.

Hervey — Possibly Rev James H Hervey; e g *The Works of J Hervey,* pub Newcastle 1787, and later editions.

Hake — Could be Thomas Gordon Hake, Edward Hake, Mrs Lucy Hake – not identified. Thomas Gordon Hake the most likely due to family acquaintanceship.

Hamiltons, Mount of Olives — Rev James Hamilton; *The Mount of Olives and other Lectures on Prayer,* London 1846.

Hamilton, Life in Earnest	Rev James Hamilton; *Life in Earnest; six lectures on activity and order,* London 1846.
Harris, Manumon (?)	John Harris, essay published 1836, *Mammon, or covetousness the sin of the Christian Church.*

J

Johnson, Dr Rasselas	Dr Samuel Johnson; *Rasselas, the Prince of Abissinia,* first pub 2 vol 1759, many later editions.
Jones, Revd., True Christian [Addition in darker ink as with Brontë entries]	Thomas Jones; *The True Christian* 1833.
Juvenal Satires 2 vol	Decimus Junius Juvenalis; *Satires* probably translated into English verse; possibly by Dryden and others; many editions beginning 1693, London; or may have been a Latin edition belonging to Richard Walker, acquired by Ellen after 1848.

L

London Review	Periodical. Published London from 1835.
Letters, Junious	Possibly *The Letters of Junious* published 2 vol by J Wheble, London 1771, or one of the many later editions.

M

More, Hannah, Strictures	*Strictures on the Modern System of Female Education with a view of the principles and conduct prevalent among women of rank and fortune.* 2 vol Cadell and W Davies, London, 1799 and later editions.
Meditations	Not identified.
Mackniel, family	Not identified.
Montgomery Rt, Omn Deity	*The Omnipresence of the Deity,* a poem by Robert Montgomery pub London 1828 and later editions.

N

Newton's Sermons	Possibly Benjamin Newton, vicar of Lantwit, *Sermons on Several Occasions,* 2 vol, London 1736; or sermons by Thos Newton, Bishop of Bristol; Rev Robert Newton D D; or Rev Samuel Newton; all of whom published sermons, or other possible authors.
Newton, Letters	Possibly Sir Isaac Newton, *Letters concerning the Greek Text of I Tim. iii 16, York 1758;* or Rev John Newton, *Letters on Religious Subjects,* London 1807; or other possibilities.

[Addition in dark ink]
National Cyclopeadia
1st vol

Not identified.

O

Ovid's Art of Love

This may be the 1 vol edition published in London 1804 by B Crosby and Co. There were numerous editions, both in English and in Latin.

P

Poetic lucubrations

Thomas Gordon Hake, *Poetic Lucubrations,* London 1828. Hake was a friend of Ellen's brother John. Ellen was likely to have known him.

Pinnock's History of England

Pinnock's *History and Topography of England and Wales, with maps.* 6 vol pub Whittaker, London 1824, or another edition.

Paley's Works

W Paley, Archdeacon of Carlisle. *The Works of W Paley,* 1825. Usually in several vols. Would include his *The Principles of Moral and Political Philosophy.*

Prayers

Not identified.

Psalter, Oxford

Not identified.

Pledge of friendship Annual

The Pledge of Friendship, an annual for 1826-8, 3 vol, London.

Patit's [?Pattil's] Theology

Not identified; Margaret Smith kindly suggested as a possibility Paley's *National Theology* of 1802. Ellen wrote 'Paley' correctly when listing his other work; against this is the point that she was presumably in sympathy with his views and might wish to have more than one representation of them.

R

Radcliffe, Sermons

Not identified.

S

Spectator

Periodical published London beginning in 1711; presumably Ellen's were bound copies.

Sacred Plays

Not identified.

Syntax Dr, 3 vol

Pen name of W Combe. Various adventures of Dr Syntax published in London at intervals from 1815.

Sue Eugene, Wandering Jew

Marie Joseph Eugene Sue, *The Wandering Jew* translated from the French in 3 vol, London 1844; but Ellen may have had a version in French.

Salmon, Modern Gazeteer

Thomas Salmon; *The Modern Gazetteer, or a short view of the Several Nations of the World,* London 1746, many later editions.

[Addition in darker ink]

Simeon, Life of 1 vol	*Memoirs of the life of Rev C Simeon* (for the most part written by himself) ed by Rev Wm Carus, London 1847 Hatchard and Son. Loaned by Ellen to Rev Patrick Brontë.

T

Thompsons, Seasons	*The Seasons* with notes philosophical, classical, biographical, historical, by Anthony Todd Thomson, London 1847.
Tompkins, Poems	Thomas Tomkins; *Poems on Various Subjects,* selected to inforce the Practice of Virtue and with a view to comprise the Beauties of English Poetry, London 1807.
Testimony of Reformers	Not identified.

V

Victor Hugo, le Rhin	*Le Rhin; Lettres à un ami,* 2 tom. Paris 1842.

W

Walker, Dictionary	John Walker; either, *A Critical Dictionary of the English Language* 1791 and later editions, or *A Dictionary of the English Language answering at once the purposes of Rhyming, Spelling and Pronouncing,* London 1755 and later editions.
Wesleys, Sermons	These exist in many versions.
Wesley's, Hymns	These also exist in many versions.
Walker, Practical Piety	Not identified.
Way of Holiness	Not identified.
Watt, Hymns	Isaac Watt; *Hymns* first edition 1707, many later editions.
Williams, The Passion	Isaac Williams; *Our Lord's Passion* 1841 is the most probable candidate for this title as Ellen was in sympathy with the Tractarian movement.
Whiston, Josephus	William Whiston, MA *The Works of Flavius Josephus;* Whiston's translation 1714. Often reprinted.
Walker, Memoirs of Medicine·	*Memoirs of Medicine including a sketch of medical history from the earliest accounts to the eighteenth century etc.* pub J Johnson, London 1799. By Richard Walker, who was Ellen's great-uncle.

Wolfs, Journal

Joseph Wolff wrote several books with *Journal* in the title, such as *Journal of Joseph Wolff for the year 1831*, London 1832; and *Journal of Joseph Wolff in a Series of Letters to Sir T Baring, bart; containing an account of his Missionary Labours from the years 1827-1831 and from 1835-1838*, London and Leeds 1839.

Y

Young, Night Thoughts

Edward Young. Usually entitled *The Works of the Author of the Night Thoughts*, this may have been the 1798 edition which was entitled *Night Thoughts by Edward Young with the life of the Author and notes etc.*

BIBLIOGRAPHY

Alexander, Christine *Charlotte Brontë: the Early Writings* 1826–1832. Blackwell 1983.

Balleine, G R *A History of the Evangelical Party*. Longmans 1909.

Babbage, B W *Report to the General Board of Health; on a Preliminary enquiry into the sewerage, drainage, and supply of water, and the sanitary condition of the inhabitants of the hamlet of HAWORTH in the West Riding of the County of York, by B W Babbage Esq.* HMSO 1850.

Barker, Nicholas and Collins, John *A Sequel to an Enquiry into the Nature of Certain Nineteenth Century Pamphlets by John Carter and Graham Pollard. The forgeries of H. Buxton Forman and T.J. Wise re-examined.* Scolar Press 1983.

Bath Chronicle newspaper for 1838, in the British Library's Newspaper Library, Colindale, London.

Benson, E F *Charlotte Brontë*. Longmans, Green and Co 1932.

Brontë *The Brontës, Their Lives, Friendships and Correspondence*. Shakespeare Head; reprinted by Basil Blackwood 1980.

Carter, John Waynflete and Pollard, Henry Graham *An Enquiry into the Nature of Certain Nineteenth Century Pamphlets* (see Barker and Collins). Constable 1934; second edition with an Epilogue, edited by Nicolas Barker and John Collins. Scolar Press 1983.

Clerical Directories before 1858. C J D and F Rivington.

Crockford Clerical Directory, issued periodically from 1858 to the present. Church House Publishing.

Cunningham, Vincent *Everywhere Spoken Against*. Clarendon Press 1975.

Dictionary of National Biography. Oxford University Press.

Farjeon, Eleanor *A Nursery in the Nineties*. Victor Gollanz 1935.

Fowler, J T *Durham University; Early Foundations and Present Colleges*. F E Robinson 1904.

French, Yvonne *Mrs. Gaskell*. Home and Von Thal 1949.

Gaskell, Mrs *The Letters of Mrs Gaskell, ed. by J A V Chapple and Arthur Pollard*. Manchester University Press 1966.

Glendinning, Victoria *Vita; the life of V Sackville-West*. Weidenfeld and Nicholson 1983

Graves, Richard Perceval *The Brothers Powys*. Routledge and Kegan Paul 1983.

Hake, Gordon *Memoirs of Eighty Years*. Richard Bentley and Son 1892.

Hartley, David *Observations on Man, His Frame, His Duty and His Expectations*. London 1749.

Hey, William *Practical Observations in Surgery*. London 1803.

Heywood, T *Two Hundred Years of Christian Witness at Gomersall, Mirfield and Wyke, 1755 to 1955*. Published privately 1955.

Holland, Sir Henry *Recollections of Past Life*. London 1872.

Holroyd, Michael *Augustus John*, vols I and II. Heinemann 1975.

Kellett, Jocelyn *Haworth Parsonage, the Home of the Brontës*. Brontë Society 1977.

Leeds Intelligencer newspaper, in Leeds Reference Library.

Lester, D N *History of Batley Grammar School*. Printed Thesis for Leicester University. J S Newsome 1968.

Martineau, Harriet *Autobiography*, vols I and II. Virago 1983.

Newspapers consulted in the British Museum's Newspaper Library at Colindale, London included those for Bath (see above), Scarborough, Dewsbury and Cleckheaton.

Nussey, Ellen *Reminiscences*. Published in *Scribner's Monthly* in May 1871, and reprinted in the Brontë Society's *Transactions* for 1898.

Nussey, John *Smithies Mill, Birstall. The life and times of an 18th century steam-driven scribbling and fulling mill in the Yorkshire heavy woollen district*. Privately published 1984.

Nussey, John 'Blake Hall in Mirfield, and its occupants during the 18th and 19th centuries'. An article in the *Yorkshire Archaeological Journal*, vol 55, 1983.

Penrose Rev John *Letters from Bath 1766/7*; edited by Brigitte Mitchell and Hubert Penrose. Alan Sutton 1983.

Ratchford, Fannie *Legends of Angria*, 1933 (with W C De Vane); and *The Brontës' Web of Childhood*, Columbia University Press 1941.

Reid, Wemyss *Memoirs of Sir Thomas Wemyss Reid 1842-1885*; edited by Stuart J Reid. Cassell and Co Ltd 1905.

Rimmer, W G *William Hey of Leeds, a re-appraisal*. Leeds Phil and Lit Society 1961.

Rolleston, Sir Humphrey *Life of Sir Clifford Allbutt*. Macmillan 1929

Scatcherd, Norrisson *The History of Morley in the parish of Batley and West Riding of Yorkshire*. S Stead 1874.

Sharpe's London Magazine of Entertainment and Instruction, VI, 1855.

Sharps, J G *Mrs Gaskell's Observation and Invention*. Linden Press 1970.

Sheard, Michael *Records of the Parish of Batley*. Robert White 1894.

Smith, Frank *The Life and Work of Sir John Kay-Shuttleworth*. John Murray 1923.

Spark, Muriel and Stanford, Derek *Emily Brontë, her Life and Work*. 1953.

Speight, Harry *Chronicles and Stories of old Bingley*. E Stock 1898.

Stevens, Joan *Mary Taylor, Friend of Charlotte Brontë; Letters from New Zealand and Elsewhere; edited, with Narrative, Notes and Appendices*. Auckland University Press and OUP 1972.

Stuart, J A Erskine *The Brontë Country*. Longmans Green and Co.

Thrale, Mrs *Dr Johnson by Mrs. Thrale. The 'Anecdotes' in their original form*; ed Richard Ingrams. Chatto and Windus 1984.

Thwaite, Ann *Edmund Gosse; a Literary Landscape*. Oxford University Press 1984.

Turner, Whiteley *A Spring-time Saunter round and about Brontëland*; The Halifax Courier Ltd 1913; then SR Publishers 1969.

White's Trade Directory for Yorkshire, 1853.

Winnifrith, Tom *The Brontës and their background, Romance and Reality*. Macmillan 1973.

York Herald, 11th August 1838, in the York Reference Library.

MANUSCRIPT SOURCES

BPM = Brontë Parsonage Museum

During the many years spent researching this book I garnered information from many sources, always giving preference to original sources and contemporary evidence, manuscript whenever possible. The main sources of this type of research material were as follows:

Charlotte Brontë's Letters.   A new and definitive edition of these is shortly to be published by the Oxford University Press, which will supersede the existing edition by Shakespeare Head. Therefore, although inevitably I used the Shakespeare Head edition a good deal, wherever possible I read the original letters. These were in the Brontë Parsonage Museum, in the Fitzwilliam Museum, Cambridge, and in the Brotherton Collection, Brotherton Library, University of Leeds. The BPM also has a collection of Charlotte's envelopes addressed to Ellen, some of which are decorated with seals bearing mottoes.

Ellen Nussey's Letters.   The Brontë Parsonage Museum contains many of Ellen Nussey's letters to various correspondents, largely in the Cadman Collection, also the Seton Gordon Collection. The Brontë Society kindly gave me permission to quote from documents in their possession. Letters include those to Mary Hewitt *née* Gorham, George Smith, Mary Robinson, Antony Nussey and Mme Cortazzo. There are letters from Ellen to Wise, Shorter, and a fragment presumed to be to George Smith, in the Brotherton Collection, Brotherton Library, University of Leeds. Letters to Wise are also in the Ashley Collection in the Manuscript Room of the British Library. The Potternewton Letters and those to Lady Morrison I consulted from copies among the Nussey family papers, made by Mildred Christian.

Mr Goodchild kindly allowed John Nussey to make many notes from a typescript copy of Ellen's letters to Mrs Atkinson of Laneside House, Churwell, which Mr Goodchild owns personally. These letters are part of the *John Goodchild Loan Collection* at Wakefield Metropolitan Library. I understand the originals are now in the possession of the BPM.

Diaries and Journals.   The BPM holds one of Ellen's diaries, written in the *Christian Remembrancer* for 1849. Ellen's Pocket Diary for 1853 is in the Harry

Ranson Research Center, Austin, Texas, USA. John Nussey kindly researched this second diary for me.

Henry Nussey's *Journal* I read in the Manuscript Room of the British Library, where it is 3268A in the Ashley Collection, and I was given permission to quote from it.

John Nussey made extensive notes for my use from William Carr's manuscript diary, which is in the West Yorkshire Archives Service Kirklees Office, Central Library, Huddersfield, reference number DDCA.

Nussey Family Papers. John Nussey gave me copyright permission for material and information from his family papers, letters, his own researches, and material anywhere to which he was in a position of holding copyright.

Reminiscences by Ellen Nussey were published by *Scribner's Monthly* in 1871 and reprinted in Brontë Society *Transactions* for 1898. The Kings School, Canterbury, have manuscript *Reminiscences* by Ellen Nussey as part of the Walpole Collection in their library. They kindly gave me permission to quote large sections of this manuscript, which has some passages not published by Scribner, and a number of small variants from the published versions.

I have also used reminiscences given by Ellen in her letters.

Nicholls' Letters. The Brotherton Collection in the Brotherton Library, University of Leeds, holds a collection of Rev A B Nicholls' letters to Ellen Nussey and other Brontë material.

Scrapbooks. The Keighley Museum holds two scrapbooks compiled by William Scruton containing many newspaper cuttings about the Brontës and Ellen Nussey. John Nussey also had a family scrapbook, useful for the earlier history of the Walker/Nussey families.

Sale Catalogue. A copy of the catalogue of Ellen Nussey's effects for sale after her death is in the BPM.

Moravian records. For the Birstall/Gomersal area these are held on microfilm at the West Yorkshire Archives Service Kirklees Office, Central Library, Huddersfield. I also visited the Moravian Church's headquarters at Muswell Hill, and was given assistance by their library and archives staff. Miss Connor of Fulneck kindly checked various points for me in the archives of Fulneck Moravian Settlement.

Richard Walker's letters on the Luddite troubles. Wentworth Woodhouse papers, Sheffield City Libraries Archive Dept.

Brontë Memorabilia. The Leeds Archives at Sheepscar, Leeds, gave me permission to quote the contents of Bundle 117 and the envelope associated with Bundle 117, part of the Hellewell and Sutton Deeds (see Appendix 3). I also researched there the Hey family records.

Chatsworth Archives.   Kim Booker discovered the records of Henry Nussey's alterations to Hathersage Vicarage in the archives of the Duke of Devonshire at Chatsworth, to which he was kindly allowed access.

Additional sources.   I used birth, death and marriage certificates from the Registrar General, St Catherine's House, Kingsway, London; parish registers including those for Batheaston and Dewsbury, in the appropriate county archive offices and the Borthwick Institute, York; census returns, which apart from the Public Record Office, Chancery Lane, London, are also available in reference libraries; wills, both from the Borthwick Institute, York, and probate registries; maps, and other sources well known to family historians.

Buildings and Artefacts.   I visited the houses of people mentioned and the sites of many of the events, and also saw surviving objects such as Ellen's silver teapot, George IV's handkerchief, various paintings, the items on display at the BPM, a hat of Ellen's and so on. When visiting Brighton I was not able to find any of the items on loan to the Royal Pavilion from the Nussey family on display, and did not have time to make enquiries.

INDEX